Islam and the West

Islam and the West

A Light on the Horizon

by
Sudibyo Markus

UHAMKA PRESS

FONS VITAE

First published in English in 2022 by
Fons Vitae
49 Mockingbird Valley Drive
Louisville, KY 40207
http://www.fonsvitae.com
Email: fonsvitaeky@aol.com

Library of Congress Control Number: 2022946029

ISBN 978-1941610-923

Printed in USA and Indonesia

Contents

Acknowledgements

THANKS FOR THE ENGLISH EDITION

As the author of the book, I would like to convey my deepest and sincerest appreciation to Prof. James L. Peacock, who has been so generous in taking the initiative to arrange for translation of the book into English and publish it in the United States. When I told him about the book, Prof. Peacock indicated his seriousness to translate and publish it immediately, even before he was really aware of what it looked like. I owe it to our long, cordial friendship, since 1970. His generous initiative was also in response to the requests for an English translation by many readers during book discussions in several universities in Indonesia, including the most recent discussions in Hamburg and Frankfurt, Germany, in the early months of 2021.

I offer my sincere thanks to Prof. William Graham, professor in Middle East Studies and former Dean of Harvard Divinity School (2002-2012), who has been so generous in facilitating the publishing process, including introducing me to Fons Vitae Publishing in Kentucky, publisher of interfaith books, including the high caliber works of the great Islamic philosopher, Imam Abu Hamid al-Ghazali.

I am grateful to Virginia Gray Henry, Director of Fons Vitae Publishing and Distribution, Sally Rother for her editing services, and the rest of the production team at Fons Vitae. Likewise, I convey my highest appreciation to Suara Muhammadiyah, Publisher in Yogyakarta and Co-Publisher of the English version, and especially to the young, energetic director, Deni Al Asyhari. Thank you to Aditya Pratama, Deputy of Publication, for the careful translation process prior to being sent to Fons Vitae for final editing, as well as Carla Jones (PhD), Jennie Smith (PhD), and Chris Belcher for their suggestions and assistance during the revision process. I would also like to acknowledge Gramedia Pustaka Utama, the publisher of the original Indonesian edition, as well as the Vatican for its importance to this book.

I would like to convey my deepest thanks to Prof. Edy Suandi Hamid, the Vice Chair of the Muhammadiyah Council of Higher Learning, Research and Development (Majlid Diktilitbang), who has been very helpful in organizing the Book Launches and Discussions in some Muhammadiyah Universities and Centers of Excellence. It was he who first indicated that the book *Dunia Barat dan Islam* should be translated into English and Arabic, then supported by Prof. Din Syamsuddin, the former President of Muhammadiyah (2005-2010 and 2010-2015), and Prof. Aflatul, Chair of the Ulama Council in South Sumatra and former Rector of the State Islamic Institute (UIN) in Palembang, South Sumatra. Prof Aflatul also underlined the need to encourage more and more dialogue for action, rather than unproductive formal dialogues, which are full of politeness, but have less real action.

I convey my sincere thanks to Dr. Yusron Ambary, Director for Public Diplomacy at the Ministry of Foreign Affairs, and Dr. Acep Somantri, the Consul General of the Republic of Indonesia in Frankfurt, for officiating the online Book Discussion within the Consulate General for the Indonesian community and diaspora in Germany.

Finally, we would like to convey our most sincere gratitude to Prof. Dr. Gunawan Suryoputro, M. Hum, Rector of the Prof. Dr. Hamka Muhammadiyah University (UHAMKA) in Jakarta, who has been so kind and generous in accepting our offer to co-publish *Islam and the West* in Indonesia. Prof. Gunawan Suryoputro has also indicated his willingness to conduct the International book launch, following the similar launch of the Indonesian version of the book by UHAMKA University on September 28th, 2019, which was attended by Prof. Dr. Haedar Nashir, M. Si, President of the Muhammadiyah movement.

Last but not least, I have to convey my most sincere appreciation to my beloved wife, Tien Sapartinah, for her patience in reading and editing my very first and original manuscript word by word. Her International Relations background and our fifty years together as of May, 2021 have made her know well my way of thinking and the directions of my thoughts and writings.

Sudibyo Markus

A Reflection for Peace

H.E. Jusuf Kalla
Former Vice President of the Republic of Indonesia
(2004-2009 and 2015-2019)
Jakarta, 1 December 2020

Religion has played a very important role in the awakening, as well as the downfall, of human civilizations. Some religious leaders have even agreed that, in the past, religions played more of a role in creating problems than solutions. Prolonged bloody wars and conflicts have occurred throughout history among the followers of different traditions. The history of the world continues to tell the ups and downs of nations and their civilizations, in peace and in conflict in search of political supremacy, territory, and natural resources. Even today, some secular states still consider religion one of the most important political instruments.

The author of *Islam and the West*, Sudibyo Markus, is known for his faith-based partnership and humanitarian work in Indonesia. In this work, he has compiled and demonstrated the interconnection of historical phases of religion into a single mosaic, including milestones such as the introduction of Islam to the European mainland by Thariq bin Ziyad in 711, the bloody two centuries of the Crusades (1095–1297), the Nostra Aetate Declaration of the Second Vatican Council in 1965, the sending of the "A Common Word" by 138 clerics and Islamic scholars to His Holiness Pope and all Church authorities in 2007, the World Humanitarian Summit in Istanbul in 2016.

Each historical milestone has its own back ground, but share many respective lessons through faith-based and cultural dialogue. Even during the Crusades, historians noted several golden events of dialogue between Christians and Muslims. The most well noted was the dialogue for peace between Saint Francis of Assisi, the Founder of the Franciscan order, and Sultan Kamil Malik of Egypt. The Crusades also witnessed the friendly exchange of medical knowledge between Muslim doctors, who had advanced methods and techniques, and the doctors of the Crusaders, whenever there was a break in the war. It was reported that even St. Thomas Aquinas was considered an Arab philosopher, as he admired the critical and elaborative translation of the great Greek philosopher's teachings by the Islamic philosopher Ibn Rushd, also known as Averroes. Still many other forms of civilizational dialogue took place during this time, when Europe was still considered in the Dark Ages, which brings doubt as to whether the Renaissance and other developments would have taken place without European interactions with the Muslim world.

However, the medieval conflict between the Western World and Islam seemed to shift upon the Reformation and Renaissance movements of Europe, including the discovery of sea routes and the resulting colonization of Muslim countries in Asia and Africa. Only in 1965, when the Second Vatican Council issued the historical *Nostra Aetate* document, the Church conveyed their respect for Islamic teachings for the first time, and invited the Muslim world to forget past conflicts. The Second Vatican Council's generous appeal was reignited in 2007, when an open letter from 138 clerics and Muslim scholars, "A Common Word," was publicly sent to the Pope and Church leaders of the world.

Moreover, the spirit to end the long inter-religious conflicts, which were marked by Nostra Aetate and A Common Word, were then renewed by Pope Francis and Sheikh Ahmed El-Thayib, the Grand Imam of Al Azhar in Cairo, in the Human Fraternity Declaration they both signed in Abu Dhabi on February 4, 2019. It is so apparent that both sides felt it urgent to renew the spirit of peace, not only among the people of the Book, but also among all the people of the world. The people of the Book, who constitute more than fifty percent of the world's population, can and must become actors for peace. Finally, the World Humanitarian Summit (Istanbul, 2016) was the first and largest global humanitarian summit to come up with a strong and realistic global agenda for a more practical humanitarian partnership in support of peace.

We hope that *Islam and the West* will broaden and deepen this reflection on peace among all people, and continue to spread the basic tenets of religions as instruments for peace worldwide.

Life of Sudibyo Markus:
A Short Sketch

James L. Peacock
Professor emeritus at the University of North Carolina, USA
North Carolina, 4 March 2019

Sudibyo Markus is an outstanding leader and scholar, whose book addresses a global need: the collaboration of Islam and Christianity.

Sudibyo's life and career include many achievements and contributions. *First*, I note our friendship. *Second*, I mention his contributions. *Third*, we examine the historical context for this topic, which entails the relations between Christianity and Islam globally, and especially in Southeast Asia, including Indonesia and Java. *Fourth*, I mention a special exposure he experienced to scholars who focused on his topic in Java.

I met Sudibyo in 1970, when I studied Muhammadiyah, an organization of 30 million members, primarily in Indonesia. Sudibyo and his friend, Amien Rais, befriended me and invited me to join the activities of Muhammadiyah. I also met Sudibyo's parents when I visited his home town, Pare, in East Java. His parents were very genteel, and his siblings showed several religious interests, ranging from Islam and Christianity to Javanese customs reflecting the influences of Buddhism, Hinduism, and other perspectives of "*agama Jawa*" (i.e. Javanese religion and Javanese culture).

However, Sudibyo had chosen Islam, and specifically Muhammadiyah, as his commitment. He also knew much about Christianity. I noticed on his bookshelf a book by Max Weber, *The Protestant Ethic and The Spirit of Capitalism*, and I thought this paralleled a Puritan stream of Islam, as explained in a book I published with the University of California Press entitled *Muslim Puritans*. In fact, Sudibyo himself seemed a strong Puritan in the broad sense of strong commitment to an ethic of upholding religious and moral values that energized good works, which build and sustain community. Muhammadiyah followed such an ethic in its remarkable works in education, health, and community.

Even as student, Sudibyo was putting into practice work for education, health and community. He expressed this commitment during study at Medical School in Gadjah Mada University, Yogyakarta. Upon completion of his study, he joined the Ministry of Social Affairs in 1973, then moved to the United Nations Development Programme (UNDP), where he served from 1988 to 1998. He also continued volunteer work with Muhammadiyah, arguably the largest Islamic humanitarian movement in the world. He was appointed Chairman of the Muhammadiyah Council of Health and Welfare from 2000 to 2005, and was later selected to be Chair of the Muhammadiyah Central Board in charge of Health and Social Development in the 45th Muhammadiyah National Congress, or Muktamar, in 2005. At present, he is Vice Chair of the Muhammadiyah International Office.

These works led to global activities. For example, in 2006 he founded the Humanitarian Forum International in London; formed a partnership between Islamic and East-West humanitarian organizations; he was a representative to the peace negotiation Team between the Moro Islamic Liberation Front (MILF) and the governement of the Phillipines; and from 2009 to the present, he has promoted partnerships with the community of Sant Edidio (Rome) to foster Muslim-Catholic dialogue in support of the peacebuilding process. He was also appointed by the Ministry of Foreign Affairs of the Republic of Indonesia to represent the Indonesian government by delivering presentations in the 2nd and 5th Asia Pacific Interfaith Conference, in Cebu, Philippines (2006) and in Perth, Australia (2010).

Returning, briefly, to the early contact between Sudibyo and me: A high point was Darul Arqam, a two-week training camp for Muhammadiyah provincial leaders held in Klaten, Central Java, in 1970, where we had many discussions with him and Amien Rais on the current and future challenges encountered by Muhammadiyah as an Islamic modernist humanitarian movement. Many years later, in 2010, I joined him and others in Yogyakarta, celebrating the first century of Muhammadiyah, which was founded in 1912. Since then we correspond frequently.

Now, let us review the history of contact between Islam and

Christianity, especially during the Crusades, but also in colonial times, especially in Southeast Asia. The Crusades expressed Christianity's fight against the expansion of Islam into Europe. As we know, Islam had spread into Spain as well as Eastern Europe. Islam also spread into Southeast Asia. In Indonesia, for example, Islamic teachers were arriving in kingdoms from around 1200 to 1500 and converting local rulers. Syncretism sometimes resulted, as in the Kingdom of Mataram in Central Java, which fused Islamic and Hinduistic or Buddhist as well as other spiritual practices and beliefs. After that, Dutch colonialism and Christianity merged in opposition to Islam, attacking the great kingdoms of Mataram represented by Sultan Agung and other figures, such as Diponegoro, whose identities combined Islam and Javanese culture and civilization. As a Javanese person with Indonesian national identities, Sudibyo Markus knew this history well and experienced the varied and sometimes conflicting identities involved.

In the 1950's, when Sudibyo was in his youth, a remarkable event happened. A group of American scholars from Harvard University undertook a study of Pare, nicknamed "Modjokuto" by the group, the community where Sudibyo lived. These scholars included Clifford and Hildred Geertz, Alice Dewey (later teacher and mentor of the mother of President Obama), Robert Jay, Rufus S Hendon, and others. They researched economics, family life, religion, and other aspects of Pare. A comprehensive study of religion was titled *The Religion of Java* by Clifford Geertz. *The Religion of Java* described three streams of spirituality: Islam, magical and ritual practices, and Hinduistic beliefs and practices. Young Sudibyo met the scholars and was interviewed by some of them. Thus, he added to his understanding of religion by contact with Westerners who sought to know his own perspective and that of his family and members of his community. This remarkable experience added to his considerable knowledge reflected in this book.

I admire and cherish Sudibyo's strong will, energy and intelligence. This book draws on those qualities to serve an urgent global need for collaboration and understanding between two great world religions. This book promises a broad and long perspective on the relationship between the West and Islam. In addition to scholarship, we can expect sharp intelligence and deep experience to open our understanding and perhaps our hearts to brotherhood and sisterhood among those of us who are children of Abraham.

North Carolina, March 4, 2019[1]

---

1. Philip K. Hitti, *History of the Arabs: From the Earliest Times to the Present* (New York: Macmillan & Co. Ltd, 1964), pp. 98–99.

The Western and Muslim World: An Introduction

Azyumardi Azra, CBE
Ciputat, 6 February 2019

This book by Sudibyo Markus, *Islam and the West*, reflects the dichotomy between the Western World and Islam, which, to me, seems out of place, given the Western World is a geographical entity, whereas Islam is a religious entity. Therefore, it should be safe to say that a more suitable dichotomy would be the Western and Eastern Worlds.

However, if the dichotomy of the Western World and the Muslim World can somewhat be accepted, it will not be without further notes: the geographical area of the Western World, arguably, is also part of the Muslim World, even though Muslims in this world are a minority. Conversely, representations of the Western World can also be easily found in many parts of the Eastern World, particularly in Southeast Asia, South Asia, the Middle East (if it can be included as part of the Eastern World) and also East Asia, where there are many Muslim areas which are inhabited by many Muslim populations. Therefore, if one has to see various kinds of porous dichotomies, one can observe an overlap amongst those dichotomies, although to varying degrees.

YET TO IMPROVE

This book extensively discusses the dynamics of the relationship between the Western World and Islam in a very long span of history. However, for the contemporary period, it is imperative to pay attention to the results of the annual Pew Research Center survey, especially since the 9/11 2001 incident that struck the United States. For example, a 2006 survey which involved 14,030 respondents—Muslim and non-Muslim—and was conducted by 15 countries, namely the United States, China, Britain, India, Indonesia, Japan, Germany, Egypt, Nigeria, Pakistan, France, Rus-

17

sia, Spain, Turkey, and Jordan, produced several findings which concluded that the relationship between the Muslim World and the Western World has yet to show a significant improvement; the relationship between the two worlds remains poor, marked by misperception and reciprocal prejudice.

It is important to note that, although the relationship between the two worlds remains bad, it hardly worsened, for there have been no extraordinary international events in the recent years which could spark increased animosity between the two worlds. Therefore, in my opinion, the opportunity for both worlds to improve their relationship remains wide open.

Furthermore, at the first level, the survey concluded that Westerners and Muslims generally have opposing views towards each other concerning major events at the international level. Generally, both parties also think of each other as violent and intolerant peoples, as well as misogynists. Muslims in the Middle East and Asia also view Westerners as immoral and selfish people; whereas Westerners condemn Muslims as fanatics.

The survey also found that the majority of respondents stated that the relationship between Muslims and the West is very bad, and both sides blamed each other for such a situation; Muslim respondents stated that the West is responsible for the poor relationship between them, while the West blamed Muslims. In follow-up interviews, Muslims generally held the view that the source of the poor relations between them was the West's continued unfair attitude towards the Palestinians, Western double standards, and so on.

Some other key findings are, FIRST, anti-Jewish sentiment remains high in Muslim countries and among Muslims in Germany, Britain and Spain. However, 71% of French Muslims have a positive view of Jews. SECOND, the majority of Muslims declare that the victory of Hamas in Palestine actually encouraged a fair solution for the Israeli-Palestinian conflicts, an opinion which is solidly rejected by Westerners. THIRD, concerning the Jyllands-Posten Prophet Muhammad cartoon controversy back in 2005, the majority of Muslims view the West as being disrespectful towards Islam, whereas the West sees protests that are waged by Muslims as proof of their intolerance.

FOURTH, the Spaniards and Germans—compared to other

Europeans—have a stronger antagonism towards Muslims. In contrast, the majority of British and French people have a more positive view of Muslims. FIFTH, European Muslims—compared to Muslims in the Muslim World—are more likely to have a positive view of Europeans. They also tend to see that the tensions between the Muslim World and the Western World are by no means a clash of civilizations.

Another thing to note from this survey is the Muslim's support or lack of support for suicide bombing. As the survey found, the majority of Indonesian Muslims do not support suicide bombing. Around 71% of Indonesian Muslims even consider suicide bombing and other forms of violence against civilians to be totally unacceptable, and Islam does not provide justification for such atrocious acts. The figure, 71%, is without question an encouraging development, given that in 2005 the figure was only 64%, and 54% in 2002.

For me, the Pew Research Center survey is important, although some people might question the methodology they use. Nevertheless, the fact that the survey is more or less a picture of the situation of relations between the West and Muslims should not be downplayed. Even when both parties are willing and have good will, the results of the research can be used as initial material for introspection, which, in turn, should be followed by various steps and concrete actions in order to improve the situation.

I am inclined to think that good and healthy relationships between the two parties are very decisive for peace, to provide support and even realization of increased welfare for humanity. If good relationships between the two sides can be fulfilled, Muslims can live their present lives and look to the future with peace and hope.

A MESSAGE FROM QATAR

The relationship between the Muslim and Western World ten years after 9/11 is still a hot topic discussed in many international, regional and local forums. This can be observed in, for example, the Doha Forum: Fourth UN Alliance of Civilization 2011 which organized a special panel to discuss this topic in the series of events which was held in December 11-13 2011. Speaking in this event were six panelists, namely representatives of the

Pew Research Center, Tariq Ramadan, Rashad Hussain (President Barack Obama's special envoy for Islamic Affairs), and myself, to discuss various aspects of dynamics and development between the two worlds in the past ten years.

The following are the messages from Doha, Qatar.

FIRST, the categorization of the Muslim and Western World in conflicting binary positions is no longer acceptable or relevant. This is based on the fact that Muslims not only inhabit Muslim-majority countries, but their population is also increasing in Europe and America, or the Western World in general. Furthermore, Muslims in the Western World, whether they are indigenous people, descendants of immigrants, or immigrants who have recently settled, generally do not stand in binary opposition to the people and governments of their respective countries.

In addition, in terms of international politics, Muslim-majority and Muslim-governed countries have good relationships with many Western countries and societies. Such healthy relationships not only apply in politics, but also in economics, culture, education, and science-technology. However, there are also Muslim countries that are in tension and involved in conflicts with certain Western countries; these conflicts should be considered as obstacles to the creation of safer and more peaceful international relations.

SECOND, based on research and annual surveys of the Pew Research Center and Gallup poll, it was found that, in general, the level of hostility and conflict between the government and Western society with the Muslim countries and community tends to be continuously declining. In recent years, a more positive perception and view of Islam and Muslims has developed among the Westerners. Furthermore, governments and societies in both worlds are generally equally concerned with extremism and terrorism; they both reject extremism, violence and terrorism in the name of religion, and mutually agree that all parties must act together to deal with it assertively, armed with fair and objective approaches and methods.

THIRD, Muslims in general are increasingly able to accept democracy, which is often associated with the Western World. They feel and perceive democracy, despite its certain weaknesses, as a better political system compared to its counterparts, such as theocracy, or military and civil authoritarianism. In accepting democracy, a serious effort was made by governments and Muslim societies to re-contextualize and popularize democracy to be more in line with the historical, demographic, social and cultural realities of the respective Muslim communities.

FOURTH, in the last ten years, more and more Muslim countries and societies have experienced economic and welfare improvements, which expose them to improvement of the quality of human resources, which, in turn, enable them to strengthen their self-confidence and self-worth. However, in the midst of increasing economic prosperity there is also growing anxiety about corruption, which seems increasingly common in various levels of government, bureaucracy and other public institutions.

Nevertheless, the message from Qatar not only contained good news, but also some unpleasant news, which required the attention and efforts of both parties to fix it at once. *First*, among the lay community in both worlds there still persisted stereotypical views as well as misperception towards one another. This is due to the lack of accurate information, knowledge and interactions among these grassroots communities.

In the meantime, the crises and economic difficulties that have plagued many countries and communities in Europe and America in recent years have prompted the birth of anti-immigrant political groups and parties, which obviously are anti-Muslim in nature. Groups and parties with such an attitude utilize the economic and social pessimism of their own communities to garner anti-immigrant and anti-Muslim zeal.

Thus, there are still a number of conditions to be eliminated—or, at least, reduced—by the government and Western society itself, notably the anti-Islamic spirit. As for the government and the Muslim community, there are also demands that are by no means light, that is, to clear the malaise and chaos in their very homes. Clearly, the chaotic and violent domestic situation in some Muslim countries is conducive to problems not only in the domestic context but also in relation to the international world.

This work of Sudibyo Markus is very helpful in bringing to light various advances that must be completed by both parties. Not only can this work enrich our literature concerning the relationship between the two worlds - Muslim and Western - throughout history, but, it can inspire us to develop a more harmonious relationship. For this work, I am very grateful to Sudibyo Markus. Congratulations.

A Light on the Horizon:
An Introduction

Franz Graf von Magnis SJ
Driyarkara Philosophy College
Jakarta, 3 February 2019

The history of Islam's relationship with Christianity is hardly encouraging. That's what Sudibyo Markus describes in the beginning of this book. And indeed it is not encouraging. True Christianity was not ready when Islam, in the seventh century, abruptly appeared on its horizon. Islam was perceived as a faith challenge as well as a political challenge. In a short time, the Arab armies carrying the banner of Islam were deployed, captured Jerusalem, conquered most of the territory of the Byzantium Empire, defeated and destroyed Persia—then an empire's greatest threat—conquered all of North Africa, and in 710 A.D., i.e. less than eighty years after the death of the Prophet Muhammad, successfully established its influence in Spain. The Island of Gibraltar, originally called Jabal Tarik, still reminds us of the name of the commander Tariq ibn Ziyad. The advances of the Arab-Muslim force could only be stopped by the Franks' forces in the Battle of Tours and Poitier, only eighty kilometers from Paris. What marked the beginning of the *reconquista*, the "recapture" of Spain from Islamic rule, which ended only seven hundred years later, was the fall of Granada in southern Spain at the hands of King Ferdinand of Aragon and Queen Isabella of Castille in 1492.

As Sudibyo Markus put it, the battle of both Christianity and Islam, the Crusades, was an attempt to recapture Christian Jerusalem and other Christian holy sites in Palestine. The eight Crusades, which ended in failure, are now considered by Christianity to be a shameful heresy, which until now has left scars in the collective memory of Muslims.

Interestingly, in fact, as Sudibyo Markus puts it, the relationship between "West" and "Islam" was not only negative in nature.

In the Medieval period, Muslim rulers themselves were mostly enlightened people. In general, they do not impose Islam on the people whose territory they conquered. In fact, until twenty years ago, one could easily find the existence of the ancient Christian minority in Egypt, Palestine, Jordan, Lebanon, Syria, and Iraq. Their numbers even reached nine percent of the total population, and they could still live and practice their faith safely (alas, the tragedy of the US invasion of Iraq in 2002 virtually destroyed the traditional balance that had lasted for fourteen hundred years, and now Christianity has almost disappeared in parts of the Middle East).

Europe, after the collapse of the Western Roman Empire in 476, was still barbaric and cruel. "The Arab world," as manifested in advanced cities like Baghdad, Damascus, Cairo, Toledo, Cordova, and Granada, is seen as the height of sophistication, adored by the world. Christian theologians and philosophers in France, Italy, Germany and England were fascinated by the works of Islamic intellectual figures, such as Ibn Sina (Avicenna) and Ibn Rushd (Averroes). It was from them that Europe got their new Aristotle-like Thomas Aquinas.

It turns out, for the first six hundred years, Islam was intellectually very open. Islamic thinkers did not hesitate to learn from and study about the classical Greek (pre-Christian) intellectuality and reflect on it. However, the beginning of a cultural change was imminent. On the one hand, by the 11th century, Romanesque and Gothic-style churches were built, some of which are still standing and admired. In the intellectual field; monks from the Dominican and Franciscan orders, supported by new universities, studied Islamic thinkers and developed their own philosophical and theological platforms, while at the same time, the great Islamic philosophers were even more rejected in the Muslim World.

It was at the University of Paris that the philosophy of Averroism was formed, which lasted for two hundred years, and the works of Ibn Rushd were actively consulted, while in Cordova (then under Muslim dominion) his books were burned and philosophy was increasingly forbidden under the pressure of sufism and Muslim jurists. When European intellectuality, inspired by Islamic intellectuality, was on the rise, the flow of Islamic intellectuality into Europe actually declined and eventually disappeared. In the 18th century, at the height of the Enlightenment, agnostics such as

Voltaire and J.W. Goethe—Germany's greatest poet—admired the wisdom of Islam. But, of course, what they meant by "Islam" was not Islam in the last seven hundred years; instead, it was the core of Islam that amazed them, the Qur'anic Islam.

Starting in the 15th century, Europe, again, was threatened by the power of the Ottoman Turks, whose troops twice reached the city walls in Vienna, Austria (in 1529 and 1683 respectively). It is very true, as Sudibyo Markus notes, that had the Arab army won the Battle of Tours and Poitiers in 746 or the Turkish army captured Vienna, European and world history would be very different. However, the defeat of the Turkish army in Vienna in 1683 at the hand of Prince Eugen (which is celebrated in many Western songs) was the beginning of the huge retreat of the Ottoman Empire, which eventually dissolved after Turkey, together with Germany and Austria-Hungary, its allies, lost in the First World War.

This fourteen-hundred-year history demonstrates why the relationship between Christianity and Islam is arguably always cold and bad. But, as Sudibyo Markus describes, in the last century a light began to emerge in the dark horizon of the relationship between the two. A process of new awareness had begun and eventually resulted in real change. This change is most evident in the Roman Catholic Church—the lighthouse for 1.5 billion (55%) Christians—and also in the Lutheran and Calvinist Protestant Churches. The Catholic Church is increasingly opening up to other churches, especially to the Protestant Churches which have been their adversaries for so long. In addition, the Catholic Church began to open up to other religions. Therefore, it is safe to say that the Catholic Church opened itself to the ideals of modernity and enlightenment. The process of enlarging that insight itself was driven by the threat of inhuman, and even evil, ideologies that emerged in the 20th century, such as fascism, racism, national-socialism, and communism.

The Catholic Church, as Markus puts it, confirmed its change of attitude at the Second Vatican Council (1962-1965). In the above-mentioned Council, the Catholic Church expressed its friendship and similarity of faith with other Churches, supported religious freedom, democracy and human rights, and emphasized its commitment to the realization of social justice.

In the Nostra Aetate, for the first time, the Catholic Church states that in other religions there are things that are "sacred and true," and hence must be respected by Catholics. And in the third point of the Nostra Aetate, the Church specifically states its appreciation towards the core Islamic beliefs, that is the oneness of God (*tawhid*).

The key text of the Council found in the Lumen Gentium Constitution (point 16) stated that God offers salvation to all humans, not only to those who are baptized, but also to those who believe in one God, and those who do not believe in the religion of monotheism, and even those who "without blame on their part, have not yet arrived at an explicit knowledge of God and with His grace strive to live a good life," provided their deeds are dictated by their conscience. As an additional explanation, it is imperative to note that Pope John Paul II emphasized that wherever there is goodness among humans, there is the Spirit of God, thus the Spirit of God also finds its existence outside the Church.

This conviction has had a profound impact on the creed of the Catholic Church mission, in which the Church's obligation is to witness the spreading of the Gospel to all mankind. Since the Church is no longer worried that people who are not baptized cannot enter heaven, the purpose of the mission is no longer to bring as many people as possible to baptism, but to guide them to a good life, and lead them to comprehend the glorifications and teachings of God, and to be the witnesses of God's love, mercy, kindness, justice, and His omnibenevolence. Therefore, the Church is expected to be a kind of catalyst that stimulates good things in man's hearts so that goodness can be manifested in real life.

Furthermore, the Church has always been very aware that it itself consists of sinners. Therefore, the Church knows that its members are not necessarily better and holier than those outside the Church. The Church has never said: "We are the best people in the world." On the contrary, since the Church is made up of people who have many weaknesses and sins, the Church believes that it is being supported by all the goodness residing in the heart of the followers of other religions. What is maintained and welcomed by the Church is: if people outside the Church are open to Jesus and they want to embrace Jesus and be embraced by Him and finally ask to be baptized, that desire must be respected.

Generally speaking, the Church demands respect for freedom

of religion, which also means freedom to follow the religion that is believed by one. If the others consider "acceptance" of Jesus and baptism as apostasy, that is their right, but they must allow anyone to follow what one felt as God's call in one's heart. Let us not interfere in the ultimate judgment affairs, something that lies only in God's hands.

The Catholic Church continues to learn and study lest it be stuck in its own parochialism. Though the preamble of his lecture in Regensburg arguably hurt the feelings of many Muslims, Pope Benedict XVI proceeded to visit the Blue Mosque in Istanbul, where His Holiness faced the pulpit, momentarily basked in silence and then prayed solemnly. Now, Pope Francis II has managed to establish a close relationship with the Grand Mufti of Al-Azhar University, Ahmed el-Tayeb, thus becoming the first Pope to visit an Arab country, the United Arab Emirates, on February 3–5, 2019.

The learning process of the Catholic Church was greatly assisted by "A Common Word between Us and You," which was sent on October 13, 2007, by 138 Muslim leaders worldwide to leaders of the Churches. It is precisely correct that Sudibyo Markus gives great meaning to the letter. In the letter, these Muslim leaders stretch out the "hand of peace" to their Christian brothers, by showing that the commandments of love towards God and love toward all human beings (love your neighbor) can actually unite Islam and Christianity, and invites Christians to work together to achieve peace.

The letter is so important and fundamental for all measures to end all kinds of chaos on earth, including violence, war and/or terrorism in the name of religion. Thus, despite the media that often depict religion as the motherlode of all things inhumane, the relationship between Christians—Catholics in particular, but also other Churches—and Muslims has reached an entirely new degree of intimacy. The closer relationship between the Muslim World and the Christian World is no less than a quintessential foundation for the "Agenda for Humanity" effort which, as previously explained by Sudibyo Markus, was initiated in 2016 by the World Humanitarian Summit.

In Indonesia alone, the emergence of radical and extremist groups has not, and will never, succeed in damaging relations between Christians and Muslims that have become increasingly close in the last twenty years. Being a pluralistic nation, Indonesian challenges which lie in their strenuous future require Indonesians to not only avoid hostility toward one another, but to respect each other deeply.

This work is an important contribution, imbued with the calls for enhancement of understanding toward one another, forgiveness of each other, and increasing respect for each other. May the light of peace and mutual respect increasingly enlighten Indonesians, and all mankind on earth.

Preface

A SMALL DEBATE IN 1970

The idea for writing this book originated in 1970, when the three of us – James L. Peacock, a professor from The University of North Carolina at Chapel Hill, Amien Rais, and I – were engaged in a serious discussion on the relations between the Western World and Islam. This issue, along with other popular issues on democratization, secularism, modernization, freedom of religion, and even proselytization were trending topics for students, after the failed communism coup effort in 1965. Amien Rais and I were both young student activists of the modernist Islamic humanitarian movement in Indonesia, the 1970 Muhammadiyah movement, and so we were very much concerned with these issues.

Between June 2-14, 1970, Amien Rais and I were assigned by the Muhammadiyah Central Board to facilitate two weeks of training sessions in a *darul arqam* (cadre training event) for the Muhammadiyah district offices throughout Central Java. The two weeks of training, which took place at an Islamic boarding School in Sobrah Lor village at the outskirt of Klaten, Central Java, was fully observed by James L. Peacock. This work between the three of us gave plenty of opportunities to share ideas.

On June 9, 1970, Amien Rais and I were both invited to give speeches in a Sunday morning religious public gathering, or *Pengajian,* for all Muhammadiyah members at Wisma Siradj House, Klaten. James Peacock was with us, attending the crowded gathering. Right after our speeches, we engaged in a small yet serious debate on the theme of my presentation, which was "The Western World and Islam." In the speech, I quoted from the book *"Islam at the Cross Road,"* written by former *Der Frankfuter Zeitung* Journalist Leopold Weiss, who converted and changed his name to Mohammed Asad. He later became a Pakistani citizen, and even later the Ambassador of Pakistan to the United Nations.

James Peacock, who had been acquainted with me for several

months, was somewhat "annoyed" when I was speaking on "the Western World and Islam" in the Sunday morning gathering, considering that no other westerner except himself was around. We shortly clarified the small misunderstanding and continued our good friendship, even noting James Peacock as one of our sincere Muhammadiyah international scholars.

While James Peacock continued his professional career in anthropology at the University of North Carolina, and Amien Rais continued as a professor in international relations at the Gadjah Mada University in Yogyakarta (beside his political career pathways, which led him to become a Speaker of the Indonesian Consultative Assembly), I focused my involvement in humanitarian and interfaith partnership. My position as former Director for NGO Affairs at the Ministry of Social Affairs, and later as one of the Chairs of the Muhammadiyah Central Board and my former involvement with the United Nations Development Programme (UNDP) Indonesia, gave me a much wider understanding of these subjects.

SHORT VISIT TO MODJOKUTO

James Peacock was very excited when I told him I was traveling through Modjokuto, East Java, a nickname for Pare in the Kediri district, and the small traditional town where his seniors, twelve doctoral students from Harvard University, attended their doctoral studies in anthropology in 1952-1954. The twelve Harvard students lived in Modjokuto to observe their respective anthropological foci of Modjokuto. One most popular among them, Cliffort Geertz, has popularized Modjokuto through his book *The Religion of Java,* which was an international bestseller after it was published by the Massachusetts Institute of Technology (MIT) in 1960. I was only an elementary school student when they were around for two years at Pare, but I knew most of the Harvard students quite well, since one of them, Donald R. Fagg, stayed with my family.

One day, James Peacock accompanied me to Modjokuto, staying with my family for two days and visiting some of the houses where the Harvard students stayed. Most of the houses were in the same condition as they were twenty years ago. He met my father and mother, who were both Elementary School masters, where he observed, just like the condition of Modjokuto itself, how multicul-

tural my family was. Since then, my friendship with James Peacock
has grown beyond a formal friendship and partnership. We lost
contact when we were busy with official duties, but were recon-
nected when Professor Peacock attended the 46th Muhammadiyah
Congress at Yogyakarta in 2010. Since then, we communicate via
email quite often. When I told him in 2019 that I was about to publish my book on the issue we disputed in 1970, "The Western World
and Islam," he spontaneously said, "I will translate and publish it
here in US."

Professor Peacock's generous idea to facilitate the translation
and publication of the book in the US, in addition to his com-
memorating my and Prof. Amien Rais deep personal long friendship with him, also arose from his sense that my idea to write the
book originated during my early encounters with the Harvard students in 1952-1954, especially Clifford Geertz. Indeed, the very first
impetus of my idea in envisioning the relation between Islam and
the West was initiated in Modjokuto, which was then groomed by
our close friendship with Amien Rais, professor in international
relations in the big "machinaries" of Muhammadiyah, the largest
Islamic humanitarian movement in Indonesia, and among the biggest in the world.

DEEPER OBSERVATION

What aroused my interest in pursuing a deeper understanding of
Westernization, secularization, and Christianization, as well as tolerance, freedom of religion and other related issues is that, at the
time, those themes were being openly discussed in the media in
Indonesia, and especially among students. Over time, due to the
social, economic, cultural and political influence of national and
global dynamics, the intensity of issues on *interreligious interrelations* gained attention as well, especially after the release of the
Nostra Aetate by the Vatican Council II.

In 1977, I was assigned by the Muhammadiyah's Council for
Religious Research and Development to give a speech in a limited
forum on the Vatican Council II. The concise paper I submitted to
the forum was published by the Antara Publishing House in 1978,
entitled *Vatican Council II: An Attitude to Revitalize the Church's Attitude towards Islam* (Indonesian: *Konsili Vatikan II: Satu Sikap Pembaharuan Sikap Geredja terhadap Islam*). Later on, the book was reviewed

in an Indonesian newspaper, *Kompas*.

Although I have divided the history of the Western World and Islam into several stages, namely (i) *Pre-Crusades*, (ii) *Crusades*, (iii) *Colonialism and Imperialism*, (iv) *Orientalism*, (v) *Cultural Missionary Adaptation*, and (vi) *Vatican Council II* - I consider the two main milestones to be the *Crusades* and the *Nostra Aetate Declaration*. Although inherently not a holy war, the Crusades remained the first and foremost milestone in the relationship between the Western World, the Church and Islam. This is because, besides being led by Pope Urban II, the Crusades were the first highly-structured, organized, continuous, and colossal effort to liberate the Holy City of Jerusalem. The Church considered that the Holy City of Jerusalem should not be under the rule of the Islamic caliphate (even though there was actually no interference from Muslim rulers against Christian pilgrims to Jerusalem). It is undeniable that the Crusades were essentially an inter-civilization dialogue, and one that was quite intensive, between Western civilization and Islam, not to mention the Crusades's role in the latter supported the creation of the International Humanitarian Law (IHL). The *International Humanitarian Law*, also a product of a long civilizational dialogue between the West and Islam, provides a code of conduct for various shared humanitarian agendas.

The statement of the Vatican Council II in 1965, Nostra Aetate—which encapsulated the attitude of the Catholic Church for improving relations with non-Christian religions, including Islam—brought a breath of fresh air to the relationship between the Church and Muslims. For the first time in history, the Catholic Church respected Islam and its teachings, and invited Muslims to forget their historical conflicts with the Church. Before that, in Indonesia, even at the beginning of the era of independence, the Church still considered Islam a blasphemous religion, and therefore legitimizing the Church's conversion and targeting of Muslims for proselytization.

Now, forty years after the first publication of my book on the Vatican Council II in 1978,—which focuses on the ups and downs of the Western World, the Church and Islamic relations from the Crusades to the Second Vatican Council—it turns out that today, the spirit of "Church-Islam reconciliation" initiated by the Vatican Council II since 1965 has changed considerably, having experienced an encouraging and more potent dynamic, and providing new hope for further developments. This new dynamic, enthusiasm and hope emerged first from the Muslim world, taking the form of an Open Letter sent to the Pope and other Christian leaders from 138 Muslim scholars and ulamas entitled "A Common Word between Us and You."

Furthermore, support for the spirit of peace and humanitarian cooperation emerged from the United Nations, which succeeded in holding its biggest historical event, the World Humanitarian Summit, in Istanbul from May 23 to 26, 2016. From this event, another call for peace through the global humanitarian program was born, the Agenda for Humanity. So, it is safe to say that these milestones are keeping the spirit of peace and humanity alive, following the two previous milestones, the *Crusades* and the *Vatican Council II.*

Following this, the Declaration on Human Fraternity was jointly signed by Pope Francis and the Al Azhar Grand Imam Sheikh Ahmaed Al Thayib in Abu Dhabi on February 4, 2019. Surprisingly, on October 3, 2020, inspired by the Human Fraternity Declaration, Pope Francis issued his 3rd Papal Encyclical, "Fratelli Tutti" or "All Brothers," which reiterates the spirit of "fraternity and social friendship" in combating the escalating global humanitarian crisis.

Therefore, considering the continued commitment for action toward a common humanity among religious leaders worldwide, I decided to change the title of the English version of the book into: *Islam in the West: A Light On the Horizon.*

The agreement to build a spirit of cooperation between Muslims and Christians, based on common values such as the Love of God and Love of One's Neighbor —the core of the open letter "A Common Word between Us and You," which was based on the Amman Message 2005—is really based on a sole motive: to establish peace between the West and Christians with the Muslim World.

The Church and Islam both recognize that there are differences among them in terms of religious doctrines that are diametrically opposed. However, in the midst of these impossible differences, the common beliefs love of God and love of one's neighbor (the first is human relations with God (*hablun minallah*), while the latter is human relations with fellow humans (*hablum minannas*) can bridge the gap of their doctrinal differences.

CONCLUDING THOUGHTS

The Indonesian version of the book has been widely discussed at different occasions in Indonesia has been widely discussed at different occasions in Indonesia, to involve some Muhammadiyah and State universities in 10 provinces, including discussions among the Indonesian students and diaspora in Hamburg and Frankfurt, by involving both Muslim and Christian participants. In addition, suggestions to translate the book into Arabic, English and some other international languages have been given by members of the audience of the discussions, and have suggested that the book could encourage interfaith partnership. There have been many partnerships scattered around different countries, whose practices could be promoted and shared to the other part of the world.

Hopefully this book will promote and broaden understanding of the importance of humanitarian efforts in combating the complex problems at the local, national and international level. What we need is international dialogue and action, which address real community problems such as poverty, poor nutrition, environmental degradation, food scarcity and hunger, maternal and newborn mortality, and others.

May Allah bless our common humanitarian endeavors, based on our shared *Love of God* and *Love of Neighbors*.

Amen

Sudibyo Markus
Jakarta, March, 2021

Executive Summary

This book is an updated version of the author's previous work *Konsili Vatikan II, Satu Pembaharuan Sikap Gereja Terhadap Islam* (*The Second Vatican Council, a Renewed Perspective from the Church Towards Islam*, Pustaka Antara Publisher, Jakarta 1978). It explains and interleaves four important historical milestones which have ushered humanity towards modernity, and driven humanity, especially religious communities, closer to peace.

The core message of this treatise is that all religious congregations must be able to transform themselves into instruments for peace.

The four historical milestones are:

The Crusades or The Holy War (1095–1297) a protracted, bloody, ignominious and useless war. Despite the Crusades being instigated by Pope Urban II at the Council of Clermont, historians generally concur that the Crusades were not an evangelical mission, as evidenced by the indiscriminate slaughter of 70,000 residents during the sacking of Jerusalem, regardless of their age or religious background.

The Crusades were more focused on territorial conquest to support the Tsar of Constantinople, whose lands were being occupied by the Turkish Seljuq, as well as to reclaim Jerusalem.

Ultimately, the Crusades failed in their mission to reclaim Jerusalem, but the protracted war did succeed in creating an important and ongoing civilizational dialogue between Western and Islamic civilizations over the 200 years of proximity and interaction. This led to the beginning of Europe's awakening through the Renaissance and the Reformation, as well as the discovery of sea routes, eventually bringing Europe into the era of colonialism and the conquest of Islamic lands.

The Second Vatican Council (1962–1965). The issuance of the Nostra Aetate (Latin for "In Our Age") is a declaration of the relationship of the Church to non-Christian religions, which includes the

Church's renewed perspective towards Islam through the expression of esteem for Islamic virtues, and calling for all to lay to rest the conflicts of the past and work together for the benefit of all mankind.

As the initiator of the Second Vatican Council, Pope John XXIII's fervent desire was to focus the Council on inter-religious discourse, however some Catholic scholars preferred to focus on prioritizing missionaries.

An open letter entitled "Kalimantun Sawa" ("A Common Word Between Us and You"), dated October 13th, 2007 and signed by 138 Muslim Scholars and Intellectuals from around the world, addressed to Pope Benedict XVI as well as all church leaders globally.

> The letter, which was inspired by the 2005 Amman Message was initiated by Prince Professor Ghazi bin Muhammad, calling on all pious peoples to jointly become the channel and instruments of peace for humanity. The open letter was overwhelmingly welcomed by all recipient Church leaders.

> The Agenda for Humanity, declared by the World Humanitarian Summit in Istanbul (23-24 May 2016), organized by the United Nations, is the first summit of its kind intended to address the worsening of the global humanitarian crisis. The Agenda for Humanity established five core tenets that provide five basic paradigms that should be adopted by all humanitarian actors when responding to the complexities of the humanitarian crisis. The Agenda for Humanity provides a structural platform for faith-based humanitarian actors for all humanitarian services and collaboration.

> In addition to discussing the phases and processes of the global interaction between Islam and the West, the book elaborates on the same processes as they occurred in Indonesia from the colonial era through to Indonesia's independence.

The book is comprised of the following parts:

PART ONE: ISLAM AND THE WEST

The Dark Ages in Europe were also the darkest time regarding Europe's perception of Islam, as this was founded in a deep-seated hatred and historical need for vengeance against the perceived threat of Islam. According to Edward Said, "For Europe, Islam was a lasting trauma."

Despite this, the on-going civilizational dialogue between the Western and Islamic civilizations through the esteemed centers of learning in Baghdad and Cairo, as well as Cordoba, Granada and Toledo in Spain, in addition to the close and prolonged interactions during the Holy War, undoubtedly provided an impetus for bringing Europe into a new era of enlightenment. Starting with the Renaissance and the Reformation, the discovery of sea routes and the introduction of some basic technologies, the West-East Pendulum had changed.

It was this discovery of sea routes combined with the growth in industrialization which fueled the need for raw materials and markets in the East, leading to the beginning of Western colonization of Islamic countries in the East.

Today, the feeling of an Islamic threat against Europe has reawakened, driven by the acknowledgement that Islam is the fastest growing religion in the world. The threat of warfare and invasion prevalent in the Dark Ages has been replaced with a sense of "soft terrorism" (John Esposito) brought about by the high level of Muslim migration seeking a better livelihood. Europe is living with a specter of a shift towards a Europe-Arab axis, or Eurabia, while European philosophers are yearning for a second spiritual renaissance.

PART TWO: THE STAGES OF RELATIONS BETWEEN
THE WEST AND ISLAM

A discussion through the consecutive stages of (i) the Dark Ages, (ii) the era of contact between Islam and the West, (iii) The Crusades or The Holy War, (iv) The Renaissance and the Reformation, (v) Colonialism, (vi) Orientalism, as the turning point or beginning of understanding and respect for Islam (vii) the era of missionary adaptation in anticipation of new era of independence and the rise of the Islamic world, and ending with (viii) The Second Vatican Council (1965) as the beginning of a new era in the relationship between the Church and Islam.

During the discussion on Orientalism, the book specifically underlines a strong rejection of a thesis claiming that Muhammadiyah was established in response to, and to counteract, intensive missionary activities, supported by colonial authorities. Muhammadiyah is the largest Islamic modernist humanitarian movement, established in 1912 in Indonesia. Muhammadiyah offered the proof that no official Muhammadiyah existed that substantiated such a claim, and furthermore the frequent meetings held by KHA Dahlan (the Founder of Muhammadiyah) with many pastors and priests was not for religious debate or proselytization purposes, but rather to simply demonstrate to his followers that they could sit and talk with Christians as fellow humans to solve problems.

Further, the main Quranic verses primarily quoted and used by Muhammadiyah are Surah Al-Ma'un (on orphans and the poor) and Surah Ali Imran: 104 (on the promotion of the best citizen), while Al-Bagarah: 120 (on proselytization) is not mentioned.

PART THREE: A COMMON WORD BETWEEN US AND YOU

The open letter entitled "Kalimantun Sawa" or "A Common Word Between Us and You" (Al-Qur'an Ali Imran 3:64) was addressed to Pope Benedict XVI and Church leaders worldwide, breaking the 50-year silence from the Muslim world in responding to the Second Vatican Council. The letter, which was jointly signed by 138 Islamic Scholars and Intellectuals, including Professor Nazaruddin Umar from Indonesia, was initiated by Prince Professor Ghazi bin Muhammad, Chair of the Royal Aal Al-Bayt Institute for Islamic thought in Amman.

The letter graciously conveyed an invitation to all world religious leaders to jointly embrace the "Kalimatun Sawa" between the two Abrahamic faiths, the essence of which is "Love of God" and "Love Thy Neighbor."

The Pope's sudden visit to the Blue Mosque in Istanbul (29-30 November 2006) in the middle of the controversy surrounding remarks he made during an address at Regensburg University, which were deemed derogatory by the Islamic community, was seen as a genuine gesture to put aside the division and hatred caused by the Christian-Muslim conflicts of the past, and reinforced the declaration made by the 2nd Vatican Council. The location was symbolic, as it was the Turks who had conquered Constantinople in 1453, and then subsequently attempted to seize Vienna in 1529 and 1683, failing in both attempts.

This symbolic visit of Pope Benedict XVI to Istanbul in 2006 and the subsequent research carried out by Abu Dhabi Gallup over a period of 5 years, commencing in 2006 and published under the title "Measuring the State of Muslim-West Relations," strongly contradicted the "Clash of Civilizations" theory proposed by Samuel P. Huntington.

PART FOUR: THE WAY FORWARD,
TOWARD THE AGENDA FOR HUMANITY

The spirit of humanization enshrined in the Second Vatican Council and Kalimatun Sawa (A Common Word) established a grounded and structural global commitment within the Agenda for Humanity, which was declared at the World Humanitarian Summit in Istanbul (23-24 May, 2016). Despite the revitalizing global momentum behind the spirit of humanization, the reality stood in stark contrast. Escalating war, primarily caused by political hegemony and competition for natural resources amongst the super powers, has resulted in the shrinking of humanitarian space.

The World Humanitarian Summit re-emphasized the importance of International Humanitarian Law, initiated by Henry Dunant (1863), as a guide for global humanitarian cooperation. It should be noted that International Humanitarian Law incorporates many Islamic contributions derived from the ongoing civilizational dialogue with Western civilizations, from the rise and spread of Islam, the Holy War, the Renaissance, Orientalism and even the Colonial era and present day.

PART FIVE: TOWARD A UNIVERSAL HUMANITY

The Second Vatican Council, Kalimantun Sawa (A Common Word) and the Agenda for Humanity all emphasized the need for civilizational dialogue while rejecting the doubtful adagium of a clash among civilizations. Dynamic, global, civilizational dialogue would facilitate the creation of a dignified and civilized global society.

The process of civilizational dialogue encouraged by religious scholars and intellectuals continues *in-situ* (within respective communities) and *ex-situ* (external or off-site). Both forms of dialogue carry out the Word of God:

> "O Men, Verily, We have created you of a male and a female; and we have divided you into peoples and tribes that ye might have knowledge of one another. Truly the most noble of you in the sight of Allah, is he who feareth Him most."

Al-Qur'an, Surah Al Hujurat 49:13

HUMAN FRATERNITY (ABU DHABI)

The Human Fraternity Declaration, which was signed by Pope Francis with Sheikh Ahmed el-Thayeb, the Al Azhar Grand Imam during his historical visit to UAE on 3-5 February 2019, represents a further commitment to humanitarian efforts by the Second Vatican Council, A Common Word and the Agenda for Humanity. The initiative was closely related to the role of the UAE Crown Prince, Shaykh Muhammed bin Zayed al-Nahyan, who was also very active in promoting dialogue on "A Common Word" through the Zayed University of the United Arab Emirates, with Yale University and the University of South Carolina (July 2008).

The historical new momentum was then followed by the issuance of Pope Francis' third Encyclical *Fratelli Tutti* (All Brothers) on October 3rd, 2020. The Encyclical Fratelli Tutti clearly indicates that it is strongly related to the Abu Dhabi Declaration on Human Fraternity. The Fratelli Tutti was the first ever encyclical to be developed and based on the Church's close encounter with Islam. Undoubtedly, the Declaration on Human Fraternity and the Encyclical Fratelli Tutti are *"two sides of the same coin"* in converging these prime historical milestones, especially the Nostra Aetate and "A Common Word."

Finally, new issues were encountered during the first launching of this book by Professor Haedar Nashir, President of Muhammadiyah in October 2019, during the preparation of publishing the English version in the United States. There were at least twelve book launches and discussions conducted by Muhammadiyah and non-Muhammadiyah Universities in Indonesia, followed by two online discussions conducted in Hamburg and Frankfurt. The one in Hamburg came upon the invitation of the Indonesian Lutheran World Federation, while the other one in Frankfurt was conducted by the Consulate General of the Republic of Indonesia in partnership with the Muhammadiyah Special Chapter (PCIM) for Greater Germany.

As a result, new sub-chapters in the English edition respectively cover the new issues we encountered in our online discussion in Hamburg and Frankfurt, especially on the church transformation, in response to the universality of mankind and the universality of salvation, as well as the launching of the Zayed Award on Human Fraternity, which has selected Antonio Guterres, Secretary General of the United Nations, and Ms. Latifa ibn Ziaten, a Moroccan-

French humanitarian activist, as honorees of the Award.

We incorporate the new sub-chapter on Voice from Frankfurt on the Church transformation in Part II: "The Stages of Relations between the West and Islam", and the Voice from Abu Dhabi on the Zayed Award for Human Fraternity in Part IV: "The Way Forward – Toward the Agenda for Humanity."

Sudibyo Markus
Author of the book
Jakarta, October 2020

PART 1

ISLAM AND THE WEST

For Europe, Islam was a lasting trauma.
Edward W. Said, *Orientalism*, Vintage Books Edition,
25th Anniversary Edition, New York, 1994, p. 59.

1

Socrates, Jesus and Muhammad

TWO BIG PROBLEMS

In the introduction to his inaugural speech as Extraordinary Professor in Arabic, Syrian, Semitology and Islamology at the University of Amsterdam on October 17, 1955, Guillaume Frédéric Pijper summarized the changes in the Western-Christian World's attitude towards Muhammad and Islam as follows:

A century ago, English philosopher John Stuart Mill stated that mankind can be hardly too often reminded that there once was a man named Socrates. A half century later, the German theologian Adolf von Harnack recognized the truth of Mill's statement but added that it is still more important to remind mankind, over and over again, that there once moved among them a man named Jesus Christ. We are living fifty years later and the English historian Arnold Toynbee considers among the greatest benefactors of mankind, beside Jesus Christ and Socrates: Mohammed (Muhammad), the founder of Islam. Mohammed is one of the greatest benefactors of humanity—it was a long time before an important writer in Western Christendom came to this realization. In the Middle Ages Mohammed was regarded in Europe as a pagan idol, or as an impostor, or as a schismatic in the Christian Church, or as a false prophet, in any case an evil man burdened with sin.

As proposed by Toynbee, only recently has understanding, acceptance and appreciation of Islam emerged in the Western-Christian World, with the hostile view toward Islam circulating up until the mid-twentieth century. In the introduction of his speech, Pijper also stated:

Later, after the rise of Arabic studies in Europe things were little better. In the seventeenth century to Roman Catholic and non-Roman Catholic scholars alike, Mohammed [was] a false prophet, the archenemy of Christendom. The enlightened Pierre Bayle, still, at the end of the century considers Mohammed as a false prophet and a fraud. Only in the eighteenth century did the opinion change. Under the influence of the two great spiritual movements, Enlightenment (Aufklärung) and Romanticism there took shape a new judgement on Mohammed and his creed, Islam. [Voltaire, an admirer of the Koran, found] much to commend in the precepts of Islam. The young Goethe [was] captivated by the personality of Mohammed; later in his life, he made the explicit declaration that he could never see Mohammed as an impostor. The historian Edward Gibbon [wrote] in his *Decline and Fall of the Roman Empire* magnificent pages in defense of the merits of Mohammed and his teaching. However, it [was] only in the nineteenth century that Oriental studies built up the historical-critical picture of Mohammed, and that [the study of] history behaved more justly towards Islam. And now comes our contemporary, Toynbee, who counts Mohammed a benefactor of mankind....

Pijper's presentation of the gradual change in the attitude of the Western-Christian World toward Muhammad reveals two fundamental problems in the Western-Christian attitude towards Islam: long historical interaction and subconscious stereotype.

LONG HISTORICAL INTERACTION

It goes without saying that Western-Christian societies needed a long historical interaction, not less than fourteen centuries, before they began to respect Muhammad as a great human being, on par with Socrates and Jesus.

However, especially at that time, the Church, both Catholic and Protestant, had not supported and approved the opinions of those great scholars that Muhammad is truly a messenger of God.

This is despite the fact that, during the period of fourteen centuries there had been quite intensive interaction between the Western-Christian World and the Muslim World. While there was significant physical interaction during the Muslim Conquests of the Byzantine Empire in the early 7th century and the penetration of Islamic civilization into Europe through the Iberian Peninsula, Crusades, and colonialism, there was also an interaction between civilizations, cultures and sciences, especially during the Western colonization of the Islamic World beginning in the 16th century. Soon after, the Portuguese explorer Vasco da Gama's voyage identified the first sea route to India from Europe.

Furthermore, while Western-Christian colonialism of Muslim provinces in Africa, Central Asia, South Asia, and East Asia in the 16th century furthered the physical interaction between the two worlds, Europe, under the influence of Romanticism, began to develop a stream of reforms which succeeded in providing an enlightened understanding of Muhammad and Islam in the Western-Christian worldview.

In turn, this understanding has improved with the emergence of Islamic studies and Orientalism, but even so, this development merely recognizes Muhammad as a *great human being* who is equal to other great figures of the world, not as a *prophet* and *messenger of God*, which is tantamount to a recognition of the truth of Islam. Therefore, in the decision of the Second Vatican Council concerning the Nostra Aetate, instead of "*acknowledges,*" the Roman Catholic Church declared that it "*regards* with esteem also the Muslims. They adore the one God...."

SUBCONSCIOUS STEREOTYPE

Presently, this centuries-long attitude toward Islam has developed into a subconscious stereotype, which cannot be altered or removed through cognitive processes or academic studies. Voltaire, Goethe, Gibbon, and Toynbee—the scholars mentioned by Pijper—are only a small group of opponents of the swift flow of subconscious stereotypes in the Western-Christian World.

This can be understood, of course, since religion, as Toynbee points out, is a "serious business of the human race," an ultimate concern or personal responsibility that is extremely fundamental and absolutely essential. Moreover, religion has dimensions of faith that are supernatural and not entirely digestible by reason, such as trust in God, the Creator, and trust in the hereafter.

Therefore, the respect for Muhammad shown by some European scholars and historians is not, and was never, a mainstream understanding that can be accepted and followed by the majority of Western-Christian societies.

There is no guarantee that all mainstream European societies will consciously agree and approve what was stated by Voltaire, Goethe, or Toynbee. Especially was this so after Pope Urban ignited the spirit of the crusaders in a synod in the city of Clermont (1095) to invade and liberate Jerusalem, a call that contributed to the outbreak of a long war that would later be known as the Crusades, and in turn gave rise to a prolonged grudge known as "Crusades syndrome."

THE WESTERN VIEW OF MUHAMMAD IN THE PAST

In just the span of the 7th century, Islam spread rapidly from the Arabian Peninsula, to the Iberian Peninsula and Indian subcontinent. The growth of Islam was facilitated by the backwardness and underdevelopment of European society at that time, which was often feudal, and agrarian. The Roman Empire, slowly but surely, had begun to collapse in the presence of a flourishing Catholic Church.

In *The Decline and Fall of the Roman Empire,* Edward Gibbon mentions that in addition to the development of Christianity in Europe, the collapse was due to various internal conflicts and the attacks of Goths and Vandals from the north. In Chapter 36 of his book, Gibbon identifies "the triumph of barbarism and religion" throughout the volume. The "triumph of barbarism" was the victory of the Goths and the Vandals, while the "triumph of religion" was the victory of Christianity, which was completed by the conversion of Emperor Constantine, who would later support

Vatican City, The Head and Heart of the Catholic Church and Catholicism, from persecution of its followers to becoming the State Religion, to its early and late middle age, to the renaissance and reform era, up to the enlightenment and modern era. The Pope has a unique influence on a significant proportion of the world's population. (*The Vatican*, Father Michael Collins. DK Limited, London 2014)

the implementation of the First Council of Nicaea and make Christianity the state religion.

It was just after these early stages of Christianity's development in Europe that Islamic civilization began to rise. Philosophy, principle and spirit based on monotheism, or the oneness of God, were the foundation for the advancement of Islamic civilization. Thomas Carlyle, a Scottish philosopher—who was also admired by Indonesia's first president, Sukarno—mentioned in *On Heroes, Hero-Worship, and The Heroic in History* that the Prophet Muhammad had changed the sands in the Arabian desert, which for centuries had been silent, into "explosive powder, blazes heaven-high from Delhi to Grenada." It is the principle of monotheism that drives such awakening and progress. Islam and its monotheistic principle have freed mankind from the idols of ignorance and hypocrisy.

The concept of the oneness of God has, in the past, has promoted unity among civilizations, because belief in one God stood above tribal, ethnic and regional diversities, as Reverend C.F. Andrews put it:

> One of the greatest blessings which Islam has brought to East and West alike has been the emphasis which at a crucial period in human history it placed upon the Divine Unity. For during those Dark Ages both in East and West, from 400 to 1000 A.D., this doctrine was in danger of being overlaid and obscured in Hinduism and in Christianity itself, owing to the immense accretions of subsidiary worships of countless demi-gods and heroes. Islam has been, both to Europe and India, in their dark hour aberration from the sovereign truth of God Unity, an invaluable corrective and deterrent. Indeed, without the final emphasis on this truth, which Islam gave from its central position,—facing India and facing Europe—it is doubtful whether this idea of God as one could have obtained that established place in human thought which is uncontested in the intellectual world today.

While it's true that Arianism, which rejected the divinity of Jesus Christ, had been suppressed at the First Council of Nicea with the backing of the Roman Emperor Constantine, the doctrine of monotheism—"the uncompromising monotheism,"[2] as Philip K. Hitti puts it—was reaffirmed and became the main foundation in Islamic teachings especially by adherence to the Qur'an, the

---

2. Philip K. Hitti, *History of the Arabs: From the Earliest Times to the Present* (New York: Macmillan & Co. Ltd, 1964), pp. 98–99.

essential scripture. Goethe's interest in studying Islam in 1771 was mainly sparked by, in addition to the highly poetic language of the Qur'an, its invitation to return to pure monotheism.[3]

As the concept of monotheism was not only the basis and backbone of Islam, but Judaism and Christianity as well, the attack on Islam by European Christians was mainly directed towards Muhammad. In the "Song of Antioch," Muhammad is mockingly referred to as "Mahom," a type of idol placed on an elephant, and as "Mohoun" or "Mahound," which is derived from Scottish-English word for "devil." Monsieur Dermenghem describes Muhammad as follows:

> They portrayed Mahomet as a camel-thief, a rake, sorcerer, a brigand chief, even as a Roman cardinal furious at not having been elected Pope. They showed him as a false God to whom the faithful made human sacrifices.

> The worthy Guibert de Nogent himself tells us that he (Mahomet) died through excessive drunkenness and that his corpse was eaten by pigs on a dung-hill explaining why flesh of this animal and wine are prohibited.[4]

Pijper also summarizes the views of his predecessor, Van der Palm, Chancellor of Leiden University in 1799, as follows:

> [Van der Palm refuted] Western lies and shortsightedness on Islam, and [provided] information about the personality, nature and spirit of Muhammad. According to Van der Palm, Muhammad had four types of virtues, namely perseverance of faith, cleverness, eloquences, and greatness. [While] Van der Palm still [regarded] Muhammad as a deceiver, it can be forgiven due to the merits of Muhammad who had succeeded in bringing back his people who worshiped idols to the belief in God Almighty.[5]

Although Van der Palm was a Western-Christian intellectual of the 18th century, this attitude generally reflects that of most Western-Christian scholars and mainstream society, who still tend to consider Muhammad as a mere con artist, regardless

3. Melanie Mohr, "Goethe and Islam Religion has no nationality," https://en.qantara.de/content/goethe-and-islam-religion-has-no-nationality.

4. O Hashem, *Marxisme dan Agama* (Surabaya: Penerbit JAPI, 1965), pp. 85–86.

5. G.F. Pijper, *Islam and the Netherlands*, 7.

of his contribution to humanity. Van der Palm's attitude epitomizes a stage when Western-Christian societies, while they may understand and appreciate his humanitarian work, still perceive Muhammad as human, not prophet, as well as a fraud. It goes without saying that with such an attitude, Van der Palm hardly acknowledges Muhammad as a messenger of God, thereby invalidating the doctrines of Islam.

Meanwhile, Gibbon and Toynbee, two great historians of the Western-Christian World in the 18th and 20th centuries, not only respected Muhammad as a messenger of God, but both historians highly appreciated and admired the capacity of Islam to improve society. In one of his works, Arnold Toynbee mentioned that Islam had the great ability to dispel racial prejudice and discrimination, as well as alcoholism.

> We can, however, discern certain principles of Islam, which, if brought to bear in the social life of the new cosmopolitan proletariat, might have important salutary effects on the "great society" in a nearer future. Two conspicuous sources of danger—one psychological and the other material—in the present relations of this cosmopolitan proletariat, with the dominant element in our modern Western society, are race consciousness and alcohol; and in the struggle with each of these evils the Islamic spirit has a service to render which might prove, if it were accepted, to be of high moral and social value.

The extinction of race consciousness between Muslims is an outstanding model achievement, and in the contemporary world there is, as it happens, a crying need for the propagation of this Islamic virtue.[6]

The great Irish poet George Bernard Shaw (1856-1950), despite claiming to be an atheist, was also known as an admirer of Muhammad:

> I have studied him—the wonderful man – and in my opinion, far from being an anti-Christ, he must be called the Savior of Humanity.[7]

It seems that there is still a long journey ahead for the Western-Christian World to recognize and respect Muhammad as not

---

6. Arnold Toynbee, *Civilization on Trial and the World and the West* (New York: Meridian Books, 1958), 181.

7. George Bernard Shaw, *The Genuine Islam*, vol 1 (Singapore: 1936) cited from David Pawson, *The Challenge of Islam to Christians* (London: Hodder & Stoughton, 2003), 200, 193.

merely a human being, let alone a deceiver, but as a prophet and messenger of God. The stereotypes were increasingly justified by 18th century European Christian scientists, who developed various official studies on everything related to Islam through the lens of the so-called Orientalism. Orientalism itself was not developed to find things that are more positive in Islam and Muhammad; rather, as stated by Reverend Andreas Yewangoe, "the study of other religions was originally intended to find their weaknesses, to be attacked and conquered."[8]Stereotypes of Muslims and the Muslim World served to facilitate the dominance of the Western-Christian World in the majority Muslim countries they occupied, including that Muhammad is a false prophet, the Qur'an is not a holy book, chapters of the Qur'an contradict one another, the prophetic tradition (hadith) was composed by Muslims after the death of Muhammad, Islam is spread with the Quran in the left hand and the sword in the right hand, Islam degrades women, etc.

INDONESIA'S CASE

The harmful residues of Orientalism were still circulating in Indonesia in the early days of independence. For example, a book published by the Tomohon Catholic Church Administration in 1949, entitled The History of the Church with its Summary (Sejarah Geredja dengan Ringkasannya), states:

> After the death of Muhammad, Abu Bakr and Umar ibn Khattab had propagated (expanded) Islam by fighting other people. After the death of Muhammad, the Qur'an was composed, which contained information about Islam – that is, all the fantasies of Muhammad. The chapters were composed repeatedly, and they contradict one another.

> As for the teachings of Islam, [these are] an embodiment of Catholic as well as Jewish influences, [while] others are influenced by idol worship (paganism). [Muslims are] ordered by the Koran to kill the unbelievers, that is to say people who are not Muslim.[9]

---

8. A.A. Yewangoe, Agama dan Kerukunan (Jakarta: PT BPK Gunung Mulia, 2009), 83. Original passage:
"Memang, studi terhadap agama-agama lain awalnya dimaksudkan untuk menemukan kelemahan mereka untuk diserang dan ditaklukkan."
9. Sejarah Geredja dengan Ringkasannya (Tomohon: Administrasi Geredja Katholik

Furthermore, Indonesia's national figure Theodorus Sumartana, a minister as well as a pioneer of the pluralist movement in Indonesia, mentioned that the Synod of the Dutch Reformed Church in 1986 also decided:

> Islam is a false religion and is a dangerous and serious threat to Christianity and humanity.[10]

Even after the Second Vatican Council officially ended the Catholic Church's hostility towards Islam in the 20th Century, the view of Islam in the West did not significantly change, as the lack of absolute power and authority over the state allowed the Church and Western countries to have different choices of opinions in relation to Islam. Samuel Huntington's *Clash of Civilizations*, as well as George W. Bush's "war on terror" campaign, for example, are nothing but repercussions and continuations of "the Crusades syndrome." Both Huntington and Bush saw Islam as a threat to Western democracies if religious faiths implied political and military conflict. They are based on the assumption that Islam is a radical religion, synonymous with violence and terrorism, a spirit of hostility that is supported by the study of Orientalism. Huntington seems inclined to preserve and exploit Islamophobia and the European historical grudge against Islam, since the failed attack on Poitiers in 732 at the hands of Charles Martel, the capture of Constantinople by Ottoman Turks in 1453, and two failed Sieges of Vienna, also by Ottoman Turks, in 1529 and 1683 respectively.

But, nevertheless, the Second Vatican Council remains an important milestone, not only in the field of religion, but for

---

Tomohon, 1949), 40. Original passages:

"Sepeninggal Muhammad, Abu Bakr dan Umar telah merambatkan (expand) Islam dengan memerangi kaum yang lain. Sepeninggal Muhammad dikaranglah Al-Qur'an, yang berisi keterangan tentang Islam, yakni yang berisi segala khayal Muhammad. Surah-surah itu dikarang ulang-berulang, serta bunyinya bersalahan satu dengan yang lain."

"Adapun ajaran Islam, sebagai pengaruh dari Katolikisme, sebagian pengaruh Yahudi, yang lain pengaruh dari pemujaan berhala (paganisme). Disuruh oleh Al-Qur'an untuk membunuh orang-orang yang tak beriman, yakni orang-orang yang tidak beragama Islam."

10. Theodorus Sumartana, *Pengantar Theologia Religionum* (Jakarta: Tim Balitbang PGI & PT BPK Gunung Mulia, 2007), 27. Original passage:

"Agama Islam adalah agama sesat (palsu) dan berbahaya mengancam secara serius terhadap Christianity dan kemanusiaan."

humanity. Although unable to immediately undermine the stereotypes and resentment and hatred of Western-Christian society towards Muslims and Islam (especially about Nostra Aetate), the Second Vatican Council has played a valuable role in transforming the pattern of relations between the Church and Islam. It has encouraged the development of theology of religion, or *theologia religionum*, which is inherently a theology of transformation to understand and appreciate all religions. It is thanks to the attitude of mutual respect and respect among fellow believers that this harmony of interfaith life can be built on earth.

2

The Western-Christian World and Islam

HISTORICAL GRUDGES

Islam once exerted considerable influence on Europe. At the dawn of its civilization, precisely only a century after the death of Muhammad (in 632), Islam expanded to two great empires, Sassanid and Byzantine. Under the leadership of Muhammad's companions, Abu Bakr (r. 632–634), Umar ibn Khattab (r. 634–644), Uthman ibn Affan (r. 644–656) and Ali ibn Abi Talib (r. 656–661), Islam was thriving and expanding very rapidly. During the reign of Umar ibn Khattab, Muslim forces succeeded in gaining control of Persia, Syria, Egypt, as well as Jerusalem in 638.

Under the leadership of the Caliph of Al-Walid (r. 705–717), Muslim forces controlled almost all of North Africa, while in 711, under the leadership of Tariq ibn Ziyad, they managed to cross to the Iberian Peninsula and mark the establishment of the Islamic caliphate of Córdoba in Spain. Karen Armstrong expressed her admiration for how the Arabs, who had been seen as inferior, suddenly and miraculously controlled various provinces with their new faith (Islam), which "extended from the Pyrenees to the Himalayas."

Córdoba became a center of culture and knowledge in Europe, giving birth to philosophers such as Ibn Rushd (Averroes). The Caliphate of Córdoba was famous for its effort to invade France through the battle of Poitiers (also known as the Battle of Tours), but was eventually defeated by Charles Martel. When the caliphate was successfully conquered by King Ferdinand of Aragon and Queen Isabella of Castille in 1492, the Sultanate of Seljuk flourished, Sultan Murad I (r. 1421–1451) in Eastern Europe even extended his power as far as Hungary. In 1453, Sultan Mehmed II (r. 1444–1446 and 1451–1481), also known as Mehmed the Conqueror, seized Constantinople, the capital of the Byzantine Empire, and later changed its name to Istanbul and made it the capital of the

Ottoman Empire.

Contrary to this success, the Ottoman Empire was also renowned for its failed attack on Vienna in 1529. After the Ottoman troops succeeded in capturing Crete in 1669, a second attack on Vienna occurred in 1683, but was again fruitless. This failure marked the beginning of its decline.

These two raids and sieges of Vienna, as well as the advent of Thariq ibn Ziyad in Europe in 711, are used by Samuel Huntington and Bernard Lewis in their arguments to preserve Western resentment towards Muslims, and are the basic argument of Huntington's clash of civilizations theory. Quoting Lewis, his teacher on Islamic issues, Huntington tries to prove that Islam is indeed an existential threat to the survival of Europe:

> "For almost a thousand years," Bernard Lewis observes, "from the first Moorish landing in Spain to the second Turkish siege of Vienna, Europe was under constant threat from Islam." Islam is the only civilization which has put the survival of the West in doubt, and it has done that at least twice.

However, Karen Armstrong states that the so-called "invasion" of Islam against neighboring provinces was never accompanied by forced conversion. The same was true for the previous period of leadership, when Muhammad, although accompanied by an army of ten thousand men, conquered Mecca in 630. In so doing he "took Mecca without shedding a drop of blood." This message of peace was also present when the Muslims captured Jerusalem in 638, the third holiest city for Islam after Mecca and Medina.

All people of various faiths living in Jerusalem are granted freedom of religion. Even Umar ibn Khattab unequivocally refused Patriarch Sophronius of Jerusalem's proposal that Umar pray in the Church of Resurrection (or Church of the Holy Sepulcher), which was built in the fourth century by Queen Helena, mother of Emperor Constantine, on the rock where Jesus is believed to have ascended to heaven. Umar only prayed on the steps outside the church gate. This refusal was deemed necessary to prevent Muslims from praying there in the future, which would have been a justification to convert the church into a mosque.

Prior to the arrival of the Crusaders, history records how peace and life between religious communities was manifested in Jerusalem for nearly half a millennium (467 years) after Umar ibn Khattab took over the city from Patriarch Sophronius in 638. The Muslim rulers provided peace in religious life, including guarding the holy sites of all three religions, Judaism, Christianity and Islam.

This is in stark contrast to the events that emerged over the next few centuries, when the Crusaders reclaimed Jerusalem in 1099 and massacred not only Muslims but Jews and other Christians, including women and children.

John William Draper describes the Crusaders' cruelty when capturing Jerusalem on July 15, 1099:

> But, in the capture by the Crusaders, the brains of young children were dashed out against the walls; infants were thrown over the battlements; every woman that could be seized was violated; men were roasted at fires; some were ripped open, to see if they had swallowed gold; the Jews were driven into their synagogue, and there burnt; a massacre of nearly 70,000 persons took place; and the pope's legate was seen "partaking in the triumph."

Then, in 1492, Isabella of Castille and Ferdinand of Aragon united and succeeded in overthrowing the Islamic caliphate in Spain, which was already seven centuries old by then, in an extensive massacre. Moreover, the Pope had activated the inquisition in Castille in 1478 by legalizing torture and mass murder. No less than 13,000 Jews were killed, while 150,000 Muslims were expelled and/or left the Iberian Peninsula.

GALLUP POLLING CHALLENGES
THE CLASH OF CIVILIZATIONS THEORY

On January 7, 2011, Sarah Reef, then the director of the Cross-cultural Department of the Common Ground Newsletter in New York, announced the results of the Abu Dhabi Gallup Center poll entitled "Measuring the State of Muslim-West Relations: Assessing the 'New Beginning.'" The poll involved more than 100,000 respondents from 2006 to 2010 and was conducted in 55 countries. This report challenges Huntington's clash of civilizations theory by showing that the majority of people surveyed view Muslim-Western interactions as an advantage rather than a threat.

The study revealed that half of the Muslims surveyed felt that the West had no respect for Muslim societies, and that the West should refrain from desecrating religious symbols. They also wanted to see more Muslim figures portrayed accurately in feature films, a powerful tool for enhancing mutual respect between Muslims and American society.

According to the survey results, people who blame religion as a source of tension are unprepared for increased interaction between Islam and the West, and are likely to remain so. They are less optimistic about peace and fear that conflict is inevitable. The Gallup poll also shows a strong correlation between education and a willingness to view increased Muslim World-Western World interactions as an advantage. Therefore, the majority of people who have graduated from secondary or higher education—both Muslims and Westerners—tend to view this interaction as an advantage.

Gallup also advised Muslims and Western leaders to put more emphasis on solving political problems rather than religious conflicts. This must be done by making policies that are fair to Western countries and take existing cultural differences into consideration. One example is to facilitate the issuance of visas for students or tourists from the Muslim World who are interested in visiting the United States of America. Such a measure would increase the number of Muslim travelers and/or tourists to the USA, and,

Samuel P. Huntington's hypothesis on 'The Clash of Civilizations' was an interpretation on post cold war global politics, providing a post cold war framework and paradigm for decision makers.

hence, reinforce cultural exchanges and encourage a better mutual understanding.

The final section of the Gallup poll revolves around the perceptions of people from three regions with acute political conflict: Afghanistan, Iraq, and Israel and the Palestinian territories. They were asked about their views on daily realities and the increased interaction between the Muslim World and the Western World. In their policy recommendation report, Gallup includes the importance of addressing local needs in Iraq and Afghanistan; however, no similar recommendations are offered for Israeli and Palestinian territories, perhaps because the issue is contentious. As this conflict is one of the greatest sources of tension between Muslims and the people of the United States, readers of the Gallup report could benefit from recommendations on this issue.

Following the speech of former United States President Barack Obama in June 2009 in Cairo, there has been an increase in Muslim-Western exchanges, such as entrepreneurship programs, student and academic exchanges, partnerships to curb disease, and programs to improve women's education in Muslim majority societies. However, critics argue that real change hasn't happened yet. In early 2020, some Arab countries' support for the President of the United States waned. This may be because Obama did not live up to expectations of change in the Arab World. This makes one thing clear: although we have made progress in improving Muslim-Western relations, there is still much to be done.

SHIFT OF THE WEST-ISLAM PENDULUM

After Pope Urban agitated the European masses to organize a Crusade on November 25, 1095, wave after wave of attacks aimed at reclaiming Jerusalem continued for two centuries. The Crusaders were a joint force from England, France, and Germany (or Prussia), under the direct command of King Richard the Lion Heart, Emperor Philip Augustus, and Emperor Frederick Barbarossa, respectively. The failure of these attacks was an indicator of the progress of Islamic civilization at that time, for it turned out that the Muslim World they wanted to conquer was more advanced and sophisticated than European civilization, which was still in the grip of the Dark Ages.

Europe lived under the influence of strong Islamic rule and civi-

An illustration of Pope Urban II delivering his Pontifical Command at the Clermont Council, November 25, 1095, to send the Crusaders to liberate Jerusalem from Muslim occupancy.

lization for no less than ten centuries, from when Islamic troops passed through the Strait of Gibraltar in 711 until improvements in navigation led to the European colonization of Africa, Central Asia, South Asia, and Southeast Asia in the 1700s. According to Edward Said, "For Europe, Islam was a lasting trauma." The experience under the rule and influence of Islam for ten centuries produced grudges toward Muslims in the form of Islamophobia, bred hatred, and fear that persist even today, when the situation of life and world civilization has changed diametrically. Now, European civilization controls and dominates the social, economic and political order of global society, including the Muslim World.

The pendulum of European-Islamic relations began to change in the seventeenth century, which was marked by the decline of the Ottoman Empire in Turkey. The historian Arnold Toynbee states: "Had the Muslim forces not been defeated and captured at Poitiers in 732, which was only 70 kilometers from Paris, and if the Ottoman Turks managed to capture Vienna in the second invasion of 1683, then the fate of Europe today is feared to be different." Additionally, Toynbee illustrates that the discovery of sea routes by European sailors in the sixteenth century is what marked the beginning of Western rule over the Muslim World. Toynbee illustrates that in the sixteenth century, it was as if Europe began to throw its "lasso rope" into the "necks" of Islamic countries which were in decline. The rope was really only tightened in the nineteenth century, choking the "neck" of the Muslim World through European colonialism.[11] Although in the early twenty-first century the Muslim World seemed to have succeeded in freeing themselves from European colonialism, politically, economically and culturally, European domination over Islam was still very strong.

SOFT TERRORISM

Symptoms of European Islamophobia in modern times have yet to subside. One could argue that they even peaked when the Arab Spring emerged in early 2011, which initially erupted in Tunisia and then spread to Egypt, Libya, and even to several Arab countries in the Middle East. In her work, *Eurabia: The Europe-Arab Axis*, Bat Ye'or asserts that there will be a political and cultural transformation in Europe due to this increasing number of Arab-Muslim migrants. John L. Esposito expressed the European fear of a new style of "invasion" by Islam today, which will no longer attack physically (such as the attacks on Poitiers and Vienna), but will take another form called "soft terrorism."

> In Europe, many news stories depict a vanishing Christianity endangered by Islam, the fastest-growing religion. The Muslim population on the Continent has grown from twelve to twenty million in a decade, and the number of mosques in countries like Britain, Germany, France, and Italy has grown exponentially.
>
> Modern-day prophets of doom predict that Europe will be overrun by Islam, transformed by the end of the century into "Eurabia." The media, political leaders, and commentators on the right warn of a "soft terrorism" plot to take over America and Europe. Bernard Lewis, a Middle East historian and adviser to the Bush administration on its failed Iraq policy, received widespread coverage when he chided Europeans for losing their loyalties, self-confidence, and respect for their own culture, charging that they have "surrendered" to Islam in a mood of "self-abasement," "political correctness," and "multi-culturalism".[12]

"Eurabia" is the feared result of the flooding of Europe by the Muslim population through the process of migration, either due

---

11. *Ibid.*, 248.

12. John L. Esposito, *The Future of Islam* (New York: Oxford University Press, 2010), pp. 25, 26.

to the Arab Spring or through normal migration in search of job opportunities, in which Europe will become dominated by Muslim or Arab populations. Fear and hatred of Islam is consistently and religiously embraced by many people throughout Europe, including scholars such as Bernard Lewis and Samuel Huntington as well as political leaders. In fact, several major European countries – France, Germany and the United Kingdom in particular – have persistently rejected Turkey's efforts to become a member of the European Union. The concerns of European Union countries are based on the belief that political upheaval in the Muslim World will spur massive and difficult to prevent waves of migrations from Muslim countries to Europe. In fact, Esposito stated that Nicholas Sarkozy's brilliant victory in the French elections was due to his consistency in refusing Turkey's efforts to become a member of the European Union.[13] Statements made by Angela Merkel and David Cameron—German Chancellor and former English Prime Minister, respectively— suggest that the failure of the multicultural movement in Europe occurred because they did not want Islamic culture to become part of European culture.

Along with Angela Merkel's opinion, the March 6, 2011 edition of *The New York Times* published a statement by the Minister of the Interior of the Republic of Germany, Hans Peter Friedrich, expressing his doubt that a person who is Muslim can become a good German citizen. Interestingly, the Lutheran Church Bishop Markus Dröge regretted this statement, since, according to him, Germany is a democracy that upholds human rights.[14] Dröge's statement suggests that a citizen's Muslim identity should not be compared to their German culture, and that Muslim citizens should become a legitimate part of a plural society.

Meanwhile, at the community level, the controversial film *Fitna* by Geert Wilders in the Netherlands, as well as the cartoon of the Prophet Muhammad published by the Danish daily, *Jylland Posten*, in 2005, reflect the stereotypes or subconscious negative attitudes of the European community toward Islam.

---

13. *Ibid*, 159. Esposito cited it from *World Economic Forum, Islam and the West: Annual Report on the State of Dialogue*, January 2008, 26 , http://www.weforum.org/pdf/C 100 /Islam_West.pdf.

14. "New Interior Minister Revives a Debate: Can Muslims Be True Germans?" https://www.nytimes.com/2011/03/07/world/europe/07germany.html

THREE CHALLENGES OF ISLAM
AGAINST EUROPEAN-CHRISTIANITY

David Pawson describes three waves of Islamic "attacks" against Europe: the military attack, the mental-cultural attack, and an attack in the form of migration of the Muslim population to Europe,[15] or what Esposito termed "soft terrorism." Included in the third wave are converts, which symbolize the increasing number of Europeans embracing Islam.

FIRST: THE ISLAMIC MILITARY CHALLENGE

The first offensives began with the invasion by Muslim forces of Gibraltar in 711, then when Muslim forces nearly captured Paris in 732, which was thwarted by Charles Martel at Poitiers. The second military invasion occurred in 1071, when the Seljuk Empire defeated the Byzantine Empire. The Seljuk Empire's attack forced the Byzantine Emperor to ask the Pope for help, thus spurring a European Christian counterattack in the form of the Crusades.

There was also the Ottoman Empire attack on Constantinople in 1453, a city which, after being captured by the Ottoman, was renamed Istanbul. Next was the Ottoman Empire's attack on Europe via Vienna in 1683, which in addition to failing also marked the beginning of the decline of the Ottoman Empire, before finally being dissolved in 1923 and replaced by a secular republic founded by Mustafa Kemal Atatürk.

SECOND: MENTAL CHALLENGES AND ISLAMIC CULTURE

Islam's second "attack" on Europe, or rather the encounter and dialogue between European and Islamic civilizations, was mental and cultural. It occurred over several events, including the introduction of Islamic universities in Spain and the development of trade involving several ports on the southern coast of Europe, such as Venice, Genoa and other emporiums.

There is no European historian or scientist who rejects the role of Islamic civilization in the birth and development of European civilization. The influence of Islamic civilization on the rise of Europe from the Middle Ages to the Renaissance, the Enlightenment, the Age of Reason, and so on has been recorded in history

---

15. David Pawson, *The Challenge of Islam to Christians*, 16.

time and again, with the peak of Islamic civilization in tenth century Baghdad and Córdoba, which had made significant developments in mathematics, medicine, architecture and art. Europe is indebted to the great Muslim philosophers there, such as Abdul Walid Ahmad ibn Rushd (Averroes), along with Al-Farabi and Ibn Sina (Avicenna). It was these thinkers, with their tradition of rationality, who inspired the scholastic thinking of the Christian World. Their astonishing interpretations of Aristotle's philosophy helped European reformist thinkers to better understand ancient Greek thought, which later influenced the development of intellect and science in the West. Without the development of an objective attitude towards science, it was impossible for the Renaissance to advance, a movement that would later give birth to great scholars such as Copernicus, Kepler, Galileo, Newton, Descartes, and others.

THIRD: MIGRATION CHALLENGES AND CONVERTS

Pawson asserts that the wave of migration that Esposito called "soft terrorism" was very difficult to prevent, since the migration was flowing from former colonies into the "mother countries" that once colonized them (for example, when Muslims from former British colonies moved to Britain, or Muslims from former French colonies to France). This pattern of migration is understandable due to the observable emotional and historical connections between the colony and mother country.

Since the Arab Spring in early 2011, migration by boat has been increasing. According to the United Nations Children's Fund (UNICEF), in addition to political and inter-community conflicts, massive migration has been exacerbated by the life-threatening difficulties of extreme climate change in African countries, particularly in North Africa and sub-Saharan Africa.[16] Europe, it was reported, has become panicked and uncooperative in the face of uncontrollable waves of boat people. By July 3, 2017, there were 103,387 migrants, with the most in Italy at 85,183 and over 2,000 migrants who crossed from Libya having died in the Mediterranean Sea. The rest were spread across Spain (6,464), Greece (10,094), and Cyprus (273), according to the International Organization for Migration (IOM). A call to action by The

16. *Kompas,* July 6, 2017, "Uni Eropa Larang Kapal LSM," 10.

This kind of private, voluntary humanitarian ship safeguards the "boat people" who endanger their lives at sea in search of better livelihoods in Europe.

United Nations High Commissioner for Refugees (UNHCR) that other European countries share in dealing with migrants has not been well received by neighboring countries, including France, Greece, Hungary, the Czech Republic, and Poland. Even Italian Prime Minister Paulo Gentilone admitted his fear that without the help of other European countries, migrants will become the victims of violence waged by native Italians.[17]

According to the Thomson Reuter Foundation, from 2011-2015 there have been more than 500,000 migrants crossing from Libya to Italy, the majority children.[18] The European Union has even banned rescue boats belonging to NGOs (non-government organizations), which were instrumental in rescuing 35% of refugees to the safety of mainland Italy.

Apart from the increasing number of Muslim immigrants, what Pawson was more worried about was the increase in Europeans converting to Islam. Pawson quoted a statement by George Bernard Shaw, found in a Singaporean magazine, *Genuine Islam*, in 1936:

> If any religion had the chance of ruling over England, nay Europe, within the next hundred years, it could be only Islam. I have prophesied about the faith of Muhammad that it would be acceptable to the Europe of tomorrow as it is beginning to be acceptable to the Europe today.[19]

---

17. *Kompas*, July 5, 2017, "Krisis Migran: 100.000 orang masuk Eropa, Italia Kewalahan," 8.

18. "E.European leaders in war of words as migrants pour across borders," https://news.trust.org/item/20150919142704-5ngcq/

19. David Pawson, *The Challenge of Islam to Christians*, 16.

In addition, Pawson also concluded that:

> Overall, Islam is the second largest and fastest-growing religion, as it is in most of the world, with mosques springing up like mushrooms.[20]

The Nobel Prize Winner in Literacy in 1925, George Bernard Shaw (1856-1950), was known worldwide for his opinion: "If any religion had the chance of ruling over England, nay Europe within the next hundred years, it could only be Islam."

FIVE THEORIES OF PHILOSOPHY OF HISTORY

In the last chapter of his book, Pawson considers the future of Islam, which according to him is growing four times faster than Christianity, so it is not impossible that one day the number of Muslims will exceed the number of Christians. Furthermore, the future of Christianity was also questioned, both in England and throughout the world, asking how long this religion could last.

He answered this question through five theoretical approaches to the philosophy of history. The *first*, the cyclic theory, is based on Greek philosophy and skeptics, who believe that history will always repeat itself in cyclic mode. The *second*, the epic theory, differs from the cyclic theory, stating that history does not repeat itself, but advances like a roller coaster, dynamically fluctuating, alternating, peace-war, win-lose, and so on.

The *third*, the optimistic theory, believes that history is like an

20. *Ibid.*

escalator that continues upwards, towards a better life. But this theory becomes increasingly unreliable as the humanitarian catastrophes grow and become more severe. The *fourth*, the pessimistic theory, states that as the world and life go on, they get worse over time, leaving only dim hope. The beginning of the twenty-first century was characterized more by human efforts to simply survive, not their efforts towards progress.

The *fifth*, the apocalyptic theory, believes that the life of the world will be so bad, only after that will it rise to grace. According to Pawson, this theory is embraced by Jews, Communists and Christians, all of which are based on the same source, namely the Hebrew prophets, even though all three faiths have different sources of power to rise and survive. Communists believe in human power, Jews believe in the power of God and Messiah, while Christians believe in the help of Jesus Christ.

Toward a Europe-Arab Axis

IS ISLAM THE FASTEST-GROWING RELIGION?

In his review of the decree of the Second Vatican Council, the Ad Gentes (announced at the Fourth Session of the Council on December 7, 1965), Stephen Bevans SVD, professor of Missiology and Culture at the Catholic Theological Union Chicago, commented on the importance of the decision to reaffirm the church as a new missionary institution. The choice is between the Church promoting "missionary work to a 'sincere and patient dialogue' with local cultures and contexts," or the Church remaining an ancient Christian institution. While "dialogue" was said to be the central theme of the Second Vatican Council at the 2012 50th Anniversary Conference held at Georgetown University, Washington DC,[21] Stephen Bevans commented that "The Second Vatican Council was funda-

---

21. Konsili Vatikan II dilaksanakan atas inisiatif Paus Johannes XXIII (1959–1963) dan berlangsung pada Oktober 11, 1962–December 8, 1965. Di tengah konsili itu sang Paus mangkat (on June 3, 1963) dan digantikan olah Paus Paulus VI (1963–1973). The Second Vatican Council 50th Anniversary Conference yang digelar di University of Georgetown, Washington DC, in 2012 menyebut bahwa konsili yang bertemakan "dialog" itu adalah momentum paling besar dalam sejarah Gereja Katolik, setelah gerakan reformasi yang dipimpin oleh Martin Luther. Konsili Vatikan memutuskan empat keputusan yang bersifat Konstitusi, sembilan keputusan yang bersifat Decree, dan tiga keputusan yang bersifat Pernyataan. Dua keputusan yang bersifat Pernyataan adalah Dignitatis Humanae (atau Pernyataan tentang kebebasan beragama) dan Nostra Aetate (atau pernyataan tentang hubungan Gereja dengan agama-agama non-Kristiani) yang merupakan keputusan penting untuk mengakhiri pertentangan Gereja Katolik dengan agama-agama lain, khususnya dengan Judaism and Islam, yang sudah berlangsung selama berabad-abad.

Sources: http://catholic-resources.org/ChurchDocs/VaticanCouncil2.htm; "Vatican II After Fifty Years," https://president.georgetown.edu/vatican-ii-dialogue/#; "How the second Vatican council responded to the modern world," The Guardian, https://www.theguardian.com/commentisfree/andrewbrown/2012/oct/11/second-vatical-council-50-years-catholicism

mentally a missionary council." Furthermore, Bevans stated:

> ... a missionary church recognizes that the world has profoundly changed in the wake of two devastating wars in the twentieth century, the demise of Communist vision in almost every place in which it once had a stranglehold, and the renaissance of the world's major religions and in particular *the ascendancy of Islam as the world's fastest growing religion and menacing radical parties within it.*
>
> *As the Western Christians find themselves in numerical decline,* they have come to recognize the need to witness to and preach the gospel in new ways and with new urgency in the pluralist and secularist societies in which they live. Mission is everywhere.[22]

It was not surprising that, in 2011, the *National Geographic Magazine* and the Pew Research Center for Religion and Public Life published the results of their studies on the development of various religions in the world over time.[23] Despite the differences in regards to the data collection methods applied by the two institutions, the reports themselves are not much different. The early 2011 issue of *National Geographic Magazine* presented a "Free Map of World Faiths" comparing the growth by percentage of the world's religions between 1900 and 2010. The report by *National Geographic Magazine* and the Pew Research Center on Religion and Public Life is close to what David Pawson had been worried about in his book (published in 2003).

The "Free Map of World Faiths" illustrates several interesting phenomena. *First*, it mentioned that, in several countries, nearly 99.9% of the population adheres to one particular religion, namely the Vatican (Christianity), Afghanistan (Islam), Somalia (Islam), Bhutan (Buddhism), Burundi (Christianity), Nigeria (Islam), Bangladesh (Islam), Kenya (Christianity), Pakistan (Islam), Yemen (Islam) and Maldives (Islam). Indonesia is not included in this category as, despite being home to the largest number of Muslims of any nation, the proportion of Muslims to the rest of the population is lower; Maldives, for example, has only 300,000 inhabitants, but

---

22. Stephen Bevans, "New Evangelization Or Missionary Church? Evangelii Gaudium and the Call for Missionary Discipleship," *Verbum* SVD 55, nos. 2–3 (2014):158–76.

23. *National Geographic Magazine*, Sacred Journey special edition, Jan 2011; Pew Research Center is a non-partisan religious, social, economic and political research institute based in Washington DC.

99.9% of those inhabitants are Muslim.

Next is the ranking of countries with a high percentage of atheists or agnostics, starting with North Korea (71.3%), followed by the Czech Republic (43.8%), China (including Taiwan) (39.5%), Uruguay (34.5%), Kazakhstan (34.4%), Sweden (32.2%), Latvia (30.4%), Estonia (28.6%), and the Netherlands (27.5%).

National Geographic Magazine also reported the growth of followers of each religion over a period of 110 years, as shown in the table below:

WORLD RELIGION DATABASE
COMPARISON BETWEEN 1900 AND 2010[24]

RELIGIONS	1900	2010
Christianity	34.5%	33.0%
traditional Chinese religions	23.5%	6.6%
Hinduism	12.5%	13.7%
Islam	12.3%	22.5%
Buddhism	7.8%	6.7%
ethnic religions	7.3%	3.9%
Agnosticism	0.2%	9.6%
Atheism	0.01%	2.0%

The table shows a drastic decline in the percentage of followers of traditional Chinese religions, consistent with the rise of the Communist Party in China, as well as an increase in the percentage of followers of Islam to almost double within a century. An increase of over fifty times the number of agnostics in 1900 is also shown. The absence of Judaism from this table suggests that Jews did not experience significant changes over the period of 1900-2010. Judaism is not a missionary religion, but rather intended for people of Jewish lineage, so population numbers do not change significantly. *National Geographic Magazine* concluded that as of 2010, 88% of the population on Earth (nearly seven billion people in 2010) is religious.

Finally, the Pew Research Center reiterated that Muslims, the largest religious community after Christians, will develop the

24. *National Geographic Magazine*, Sacred Journey special edition, "World Religion Database.".

fastest among the followers of other religions in the world. In the period of 2015–2060 it is projected that Muslims will make up 70% of all religious communities in the world, followed by Christians with 34%, Hindus with 27%, and Jews with 15%, with an average growth rate of 32%.[25]

GROWING NUMBER OF MUSLIMS IN EUROPE

The following report by the Pew Research Center Forum on Religion and Public Life, "The Future of the Global Muslim Population: Projection for 2010–2030," was published on January 27, 2011:

> The world's Muslim population is expected to increase by about 35% in the next 20 years, rising from 1.6 billion in 2010 to 2.2 billion by 2030. *Globally, the Muslim population is forecast to grow at about twice the rate of the non-Muslim population over the next two decades-* an average annual growth rate of 1.5% for Muslims, compared with 0.7% for non-Muslims. If current trends continue, Muslims will make up 26.4% of the world's total projected population of 8.3 billion in 2030, up from 23.4% of the estimated 2010 world population of 6.9 billion.[26]

The Pew report also predicted that the Muslim population in Europe would grow by almost a third over twenty years, from 44.1 million to 58.2 million, or 6% of the total population of Europe in 2010, to 8% in 2030. This does not include the 80 million Muslims in Turkey, which, should Turkey enter the European Union, would significantly increase the population of European Muslims.

Several European Union countries will witness rapid growth in the Muslim population by 2030. In Belgium, for example, the Muslim population will increase from 6% in 2011 to 10.2% while Muslims in France will increase from 7.5% in 2011 to 10.3%. Furthermore, the Muslim population in the UK is predicted to increase from 4.6% in 2011 to 8.2% in 2030, and in the same year Russia is predicted to become the country with the largest Muslim population in Europe of 18.6 million, or 14.4% of the total Russian population.

Pew Research Center Forum on Religion and Public Life also reported the development of Muslims in several European coun-

---

25. Pew Research Center, "The Changing Global Religious Landscape," https://www.pewforum.org/2017/04/05/the-changing-global-religious-landscape/

26. Pew Research Center, "The Future of the Global Muslim Population," https://www.pewforum.org/2011/01/27/the-future-of-the-global-muslim-population/

tries, as follows:

In 2030, Muslims are projected to make up more than 10% of the total population in 10 European countries: Kosovo (93.5%), Albania (83.2%), Bosnia-Herzegovina (42.7%), Republic of Macedonia (40.3%), Montenegro (21.5%), Bulgaria (15.7%), Russia (14.4%), Georgia (11.5%), France (10.3%) and Belgium (10.2%).

Russia will continue to have the largest Muslim population (in absolute numbers) in Europe in 2030. Its Muslim population is expected to rise from 16.4 million in 2010 to 18.6 million in 2030. The growth rate for the Muslim population in Russia is projected to be 0.6% annually over the next two decades. By contrast, Russia's non-Muslim population is expected to shrink by an average of 0.6% annually over the same period.

France had an expected net influx of 66,000 Muslim immigrants in 2010, primarily from North Africa. Muslims comprised an estimated two-thirds (68.5%) of all new immigrants to France in the past year. Spain was expected to see a net gain of 70,000 Muslim immigrants in 2010, but they account for a much smaller portion of all new immigrants to Spain (13.1%). The U.K.'s net inflow of Muslim immigrants in the past year (nearly 64,000) was forecast to be nearly as large as France's. More than a quarter (28.1%) of all new immigrants to the U.K. in 2010 are estimated to be Muslim.[27]

PEW RESEARCH CENTER'S PREDICTION FOR 2050

The Pew Research Center has predicted that the number of Muslims in Europe in 2011 will triple by 2050.[28] Even if all European Union countries (twenty-seven countries in 2020) close their borders, the population of European Muslims will continue to increase due to a considerable number of youth and a high fertility rate.

According to the Pew Center, in 2016, the European Muslim population significantly increased, from 19 million in 2010 to 25.8 million, or from 3.8% to 4.9% of the total population of Europe. The number of Muslim immigrants alone has reached as high as 500,000 over the past four years, particularly since the Arab Spring in 2011 and the following armed conflicts in Syria, Iraq and Afghanistan.

The Pew Research Center considered three main scenarios for the intensity of this migration. *First*, zero migration from 2016 to

---

27. *Ibid.*
28. *Ibid.*

2050; *second*, medium migration, in which migration generally stops but migration for personal reasons still occurs; *third*, high migration, in which large-scale migration patterns such as that which occurred in 2014–2016 continue to occur with the same religious composition.

In the zero-migration scenario, the European Muslim population would increase from 25.8 million (4.9%) to 35.8 million (7.4%), except for Cyprus, which already had a total Muslim population of 25.4% (most of whom settled in North Cyprus for historical reasons). By 2050, the total population of Muslims in France would increase to 8.6 million (12.7%), from only 5.7 million (8.8%) in 2016.

Under the medium migration scenario, by 2050 Sweden would have a Muslim population of 20.5%, the UK will increase from 6.3% in 2016 to 16.7%, and Finland will increase from 2.7% in 2016 to 11.4%. Likewise, Western European countries, where the Muslim population will increase notably by 2050.

Finally, under the high migration scenario, the population of Muslims in Sweden will grow to 30.6%, in Finland 15%, and in Norway 17%. In Eastern Europe, the average population growth of Muslims will be low, except for Greece and Hungary, which will see an even higher increase of Muslims.

Apart from the influence of the migration factor, the increasing number of Muslims in Europe is also driven by high fertility. The study shows that the fertility rate of the Muslim population compared to the population of non-Muslims in Europe is 2.6:1.6.

The European Muslim population is also much younger on average than the non-Muslim population. Approximately 27% of the total Muslim population is under 15 years of age, compared to 15% of the total population of non-Muslims.

While the Muslim population is projected to continue to grow under all three scenarios— more than double under the medium and high migration scenarios—the number of non-Muslim residents will decline in all three scenarios, as predicted by the Pew Research Center.

SUMMARY

Aside from typical factors such as fertility and death rates, the Arab Spring revolutions beginning in Tunisia, then Egypt, Libya and several other Arab countries since 2011 has created a new trend of extraordinary events affecting the development of Islam

Regent's Park Mosque in London, built by the British government in appreciation of the support of the Muslim people during the Second World War. https://www. idntimes.com/travel/destination/amanda-putri/8-masjid-termegah-di-eropa-arsitekturnya-bikin-kagum-nih-c1c2/full

in Europe. Furthermore, climate change has led to increased emigration from parts of Northern Africa and Sub-Saharan Africa as victims flee a damaged environment which can no longer support their livelihoods or provide food security. Since 2017, there have been half a million migrants from North Africa to Europe, the largest of which is through the North Coast of Libya to Italy.[29] Italy is a destination for migrants from Libya not only due to its geographical proximity to Libya, but because of a kind of emotional relationship between Libyan migrants and Italy, the "motherland" of Libya, to borrow David Pawson's term. A number of media reports said that on Friday March 18, 2011, the first ship carrying 350 migrants from Libya (mostly women and children) had landed in Italy. It is not impossible that other ships carrying migrants will follow, apart from migrants who come individually or in small groups.

Unfortunately, in most cases, friction between religious communities is the source of prolonged bloody conflict, whether directly or indirectly, which is downright contradictory to the spirit of salvation and brotherhood that is preached by every religion.[30] Although in all religions there are fundamental differences, followers of all major religions in the world agree that humans

29. *Kompas*, July 5, 2017 and July 6, 2017.

30. David M. Cordis, "The Role of Religion in History," in David M. Cordis, George B. Grose and Muzammil H. Siddiqi (eds.), *The Abraham Connection: A Jew, Christian and Muslim in Dialogue* (Cross Cultural Publications, 1994).

were created and sent down to Earth to achieve their own welfare and peace, earthly and heavenly. If these followers can focus on and carry out this mission and responsibility that they carry in accordance with their religious teachings, then it is safe to say that the seven billion religious people (or 88% of the total human population) on Earth is a tremendous force for realizing prosperity and peace on Earth.

4

The Future of The Western World and Muslim World Relations

EUROPE AS A CHRISTIAN CONTINENT

A 2018 survey of fifteen Western European countries by the Pew Research Center found that, while most European Christians are non-practicing in religious matters, Christianity remains central to their identity in social and cultural terms. Pew Research analyst Neha Sahgal also observes that, according to the survey, one's Christian identity can influence attitudes towards immigration, national identity and pluralism. She identified the following ten points, which summarize the level of diversity of European Christians on developing socio-cultural issues in Europe.

First, even though secularization is so widespread in Western Europe, the majority of European people still identified themselves as Christians, including 71% in Germany and 64% in France.

Second, although most Europeans still claim to be Christians, only a few of them worship in church. With the exception of Italy, more Western Europeans are classified as non-practicing (attending church only once or twice a year) than practicing or churchgoing (attending church once a month or more). In the UK, the number of Christians who are non-practicing is 50%, while only 18% of Christians are churchgoing.

Third, most Christians in Western Europe, including those who are non-practicing, believe in a higher power. Although many non-practicing Christians say they do not believe in God "as described in the Bible," they do tend to believe in some other higher power or spiritual force in the universe. By contrast, most church-attending Christians say they do believe in God "as depicted in the Bible." Those who are religiously unaffiliated do not profess to believe in God or any higher power in the universe. Non-practicing Christians are also more likely than those who are religiously unaffil-

Majorities across Western Europe identify as Christian

% who say they are Christian

■ 0-49% ■ 50-64% ■ 65-74% ■ 75%+   □ Non-surveyed country

Note: Respondents were asked "What is your present religion, if any? Are you Christian, Muslim, Jewish, Buddhist, Hindu, atheist, agnostic, something else or nothing in particular?"
Source: Survey conducted April-August 2017 in 15 countries. See Methodology for details.
"Being Christian in Western Europe"

PEW RESEARCH CENTER

Despite only 50% of the people in the UK identifying as "non-church attending," and only 18% "church attending," the population of Western Europe still considers themselves to be Christians.

iated to believe in a spiritual force that cannot be illustrated in orthodox theologies.

Fourth, while the majority of Western Europeans surveyed answered that they are willing to accept Muslims as part of their families or in their neighborhoods, there is still a kind of uncertainty towards multiculturalism. They do not unequivocally agree on whether Islam is compatible with their national values and culture; at the very least, they want flexibility in terms of Muslim women's clothing. In general, Western Europeans think that it would be better if a person were born in the local country. For example, roughly half of Finnish adults say that it is important to be born in Finland and to have Finnish family background to be considered Finnish (51%).

Fifth, Christian identity in Western Europe is associated with relatively high levels of nationalism and negative sentiment toward immigrants and religious minorities. Both non-attending and churchgoing Christians surveyed thought that Islam is inherently incompatible with their values and culture. In Germany, as in several other European countries, the public has varying opinions about Islam's compatibility with local values and culture, with 55% of churchgoing Christians agreeing that Islam is incompatible with German values and culture, compared to 45% of non-practicing Christians and 32% of religiously unaffiliated adults. In addition, both churchgoing and non-church attending Christians thought that their values and culture were superior, and wanted limitations on Muslim immigration, whereas those who are religiously unaffiliated felt the opposite.

Sixth, aside from religious identity, other factors—such as education, political ideology and personal familiarity with Muslims—can also influence levels of nationalist, anti-immigrant and anti-religious minority sentiment. Highly educated Western Europeans, for example, do not consider their culture to be superior, nor do they necessarily reject the presence of Jews and Muslims in their family circle. Regarding political ideology, those who belong to the political right are stronger in rejecting the presence of Jews and Muslims compared to those in the political left.

Seventh, the current attitudes of Western Europeans toward Jews and Muslims are highly correlated. Although the current discourse on multiculturalism in Europe is more related to Islam and Muslims, people who say they would be unwilling to accept Muslims in their family are also more likely than others to say they would be unwilling to accept Jewish people in their family. Those who think that Muslims tend to spread the Sharia around them are more likely to agree with the statement that "Jews always pursue their own interests and not the interests of the country they live in".

Eighth, the majority of Christians in Western Europe tend to accept same-sex marriage and abortion. The same attitude was also embraced by those who were not affiliated with a particular religion and also non-practicing Christians who supported the legalization of same-sex marriage and abortion. Although the churchgoing Christians tend to oppose same-sex marriage and abortion, gay or lesbian marriage and abortion are somewhat supported in Denmark, France, Sweden, Switzerland and the UK.

Ninth, a view that resonates in Western Europe is the separation of church and state, thus religion from politics. In Sweden 80% of respondents support the separation of religion and politics, while in Belgium 72% of respondents think so. Meanwhile, 38% respondents in the UK and 45% in Switzerland stated that government policies should support religious values and beliefs in the country, a stance more popular among churchgoing Christians than among non-practicing Christians. Meanwhile, respondents who are religiously unaffiliated do not support "intimacy" between the church and the government.

The tenth point is about the difference between the "religiously unaffiliated" in Western Europe and the United States. Although about a quarter of Americans (23% in 2014) say they are atheist, agnostic or "nothing in particular," similar to the shares of religiously unaffiliated adults in the UK (23%) and Germany (24%), the religiously unaffiliated people in the US are more likely to pray and believe in God than their counterparts in Western Europe. Likewise, the lives of Christians in the US are more religious than their counterparts in Western Europe.[31]

It is observable that the attitude of the Western European community towards Muslims and Islam, for those who claim to be churchgoing (or church-attending) as well as the religiously unaffiliated, is strongly influenced by their level of education and their belief in the superiority of Western European values and culture. The findings of Sahgal's study will be even more interesting when juxtaposed with Richard Wike's study, which shows that what is more influential is not their knowledge of Islam, but the level of familiarity of the Western European community with Muslims.

It's easy to imagine the impact of this familiarity. Muslim public figures who are known, admired and revered by the Western European community at large have surely contributed to changing the perception of the European non-Muslim population towards the Muslim population. Zinedine Zidane, for example, is a Muslim footballer (soccer player) born in Marseille of Algerian descent

---

31. Nesa Sahgal, "10 key findings about religion in Western Europe," https://www.pewresearch.org/fact-tank/2018/05/29/10-key-findings-about-religion-in-western-europe/.

PEW's surveys indicated that familiarity with certain Muslims is much more important for attitudes toward Islam than knowing the Islamic teachings. Positive images of somebody like Zinadine Zidane strongly influence the degree of acceptance of Muslims in general.

who is known and revered by almost all Europeans. Legendary footballer like Zidane have certainly made a considerable contribution in changing the non-Muslim population's perception of Islam and Muslims, especially Muslim migrants, from negative to positive.

In a similar vein, who doesn't know Mohammed Salah, the Egyptian footballer (soccer player) who contributed forty-four goals for Liverpool in the English Premier League 2017/18 season? Even though he is not a migrant, "Mo" Salah's contribution to European football clubs has also helped build the European non-Muslim population's familiarity with Muslims and Islam. In addition, as it happened in the UK, the number of Muslim migrants in important public positions across Western Europe is increasing, including mayors, members of parliament, and even ministers. As Muslim figures become more prominent in Western Europe, the acceptance of Muslims should improve over time.

French Views of Muslims, 2014-15

% with favorable view of Muslims in France, by political ideology

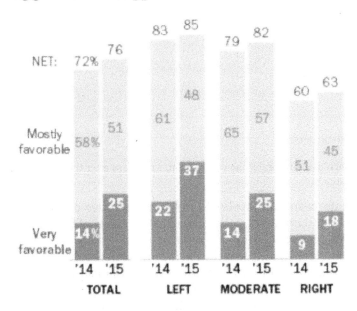

Source: Spring 2015 Global Attitudes survey.

PEW RESEARCH CENTER

The increase of positive public attitudes towards Muslims after the Charlie Hebdo on January 7, 2015.

CURRENT AND RECENT ATTITUDES IN THE WEST TOWARD MUSLIMS

Following are some findings of recent surveys to assess European views of Muslims. As will be noted, such views are complex and in process. A June 2015 Pew Research Center study entitled "Ratings of Muslims rise in France after *Charlie Hebdo*, just as in U.S. after 9/11" [32] conducted in fifteen European countries suggested that

---

32. *Ibid.*

U.S. Views of Muslim Americans Improved After Sept. 11 Attacks

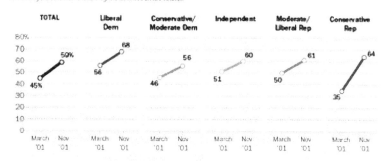

% with favorable views of Muslim Americans

Source: Pew Research Center Post 9-11 Attitudes survey, Dec. 6, 2001

PEW RESEARCH CENTER

The increase of favorable views of Muslim Americans after the September 11th, 2001 attacks.

the European non-Muslim population's positive opinion of Muslims and Islam was directly related to their level of familiarity with the Muslim population. In fact, the attack carried out by several migrant Muslims against the *Charlie Hebdo* magazine office in Paris on January 7, 2015—which killed twelve and injured eleven, as did the September 11 attacks but with a greater degree of destruction—seemingly did not affect the European non-Muslim population's opinion of Muslims and Islam itself; however, according to the study, "knowing something about Islam—as opposed to personally knowing a Muslim—is less associated with these positive feelings."[33] What is trying to be assessed from the European non-Muslim population is "whether they think Islam is compatible with their country's culture and values and whether they would be willing to accept a Muslim as a member of their family."

Since the *Charlie Hebdo* attacks in 2015, there has been a wide range of discourse both in France and globally on the radicalization of around 5 million French Muslims, particularly regarding their role in secular France. Surprisingly, no extreme overreac-

---

33. Scott Gardner and Jonathan Evans, "In Western Europe, familiarity with Muslims is linked to positive views of Muslims and Islam," https://www.pewresearch.org/fact-tank/2018/07/24/in-western-europe-familiarity-with-muslims-is-linked-to-positive-views-of-muslims-and-islam/.

tion or backlash that could be categorized as radical or a terror of aggression against the French people has occurred. On the contrary, the attitude of the French public towards Muslims only months after the *Charlie Hebdo* attacks had gotten better. The Pew Research Center survey shows that in 2015, 76% of the French population had a positive view of Muslims, slightly higher than the survey results a year earlier (72%). In fact, those who expressed views that were very positive (very favorable) increased from 14% in 2014 to 25% after the *Charlie Hebdo* attacks. A more positive attitude was shown not only by those from the political left, but from all positions across the ideological spectrum.

This pattern also applied to the perspectives of the American non-Muslim population soon after the September 11 attacks. In fact, favorable opinions towards the American Muslim population increased from 45% in March 2001 to 59% in November 2001, that is to say, two months after the occurrence of the devastating tragedy in New York. This increase occurred in all partisan groups and ideological groups, with the highest increase in the Republican party, which is considered conservative.

After the *Charlie Hebdo* attacks and September 11 attacks, there was a widespread call for national unity. Meanwhile, the leaders of France and the USA at the time, François Hollande and George W. Bush respectively, stated that violent extremists do not represent

Police and journalists crowded in front of the Charlie Hebdo magazine after the fatal attack by two gunmen on January 7, 2015

Islam. However, while there has been no extreme overreaction or backlash against Muslims in either country, violence against Muslims has increased ever since. This is due perhaps to a small group of non-Muslims, who from the beginning have had negative views of Muslims.

It should be noted that in 2007, the positive perspective on Muslims in America did decrease slightly to 53%, a decrease of 6% compared to November 2001 (59%), although this figure is still better than the poll results in March 2001 (45%). Another thing that needs to be considered is that there have been several shifts in the perspective of the American non-Muslim population regarding Islam and violent tendencies. In March 2002, eight months after the September 11 attacks, only 25% of American non-Muslim respondents thought that Islam encourages violence. However, in July 2003, this figure had increased to 40%, and in September 2014, a Pew Research Center poll found that 50% of respondents thought this way, or half of the American population.

MEASURING THE FUTURE OF WESTERN WORLD
AND MUSLIM WORLD RELATIONS

A change in approach to intercultural dialogue is apparent. The January 2011 Abu Dhabi Gallup Center poll mentioned in Chapter 2 concluded that the majority of respondents (from a total of 100,000 respondents) from fifty-five countries view Muslim-Western interactions as an advantage rather than a threat.[34] Likewise, the 2015 Pew Research Center study, which shows the increasing sympathy of the non-Muslim population in Europe and the United States for Muslims, questions that the post-Cold War confrontational approach, e.g. that embraced by Bernard Lewis and Samuel Huntington, is somewhat overstated. Rather, the approach in the second millennium, especially after the Second Vatican Council, emphasizes the importance of intercultural dialogue. The Second Vatican Council 50th Anniversary Conference held at Georgetown University reminds us that although a small group of missionaries claimed that a central theme within the Second Vatican Council is strengthening the missionary church, the Christian World widely affirms that the central theme of the Council is primarily dialogue, whether it's internal dialogue within

---

34. Gallup Inc., "Measuring the State of Muslim-West Relations..."

Centro Islamico Culturale d'Italia Grande Molschea, the Mosque and Islamic Cultural Center in Rome using ancient Roman architecture

the Catholic Church, dialogue between the Catholic Church and followers of non-Christian religions, or even dialogue with those who are non-religious.

The Gallup poll suggests possibilities for interaction and negotiations between Muslims and others. Moreover, Pope Benedict XVI's visit to the Blue Mosque in Istanbul, in November, 2006, —arguably inspired by Nostra Aetate— amidst the protests by Muslims regarding his speech at the University of Regensburg on September 12, 2006, suggested such possibilities, in Istanbul and Turkey. These instances are both epitomes of negotiation to overcome Western grudges toward Islam (still reflecting past events such as when in 1453, Turkish forces, under the Ottoman Sultanate, seized Constantinople from the Byzantine Empire, and launched two failed attacks on Vienna, in 1529 and 1683 respectively).

The future-oriented themes of Muslim-West relations in the Gallup poll are increasingly finding their operational constructs in Scheherazade S. Rehman and Hossein Askari's research, "How Islamic are Islamic Countries?" In this study, two researchers used four Islamicity indexes, namely economic, legal and governance, human and political, and international relationships. [35]

Surprisingly, the countries that are considered the most Islamic

35. Scheherazade S. Rehman and Hossein Askari, "How Islamic are Islamic Countries?" *Global Economy Journal,* Vol. 10, No. 2 (2010).

are in fact secular Western countries where the majority of the population is Christian, which are, at the same time, countries with a high level of progress in terms of life in their society, nation and state. These countries include New Zealand, followed by Luxembourg, Ireland, Iceland, Finland, Denmark, Canada, the United Kingdom, Australia, Norway, Switzerland, Belgium and Sweden, most of which are Western European countries. This seeming paradox doubtless reflects the poll's measurement of Islamicity but may also suggest that Muslim minorities in non-Muslim countries bend over backwards to retain and accentuate their own faith in a sea of non-Muslims.

Meanwhile, Muslim-majority countries are actually left behind, some even very far behind, such as Malaysia (38), Kuwait (48), Bahrain (64), Brunei Darussalam (65), United Arab Emirates (66), Turkey (103), Qatar (112), Saudi Arabia (131), Indonesia (140), Pakistan (147), Egypt (153) and Iran (163).

The direction and findings of the Gallup study and the Islamicity rate survey relate to the opinion of the translator of the Qur'an into English, Muhammad Marmaduke Pickthall, a son of an Anglican priest of English descent. In his work entitled *Cultural Side of Islam*, Pickthall writes:

> Islam offers a complete political and social system as an alternative to socialism, fascism, syndicalism, bolshevism and all other "isms," ... a system which is manifestly threatened with extinction. The system of Islam has the great advantage over all these nostrums, [in] that it has been practiced with success—the greater the success the more complete the practice. Every Muslim believes that it must be eventually adopted in essentials by all nations whether as Muslims or non-Muslims in the technical sense, because its laws are the natural (or divine) which govern human progress, and men without revelation of them must find their way to them, in course of time and painfully, after meeting, trying every other way and meeting failure.[36]

From his explanation, Pickthall believes that there are actually many countries in the world that are technically yet unknowingly implementing the Islamic life order. According to him, this could happen because "its law is the natural (or divine) which governs

---

36. Muhammad Marmaduke Pickthall, *Cultural Side of Islam* (Madras: The Committee of Madras Lectures on Islam, 1927), pp. 19–20

William Mohammed Marmaduke Pickthall, the British convert who translated the Qur'an into English in 1930. The first English translation, 'The Qur'an from Mohammed,' was made by George Sale in 1734.

human progress, and men without revelation of them must find their way to them, in course of time." According to Rehman and Askari's research, technically a series of trials and errors can be said to be Islamic, because they are the same as Islamic teachings, although they are not based on Islamic faith.

The Qur'an teaches that Islam is a religion of nature (*fitrah*),[37] a religion bestowed by God in accordance with human nature and

---

37. Is the state of purity and innocence Muslims believe all humans to be born with. The word *fitrah* is derived from *fathara*, which means 'to make'. Etymologically, fitrah means original event, religion, creation, original nature, basic potential, and holiness. There are several other definitions of fitrah: *first*, according to Ibn Al-For Qayyim and Ibn Al-Katsir *fitrah* means a state resulting from creation, since *fatir* means creating.

Second, based on the *hadith* narrated by Ibn Abbas, *fitrah* is the beginning of human creation, since the word *fitrah* has never been stated by the Qur'an in any context other than humans. *Third*, in the *Al-Munjid* dictionary, the oldest Arabic language dictionary, the word *fitrah* means provisions, events, character. *Fourth*, according to Syahminan Zain (1986:5) *fitrah* is a latent potential or strength in humans, which is carried by all humans from birth.

needs. Humans are "created by" God, while Al-Qur'an is a "direction for use," which is also from God. Only God knows best about all his most abstruse nature and behavior. Therefore, only God best understands what kind of rules are needed to govern humans. Muslims get "direction for use" from God, but other human beings can also seek it through a process of trial and error, a long trial, until they get the same "direction for use" that was bestowed by God through Islam.

This is in accordance with the word of Allah in Al-Qur'an, Surah Ar-Rum verse 30:

> So direct your face toward the religion, inclining to truth. [Adhere to] the fitrah of Allah upon which He has created [all] people. No change should there be in the creation of Allah. That is the correct religion, but most of the people do not know.

Alexis Carrel, a Nobel Prize laureate in Physiology or Medicine in 1912 stated in his book, *Man, The Unknown*, that humans are very complex creatures, and that "We must realize clearly that the science of man is the most difficult of all sciences."[38]

However, it is precisely the science of man, that is to say, the science of human nature, that is only in the knowledge and power of God. The science of man is the basis of the Islamic theological system, the basis of faith, Islam, creed and sharia (Muslim law) in shaping the Muslim person. Only God, through the Qur'an, is able to explain in detail the origin of human events, the human traits of being stingy and loving wealth, complaining in times of difficulty, being ungrateful when getting pleasure, and being gluttonous and lustful. Humans in modern times are able to travel through space, control uranium and plutonium but struggle to recognize these behaviors and control themselves.

Through the Qur'an, God explains the facts about man, his origin, traits and nature, and even his eventual demise. Through the creed and sharia created by God, as a "direction for use" for humans who are "the unknown," Islam can change negative traits into positive and utterly benevolent traits.

Modern countries that do not know Islam in the fashion where Islam is the faith of citizens, i.e. countries such as New Zealand—such as New Zealand and Western European countries that rank

---

38. Alexis Carrel, *Man, The Unknown* (London: Pelican Books, 1935), 23.

high in Islamicity rate in the fields of economy, law, governance, humanity, political rights and their relations between nations— have worked hard through a series of trial-and-error processes and a long search to become developed nations, using virtues and systems akin to those taught by Islam, which they may or may not know. On the other hand, other modern countries are limited to seeing Islam as a way of life, as a virtue, which teaches various values and systems of life in society and a good and ideal state. Muslims might believe that such countries have never succeeded in achieving and realizing the ideal life order. Hence, they only partially achieve that virtue, simply because they do not carry out the life order in its entirety.

On the contrary, Muslim-majority countries that should be able to show a higher Islamicity rate in state and social affairs are unable to realize the virtues of the Islamic system since they cannot fully practice Islam, so that only, in Said's language, "reduced Islam" is manifested.

EURABIA: REVIEWING THE NEW BEGINNINGS OF THE WEST-ISLAM RELATIONSHIP

There is a sharp difference in point of view between a view of humanity articulated by an emerging global perspective, Bernard Lewis, Samuel Huntington and a large number of Western rulers, colonial governments, and Orientalists, who are still under the illusion of living in an era of colonialism and Christianization of the Muslim population. It is very clear that after the Second Vatican Council the illusion that the Qur'an is a false Holy Book and Muhammad is a false prophet has been abandoned even by the Church itself, with a change in perspective for mutual respect and demands for dialogue between religious believers in modern times.[39]

Islamophobia is becoming increasingly abandoned. Now, the Church also respects non-Christian teachings, and—for the sake of world peace, especially among religious believers—they need to have a dialogue with followers of non-Christian religions, including Muslims. The present era is the era of dialogue, for building cooperation between civilizations and religious believers, in the context of realizing world peace. In fact, the call for peace between religious believers has also been supported by the United Nations,

---

39. See, Nostra Aetate, Appendix I.

which stipulated the first week of February as the International Interfaith Harmony Week.[40]

Thus, the view of the occurrence of a European-Arab Axis, or "Eurabia," as well as migration as a form of "soft terrorism" by Muslims, is incorrect. First, the massive migration of Muslims to Europe came not only from Arab ethnicities, but also from non-Arab ethnicities in Africa and Asia. Second, the meeting between the non-Muslim population and the Muslim population of Western Europe and America —as recognized by the Second Vatican Council—is nothing less than a dialogue between them, with more benefits than disadvantages[41] and improves positive attitudes towards Muslims,[42] unlike in Huntington's clash of civilizations theory. It is hoped that the dialogue between the West and Islam will give birth to new intercultural variants and to a new human civilization, where various virtues of Islam meet the more developed and structured cultural order of Western European and American societies, both in the social, economic, humanitarian, political fields and relations between nations.[43]

In fact, the reason the majority of Western Europeans still associate themselves with Christianity, even though they are divided into non-attending and churchgoing with a fairly good level of acceptance of Muslims,[44] can be more easily explained through Edward Said's perspective. In his book, *Covering Islam*, Said distinguishes between Westerners and Christians:

> And we must note immediately that it is always the West, and not Christianity, that seems pitted against Islam. Why? Because the assumption is that whereas "the West" is greater than and has surpassed the stage of Christianity, its principal religion, the world of Islam—its varied societies, histories, and languages notwithstanding—is still mired in religion, primitivity, and backwardness. Therefore, the West is modern, greater than the sum of its parts, full of enriching contradictions and yet always "Western" in its cultural

---

40. Mu'assasat Āl al-Bayt lil-Fikr al-Islāmī, *A Common Word between Us and You*, 5-Year Anniversary Edition (Amman: Royal Aal Al-Bayt Institute for Islamic Thought, 2012), pp. 11–50.

41. Gallup Inc., "Measuring the State of Muslim-West Relations...".

42. Richard Wike, "Ratings of Muslims rise in France...".

43. Rehman and Askari "How Islamic are Islamic Countries?"

44. See, Sahgal, "10 key findings about religion in Western Europe".

identity; the world of Islam, on the other hand, is no more than "Islam," reducible to a small number of unchanging characteristics despite the appearance of contradictions and experiences of variety that seem on the surface to be as plentiful as those of the West.[45]

Said's perspective makes it easier to explain the resistance of the Western European community to the Muslim population, or more precisely Muslim immigrants. The resistance tends to decline, since, although Western Europe still envisions itself as a Christian community, they are actually Westerners, not Christians, who are interacting with Muslims. Said's approach can also be used to explain the polling results of the Gallup Center Abu Dhabi.

As a matter of fact, Said's perspective can also be employed to explain and support the dialogue between the West—which is more advanced, modern and "more Islamic"—and Islamic "representatives," or immigrants who are "reducible to a small number of unchanging characteristics" which are scattered across their respective "mother countries" in Western Europe.

The Western and Islamic dialogue in contemporary and future Europe is increasingly finding urgency, significance, and justification due to the following factors:

LONGING FOR A NEW SPIRITUAL RENAISSANCE

On June 26, 1972, an Indonesian newspaper, *Kompas*, published a report on the results of a study by Han Fortmann, who was a pastor as well as professor of comparative psychology and culture at Nijmegen Catholic University, the Netherlands, and the leader of the *aggiornamento* (reformation) program of the Dutch Catholic church. The church is considered "radical" when compared to other Catholic churches in Europe. In his report, *Oostersche Renaissance: kritische reflecties op de cultuur van nu (Eastern Renaissance: Critical Reflections on the Culture of Today)*, which was published only two years after his death in 1970, Fortmann states that:

> The rise of science and technology in the West caused a spiritual crisis, so that the West yearned to pass the Eastern ways to achieve balance.

> The West is not satisfied with rationalistic values and objectivity that are biased and ignore human values.

---

45. Edward W. Said, *Covering Islam: How the media and the experts determine how we see the rest of the world* (London: Vitage Books, 1997)

Der innere klang (inner voice), which is still preserved in the East, can no longer be maintained in the West.[46]

Indeed, the modernization and secularization of Europe now has a negative impact in the form of spiritual dryness. Secularization is not only at the macro level or in state politics, but also at the micro level – consequently, there are now more and more non-attending Christians and religiously unaffiliated people in Europe, while churchgoing Christians are becoming fewer and fewer. According to Fortmann, the spiritual vacuum caused by this secularization needs to be filled immediately by upholding an Eastern spiritual renaissance.

Meanwhile, for Fortmann, the meaning of longing for *der innere klang* is that "Eastern" can have a broad meaning; it could be that it refers to the spirituality of ancient civilizations in India and China, or Islam, which grew and developed recently but has a close and very meaningful connection in the history of Western development. Thus, the term "Eastern" in the nomenclature and context of Western history is more associated with and directed towards Islam than the other two old civilizations in the East (India and China), especially if it starts with the term Orientalism, which means nothing but the study of Islam. In fact, Johann Wolfgang von Goethe's famous work, *West-östlicher Divan*, which was reputedly inspired by Al-Baqarah verse 115, strongly refers to Goethe's closeness to Islam.

This *West-östlicher Divan*, which was influenced by the book of poetry written by his Persian friend, Hafez, contains Goethe's admiration for Islam and Muhammad. It is a marvelous collection of poems that reveals admiration of the religion of Islam. Goethe writes:

East belongs to God, West belongs to God.
Likewise North and South. Everything is peace in His hands.[47]

It can be seen that there are similarities between Goethe's verse above and Al-Baqarah verse 115, which states:

---

46. *Kompas*, July 27, 1972; "Fortmann, Herman Joannes Henricus Maria (1904-1968)" http://resources.huygens.knaw.nl/bwn1880-2000/lemmata/bwn3/fortmann

47. Johann Wolfgang von Goethe, *West-östlicher Divan* (Stuttgart: Cotta, 1819). Original passage: "Gottes ist der Orient! // Gottes ist der Okzident! // Nord-und südliches Gelände // Ruht im Frieden seiner Hände".

"West-Ostlicher Divan," or "Compilation of Western and Eastern Poems," was written by Johan Wolfgang von Goethe, having admired Qur'anic poetry. It was published in Stuttgart in 1819. His colleagues suspected that he converted to Islam, but there was no proof of that from Goethe.

> "And to Allah belong the east and the west. So wherever you [might] turn, there is the Face of Allah. Indeed, Allah is all-Encompassing and Knowing."

As such, it is not surprising that people thought that Goethe had secretly embraced Islam, an assumption which he did not confirm until the end of his life. The "Eastern" values embodied in Islam admired by Goethe will no doubt once again fill the spiritual void of the West that is sweeping Europe today.

EXPERIENCE EUROPEAN HISTORY

In her book, *Allahs Sonne über dem Abendland* (*Allah's Sun over the Occident*), Sigrid Hunke, a historian and religious writer who was a member of the German Sciences Service of the Schutzstaffel, emphatically points to Europe's debt to Islam. According to her, it was the spirit of Islam that had liberated Europe from the Dark Ages by introducing intercultural dialogue through the establishment of scientific centers in Baghdad, Cairo, Cordova and Toledo in Spain as well as the Crusades. Like George Bernard Shaw, Hunke praised Islam's role in giving birth to a new Europe, and in this regard is the only Western intellectual who dared to say the following:

Europe has become the new Europe, modern Europe, and it is the

Soul of Islam that is the midwife. Europe is not only the cultural heritage of Greece and Rome, but also the intellectual heritage of the Muslim world.[48]

In the same vein, George Bernard Shaw also expressed his belief that:

If any religion had the chance of ruling over England, nay Europe, within the next hundred years, it could be only Islam.[49]

Without a doubt, Islam will once again revive a secular Europe that has lost its spiritual values, as Fortmann stated.

THE MUSLIM DIASPORA IN EUROPE
AND INTERCULTURAL DIALOGUE

The situation of Muslims in Europe is very different from the situation in the eighth and fifteenth centuries. Rather than a developed Islamic civilization providing a center of learning for underdeveloped European societies, today there are Muslims from countries that are less developed and have low Islamicity rates spread across Western European countries with highly developed social, economic, legal, political and governance systems (high Islamicity rates). Because of this diaspora, it is hoped that there will be intercultural interaction or dialogue between these Muslims, who only carry the virtues of Islam (or only practice a "reduced Islam"), and Western societies, who have reached an advanced form of life that is technically Islamic, but lacks Islamic virtues and spirituality. Through the process of intercultural interaction and dialogue, Muslim communities can increase their Islamicity rate in terms of social, economic, legal, political and governance, while Western European societies that feel the emptiness of spirituality can truly regain momentum toward a second Renaissance in the spiritual realm.

---

48. Sigrid Hunke, *Allahs Sonne über dem Abendland* (Hamburg: Fischer Bücherei, 1965), http://islamische-akademie-berlin-de./index.php./geschichte/156-allahs-sonne-ueber-dem-abendland-1. Original passage: "Das Abendlandes war ein anderes Abenlanden geworden, das moderne Abendland, und der Islamische Geist war sein geburdhelper. Das Abendlandes ist nicht allein Erben Griechenlands und Roms—sondern ebenso der Arabischen Geisteswelt".

49. In David Pawson, *The Challenge of Islam to Christians*, 16.

PART 2

THE STAGES OF RELATIONS BETWEEN THE WEST AND ISLAM

All the savage lands in the world are going to be brought under subjection to the Christian Government of Europe. The sooner the seizure is consummated, the better for the savage. The end of the geographical feat is the beginning of the missionary enterprise.

> Rev. S.M. Zwemer, F.R.G.S.
> *Arabia, The Cradle of Islam,*
> Eidenberg and London, 1900. p. 223

Islam is the only civilization which has put the survival of the West in doubt, and it has done that at least twice.

> Samuel P. Huntington

5

Europe's Dark Ages

THE PEAK OF THE ROMAN EMPIRE

Historians agree that what is meant by the "Middle Ages," or in the case of Europe what is often called the "Dark Ages," is the age between the fifth and fifteenth centuries. The fifth century was marked by the fall of the Roman Empire in 476, while the fifteenth century was marked by the fall of Constantinople to the Ottomans in 1453. Historians refer to this span of ten centuries as the Age of Darkness, because, compared to the splendor of the earlier Roman Empire, there was such a disrepair afflicting various public institutions and the domination of no less corrupted religious institutions. These institutions curbed the development of science, while armed inquisition institutions persecuted and killed those who opposed church doctrine and power.

The world-renowned historian Edward Gibbon argued that the Roman Empire reached its peak in the second century. Gibbon asserted that "In the second century of the Christian Era, the Empire of Rome comprehended the fairest part of the Earth, and the most civilized portion of mankind."[50] The territory of the Roman Empire stretched very broadly, covering England and Gibraltar in the West, the Rhine and Danube rivers in the North, the Euphrates River in the East, southern Egypt, and even Persia. Such expanse and grandeur also illustrate how advanced the infrastructure of Rome and the urban centers of the Roman Empire were, all of which facilitated the movement of troops, merchants, and even evangelists. Consequently, Christianity developed more rapidly in Rome's territory than in Christianity's homeland, in the Middle East.

Under four emperors, Nerva, Trajan, Hadrian and Antoninus

---

50. Edward Gibbon, *The Decline and Fall of the Roman Empire* (New York: Dell Publishing, 1966), 27.

Pius, the Roman Empire reached the peak of its progress. According to Gibbon, the security and welfare of the people were well guaranteed, so that the life of the Roman population was arguably luxurious. Laws were well enforced by the four emperors. Rome's relations with all governors in the western, northern, eastern and southern provinces were well maintained. Thus, Gibbon wrote:

> The progress of Christianity has been marked by two glorious and decisive victories: over the learned and luxurious citizens of the Roman empire, and over the warlike barbarian of Scythia and Germany, who subverted the empire and embraced the religion of the Romans.[51]

In the early stages of its existence and development, Christianity was considered to be one of the "sects" of Judaism, and it was only later that the rulers of Rome understood that Christianity was completely different from Judaism, for they were followers of Christ who died on the cross because of the trial by Roman rulers. Thus, they were then considered not to be part of the Roman "national religion," and were considered to have no loyalty to the empire.

Despite the torture, even arson, of Christian congregations by Emperor Nero (r. 54–68), the real obstacles only emerged intensively during the reign of Emperor Decius (r. 249–251). The notorious Nero alleged that Christians were responsible for the great fire of Rome in 64, even though, as it is believed, the fire was deliberately set by Nero himself.

During Decius' reign, the intensity of attacks by the Huns from Central Asia and the barbarians of Germany in the North towards Rome increased, coinciding with the weakening of Roman authority. In the face of the growing number of Christians and the increasing intensity of attacks by Rome's enemies, Roman rulers assumed that the decline of the empire was a manifestation of the anger of their gods for the development of Christianity, a religion that was not a "national religion" and hence in constant conflict with the original Roman culture.

As a result, the cruelty of the Roman rulers to Christians increased and was extensive. This was done no longer to gauge Christians' loyalty to the Roman rulers, but to appease the Roman gods and prevent them from punishing the weakening empire.

---

51. *Ibid.*, 617.

By writing that "I have described the triumph of barbarism and religion,"[52] Gibbon argues that the fall of the Roman Empire at that time was indeed influenced by internal factors, namely the entry of Christianity as the state religion displacing the Roman gods, and the invasion of barbarians from the North that flowed relentlessly.

STATE'S CHURCH

In the midst of the advancement of Roman civilization and the support of good public service infrastructure, Christianity spread very rapidly to every corner of the Roman Empire. By 180, the Gospels had begun to spread in Germany, England, Spain and Armenia. Meanwhile, in the third century, the Bible even spread in the East to Persia and India. However, along with this speed of development came differences in the understanding and interpretation of the doctrines of Christianity. This rapid development of Christianity also created political problems for Rome. The peak of the obstacles to the growth of Christianity continued until the reign of Diocletian (r. 303–311) who took firmer actions, including "cleaning" the state apparatus by dismissing the followers of Christ from public positions, as well as continuing to use torture and murder. Finally, this suffering ended during the reign of Emperor Constantine, who eventually embraced Christianity. In 313, he issued an Edict of Milan stating that Christians were free to carry out their religious activities, and that all their property confiscated by the state would be returned.

Although Christianity was only officially made the state religion by Theodosius in 380 through the Edict of Thessalonica,[53] the process toward that direction actually started long before, namely with the emergence of the First Council of Nicea in 325. This council was an initiative of Emperor Constantine, which was held to end the theological conflict between the Arians and the Bishop of Alexandria as well as most other priests and theologians. The main controversy that led to the emergence of the First Council of Nicea was the difference in views regarding the substantial relationship between God the Father and Jesus Christ, especially the Arians' view of the divinity of Jesus. The Arians insisted that God the Son

52. *Ibid.*, 704.
53. Greg Forster, *The Contested Public Square: the Crisis of Christianity and Politics* (Illinois: InterVarsity Press, 2010), 41.

Nicea Council 325, supported by Emperor Constantine. Emperor Constantine, along with some Bishops, holding the Nicea Declaration, ending the dual theological factions within the Church. Arianism, which opposed the Divine status of Christ, was banned.

was a Creation, born of nothingness. This led to the splitting of the churches into two theological factions. The prolonged schism in the theological doctrine of Christianity was perceived by Constantine as something that not only jeopardized Christianity, but also weakened the state.

The council was held in Nicea, a small town near Constantinople, hence it was easily accessible to various bishops from all provinces in the Roman empire. Constantine, accompanied by Bishop Hosius of Corduba (now Córdoba, Spain), organized and presided over the proceedings of the Council as did the Senate sessions of the Roman empire. The Council was attended by about 1,800 bishops, consisting of 1,000 bishops from Eastern Provinces and 800 bishops from Western Provinces. The bishop of Alexandria was represented by Athanasius, while Pope Sylvester I was unable to attend due to his illness. One important decision of the First Council of Nicaea, in addition to determining Easter (an important milestone of the Church), was to break the Arian view against the equality of Jesus Christ and God the Father, and that view became a major part of the Nicene Creed, the council's decision.[54]

The Council of Nicea in 325 was a milestone in the history of the unification of church theology after Christianity was 'legalized' by

54. https://en.wikipedia.org/wiki/First_Council_of_Nicaea

Constantine through the Edict of Milan in 313, and the status of Christianity as the state religion was declared by Theodosius in the Edict of Thessalonica in 380.

CHURCH IN THE DARK AGES

Dark History of the Popes

The dark age of the Roman Empire, which was full of violence, torture and murder, including witchcraft and corruption, seems to have played a role in influencing the development of culture and various practices of church life that should not have happened in this sacred institution. As an institution that had a major role in state affairs, the Church had wide autonomy and was beyond the control and interference of the Roman government. However, various models of regal clothing, namely the robes of the Popes and church officials (which are actually very far from the spirit of suffering and simplicity of Jesus Christ, who died on the cross with a crown of thorns), may very well be influenced by Roman Empire culture itself.

Brenda Ralph Lewis, in his book, *Dark History of the Pope: Vice, Murder and Corruption in the Vatican*, wrote:

> The Pope in Rome holds the oldest elected office in the world. In the nearly 2,000 years it has existed, the Papacy has helped forge the history of Europe, and has also reflected both the best and the worst of that history. Several popes schemed, murdered, bribed, thieved and fornicated, while others committed atrocities so appalling that even their own contemporaries were shocked.[55]

Lewis wrote several chapters about the papacy scandals that should have never existed, including the cadaver synod, the rule of the harlots, the Vatican's scandals, the genocide of the Cathars, the relationship between the Popes and witches, Galileo's suffering in the face of the Inquisition due to his support for the heliocentric theory, and the Pope's relationship with the Nazis.

Towards the ninth century, the holy and papal thrones became a kind of play item for noble families, such as the Spoleto family, who controlled cities such as Venice, Milano, Genoa, Pisa, Florence

---

55. Brenda R. Lewis, *Sejarah Gelap Para Paus: kejahatan, pembunuhan, dan korupsi di Vatikan* (Jakarta: Elex Media Komputindo, 2010), 7, translated from *Dark History of the Popes: vice, murder and corruption in the Vatican* (London: Amber Books Ltd, 2009).

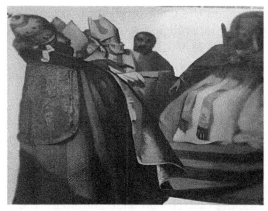

Illustration of Pope Stefanus interrogating the remains of Pope Formosus, which had been buried for nine months. The remains were dressed in Papal robes and seated upon the Pope's throne. (*Dark History of the Popes*, PT Elex Media Komputino Kompas Gramedia, 2010 p.16)

and Siena. With their wealth, influences and connections, and the support of armed militias, these families became a feudal aristocratic group that freely controlled the Pope, even since the papal conclave.

During the so-called "papal pornocracy," that is, in the early tenth century, the Popes were manipulated, exploited and mobilized for vicious purposes by these noble families, or their "dark lovers," who used them as pawns in the game of power. With justification, this is what is called the "rule of the harlots."

The variety of the brutal deaths that the Popes have suffered during the "papal pornocracy" era is astonishing. Pope John VIII (r. 872–882) was assassinated in 882. After being poisoned but not immediately killed, the assassins then hit his head with a hammer until he died. Later, Pope Stephen IX (r. 939–942) suffered terrible wounds when his eyes, lips, tongue, and hands were cut off. Miraculously, this Pope escaped death, but never again showed his mutilated face in public. Allegedly, Pope Benedict V fled to Constantinople in 964 with a young girl, along with papal treasure.

Cadaver Synod

The Spoletto family of central Italy along with its notorious ruler, Duchess Ageltrude, managed to force Pope Stephen VII, widely known as a lunatic, to become Pope (r. 896–897) for only fifteen months, in order to orchestrate her own revenge against the former Pope, the late Pope Formosus (r. 891–896). Ageltrude had a grudge against Pope Formosus for rejecting her young son Lambert as future emperor of the Holy Roman Empire. Pope Formosus, known as a very wise man, instead chose another candidate to become emperor of the Holy Roman Empire on February 22, 896, namely Arnulf of Carinthia, who was a descendant of Charlemagne.

Pope Formosus died six weeks later, on April 5 896, supposedly poisoned by Ageltrude, and his remains were buried in the Papal Tomb. However, in January 897, Pope Stephen VII announced that he would "try" Pope Formosus' body at the Church of St. Johannes Lateran. The body of Pope Formosus, which had been buried for nine months, was exhumed, dressed in papal robes, seated on the papal throne and tried by Stephen in a dramatic cadaver synod. Finally, Formosus' lifeless body was deemed guilty and was reburied in a public cemetery without the majestic papal robes. Not long after, the body was exhumed and thrown into the Tiber River, and his right hand which was used to give blessings was also cut off. The amputated right hand was handed over to Ageltrude who ordered the cadaver synod.[56]

Four centuries later the cadaver synod was repeated by Pope Boniface VIII (r. 1294–1303) who was very autocratic and decreed that all monarchs must submit to the Catholic Church. This decision angered King Philip IV of France, who accused the Pope of heresy and urged him to resign. Pope Boniface was reinstated and detained at the Lateran Palace, but died on October 11, 1303. Philip IV, who still held a grudge against the former Pope, asked Pope Clement V, who had once railed against Formosus' heretical trial, to delay the trial until the decision was not passed.[57]

Inquisition Against Heresies

When Pope Urban succeeded in mobilizing the Crusaders to invade Jerusalem in waves and liberate the Holy City from Islamic rule (1095–1272), the Church was actually facing two big problems. *First*, there were the Crusades in Europe, in a war against heresy (a massive deviation from the true teachings of the Church), that is, an attempt to finish off the Cathars. The Cathars were a religious

56. *Ibid.*, pp. 9–17.
57. *Ibid.*, 35.

sect that emerged in 1143 in northwestern France, and, thanks to the support of many European monarchs, its influence spread rapidly to Spain, Belgium, Italy and Germany. In fact, there was a suspicion that some Catholic bishops in some areas had collaborated with the Cathars. Second was the war against demons in the form of the remains of pagan beliefs that were still lingering, thriving and becoming a common belief in Europe.

From the beginning, the Popes had been wary of the Cathars movement, which they considered heretical with a religious understanding that was subversive to the Church. Catharism is considered a "dualistic" religion that is similar to the religious beliefs of Persia, Zoroastrianism. According to Catharism, humans are born through a series of reincarnation processes, until they are truly born with a pure soul. The Cathars perceived Catholic doctrine in the Vatican as immoral, politically and spiritually corrupted.

Various attempts of negotiation with the Cathars were more or less fruitless, so that Pope Gregory IX (r. 1227–1241), in addition to sending the Crusaders to subdue the Cathars' strongholds in western and northern Europe, founded the Inquisition in 1231. The aim was to judge the heretics, mainly the Cathars, so it was very appropriate when most of the Crusaders were associated with genocide. This inquisition bestowed additional limits on the authority of the inquisitors, which were already large in scale.

The description of the trial of the Inquisition, namely inquisitio *haereticae pravitatis*, has two connotations. *First* was the horror of torture in order to make the heretics admit their guilt, to the imposition of the death penalty in ways that are beyond humane. *Second*, the authority of the inquisitors was expanded to not only prosecute heretics, but also to try superstitious persons, who were controlled by demons. The Church and society at that time believed that the followers of the devil and the superstitious person greatly disturbed the expansion of the Church's influence, and also disturbed the peace and life of the people, not only spiritually but also economically since they were thought to have caused drought which caused the decline in cow's milk production.

This crusade and the inquisition against the Cathars went on for a long time. The last of the Cathars could only be finished at the end of the thirteenth century, that is to say longer than the Crusades and the trials of the Inquisition which lasted for 112 years, under the leadership of nineteen different Popes.[58]

Inquisition Against the Witches

Unlike the Crusades, the inquisition against the Cathars, which were considered heretic, were easier to deal with since they were easier to track down, namely in enclaves or certain areas they controlled. On the other hand, the war against the devil, that is to say against the witches, cannot be fought openly, for the belief in demons—including various superstitions that have been ingrained in the life of the wider communities—had developed over the centuries even before the Church developed.

The Church considers the existence of belief in the devil and various superstitious practices as an obstacle and a barrier to the spread of the Church's mission. Moreover, all this time the various practices of belief in the devil also seemed to be part of the official state culture during Roman rule. Thus, when Pope Gregory decided to hold an inquisition court to face the Cathars, the role of the inquisitors was expanded to prosecute people who were considered followers of the devil, magicians, and practitioners of superstition.

Allegedly, Pope Gregory, as the originator of the inquisition court, was involved quite profoundly in determining the election of Dominican priests as inquisitors, making them his confidants, and it was very easy to believe in what they reported. Pope Gregory was also involved in detailed drafting of the expanded inquisition. In the "Vax Rama" issued in 1233, it is stated that the devil regularly attended every gathering of witches and appeared as a frog or black cat. In fact, the Papal Bull "Vax Rama" mentions that the black cat is an incarnation of Satan and therefore can vanish in the dark. Pope Gregory was very serious about targeting black cats and their owners as targets of an inquiry hunt.

In fact, the inquisitors also suspected the ugly and hunchbacked old women as the valid image of witches. Many husbands suspected that their wives were demons and witches and thus suspected that their children were also demons. In 1252, Pope Innocent IV (r. 1243–1254), in lieu of Pope Gregory IX, who died in 1241, decided that torture was the official method of obtaining confessions from the witches.

Until the fifteenth century, the inquisition court in Switzerland

---

58. *Ibid.*, pp. 67–69.

still persecuted witches, and became increasingly brutal and cruel. The inquisition court thought that witches could fly away, destroy crops, make husbands and wives infertile, make cows unable to produce milk, and even feast on children in witches' gatherings.

Compared to the 112 years of Crusades and the inquisition against the Cathars under the leadership of nineteen different Popes, the inquisition against the witches lasted significantly longer. Pope Innocent VIII (r. 1484–1492) issued two Papal Bulls to activate the Inquisition. On December 5, 1484, Pope Innocent VIII again tightened the implementation of the Inquisition by issuing a Papal Bull "Summis Desiderantes," which gave an indication that the inquisition court process was permitted to use more stringent methods in trying witches and witchcraft in Germany.

Subsequently, in 1486 the Pope commissioned two Dominican priests, Heinrich Kramer and James Sprenger, commonly known as the Apostle of the Rosary, to compile a witchcraft and witch-hunting manual called the *Malleus Maleficarum*. This book contains instructions on how to identify and punish witches. The book contains all the folk beliefs in that era, which are considered to be part of paganistic witchcraft. Although it was rejected by the Faculty of Theology at the University of Cologne, the book was successfully reprinted many times, including a falsification of Heinrich Kramer. Pope Innocent VIII himself was in accord with this brutal inquisition. Finally, in 1490 *Malleus Maleficarum* was included in the forbidden book index. However, the Inquisition was still ongoing.

Inquisition in Spain

On January 2, 1492, the Muslim Kingdom of Granada, which existed since 711, was conquered by King Ferdinand of Aragon and Queen Isabella of Castille. On that day King Abu Abdillah Muhammad ibn Al-Ahmar Ash-Shagir handed over the keys to the Córdoba Palace to Ferdinand and Isabella, and was allowed to leave Spain. However, Spanish Muslims living in the country had to face three difficult choices, embrace Christianity, leave Spain, or face an inquisition. In fact, the inquisition in Spain, especially in Northern Spain, which was far outside the influence of the Muslim caliphate, had been held since 1478, not under the authority of the Pope in the Vatican, but under Ferdinand and Isabella. This inquisition

Illustration of witch doctors who were burned at the Berneburg Castle, near Hannover, from a book published in 1555. (*Dark History of the Popes*, p. 113)

occurred after King Ferdinand pressured Pope Sixtus VI (r. 1471–1484) to be allowed to hold his own trial of inquisition; otherwise, King Ferdinand and Queen Isabella would not send troops to retake Constantinople after its falling to the Ottomans in 1453. Different from the implementation of the inquisition in The Papal Territory, the inquisition in Spain, celebrated and witnessed by a flock of people, became public entertainment and was accompanied by large and magnificent processions.

This inquisition against Jews and Muslims was commissioned by the inquisitor general Thomas de Torquemada, a Dominican priest and abbot of the Santa Cruz monastery in northern Spain, who was appointed leader of the inquisition in Spain by Ferdinand and Isabella in 1483. The inquisition against Jews and Muslims, as well as against heretics in Spain, was the worst in the history of the Inquisition. Because many people hated Torquemada for his unspeakable cruelty and brutality, it was reported that he always carried an antidote with him. De Torquemada might have died a natural death, but his terrible reputation as an inquisitor made the revenge of the Spanish people an enduring hope. In fact, it is reported that in 1832, that is, three hundred years after his death and two years before the Inquisition was finally officially banned, a number of people broke into the fence of the tomb, dug up the tomb and burned Torquemada's remains.[59]

---

59. *Ibid.*, pp. 124–127.

Illustration of women who were undressed by an acquisitor or inquisition judge in the 16th century. The acquisitor was well equipped with horrible instruments for torturing the victims. (*Dark History of the Popes*, p. 109)

Galileo Galilei

One major church scandal at the end of the Dark Ages is the controversy between the Church and science involving Galileo Galilei. Galileo was the heir to Nicolaus Copernicus and his heliocentric theory, perpetuated in the *De Revolutionibus Orbium Coelestium* (1543), which was included in the index of forbidden books by the Vatican on March 3, 1616.

Contrary to Copernicus and Galileo, the Church followed the geocentric theory, and considered the theory to be absolute truth since it was based on Psalm 104:5 which stated that: "He set the earth on its foundations; it can never be moved." Copernicus realized that his theory was against the doctrine of the Church's geocentric theory, hence was very susceptible to being called heretical and very likely to be confronted with inquisition. Especially noteworthy at that time, the Reformation movement launched by Protestants in Germany supported the heliocentric theory. Therefore, Copernicus tried to ingratiate himself with Pope Paul III by giving the Pope the *De Revolutionibus Orbium Coelestium*, and delaying its publication while he was alive. The publication was successful after the manuscript of this book was smuggled into Germany.

In his lectures at Bologna and Padua, where he taught, Galileo always criticized geocentric theory. A friend of his, Cardinal Roberto Bellarmine who later became Pope Urban VIII (r. 1623-1644), reminded him of his risk, namely facing the trial of the

Inquisition, interrogation, torture and incarceration. Moreover, a previously Dominican priest, Giordano Bruno, was burned to death because of the same case in 1600. Pope Urban VIII's attitude, which was initially more friendly towards Galileo, became violent when Galileo published several of his books detailing the results of his observations of the solar system using his own telescope, which could magnify celestial objects up to 32 times.

Pope Urban VIII was then even more angry when Galileo published *Dialogo Del Massimo Sistemi*, followed by *Sidereus Nuncius*. He submitted Galileo to the Inquisition in 1632 as news of the Protestant movement in Germany and its support of the Copernican theory became more widespread. Galileo, who was 68 years old at that time, tried to delay his appearance at the trial of the Inquisition, but Pope Urban VIII refused.

Initially, Galileo persisted in defending his heliocentric theory, so that the inquisitors were confused about how to handle this case. However, when faced with the final inquisition trial, in which the inquisitors displayed various torture devices, Galileo finally gave up. He was forced to make a statement that humiliated himself by withdrawing his support for the heliocentric theory for which he spent a lifetime.

Furthermore, under Pope Urban's orders, Galileo's "defeat" confession was read out in every church all over Europe, so that every congregation knew that the great Galileo had been successfully broken by the Inquisition. Subsequently, he was locked up in a prison located under the Apostolic Palace, Vatican. Despite finally obtaining relief and receiving treatment at his home in Arceti, Galileo remained under house arrest and tried to write books on mechanics, although none of the publishers dared to publish them.

On January 8, 1642, Galileo died at the age of 78, blind from his prolonged observation of the solar system. Even so, Pope Urban VIII still held a grudge against him because of the "scandal and grave sins he had committed against the Christian kingdom," and, as a result, his body was prohibited from being buried in a public cemetery. Finally, his remains were hidden, buried underneath the Church of Santa Groce in Florence. However, nearly a century later Pope Clement XII ordered a proper re-burial of Galileo's body and a monument to him in Santa Groce. Only three hundred years later, in 1972, Pope John Paul II reversed previous decisions and

Galileo Galilei (1564-1642) who was a follower of Nicolaus Copernicus' heliocentric theory (that the earth circulates the sun, not the other way around) was declared guilty by the inquisition judge. The penalty was considered a scandal by the church, which opposed the development of science following the renaissance and reform movements. (*Dark History of the Popes*, p. 109)

confirmed Copernicus' heliocentric theory supported by Galileo.[60]

Some Vatican Vocabulary

In addition to the Inquisition, Brenda Lewis introduces a number of distinctive vocabularies from the Vatican. These include:

1. *Simoni*, derived from the name Simon the Sorcerer, is a figure deemed to have committed a serious crime by selling or paying for a certain position in the Church.
2. *Nepotism* is derived from the Latin word, *nepos*, meaning nephew or grandson, and is used to describe the pleasure of popes in giving certain positions in the Church to their relatives or friends.
3. *Excommunication*, which means placing someone outside the fellowship of the Catholics so that they are separated from the life and protection of the Church as punishment for their wrongdoing.
4. *Anathema* is a heavier punishment than excommunication. This

---

60. *Ibid.*, pp. 161–183.

punishment is given to people who are considered to adhere to a doctrine condemned by ecclesiastical authority.

5. *Index of Forbidden Books (Index Librorum Prohibitorum)*, is a list of books that Catholics are prohibited from reading. *De Revolutionibus Orbium Coelestium* is one of those forbidden books.

6. *Purgatory* is a process in which souls who have died in a miserable condition are purified and given temporary punishments in preparation for entering heaven.

7. *Indulgence* offers pardon from the punishment of purgatory. Martin Luther, initiator of the Reformation, originator of the Reformed church, and figure behind the emergence of the Protestant church in Germany, protested against this doctrine, which he considered insulting and thought it was a lie. He thought it was an exploitation of Christians for the Church to rebuild Saint Peter's Basilica, and believed that faith alone is what determined freedom from purgatory.

8. *Papal infallibility,* established in the First Vatican Council on July 18, 1870, holds that the Holy Spirit is actively guiding His Holiness so that he does not make mistakes in the Church's official statements about belief and morals. In fact, this doctrine was only employed once by Pope Pius XII in 1950, who stated that Mary, the mother of Jesus Christ, was raised to heaven as a whole body and soul.

6

The Encounter of Islam and the Western World

Muhammad bin Abdullah, who was born in 570 and received the first revelations in the Cave of Hira in 610, lived in an environment in which two Abrahamic religions, Judaism and Christianity, had developed widely throughout Arabia, Syria and beyond, even as far as Yemen and Abyssinia on the Horn of Africa. Therefore, Muhammad's life journey was often entangled with the life journey of the Jews and Christians in those regions. The initial relationship between Muhammad and the Jews and Christians, including religious leaders, demonstrated their closeness, not hostility. Hostility was shown by the Qureishis, the natives of Mecca, who by all means wanted to prevent the spread of Islam, including harming Muhammad.

Because their safety was threatened by the actions of the Qureishis, a number of early Muslims migrated to Abyssinia, which was under Christian rule. This was after the Christian king of Abyssinia, Najashi, learned that Muhammad taught Islam, which commanded to worship God, and respected Jesus and his mother, Mary.

There are several things to be noted in the journey of Muhammad's life. *First*, Muhammad's encounter with a Nestorian monk named Bahira when Muhammad, who was nine years old (twelve years according to another source), was invited by his uncle, Abu Talib, to trade in Syria. *Second*, the remark of Waraqah ibn Naufal, who was the uncle of Muhammad's wife, Khadijah, and himself a Christian and the translator of the Bible into Arabic. *Third*, the responses of Emperor Heraclius of Rome (r. 610–641) when he received an invitation to embrace Islam from Muhammad through a letter he sent to him by a courier.

The Encounter of Islam and the Western World

Young Muhammad and Bahira

In his ceremonial speech when receiving the Eigen Biser Award on November 22, 2008 in Munich, Germany for his services in building the Muslim-Christian dialogue, Prince Ghazi bin Muhammad of Jordan gave his background on writing "A Common Word between Us and You," a letter to Pope Benedict XVI and all the top leaders of Christianity. Also in his speech, he specifically told the story of Muhammad's travels with his uncle to trade in Syria at the age of nine. At the end of his speech, Ghazi presented an important but little-known account of Muhammad's life that caught the attention of Islamic observers and historians:

> In the middle of the eastern Jordanian desert, in a place called Safawi, miles away from anything, distant from any landmark or any human traces, there stands a unique, solitary tree. This tree is around 1,500 years old and there are no other trees to be seen for dozens of miles in any direction. Despite its age and breadth, it is only about 6-8 meters tall. It is a *butum* tree, a kind of pistachio tree to be found in our part of the world.... Despite today being in a completely desolate place, there lay until the last century not far from this tree the clear remains of an ancient Roman Road and of a later, but also ancient, Byzantine Monastery.

> And according to the earliest Islamic historical sources, some 1400 years ago, on one of the caravan roads from Arabia to Syria, a nine-year-old Meccan boy named Muhammad bin Abdullah from the clan of Hashem (may peace and blessing be upon him) travelled with his uncle Abu Talib to Syria from his home in Eastern Arabia. A cloud hung over him wherever he went, and when he sat under a tree in the desert, the tree too lowered its branches to shield him from the desert heat.

> A local Christian monk named Bahira noticed these two miracles from a little distance, and summoned the caravan and the boy. After courteously examining and speaking to him, Bahira witnessed the boy as a future Prophet to his people. The monk had a book with him that led him to expect a Prophet among the Arabs, who were descended from Ishmael the eldest son of the Prophet Abraham (peace be upon him). Perhaps it was the Torah, for Genesis 49:10 and Deuteronomy 18:15 seem to predict a prophet that is not the Messiah and not Judah but from the 'brethren' of the Jews, but we do not know.[61]

---

61. Prince Ghazi bin Muhammad, "A Common Word between Us and You: Theo-

113

Prince Ghazi explained at the end of his speech why he quoted the history of the encounter between monk Bahaira and young Muhammad and the meaning of the *butum* tree. *First*, the encounter between Bahira and Muhammad is "the first harmonious contact between the founder of Islam and Christianity." *Second*, the *butum* tree itself is a similitude which likens Islam and Christianity to two "good trees" which are "giving its fruit at every season." As mentioned in Surah Ibrahim verses 24 to 27:

> Seeist thou not how Allah coineth a similitude: A goodly saying, as a goodly tree, its root set firm, its branches reaching into heaven. // Giving its fruit at every season by permission of its Lord? God coineth the similitudes for mankind in order that they may reflect. // And the similitude of a bad word is as a bad tree, uprooted from upon the ground, possessing no stability. // God confirmeth those who believe by a firm saying in the life of the world and in the Hereafter, and God sendeth wrong-doers astray. And God doeth what He will.

By quoting Surah Ibrahim verses 24 to 27, Ghazi shows that *love your God* and *love your neighbor* are like the two "main fruits" of the strong and shady trees, Islam and Christianity, and are the heart of the message "A Common Word between Us and You." The open letter, from 138 Muslim scholars and ulamas on October 23, 2007, received very positive responses from all Church leaders and has even produced several real actions and measures from the Vatican, the Christian World and the Muslim World. Moreover, the general assembly of the United Nations has proclaimed the first week of February as the World Interfaith Harmony Week.

---

logical Motives and Expectation," delivered in Eugen Biser Ceremonial Speech, Munich, Germany (November 22, 2008), https://www.acommonword.com/a-common-word-wins-the-eugen-biser-award/.

Prince Ghazi bin Muhammad, apart from being an adviser to King Abdullah of Jordan and Director of The Royal Aal Al-Bait Institute for Islamic Thought, is also an important figure behind "A Common Word between Us and You," an open letter to Pope Benedict XVI and all Church top leader around the world. This letter, sent on October 13, 2007, and signed by 138 Muslim scholars and ulamas, contains a call for peace, friendship and humanitarian cooperation. This letter received a positive response and has resulted in several real agreements and cooperation between Muslims and Christians in the religious and humanitarian fields. This open letter is considered an important breakthrough from Muslims, after the "Nostra Aetate" which was coined at the Second Vatican Council in 1965. "A Common Word between Us and You" will be specifically discussed in Part Three.

A pistachio tree growing in East Jordan, where the young Muhammad and his uncle Abu Thalib made a business trip and took a rest under the shade of the 1500 year-old tree, near an old monastery. Bahira, the priest who led the monastery, invited Abu Thalib and Muhammad to visit the monastery. Bahira advised Abu Thalib to take good care of Muhammad since he would be an important person one day.

In his book, *Muhammad: His Life on the Earliest Sources*, Martin Lings provides a more detailed explanation of Bahira's encounter with young Muhammad. As he described, in an old monastery located not far from the caravan halt, ancient Christian manuscripts are stored that predict the arrival of a Prophet from the Arabs. At the end of the encounter, Bahira advised Abu Talib,

> Take thy brother's son back to his country, and guard him against the Jews, for by God, if they see him and know of him that which I know, they will contrive evil against him. Great things are in store for this brother's son of thine.[62]

Waraqah ibn Nawfal on Muhammad's Prophetic Life

In Arabia, in both Mecca and Medina, lived a community of Jews and Christians, including some people who were close to Muhammad's family when he was born in 570. Before receiving the rev-

---

62. Martin Lings, *Muhammad: His Life on the Earliest Sources* (Cambridge: The Islamic Texts Society, 1983), 30.

elation, Muhammad already knew a Christian slave named Jabar, and often chatted with him. The Qureishis therefore criticized what Muhammad conveyed, including the revelations he received, as delusions and fabrications which he created based on what he heard from Jabar.

When Muhammad received the first revelation and was shivering with anxiety as he searched for its meaning, his wife, Khadijah, secretly consulted Waraqah ibn Nawfal, her cousin and a devout Christian and avid reader of the Bible, who even had it translated into Arabic. Hearing Khadijah's story about what happened to Muhammad in Hira Cave (when he received his first revelation), Waraqah replied:

> Most Holy He is, Most Holy. For the sake of Him who holds the life of Waraqah, believe, Khadija, that he (Muhammad) has received *an-namus' al-akbar* as Moses had. And really he is a prophet of this people. Tell him to stay strong.[63]

The presence of several Jews and Christians around Mecca, including Waraqah, led the Qureishis to claim that what Muhammad conveyed, including the revelations he received, was compiled from what he heard from Christians in Mecca and its surroundings. Likewise, some Western Orientalists also assumed that all of Muhammad's teachings were nothing more than his imagination and his own creation from hearing pieces of Christian teachings by several local Christians, including Waraqah.

Muhammad's Letter to the Roman Emperor

At the time of Muhammad's prophecy, there were two empires whose domains included the Arabian Peninsula: Rome, under the leadership of Emperor Heraclius, and the Sassanid Empire, under the leadership of Khosrow II. Wars between the two great empires occurred frequently, with successive victories. In the beginning, the victory was on the side of the Sassanids, who succeeded in

---

63. Muhammad Husain Haikal, *Sejarah Hidup Muhammad* (Jakarta: Tintamas, 1992), 83. *An namus' al-akbar* derives from *namus*, namely Jibril. Montgomery Watt notes that the word *namus* is usually taken from the Greek word, *noms*, which means law or revealed scripture. On the other hand, *namus* is not the Qur'anic term, since the Qur'an uses *Torah* to refer to the book that was revealed to Moses. See William Montgomery Watt, *Muhammad at Mecca* (Oxford: Oxford University Press, 1953), 51.

controlling Egypt, Palestine and Jerusalem. On that occasion, the Persian rulers captured The True Cross, a physical symbol of the majesty of Jesus Christ and Roman power. However, when foreign troops regained control of Egypt, Syria and Jerusalem, Heraclius took back the cross.

Some kingdoms, such as Yemen and Iraq, were under Persian influence, while Egypt and Syria were under the influence of the Roman Empire. These kingdoms did not dare to challenge Roman or Persian authority. Therefore, Muhammad's companions were very surprised when the Prophet suddenly conveyed the idea of sending letters to all kings in Arabia and its surroundings, including the rulers of Rome and Persia, the two superpowers at that time. The letters were sent by special couriers, and contained teachings to embrace Islam and accept the concept of oneness of God, tawhid. Not in the slightest was Muhammad worried about the possible consequences of that measure. For this purpose, the Prophet made a silver ring that reads "Muhammad the Messenger of God" as a kind of identification for the couriers who were leaving simultaneously. The letter to Emperor Heraclius was delivered by Dihya ibn Khalifa; the letter to Emperor Khosrow II was delivered by Abdullah ibn Hudhafa; the letter to King Najashi was delivered by Amir ibn Umayya; the letter to Muqawqis the Roman viceroy of Egypt was delivered by Hatib ibn Abi Balta'ah; the letter to ruler of Oman was delivered by Amir ibn Al-Ash; the letter to the ruler of Yemen was delivered by Salit ibn 'Amar; the letter to the ruler of Bahrain was delivered by Al-A'la ibn Al-Hadzimi; the letter to King Harith Al-Himyari of Yemen was delivered by Muhajir ibn Umayya; and the letter to Raja Harith Al-Ghassani of Syria was delivered by Syuja ibn Wahb.

Actually—given Muhammad's position as a messenger of God—his desire to send letters to the rulers, especially Christian rulers, is understandable. When viewed from the standpoint of Islam as the ultimate revelation in the evolutionary process of revelation, it can be understood that Islam is by no means a new religion, but a continuation and ultimate form of a series of evolutions of Allah's revelation. Thus, Islam and Muslims never see Christianity and Christians as others. This is mentioned in Surah Al-Maidah verse 82:

> ... and you will find the nearest of them in affection to the believers who say, "We are Christians." That is because among them are priests

and monks and because they are not arrogant.

In fact, Islam and Muslims also indiscriminately respect all religions taught by all previous prophets as messengers of Allah, as explained in Sura Al-Baqarah verse 136:

> Say, [O believers], "We have believed in Allah and what has been revealed to us and what has been revealed to Abraham and Ishmael and Isaac and Jacob and the Descendants and what was given to Moses and Jesus and what was given to the prophets from their Lord. We make no distinction between any of them, and we are Muslims [in submission] to Him."

It is in the spirit of the brotherhood of Abrahamic religion that Muhammad sent letters to those rulers. The responses to Muhammad's letters also varied; some rejected them rudely and tore up the letters, such as Khosrow II, and there were others who kindly accepted Muhammad's invitation and eventually embraced Islam, as was the case for the ruler of Yemen. It should be noted that, although they did not accept Muhammad's invitation to embrace Islam, the Christian rulers, namely Heraclius, Muqauqis and Najashi, were polite in their refusal. In fact, Muqauqis sent several gifts to Muhammad through Habib ibn Abi Balta'ah. Meanwhile, Najashi of Abyssinia, who is widely known for giving asylum to Muslim refugees, ignored the Qureishis' persuasion to reject the refugees.

Most interesting is the attitude of Emperor Heraclius, who first sought information about who Muhammad really was before responding to his letter. Incidentally, Abu Sufyan, who at that time was the leader of the Qureishis and still Muhammad's great enemy, was on a trading expedition not far from the tent of the Emperor who was then leading an attack on the Persian empire. Even though Abu Sufyan was extremely hostile to Muhammad, he could not lie to himself and answered Heraclius' questions honestly. In the dialogue, it appears that Abu was impressed to learn that the intelligent Heraclius respected Muhammad, so that Abu Sufyan and all his caravan members mistakenly thought that Heraclius had accepted Muhammad's invitation and secretly embraced Islam.

However, several historians, including Martin Lings, have argued that the great Emperor Heraclius also had knowledge of the prediction of a new prophet of Arab descent, and that all the honest answers from Muhammad's enemies (Abu Sufyan and his companions) further reinforced the truth of the fact that Muhammad is indeed in accordance with the characteristics of the promised prophet. However, when Heraclius conveyed his desire to embrace Islam to the Byzantine officials, who were also present in his dialogue with Abu Sufyan, anxiety arose. The Emperor immediately corrected and hid his desire by saying that "I am testing your loyalty and faith."[64]

Da'wah Communication

According to Prince Ghazi bin Muhammad, young Muhammad's encounter with Bahira, Waraqah's testimony on the Muhammad's prophetic ability, and Heraclius' friendly attitude towards Muhammad's letter are some cases that can be said to be "the first harmonious contacts between the founder of Islam and Christianity." The lesson that can be learned is that, given that both Islam and Christianity are *da'wah* religions, or missionary religions, communication in preaching is a very important and fundamental thing to continue to be developed. On the way forward, *da'wah* communication between Islam and Christianity, as fellow Abrahamic religions and *da'wah* religions, needs to be continuously improved.

DIRECT ENCOUNTER BETWEEN ISLAM AND THE WESTERN WORLD

The first revelation of Allah that Muhammad received in the Cave of Hira was the command to read, namely *iqra*, or recite. The command to read can be understood literally, so that humans can read and write, which is a technique and gateway for humans to more intensive and massive learning in the era of Muhammad and beyond. The command to read can and should be understood as a command to read all natural and life phenomena, from reading macro natural phenomena in the form of the universe and all the contents and events in it, to reading micro natural phenomena that are human and in life. By doing so, in the end, man, if he uses his mind, will be able to "encounter," acknowledge and admire the greatness of God, the Creator of the Creator and Ruler of the Universe and its contents. In addition, humans can gain understanding of natural laws, namely God's provisions that cannot be prevented or avoided by humans and all of His creation.

---

64. Martin Lings, *Muhammad: His Life on the Earliest Sources*, pp. 453–455.

God said in the first revelation that Muhammad received, and as it is stated in Surah Al-'Alaq verses 1-5:

Recite in the name of your Lord who created // Created man from a clinging substance. // Recite, and your Lord is the most Generous // Who taught by the pen // Taught man that which he knew not.

The first revelation, in the form of an order to Muhammad to read, encouraged all humankind to be prepared to become agents of change and progress in the future with a scientific perspective. Thus, Islam developed and spread from the Arabian Peninsula eastward and westward very fast. Thomas Carlyle explains that the sands in the Arabian desert, which for centuries had been silent, expanded into "explosive powder, blazes heaven-high from Delhi to Grenada." Historians noted that the rapid development of Islam to the east and westward, as well as controlling the two territories of the Roman and Sassanid Empire, was not only territorial expansion, but the advancement of new knowledge and civilization.

In *Islam, A Short History*, Karen Armstrong wrote:

A century after the Prophet's death, the Islamic Empire extended from the Pyrenees to the Himalayas. It seemed yet another miracle and sign of God's favor. Before the coming of Islam, the Arabs had been a despised outgroup; but in a remarkably short space of time they had inflicted major defeats upon two world empires.[65]

Arab societies that were unknown, even considered inferior, suddenly became highly civilized when they found Islam in their lives. They became historical actors, people who are forward-looking, who change and transform themselves first and then change other societies, as explained in Surah Ar-Ra'd verse 11:

Indeed, Allah will not change the condition of a people until they change what is in themselves.

In that swift victory, the Muslims were not complacent, nor did they slaughter those they conquered, or force them to embrace Islam, or take their property. Muhammad himself gave an example: when the ruler of Mecca broke the Hudaibiyah agreement, the Prophet conquered Mecca with his 10,000 followers in 630, but

---

65. Karen Armstrong, *Islam, A Short History*, 29.

The Church of Resurrection, or The Holy Sepulchre, was built by Queen Helena, Mother of Emperor Constantine. Caliph Umar bin Khattab visited Jerusalem in 638 for handing over of Jerusalem from Patriarch Sophronius. When he went back to Mecca, he let his assistant Nusaibeh stay to keep watching the Holy Church. Today, descendents of Nusaibeh are in charge of watching the church, to avoid any conflict between the different denominations who are occupying certain parts of the historical holy church.

not a single drop of blood was spilled. All residents of Mecca who used to be hostile to Muhammad and Muslims, so that they had to migrate to Medina, were forgiven. Historians like Stanley Lane-Pole and Philip K. Hitti greatly admired Muhammad's attitude; he did not hold a grudge against his former enemies and never forced them to embrace Islam.

The example given by Muhammad was followed by Caliph Umar ibn Khattab, mentioned in Chapter 2, when he came to Jerusalem in 638 at the invitation of Patriarch Sophronius of Jerusalem for the handover ceremony of the keys to the City of Jerusalem.[66] F. Buhl, in *Shorter Encyclopedia of Islam*,[67] specifically discussed how peaceful the key-handing ceremony was. This is in stark contrast to the events that emerged over the next few centuries, when the Crusad-

---

66. *Ibid.*, xii.
67. H.A.R. Gibb and J.H. Kramers, *Shorter Encyclopedia of Islam* (Leiden: E.J. Brill, 1953).

ers reclaimed Jerusalem in 1099 and massacred not only Muslims but Jews and other Christians, including women and children.

Umar came in a dirty robe due to the long road trip to Jerusalem, carrying a jug in hand and only one camel to ride in turns with his bodyguard. When he entered Jerusalem and was greeted by Sophronius in his majestic robe, Umar was actually having his turn leading the camel, while the guard, Nuseibeh, was riding the camel. Umar warmly hugged Sophronius, after which the time for prayer arrived and, rather than pray inside, Umar prayed on the steps outside the gate of the Church of Resurrection. The 4th Century church, built by Queen Helena, mother of Emperor Constantine on the rock where Jesus is believed to have ascended to heaven, was destroyed by the Sassanid Empire under Khosrow II when they conquered Jerusalem. It was later rebuilt by Patriarch Modista in 617. For the sake of the safety of the church, Umar even assigned his bodyguard, Nuseibeh, to remain in Jerusalem and maintain this historical and sacred church. Until now, even though Jerusalem has been led by different rulers in turn, Nuseibeh's children and grandchildren are still trusted to be the custodians of the Church of the Holy Sepulcher.

There is an interesting story about why all the denominations who have 'their respective plots' in the four-story church believe in neutral Muslims, that is to say Nuseibeh's children and grandchildren, to become the custodians instead of having custodians from each of them. David Holden wrote about this in his article entitled "The Unholy Row over the Tomb of Christ,"[68] which was published in the final issue of The Saturday Evening Post in 1968. Once there was a pastor who died on the fourth floor of the church, but all the priests downstairs did not allow the pastor's body to be carried down through their 'holy territory'. Eventually, the Jordanian government sent a helicopter to evacuate the pastor's body.[69]

THE ENCOUNTER OF TWO CIVILIZATIONS

The arrival of Muslim troops in Europe via Gibraltar under the leadership of Thariq ibn Ziyad in 711 was the beginning of a direct,

---

68. David Holden, "The Unholy Row over the Tomb of Christ," Saturday Evening Post, 6 Apr, 1966.

69. Sudibyo Markus, Konsili Vatikan II: suatu Pembaharuan sikap Gereja terhadap Islam (Jakarta: Pustaka Antara, 1978), 16.

physical encounter between Islam and the West, although previously the Byzantine authorities had been associated with the Muslim World in the East, particularly in the Balkans, and when Byzantium defeated the Sassanid Empire. This physical interaction lasted until 1492, when the Muslim Kingdom of Granada, which has existed since 711, was conquered by King Ferdinand of Aragon and Queen Isabella of Castille. However, before Granada's fall, the Ottoman Empire in Anatolia emerged in 1288, then flourished under Orkhan, son of Uthman (r. 1323–1362). The Ottoman Empire reached its peak during the reign of Murad I (r. 1421–1451), who succeeded in controlling Hungary, and under his successor, Mehmed II, conquered Constantinople in 1453 and changed its name to Istanbul.

For most Europeans, even some Western scholars, Istanbul and the Hagia Sophia are the epitome of revenge and invoke a sense of threat on their part. As the capital of the Eastern Roman Empire, Constantinople—which enshrines the name of the Great Constantine (r. 324–337), the Roman Emperor who was instrumental in the unification and development of Christianity—and more specifically the Hagia Sophia, a church before it was converted to a mosque, are some of the causes of "everlasting trauma to the West against Islam," according to Edward Said. Events considered to be traumatic include the rule over Hungary under Murad I, the capture of Constantinople by Mehmed II, and two failed Sieges of Vienna in 1529 and 1683 respectively, also by the Ottomans, which was precluded by the failed attack on Paris but was thwarted by Charles Martel in Poitiers in 732.

Meanwhile, the two main civilizational interactions, namely the Western World and the Muslim World, occurred through, *first*, the educational and cultural sectors of the civilization centers in Spain (Andalusia) in the West and Iraq (Baghdad) and Egypt in the East. The *second* occurred through warfare, especially the Crusades. It turns out, in addition to physical combat, the Crusades can also be viewed as civilizational interactions, since along their journey to Jerusalem the Crusaders could see that the Muslims they were fighting had a higher level of civilization than they had at that time.

Islam was born six hundred years after the birth of Christianity. When Islam grew and thrived in the 7th century, the Eastern

The fall of Toledo, one of the cultural centers in Europe on May 25, 1085. The Christian authorities in Toledo continued developing Toledo as a cultural center, including further translation of Aristotle into Arabic, Latin and some other European languages. UNESCO has recognized Toledo as a modern cultural center.

Roman (Byzantine) Empire was in a period of decline, and the Church was trapped in an era of darkness. Indeed, Christianity was made the official religion of the Roman Empire at that time, but de facto Christianity was not the main pillar of Western civilization. That role was actually held by Greek civilization, and it is unfortunate that Christianity was unable to nurture and take full advantage of the various intellectual and philosophical souls of Greece that had been the foundation of Western powers in the past.

Rom Landau pointed out that all kinds of scientific treasures existed in the past that have succeeded in supporting the greatness of Greek civilization and were neatly stored in the church libraries, but Western-Christianity deliberately did not take full advantage of that treasured heritage.

> It is true, however, that these Greek manuscripts existed in Europe during the Middle Ages. However, the manuscripts were hidden under the dust of the monasteries, and the guards were too ignorant to understand them.[70]

The Church has paid serious and deep attention to Islam since its growth and development in the seventh century because, in addi-

---

70. Rom Landau, *Batu Sendi Peradaban Barat yang Diletakkan oleh Sardjana-sardjana Islam* (Jakarta: P.T. Penerbit & Balai Buku Ichtiar, 1964), 8, translated from Rom Landau, *The Arab Heritage of Western Civilization* (New York: League of Arab States, 1974).

tion to the notion that Islam is a heretical religion (and therefore Muslims need to be saved), Islam would become a real threat to Europe and the Church. The Church started its relationship with Islam at that time with a suspicious attitude, which increased until it considered Islam a threat to the rules and domination of the Church in Europe. Moreover, at that time, the strength of the Roman Empire and European civilization, which became the support of the Church, was in decline. Historians have described how the destruction of the Roman Empire occurred as the Church grew and struggled, both in terms of internal conflicts over its religious doctrines and in the struggle for worldly power. Of course, in such a situation the Western-Christian World was unprepared to confront Islam, which was already spreading its influence to Europe.

Since the Muslim World was outside the jurisdiction of the Roman Empire and the Church's authority, all that the Western-Christian World could do to prevent further progress of Islam was instill hatred against it, massively and systematically. Indeed, at the same time the Church was busy condemning and prosecuting "heresies" and witchcraft in a deadly inquisition a "mental barricade" of all sorts of falsehoods about Islam were disseminated..

In the first physical contact—which occurred in the Dark Ages, when Europe and the Church were still busy holding inquisitions—Islam entered Europe with advanced knowledge and a friendly attitude, even protecting Catholics. The Catholics in Western Europe, especially in Northern Spain, at the time faced an inquisition that was more violent than the one in Eastern Europe; meanwhile, Catholics in the Islamic region of southern Spain were free to take advantage of the existence of education centers in Al-Andalus, namely those in Cordoba, Toledo and Granada. Likewise, Catholics in the East, especially in the provinces contested by the Sassanid Empire and in the Eastern Roman Empire, could still study in Baghdad and Cairo.

Until their fall, in 1492 and 1258, respectively, Granada and Baghdad were centers of learning for a large number of European scholars, both Jews and Christians, such as Moses Maimonides and Thomas Aquinas. Even in the 19th century, philosopher Ernest Renan still praised Ibn Rushd (Averroes) "as a free spirit, an early champion of rationalism against blind faith."[71]

---

71. Karen Armstrong, *Islam, A Short History*, pp. 83–84.

The debt of the Western World to the Muslim World is also acknowledged by historians, although slowly but surely the Western World defeated the Muslim World in their own home, through the control of the sea route, the Renaissance, Church reformation and capitalism. Rom Landau stated that:

> It seems surprising that Christianity, although founded six hundred years earlier than Islam, in one important way not only followed in the footsteps of Islam, and even found itself deeply indebted to the latter.[72]

Furthermore, he pointed out:

> Even though the spiritual and moral foundation that underpins Western civilization was the gospel of Christ, it is the Greek legacy that enabled that civilization to progress in the intellectual field. The principal systems of rule in intellectual and scientific fields originate from Aristotle, Plato, Pythagoras, Euclid, Hippocrates and Galen. However, by the time Christians' 'cornerstones' were firmly laid down, our intellectual completeness was too weak and there was a deep gap between belief and reason.[73]

It is recorded in history that the development of science at that time, both in Spain (West) and in Baghdad and Cairo (East), contributed to the future intellectual development of the West, which was based on Greek science. Under the rule of Caliph Al-Ma'mun (r. 813–833), son of the Caliph Harun Al-Rasyid, the Arabs already recognized the knowledge inherited from the Greeks. Al-Ma'mun founded a special translation agency called Darul Hikmah, whose leadership was entrusted to a Nestorian named Hunayn ibn Ishaq. Furthermore, Hunayn employed Christians, Jews and Muslims to carry out the task of translating the Greek works.

This fact shows that, at that time, religious and national tolerance could in fact be enforced in the form of cooperation in the intellectual and religious fields. All Greek intellectual works were translated in the fields of science, medicine, botany and of course philosophy as the foundation for building values. Thanks to the merits of the Arabs, the intellectual works of Aristotle, Plato, Euclid, Heraclitus and Galen came to the surface and were saved from oblivion. Without their services the West's Renaissance and

---

72. Rom Landau, *Batu Sendi Peradaban Barat*, 7.
73. *Ibid.*

Enlightenment would have been impossible.

Although in the 13th century Moorish civilization in Spain was politically rivaled by Christian power, Spain remained a center of knowledge for the civilization. Some of the most famous Muslim scholars from Spain include Ibn Hazm, Ibn Thufail and Ibn Rushd. Ibn Rushd, also known as Averroes, is the driver of change in Christian scholasticism. Armed with his outstanding explanation of Aristotle, Ibn Rushd succeeded in reintroducing Greek philosophers to European intellectuals, and therefore considered to have expanded new scientific horizons in the West.

In present-day Spain, there are a number of universities, such as those in Córdoba (Qurtubah), Malaga (Malaqoh), Granada (Gharnatah) or Seville (Isbiliyah). One university in Córdoba was founded by Caliph Amir 'Abd al-Rahmān (r. 929–961), earlier than the founding of Al-Azhar University in the 970s by Caliph Abu Mansur Nizar (r. 976–996). The university in Córdoba attracts both Muslim and Christian students, and not from Europe, but Africa and Asia as well.

The new insights and teachings developed by Ibn Rushd were based on Aristotle's teachings and included philosophy, exact science, astrology and medicine. Thanks to the efforts of Ibn Rushd, European scholars succeeded in developing an objective and open attitude towards science, without which the Renaissance—a movement that gave birth to numerous world-renowned scholars, such as Copernicus, Keppler, Galileo, Newton, Erasmus and Descartes—would not have been able to grow and thrive in Europe.

However, the indebtedness of the West to Arab scholars, through their own discoveries or their translation of numerous Greek science books, was never publicly acknowledged, especially when Orientalism was developing. The one exception was during the Renaissance, and when in 1472 King Louis XI decreed that Aristotle's philosophy should be taught with an explanation from Ibn Rushd.

Later, in 1552, a complementary work of Ibn Rushd was published by the University of Padua. Rom Landau stated the difference in the amount of public trust between Ibn Rushd's work and Aristotle's book which he translated:

Many of the Christian thinkers believed Ibn Rushd more than Aristotle himself. Albertus Magnus, a Dominican friar and German philosopher, placed faith in the way Al-Farabi and Ibn Sina viewed Aristotle, but his pupil, Thomas Aquinas, became increasingly oriented towards Ibn Rushd's work on philosophical matters, and to Al-Ghazali regarding matters of religious science.

Among Christians, St. Thomas Aquinas became an influential expert in Arab studies, so that his greatest works, which later became the basis of Christian theology and philosophy, were full of Arab teachings.

Averroism became a major teaching in the philosophical schools of Paris, Padua and Bologna, and it is clear that in Venice Averroism helped lay the foundations of the Renaissance.[74]

TOLEDO AS EUROPE'S CULTURAL CENTER

Among the several centers of Islamic civilization in Spain is Toledo, which is located in northern Spain, near Madrid. In 1986, Toledo received an award from UNESCO as a world heritage site, and was also crowned the city of three cultures, because it is the only city in Europe with a lively harmony between Christians, Jews and Muslims. This admission is a rare and unusual sight in Europe in the past, especially considering the genocide against Jews before the Islamic Caliphate came to power there, respectively in 633, 653 and 693, which then repeated itself after the fall of the Islamic Caliphate, namely in 1368, 1391, 1449 and 1486.

Seville, Granada and Córdoba, which are located in southern Spain, are also known as centers of literacy. Different from northern Spain, which in the Dark Ages was under Vatican rule and still practiced inquisition against heresies and witches, in southern Spain religious freedom was upheld. Although on May 25, 1085, Toledo finally escaped the grasp of the Muslim caliphates, four centuries was enough for Muslim rule there to establish a foundation and awareness for the advancement of civilization, including the development of tolerance for local government and church leaders. The year 1085 was the starting point for European openness to science, and Christian scholars in Toledo were the first to represent Europe in understanding and mastering Greco-Arab science.

Archbishop Raymond I (r. 1126–1151) founded a translation institute in Toledo, which flourished until the end of the 13th cen-

---

74. *Ibid.*, pp 14–15.

tury. In that century, Europe became ready to accept all Arab science and philosophy, including the translation of Aristotle's philosophy developed by Ibn Rushd from Arabic to Latin and various other languages in Europe.

Three centuries earlier, in 830, the Caliph Al-Ma'mun of Baghdad founded Baitul Hikmah, the House of Wisdom, which was not just a translation and library institution, but an academy where the ins and outs of Aristotle's philosophy were studied. At that time, Europe was completely unfamiliar with the Greek mindset. When the Caliphs Harun Al-Rashid and Ma'mun immersed themselves in Greek and Persian philosophy, in Europe Charlemagne and the aristocrats were, some say scornfully, engrossed in writing their own names.[75]

ZERO: THE DEVELOPMENT OF ALGEBRA

The zero may look like a valueless number, but when zero is written after another number, the value of that number increases. The number 1 without being preceded by a zero will still read as one, but when one is added to a zero (or zeroes), it can become ten, one hundred, one thousand, and so on. Perhaps people think that zero has existed from time immemorial. In fact, Europe took the concept of zero from Arabs in the thirteenth century. Prior to that, the numerical system used in Europe was Roman numerals which were very impractical. So, a simple number like 1959 should be written as MCMLIX. Imagine the difficulty of filling in the matrices or tabulations that are increasingly used in Microsoft Excel today with Roman numerals.

Indeed, zero was originally introduced by the Hindus in 876, but it was the Arabs who later developed it along with the widespread influence and development of their knowledge in various cultural centers. The European community initially refused to use zero, assuming it is said that it is meaningless to have a number with no value.

Meanwhile, Al-Biruni (973–104), reputedly one of the greatest scholars of all time, had discovered latitude and longitude six hundred years before Galileo revealed the earth's rotation. Al-Biruni also explained the relative speed of sound and light. Meanwhile, Al-Khwarizmi (d. 850), in addition to developing algebra (which

75. *Ibid.*, 106.

was invented for the first time by the Hindus), contributed to the development of astrology, earth science and music theory.[76]

MEDICAL SCIENCE DEVELOPMENT

Apart from the translation of Greek books, for the Arabs, medical science started from the teachings of Muhammad himself. The prophetic traditions (hadith) compiled by Bukhari discuss many things about health science, such as burning, bleeding using a bowl, the benefits of honey, or the suggestion to sleep on your right side. There are also several diseases identified by the Prophet, for example eye inflammation, pleurisy, leprosy and bubonic plague. In addition, Muhammad also advised not to visit a country that was hit by the bubonic plague; this showed his awareness of infectious diseases.[77]

Rom Landau described the superiority of Arab medicine over European medicine. When European and Arab physicians met in Syria during the crusades, they exchanged ideas about various rescue ceremonies for injured patients. The treatment widely used by European physicians to treat severe wounds on the hands and feet was to cut the body parts with an ax, which actually made death inevitable. Those European physicians also performed treatment by shaving the head, then cutting and painting the sign of a cross on the flesh of the affected body part, and performing exorcism on the patient's body. This was clearly an impact of the witch hunts in Europe. Meanwhile, Arab physicians used medical science inspired by Greek, Hindu and Islamic medicine.[78]

In Europe, especially Muslim Spain, scholars viewed Arab science and medicine with a mixture of fear and respect. Hence, until the 16th century, all teaching of health science at European universities required knowledge of *Qanun Avicenna* or *Avicenna Medicine*. Medical schools in Europe would not have been born without a source of basic medical knowledge from these Arab books, especially from Ibn Sina (Avicenna). When medical schools were established in Paris (1110), Bologna (1113), Montpellier (1181), Padua (1222), and Naples (1224), the teaching plans or curricula there were practically dominated by Arab medical science.[79]

---

76. *Ibid.*, 32.
77. *Ibid.*, 46.
78. *Ibid.*, 48.
79. *Ibid.*, 50.

7

The Crusades

PRE-CRUSADES

Since the beginning of its development in the Dark or Middle Ages of Europe to the recent study of Orientalism, Islamic studies has been inseparable from the original intention behind its creation: to discover the various weaknesses of Islam.[80] Only in its later development has Islamic studies become truly academic and objective. Thus, the prejudice, rumors and bad news about Islam are unlikely to have been completely eliminated. Indonesian religious scholar Agus Salim states in his book, *Islam: Got's Laatse Boodschap, De Universelle Godsdient* (*Islam: the Ultimate Revelation, Religion for All Humankind*):

> The religion of Islam, the youngest form, and, according to Haeckel, the purest form of monotheism, is the religion that is the most widely opposed and slandered of the other world religions. Under the influence of such a propaganda, which is false, fraudulent, lying, which is carried out continuously, Islam is like being surrounded, locked up by a living fence consisting of plants that are in the form of misunderstanding, wrong or prejudice, which always depicts Islam as an inferior religion, with low human morals as well.[81]

The hate campaign against Islam also began in the Dark Ages, with a long list of those who succeeded in spreading bad news, slander and misinformation about Islam as well as instilling grudges and hatred against Muslims. Their names include Johannes Damascendi, Theophanes the Confessor, Nocotas Byzantinus, Prideaux, Bibliander, Rudolf de Ludheim, Nicholas of Cusa, Vives, Marracei and Hottinger. The misunderstanding of Islam has proven to

---

80. A.A. Yewangoe, *Agama dan Kerukunan*, 83. Original passage:
"Memang, studi terhadap agama-agama lain awalnya dimaksudkan untuk menemukan kelemahan mereka untuk diserang dan ditaklukkan".
81. Sudibyo Markus, *Konsili Vatikan II: Satu Sikap Pembaharuan Gereja terhadap Islam* (Jakarta: Pustaka Antara, 1978), 14.

be difficult to eliminate in modern times, even among Christian scholars. In fact, renowned modern scholars like Samuel P. Huntington cannot be separated from these historical grudges.

In Indonesia, precisely in the early days of independence, there are still remnants of this misunderstanding of Islam, as explained by Andreas Yewangoe:

> After the death of Muhammad, Abu Bakr and Umar ibn Khattab had propagated (expanded) Islam by fighting other people. After the death of Muhammad, the Qur'an was composed, which contained information about Islam, that is, all the fantasies of Muhammad. The chapters were composed repeatedly, and they contradict one another.

> As for the teachings of Islam, as an embodiment of Catholic influence, as well as some Jewish influences, others are influenced by idol worship (paganism). [Muslims are] ordered by the Koran to kill the unbelievers, that is to say people who are not Muslim.[82]

Meanwhile, a daily prayer book for the Indonesian Catholics still contains a prayer entitled "Prayers Asking for the Conversion of Muslims" (Sembahyang Nyuwun Mertobatipun Bongso Islam), which includes:

> O Lord Jesus Christ, our Lord, True God, True Man, Redeemer of

---

82. *Sejarah Geredja dengan Ringkasannya*, 40. Original passages:
"Sepeninggal Muhammad, Abu Bakr dan Umar telah merambatkan Islam dengan memerangi kaum yang lain. Sepeninggal Muhammad dikaranglah Al-Qur'an, yang berisi keterangan tentang Islam, yakni yang berisi segala khayal Muhammad. Surah-surah itu dikarang ulang-berulang, serta bunyinya bersalahan satu dengan yang lain".
"Adapun ajaran Islam, sebagai pengaruh dari Katolikisme, sebagian pengaruh Yahudi, yang lain pengaruh dari pemujaan berhala (paganisme). Disuruh oleh Al-Qur'an untuk membunuh orang-orang yang tak beriman, yakni orang-orang yang tidak beragama Islam".
Al-Qur'an was not written by Muhammad, let alone Abu Bakr or Umar ibn Khattab. Surat An-Najm verse 3 and Al-Ar'af verse 184 refresh the belief that the Qur'an was not written by Muhammad, but he is only a messenger, the Prophet chosen by God to deliver Islamic messages. In his time, Al-Qur'an was completely revealed, it could only be recorded after he died. After the death of the Prophet, the leadership of the Muslims was in the hands of Abu Bakr, and at that time Musailamah emerged as the false prophet. He caused conflicts and battles to occur. Although Musailamah was killed in battle, seventy memorizers of the Qur'an were also killed. Consequently, Umar suggested to the Caliph Abu Bakr to collect the Qur'an texts that were scattered into one book.

all people, with all humility we ask You, in line with the grace of the Immaculate Mary, may God be pleased to bestow mercy on all nations who have long been under Islamic oppression.[83]

When the entire European empire was under Vatican influence, and the spirit of hatred toward Islam had spread extensively, a new stage began: a physical confrontation with Islam. With the division of the Islamic kingdoms, especially in Andalusia, it seemed it was time for the West to rise up and attack Islam. In his agitative sermon delivered on November 25, 1095, at the Council of Clermont, Pope Urban II was successful in inflaming the passions of all major empires in Europe to unite in sending his troops to carry out a holy mission, liberating the Holy City of Jerusalem. Incidentally, the heightened enthusiasm for liberating Jerusalem coincided with a call for help from the Byzantine Emperor in Constantinople, who began to sense the disturbance from the Seljuk Turks.

Since Jerusalem fell to Arabs in the 7th century, Christian pilgrims from Europe had felt disturbed and harassed, and hence were eager to reclaim the Holy City. As a result, Richard the Lionheart of England, Philip Augustus of France, and Frederick Barbarossa of the Holy Roman Empire united to move their troops towards the Holy Land. However, although the war was a holy war, the aim was solely to liberate the Holy City, with no intention of spreading the Gospel among Muslims.

Given that the Crusades were by no means evangelistic in nature, in practice the war was no different from other wars in general, and hence it ended with the massacre of the losing party.[84] As described by Karen Armstrong, once the Crusaders captured and entered Jerusalem on July 15, 1099, the first thing they did was massacre all the inhabitants of the city, regardless of religion or age. Reportedly, 40,000 Muslims and non-Muslims in Jerusalem were killed in the first two days, followed by the massacre of 70,000 people in the following days. Gustave LeBon described the Crusaders' abomination in releasing their grudges in the Holy City as "Heaps of heads, hands and feet [which] can be seen all over the streets and squares of the city."[85]

---

83. *Buku Doa Harian Keuskupan Agung Semarang* (Semarang: Keuskupan Agung Semarang, 1950), pp. 195–196.

84. I.H. Enklaar, *Sejarah Geredja Ringkas*, third edition (Jakarta: PT BPK Gunung Mulia, 1996), 36.

85. Philip K. Hitti, *History of The Arabs* (New York: Macmillan International High-

Two weeks after the fall of Jerusalem, Pope Urban II, father of the Crusades, died. Even so, "he would have been horrified by the massacre in Jerusalem," wrote Karen Armstrong. Many people in Europe were shocked by the news. However, on October 2, 1187, Salahuddin Al-Ayyubi managed to reclaim Jerusalem. After that, for 800 years, Jerusalem was under the rule of successive Islamic caliphates before finally being captured by Israel in 1967. This seemed to spark a new holy war, this time against Zionism.[86]

Young people also acknowledge the Crusades as the greatest war in history. Not surprisingly, when three hundred pastors heeded the invitation of Yale Divinity School, Yale University, on 18 November 2007, in order to welcome "A Common Word between Us and You," they responded positively to the pastors' letter and first apologized to Muslims for the actions of the Christians which occured both in the past and present, the Crusades and the war on terror, respectively, along with all the excesses that are bad for Muslims.[87]

BEGINNING OF THE CRUSADES

With the fall of Toledo on May 25, 1085, when the Islamic rulers of Al-Andalus were divided, Christian rulers began to understand that Islamic rule was no longer unified, complete and strong. Therefore, when in 1094 the Pope and Christian rulers in Western Europe received requests for help from Byzantine emperor Alexius Comnenus I to fight the infiltration of the Seljuks, the Pope and the rulers of Western Europe responded immediately.

In his agitative sermon at the Council of Clermont, Pope Urban II mentioned two things that all kings, heroes and defenders of the Christian church throughout Europe would have to succeed in at all costs. *First*, they would have to drive back the Seljuk Turks, the Muslim barbarians who had dared to harass Byzantium by attacking Anatolia in Asia Minor. *Second*, they would have to continue southward to reclaim Jerusalem, the Holy Land, from the occupation of the infidels. It was unacceptable to the Christians that their holy lands were under Islamic rule.

---

er Education, 2002), 816.

86. Karen Armstrong, *Holy War: The Crusades and Their Impact on Today's World* (New York: Random House, 2001), pp. 178–180, 258.

87. *A Common Word Between Us And You 5-Year Anniversary Edition* (Jordan: The Royal Aal Al-Bayt Institute for Islamic Thought, 2012), pp. 143–162.

The statue of Pope Urban II, who declared his Pontifical command for sending the Crusaders to liberate Jerusalem at the occasion of the Clermont Council, November 25, 1095.

Furthermore, Philip K Hitti added that, for Pope Urban II, the request of Emperor Alexius Comnenus I was an opportunity to reunite the Greek and Roman churches which split between 1009 and 1094.[88] Moreover, the position of Constantinople was more important than Rome at that time, as it was the location of Byzantium, as well as the center of power and the Greek church, which was still intact when compared to the Western Roman Empire, which had collapsed.

The response of the religious leaders, the troops, the community and the Christians in general was overwhelming. In the spring of 1096, they had gathered 60,000 soldiers, consisting of professional soldiers as well as volunteers, who were ready to go to the east with their families. Realizing that the journey to liberating the Holy Land was a long-term journey, many of them sold their belongings to get provisions during the trip. In the following season, 100,000 soldiers were successfully dispatched and, of course, accompanied by priests and volunteers. Since many of them had sold their property, not a few of them expected the booty of war.

Karen Armstrong argues that the uniforms of the troops - vests dec-

---

88. Philip K. Hitti, *History of The Arabs*, 811.

orated with the symbol of the cross – were an attempt to raise their pride as a Western nation who was just emerging from the Dark Ages.

> In the eleventh century Western Christians were beginning to recover from the trauma of the Dark Ages and were trying to create a new Western identity which could enable them to shake off their sense of inferiority toward their more powerful and cultured neighbors.[89]

While the Western Roman Empire fell, Byzantine rule remained intact, with the emperor as the supreme leader of the religious state and all religious activity. The Patriarch of Constantinople still recognized the supremacy of the Pope in the Vatican, and there were no differences in religious doctrine between Constantinople and the Vatican. There were only psychological and cultural differences: while the Western Roman Empire was influenced by Latin culture, the Byzantine Empire was closely related to Greek culture. Meanwhile, the rising Anglo-Saxons, along with the barbarians of western and northern Europe, supported the revival of the Roman Empire, although there was also some objection to the fact that Rome was only a "satellite" to Byzantine at that time.

STAGES OF THE CRUSADES

There is no single approach to determining the stages of the Crusades. The Crusades had been ongoing since 1095, from the time Pope Urban II's agitative sermon was delivered at the Council of Clermont until the recapture of Jerusalem by Salahuddin Al-Ayyubi in 1297. However, the Pope's orders to dispatch gradually into the battlefield that stretches between Constantinople and Jerusalem could be considered one stage.

The so-called Second Crusade was a period of revival of the Muslim armies after their defeat and loss of Jerusalem in 1099. The resurrection took place under the leadership of Imad al-Din Zengi (1085–1146), the Governor of Mosul who won the trust of the Sultan of Seljuk, Malik Shah, as warlord and managed to reclaim Edessa on November, 28, 1144, after having been ruled by the Crusades for four decades. The Crusaders' attempt to reclaim Edessa by deploying additional troops from Antioch, Tripoli and Jerusalem were at first fruitless. However, after successfully capturing Edessa, Antioch, Tripoli and Jerusalem, the Crusaders immediately

---

89. Karen Armstrong, *Holy War*, 47.

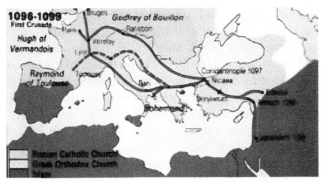

The route of the Crusade I, where all the soldiers went by land, first to secure the Turkish Seljuk from the Byzantine territory in Anatolia and Minor Asia, then move south to Jerusalem.

established governments in the four cities.

It was Imad al-Din Zengi who revived the spirit of resistance against the Crusaders, since after the Muslim defeat in Jerusalem in 1099, Muslim polities remained divided. Some polities even made peace with the Crusaders. The leadership of Zengi and the recapture of Edessa, the first Crusader state, were the turning points for the rise of the Muslim army. Pope Urban II may have succeeded in arousing the spirit of the masses to mobilize the First Crusade, but Zengi succeeded in reviving the jihad spirit of the Muslim forces to reclaim the areas occupied by the Crusaders. Imad al-Din Zengi's leadership was continued by his sons, two siblings, Nuruddin Mahmud ibn Imad al-Din Zengi, the Governor of Aleppo, and Saifuddin Zengi, the Governor of Mosul.

The First Crusade: the fall of Jerusalem

The Crusaders departed before the First Crusade through the inland journey, but the hardships they experienced would later lead the next group to take the sea route instead. The leaders of the first troops had to work hard to prevent the looting of property along the way to Constantinople. When they arrived at the city, all troops who came from Western Europe were amazed by the condition and progress of the people of Constantinople who were more advanced than Western European cities, in terms of the conditions in the palaces, churches, and gardens all over the city. The mission of the first batch of troops was to help Emperor Alexius seize Anatolia and Asia Minor from the hand of the Seljuks. Emperor Alexius was actually worried that if the Crusaders of Western Europe did succeed in capturing Asia Minor, then they would continue to occupy the province, and would not hand it over to the Byzantines.

Emperor Alexius did not allow the Crusaders to linger in Constantinople, considering the background of the former rioters in their respective territories, ordering them to immediately cross the Bosphorus in preparation for attacking the Seljuks, camping near Nicea. In June 1097, the Crusaders achieved their first success in crossing Anatolia, conquering the Seljuks' capital, Iznik. Finally, the Seljuks, led by Sultan Qilij Arslan, were totally defeated in the battle of Dorylaeum.

On March 10, 1098, the Crusaders succeeded in capturing Edessa, a city controlled by Armenian Christians, where they established the first Crusaders state. After besieging Jerusalem for three weeks, 40,000 Crusaders managed to capture a city defended only by the 1,000 strong Turkish garrison. Then, like the fall of Antioch, the fall of Jerusalem was followed by the massacre of no less than 70,000 inhabitants, which marked the ending of the First Crusade.

The Second Crusade (1147-1149)

The fall of Edessa in 1144 worried the Pope, Eugene III at that time, and European monarchs, for it was indeed followed by other provinces that the Crusaders managed to tackle in the previous war. Edessa was perceived as a holy city for the Crusaders, thanks to many sacred churches there. Jesus' handkerchief was even found there as well.

The main character who called for the Second Crusade to liberate Edessa was the French priest Saint Bernard Clairvaux who succeeded in moving King Louis VII of France, Emperor Conrad III of Germany, and King Baldwin of Jerusalem. Emperor Conrad III's troops, following in the footsteps of the First Crusaders by entering via Asia Minor, were intercepted by the Seljuks and forced to retreat to Nicea. Then, they returned to Constantinople to continue their voyage to attack Damascus by sea, along with King Louis VII's troops.

In June 1148, the joint forces led by King Louis VII, Emperor Conrad III and King Baldwin had besieged Damascus and its king, Mu'in ad-Din Unur, who had previously entered into an agreement with the Crusaders. The Crusaders, initially convinced of taking

The fall of Jerusalem to the Crusades in 1099, where 70,000 people, regardless of their religion and age, were slaughtered by the Crusades soldiers.

Damascus with little fuss, were forced to retreat when the troops of the Zangi brothers, from Aleppo and Mosul respectively, came to Mu'in ad-Din Unur's aid. The cost of the defeat in Damascus to Louis VII and Conrad III was so devastating that they decided to return to Europe, an event that marked the end of the Second Crusade. It was Nur al-Din Zengi who had the leadership and ability to unite Muslim leaders in the spirit of jihad to reclaim Damascus, Antioch and Egypt in 1147, 1149, and 1169, respectively. It was only on October 2, 1187, that Jerusalem was successfully liberated by Salahuddin Al-Ayyubi.

The Third Crusade (1187-1191)

The defeat of the Crusade polities and army, which began with the fall of Edessa and was followed by the fall of Antioch and Jerusalem, prompted Europe to deploy the Crusaders under the leaderships of King Richard the Lionheart of England, Emperor Philip Augustus of France and Emperor Frederick Barbarossa of the Holy Roman Empire. Some troops took the sea routes, while Barbarossa, who went through the inland route, drowned in Saleph River in Armenia, near Edessa; thus, most of his troops returned to Germany. King Richard and Philip Augustus, who took the road overland, met Salahuddin Al-Ayyubi's troops in Sicily, and then Philip

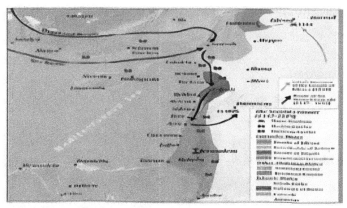

The sea route of the Crusades

Augustus chose to leave Sicily and defend Egypt.[90]

The Fourth Crusade (1202–1204)

It was at this stage that the Crusaders from the Latin countries of Western Europe took over the government of Alexios III in Constantinople. The Crusaders changed their strategy for control of Egypt under the rule of the Ayyubid Dynasty, which was considered to have the most prominent Islamic leadership that could serve as a stepping stone for the Jerusalem recapture. However, the Crusaders, assisted by the Greco-Venetian troops, only made internal agreements with the Egyptian government in 1203–1204 and 1210–1211, and as a result the Egyptian government allowed Christians to make pilgrimages to Jerusalem peacefully.

The Fifth Crusade (1217–1221)

This war was still colored by the fight between Latin and Greek kingdoms over Constantinople, involving Jeanne Brunne, Cardinal Pelagius, and the King of Hungary.

An unprecedented meeting occurred in the Fifth Crusade between St. Francis of Assisi and the ruler of Egypt, Sultan Malik Al-Kamil. The meeting was aimed at ending the protracted Crusades, and was recorded as a monumental interfaith dialogue. So important, monumental and historical is the dialogue that Paul

90. "Sejarah Lengkap Perang Salib," August, 30, 2016, https://www.Islamedia.com/sejarah-lengkap-perang-salib/

Moses described the meeting between the two adversaries as a dialogue full of politeness. It is hard to imagine that this could happen
in the midst of the Crusades, a vicious yet futile war.[91]

The Sixth Crusade (1228-1229)

Led by Frederick II of the Holy Roman Empire and a king from Italy,
who later became the viceroy of Jerusalem, this crusade had no war,
but brought a 10-year peace agreement with Sultan Al-Malik Al-
Kamil, nephew of Salahuddin Al-Ayyubi. This agreement was later
taken over by Sultan Al-Malik Al-Saleh Najamuddin Ayyub in 1224.

The Seventh Crusade (1248-1254)

This crusade was led by King Louis IX of France, who managed
to seize Damietta (Dimyath) in 1249. When Louis IX failed to take
Antioch, which was controlled by Sultan Malik Zahir Bay, and then
set his sights on Tunis, he and his troops were captured on April
6, 1250, in a battle sea around Egypt. They were later released by
paying a ransom and allowed to return to France.

The Eighth Crusade (1270)

During the war of the Eighth Crusade, it was rumored that Louis
IX died on November 25, 1270, possibly due to illness. Historians
agree that this war did not continue since Aere, which was then
occupied by the Crusaders, was captured by Muslim troops.

The Ninth Crusade (1271-1291)

These events consisted only of skirmishes between the Crusaders and
the Muslim troops, which marked the ultimate end of the Crusades.

PERIODIZATION OF THE CRUSADES

The following summarizes the nine Crusades above into four periods.

First period

This period is also known as the period of conquest (1009–1144).
Hasan Ibrahim Hasan[92] argues that the First Crusade, which was

---

91. Paul Moses, *The Saint and the Sultan: Crusades, Islam and Francis Asisi's Mission
of Peace* (New York: Doubleday Religion, 2009) in Trias Kuncahyono, "Memaknai
Pertemuan Paus Fransiskus dan Imam Besar Al-Thayeb," Kompas, February 9, 2019.
92. Trias Kuncahyono, "Memaknai Pertemuan Paus Fransiskus dan Imam Besar

led by Pierra Permite, was a war of an undisciplined and unprepared commoner who had no war experience,

The next Crusaders were led by Godfrey of Bouillon more competently. They succeeded in occupying Jerusalem on July, 7, 1099. The victory of the Crusades in this period changed the map of the Muslim world and triggered the establishment of Latin-Christian Crusader states in the East, such as the Kingdom of Jerusalem (in 1099) under the leadership of King Godfrey, the County of Edessa (1098) under King Baldwin, and the County of Tripoli (1102) under King Raymond IV.

Second period

This period is also known as the Muslim reaction period (1144–1192). The victory of Muslims was evident after the appearance of Salahuddin Al-Ayyubi, who succeeded in liberating Jerusalem on October 2, 1187.

In this war, Richard the Lionheart and Salahuddin agreed to a ceasefire and treaty, which was settled on November 2, 1192. It provided that the coastal area belonged to the Latins, while the interior belonged to the Muslims, and that any pilgrims who came to the Holy City could not be harassed. The next year, on February 19, 1193, Salahuddin fell ill in Damascus and died on March 2, 1193 at the age of 55. His tomb, which is adjacent to the Umayyad Mosque, is still an attraction for the capital of Syria.

Third period

This period (1193–1291) is better known as the period of skirmishes, or the period of internal decline of the Crusaders. During this period, heroes such as Syajar Ad-Durr appeared, who demonstrated the greatness of Islam by liberating and allowing King Louis IX to return to his country, France.

THE IMPACT OF THE CRUSADES ON THE MUSLIM WORLD

Broadly speaking, it can be concluded that the Crusades were won by Muslims, but the negative impact caused by the Crusades was enormous, including the ruin of the economy, since the Crusades occurred in Islamic territory. The political power of the Muslims was also weakened, as they were increasingly divided. Many small

Al-Thayeb," *Kompas*, February 9, 2019.

dynasties broke free from Abbasid rule in Baghdad.

Even though the European Christians also suffered losses in the Crusades, they had the invaluable opportunity to become acquainted with the advancements of Islamic civilization, an encounter which in turn gave birth to the Renaissance in the West. Some of the advancements adopted by the West are as follows:

- Military. The West encountered weapons and warfare techniques such as the use of gunpowder to launch projectiles, armed combat while on horseback, techniques to train pigeons for military information purposes and the use of percussion to encourage troops on the battlefield.
- Industry. The West found woven fabrics, along with the tools for making them, in the Islamic world, which they later brought to Europe, such as muslin, satin and damask. They also found various types of fragrances, incense and Arabic resins that could scent the room.
- Agriculture. The West brought the agricultural systems encountered by the Crusaders in the Muslim East to the West, such as an enhanced irrigation system, and cultivation of various plants and fruits, especially sugar.
- Trade. The West began to recognize the monetary system used in buying and selling from Islamic civilization; previously they only used the barter system.
- Science and medicine. The science of astronomy that had been developed by Muslims since the ninth century has certainly influenced the appearance of various observatories in the West. In addition, the West also imitates the hospitals that had previously been developed in the Muslim World.[93]

The Role of the Order of the Knights Templar

In addition to the official forces from the Kingdom of England, France and Germany, as well as a number of volunteers who wanted to start a new life in the war, the Crusades were also supported by a number of special forces who were superior in terms of combat and military strategy, and were well-organized. These troops were the Knights Templar.

The Knights Templar is a religious military order formed after the success of European Christian armies in capturing the Holy

93. https://www.rangkumanmakalah.com/perang-salib

Land and a number of provinces during the First Crusade (1095–1099). This order was also formed to provide assistance in defense, administration, and even medicine. One of their extra duties was to escort and protect pilgrims to the Holy Land. The Knights Templar special forces had a wide and firm network. They consisted of young Frankish knights of rich noble families, and were supported by other wealthy aristocrats.

As the Knights Templar became increasingly large and respected, they also received special support from the Pope. The Pope gave them special rights and permits to set up a financial repository, so that all royals could keep their money. From this business network they reportedly owned 870 castles, schools and houses.

This infuriated Philip IV of France, who made a false report to Pope Clement V (allegedly a puppet of Philip IV whom he raised up after overthrowing Pope Boniface VII in 1303), provoking the latter to destroy the order. As a result, the Knights Templar, who had a strong organization and network for no less than two centuries, was successfully disbanded by the Pope in just eight months, through methods which included trial and torture.[94]

LESSONS FROM THE CRUSADES

The Crusades ended with the failure of the Holy War's mission to liberate Jerusalem from Islamic occupation. However, behind this failure there were a number of both positive and negative lessons that both parties managed to learn.

First, intercultural and intercivilizational dialogue developed. Along the way to Constantinople and Asia Minor before traveling south to Jerusalem, via Edessa, Antioch and Tripoli, the Crusaders saw that Islamic culture was more advanced than their nations in Western Europe, which at that time were still languishing in the Dark Ages.

Besides a monumental interfaith dialogue between St. Francis of Assisi and Sultan Malik Al-Kamil, there was also an exchange of experiences on how to treat prisoners, and between Christian and Muslim physicians, in which the latter were more knowledgeable. Muslim physicians had to be called to treat a Crusades commander, who was badly injured.

---

94. Brenda R. Lewis, *Sejarah Gelap Para Paus*, pp. 106–107.

Second, this experience encouraged Europe to increase its scientific and technical activities from the centers of Islamic civilization in Baghdad and Cairo in the East, as well as from Islamic civilization in Toledo, Seville and Cordoba in the West. In fact, in Toledo, a translation agency had previously been established which had grown rapidly until the thirteenth century. The institute, which was founded by Archbishop Raymond, succeeded in translating several philosophical works and works of Aristotle from Arabic, which had previously been developed by Ibn Rushd.

Third was the long-term impact on Muslim-Christian relations. Karen Armstrong argues that all the prejudice and grudges toward Islam that were developed in the Crusades over two centuries contributed to the conflict between the Western World and the Muslim World to this day.[95]

Meanwhile, Arnold Toynbee argues that Europe, after going through a long historical process leaving the Dark Ages, slowly but surely succeeded in conquering the Muslim World. In the sixteenth century, along with the discovery of the sea route by Columbus, Europe succeeded in throwing its "lasso rope" onto the "necks" of Muslim countries which were in decline, and then pulled it in during the nineteenth century through colonialism.[96]

---

95. Karen Armstrong, *Holy War,* ix.
96. Arnold Toynbee, *Civilization on Trial,* 248.

8
Renaissance and Reformation

While other historians still debate the existence and extent of the relationships between the Renaissance and the Reformation (which took place in the fourteenth and sixteenth centuries, respectively), Crane Brinton, professor of ancient history at Harvard University, emphatically states:

> We call the Protestant Reformation and the Renaissance somehow the same in inspiration and purpose. One was directed toward religious freedom, the other toward artistic freedom, and both together worked for moral freedom, and, of course, for what became in the nineteenth century democracy.[97]

The Renaissance and Church Reform movements went hand in hand to realize moral and religious freedom and progress, and in the end to pioneer democracy. Both had the same aspirations and goals, the former having emerged for the sake of artistic freedom, the latter for religious freedom. Both aimed to realize moral freedom, independence, and a critical attitude, which in turn became the basic capital for the development of democracy.

Moral freedom is the freedom to criticize the establishment of culture and power in favor of one's own values and beliefs. Both the Renaissance and Church Reform movements meant to realize this through a movement called humanism, and together freed mankind from the shackles of oppression and superstition, including various threats to freedom of thought that dominated human life in the Middle Ages.

Historians agree that the Renaissance and Reformation "marked the transition from Medieval to Modern Times."[98]

---

97. Crane Brinton, *The Shaping of Modern Mind* (New York: Mentor Books, 1956), pp. 21–22.
98. *Ibid.*, 22.

RENAISSANCE

Cultural movement

The Renaissance is a cultural movement that was born in Florence, Italy, then developed throughout Europe, defined by the *American Heritage Dictionary* as "the humanistic revival of art, literature and learning in Europe."[99] . Inherently, it was an effort to develop new cultural options, shifting away from traditional Roman-Christian culture that was already familiar to European society.[100] Thus, historians regard the Renaissance as a bridge between European medieval and progressive ages. Though its development was uneven, the spirit of the Renaissance could be felt throughout Europe, supported by the invention of paper and, later, Gutenberg's printing press. The Renaissance cultural movement succeeded in developing elements not only in art and culture, but gave birth to intellectual and socio-political changes, even in the field of diplomacy. Famous Renaissance figures, such as Leonardo da Vinci and Michelangelo Buonarotti, who were known as both polymaths and figures of artistic reform, are called Renaissance men.[101]

Renaissance humanism

After the fall of Constantinople in 1453, many Greek immigrants headed to the West. Greco-Roman culture was a culture that emphasized humans as the main subject. Greek philosophy describes humans as beings who constantly ponder in order to understand their environment and determine the principles of their life, and realize the actions they can take toward obtaining self-happiness.[102] Literature, in Greek myth, also teaches courage to explore the world and realms that are full of challenges. In fact, Greco-Roman architecture also reflects the human ability to harmonize law, power and beauty.[103] The immigrants carried with them precious ancient manuscripts, many of which ended

99. *The American Dictionary of English Language* (New York: Dell Publishing Co. Inc., 1976), 597.

100. John Hale, *The Civilization of Europe in the Renaissance* (New York: Simon and Schuster, 1995), 648.

101. BBC Science and Nature, Leonardo da Vinci, retrieved May 12, 2007.

102. BBC History, Michelangelo, retrieved May 12, 2007.

103. Stella Fletcher, *The Longman Companion to Renaissance Europe, 1390–1530* (London: Routledge, 2000), 347.

in obscurity until they encountered Arabic or Greek philosophy and mathematics, especially Aristotelian manuscripts (which had been translated into Arabic by Ibn Rushd of Spain). However, many Christian Greek works, including the Greek version of the New Testament, were transported from Byzantine to Western Europe where they were studied by European scholars. Studies of Christian Greek works, especially their application to studying the New Testament, as promoted by humanists such as Erasmus, paved the way for the birth of the Reformation.

The Renaissance was aimed at reviving classical humanism which emphasized humans as part of nature, or polis; an individual, as part of nature, can think critically and determine his or her own choices as part of his or her control over nature. Classic humanism was hampered by Medieval scholasticism, which did not give space for critical attitudes. Humanists strove so that people, including women, could express opinions critically, eloquently and clearly, which was believed to be achieved through humanitarian studies (*studia humanitatis*), now known as humanities, which includes grammar, rhetoric, history, poetry and moral philosophy.[104] Renaissance scholars used humanist methods in research, as well as searching for realism and human emotions in art.[105]

SOME RENAISSANCE FIGURES[106]

Art and culture

1. Erasmus

Desiderius Erasmus of Rotterdam (1466–1536) was a Dutch theologian, teacher, social critic, Catholic priest, and Renaissance humanist. Erasmus was also a classics scholar and wrote in a pure Latin style. Among humanists he was nicknamed "the Prince of Humanists," and also known as the Christian humanists' crown of glory.[107] Using humanist techniques to work on texts, he compiled a new edition of

---

104. Marvin Perry, J. Wayne Baker and Pamela Pfeiffer Hollinger, *The Humanities In The Western Tradition: Ideas And Aesthetics, Volume I: Ancient to Medieval* (Boston: Cengage Learning, 2002), chapter 13.

105. Paul F. Grendler (ed.), *The Renaissance: An Encyclopedia for Students* (New York: Scribner, 2003), 970.

106. Wikipedia Indonesia.

107. Gordon Campbell, *The Oxford Dictionary of the Renaissance* (Oxford: Oxford University Press, 2004), 862.

the Greek and Latin New Testament, two books that were considered extremely important, raising issues that would later be influential in the Reformation and Counter-Reformation.

2. Donatello

Donatello di Niccolò di Betto Bardi (1386–1466) was an Italian artist and sculptor, originally from Florence. He is known as one of the best sculptors of his era. He employed a special type of sculpting technique which made his works look very realistic.

3. Leonardo da Vinci

Leonardo da Vinci (1452–1519) was an Italian Renaissance architect, musician, writer, sculptor, and painter. He is described as a "Renaissance man" and universal genius. Leonardo is known for his masterful paintings, such as "The Last Supper" and "Mona Lisa," and for designing many creations that anticipated modern technology but were only touched on during his lifetime. For example, his ideas about tanks and cars were poured into two-color drawings. In addition, he also promoted anatomy, astronomy and civil engineering, and even culinary arts.

4. Michelangelo

Michelangelo Buonarotti (1475-1564) was an Italian sculptor, painter, architect, poet, and engineer whose influence in the development of Western art is unmatched. He is well known for his contributions to fine arts, including his best works: "David," "Pietà," and the fresco on the ceiling of the Sistine Chapel.

Exploration

5. Christopher Columbus

Christopher Columbus (1451–1506) was an Italian explorer and merchant from Genoa who crossed the Atlantic Ocean to the Americas on October 12, 1492. The trip was funded by Queen Isabella of Castille after the Queen conquered Andalusia. He believed that the earth was round and assumed that a ship sailing west would be able to return to the east.

Columbus was not the first to arrive in America, for in the 11th century the continent had been touched by the Vikings of Northern Europe, who founded a colony called L'Anse aux Meadows in a short period of time.

Desiderius Erasmus, known as Erasmus from Rotterdam, a Catholic priest who was noted as the Prince of Humanism.

6. Ferdinand Magellan

Ferdinand Magellan (1480–1521) was a Portuguese explorer who sailed from Western Europe to Asia, navigated the Pacific Ocean, and was the first to lead an expedition around the world to the Spice Islands, Moluccas. Magellan himself was killed by Datuk Lapu-Lapu in the Philippines while stopping in the East Indies before heading to Europe, but the crew of eighteen and his fleet managed to return safely to Spain in 1522.

Science

1. Johannes Gutenberg

Johannes Gensfleisch zur Laden zum Gutenberg (1400–1468) was a German metalsmith who invented the printing press in the 1450s, including metal alloy character molds and oil-based ink. By combining these elements in a production system, printing could be done quickly; hence, the printing press invented by Gutenberg spurred the information boom in Renaissance Europe.

2. Nicolaus Copernicus

Nicolaus Copernicus (1478–1543) was a Polish astronomer and mathematician who developed the heliocentric theory. He was also a church canon, governor and administrator, judge, astrologer, and physician. His heliocentric theory overturned the traditional geocentric theory and is considered to be one of the most important discoveries in the history of mankind, as well as a fundamental starting point for astronomy and modern science, as it gave rise to scientific revolutions. His theories also affected many aspects of human life from astrology to theology.

3.   Galileo Galilei

Galileo Galilei (1546–1642) was an Italian astronomer, philosopher and physicist who played a significant role in the scientific revolution. He is called the "father of observational astronomy," "father of modern physics," "father of scientific methods" and "father of science."

His contributions to the world of science include the improvement of telescopes, various astronomical observations, as well as the second and third law of thermodynamics. In addition, Galileo is also known as a supporter of the Copernican heliocentric theory.

As a consequence of his stance of the sun as the center of the solar system, which deviated from the belief that the earth was the center of the universe widely held by European society and the church at that time, he was submitted to the Italian Inquisition court on June 22, 1633. He was required to wear a white robe and a conical hat, as a sign of confessing sinners, and kneel before the judge to hear the decision of the Inquisition court. Galileo surrendered before the Inquisition court due to his old age and fear, and was propagated by the Church throughout Europe to humiliate him. He was sentenced to exclusion (house arrest) until he died. It wasn't until 1992 that Pope John Paul II officially stated that the sentencing decision was wrong. In a speech he gave on December 21, 2008, Pope Benedict XVI stated that the Roman Catholic Church was rehabilitating his name as a scientist.

4.   Johannes Kepler

Johannes Kepler (1571–1630) was an important figure in the scientific revolution. He was a German astronomer, mathematician, and astrologer. He is best known for his laws of planetary motion. At the age of 29 Kepler, became the mathematician of the Holy Roman Empire, as well as advisor to General Wallenstein, a position he held until his death. Kepler was highly respected not only in mathematics, but also in the field of optics and astronomy.

Despite a number of objections to the influence of the Renaissance by the Reformation movement driven by Martin Luther (1483–1546), there are some obvious intersections and points of contact between the two. For example, Erasmus' translation of the New Testament from the Greek language is thought to have influenced Luther's change of view and translation into local languages including German. Erasmus himself, as a Renaissance figure, initially supported Luther who courageously challenged the practices of the Catholic Church, but later withdrew when he saw the danger that threatened Luther, which was exerted by the Pope and German emperor. Erasmus is depicted as a true priest who chose tranquility in life and shunned 'turbulence' in the Church. However, Ulrich Zwingli (1484–1531), one of Erasmus' followers and known as one of Luther's supporters besides Johannes Calvin (1509–1564), came forward to improve church life in Zurich by replacing mass with ordinary sermons and reducing ornamentation.

At that time, Church practices were still entangled with the Inquisition trials against heresies and witches. The case of Galileo,

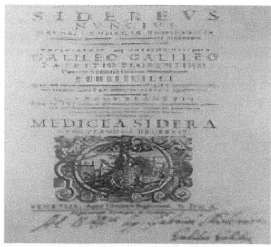

SIDEREUS NUNCIUS or "Message from the Stars," the front cover of Galileo's book which was published in 1610, telling his experiences in observing the night skies over one month. (*Dark History of the Popes*, p. 168)

which was brought before the Inquisition court in 1633, shows a sharp intersection between the Renaissance and the Reformation illustrated by Martin Luther in 1517. Previously, Copernicus's *De Revolutionibus Orbium Coelestium* was included in the index of forbidden books by the Vatican in February 1616 and a Dominican priest, Giordano Bruno, was burned to death in 1600 for supporting the heliocentric theory.[108]

Negative Renaissance

Besides the positive Renaissance of new awareness in the fields of art, culture, science and technology driven by classical humanism, there was also a negative Renaissance called "infidel humanism," which was developed by Niccolò Machiavelli (1469–1527). Machiavelli, who was raised in the environment of a corrupt government bureaucracy, wrote in his *Il Principe* that the state should do whatever necessary to maintain its security and power. In his view, known as 'Machiavellianism,' religion and religious morality are completely unimportant for the state, for the state has its own morals. Murder, violence, and treason can be employed by the government to achieve its aims.[109]

REFORMATION

Background

In the fifth and sixth centuries, Europe experienced great turmoil. The Huns, under Attila's leadership, defeated the Roman Empire and forced Roman rule to move to Constantinople in the east. Thus, the power of the bishop in Rome became stronger and was considered the leader of the highest church, even rivaling the Pope. Pope Leo I (r. 440–461) who dared to face Attila was considered the first 'great Pope'.[110]

Evangelism continued throughout Europe, and by the 11th century the whole of Europe, from Western Europe to Eastern Europe, was successfully Christianized. Pope Gregory I (r. 590–604) is considered the most instrumental in the history of Christian dominion

---

108. Brenda R. Lewis, *Sejarah Gelap Para Paus*, 170.

109. Herman Embuiru, *Geredja Sepanjang Masa* (Ende: Penerbit Nusa Indah, 1967), pp. 177–178.

110. I.H. Enklaar, *Sejarah Geredja Ringkas* (Jakarta: Badan Penerbit Kristen, 1966), pp. 33–34.

expansion in those difficult times. There was one very important event in the history of Christian Europe, namely the services of Charles Martel, who thwarted the advances of Muslims to Poitiers. History would have been different had the Moorish troops succeeded in occupying Paris at that time.

LETTERS OF INDULGENCE

One Vatican practice which Martin Luther strongly opposed was the sale of letters of "indulgence" issued by the Vatican to finance the construction of the magnificent and costly St. Peter's Basilica, as well as to increase profits for the church itself. In this case, Pope Leo X conspired and entered into a clandestine agreement with Archbishop Albrecht of Mainz. The power of attorney given by Pope Leo to the Archbishop Albrecht claimed that these letters of indulgence could not only wash away sins, but could be used to atone for sins.[111]

Johan Tetzel, a Dominican priest as well as the chief seller of these letters, launched a massive campaign arguing that the acquittal of sins from buying letters of indulgence also applied to his brothers as well as himself. Johan Tetzel's well-known propaganda motto was:

As soon as the coin in the coffer rings, the soul from purgatory (also attested as 'into heaven') springs.[112]

Such letters of indulgence could even be sold by the priest to someone who is dying – so that people could sin without consequence until the penultimate minute of their lives.

The sale of letters of indulgence was only one example of the Catholic Church's damage in the Dark Ages. The practices of the Inquisition against heretics and witchcraft, as well as the prohibition of publishing scientific works considered contrary to Church beliefs, continued during the Renaissance period and were increasingly widespread in Europe.

---

111. H. Berkhof and I.H. Enklaar, *Sejarah Gereja* (Jakarta: PT BPK Gunung Mulia, 2010), pp. 126–127.

112. Charles Herbermann (ed.), "Johan Tetzel", in *Catholic Encyclopedia* (New York: Robert Appleton Company, 1913).

The East and West Church Schism. The first schism was the split between the Vatican Church, headed by the Pope, and Constantinople's Church, headed by a Patriarch. The second schism was the split between the Vatican and Avignon as head of the Catholic Church (1309-1377). The red area supported Avignon, while the blue supported the Vatican.

THE SCHISM, THE RIFT OF THE CHURCH

Apart from these corrupt attitudes and practices, the Catholic Church also faced two serious structural weaknesses – two schisms – that caused the rift of the Church.[113] The first schism was the duality of the Roman Catholic Church, which was based in the Vatican, and the Eastern Orthodox Church, which was based in Constantinople. While the Roman Catholic Church was subject to the pope in the Vatican, the Eastern Orthodox Church was ruled by a high bishop called a patriarch. Until the fall of Constantinople in 1453, the patriarch of Constantinople had strong support and influence from the Byzantine emperor and other important bishops, such as the Bishops of Alexandria and Antioch. Political support of this kind had not been received by the Pope in the Vatican since the fall of the Roman Empire, but he received similar support from European empires, such as France, England, and Germany. Therefore, Pope Urban II's campaign for

---

113. Christiaan de Jonge, *Pembimbing ke dalam Gereja* (Jakarta: PT BPK Gunung Mulia, 2009), pp. 62-68.

instigating the Crusades on the pretext of liberating Jerusalem, a call that was also supported by the emperor of the Holy Roman Empire and the kings of England and France, actually contained a hidden political mission to match the Patriarch of Constantinople, who was supported by Byzantine emperors.[114]

The second schism was the Pope's dualism. The vacuum of power in the absence of a Roman emperor was exploited by Philip IV of France. With such influence, Philip IV overthrew Pope Boniface VII and crowned Pope Clement V (r. 1305–1314), who was practically his "puppet". In fact, from 1309 to 1377 the Popes no longer resided in the Vatican after Pope Clement V ordered his palace to be moved to Avignon in southern France. He established a separate curia council in Avignon, which consisted mostly of a number of French cardinals. Pope Clement V, along with King Philip IV, managed to destroy the order of the Knights Templar, who had served in the Crusades. Pope Gregory XI (r. 1370–1378) was the last Pope to live in Avignon, before the papal palace finally returned to the Vatican in 1377. However, one year apart from Gregory XI, the king of France tried to appoint a new Pope of French origin in Avignon, and was supported by the French curia council. The existence of these two popes in the Vatican and Avignon is what is called the western schism (1378–1415).[115]

The Indonesian theologian Herman Embuiru maintains that the Protestant revolution did not happen suddenly. The emergence of the reform movement and its success was triggered by the corruption within the Catholic Church that had occurred for a long time, allegedly since the 13th century.[116] Various internal improvement efforts directed at church leadership from top to bottom—as outlined by the Council of Konstanz, Basel and Lateran—never bore fruit. The life of the Pope and his monks, who continually forgot their spiritual mission, was contrary to the spirit of Christ; hence, the Pope and the Church lost sanctity.

From Wittenberg against the Pope

On October 21, 1517, Martin Luther rebelled against the Catholic Church with a Latin poster containing 95 theses, posted on

---

114. *Ibid.*, 66.
115. *Ibid.*, 68.
116. Herman Embuiru, *Geredja Sepanjang Masa*, 183.

the gates of All Saints' Church in Wittenberg. Luther criticized not only the sale of letters of indulgences, but also the position of the Pope as supreme leader of the Catholic Church. Luther's demands received a warm and wide reception in Germany, and immediately resulted in a slump in sales of indulgences. The German people were tired of blackmail by the Vatican through the letters of indulgences.

Pope Leo X, apart from asking Luther to withdraw the demands and regret his actions, asked him to appear before the judges in Rome within sixty days. He sent Cardinal Cajetan to Augsburg to examine Luther, but the effort did not work. Finally, on June 15, 1520, the Pope issued a papal bull condemning Luther's teachings as heresy, but Luther countered by calling the Pope anti-Christ. Even more extreme, on December 10, 1520, Luther publicly burned the papal bull at the gate of Wittenberg. On January 5, 1521, the Pope once again issued a papal bull containing condemnation against Luther, but no one in Germany heeded this papal bull, believing that the church no longer had to submit to the Vatican.

On May 26, 1521, Emperor Charles V convened the Diet of Worms, which condemned Luther and his followers. As a consequence, all of Luther's writings were burned. Hiding for ten years in Wartburg Castle, Luther succeeded in translating the New Testament from Latin to German, thus giving further insights and inspiration to his followers in Germany. The reform movement developed rapidly, even though it began to fall prey to the conflict between pro-Reformation and pro-Roman Catholic groups. In those years, the Diet of Worms received little attention, especially since the Emperor was busy fighting the French and Turks. In 1555, after the Reformation and a long war, the Peace of Augsburg was held in which Charles V recognized the existence of the Reformed Church as an official church, which was equal and had the same rights as the Roman Catholic Church.[117]

Ulrich Zwingli

Zwingli was one of Martin Luther's main supporters. He was located in Switzerland, especially in Zurich, and also a follower of Erasmus. Since 1520, Zwingli made several changes to the church, such as removing crosses and statues. The Mass was completely stopped

---

117. I.H. Enklaar, *Sejarah Geredja Ringkas*, pp. 52–54.

The Castle Church in Wittenberg, Germany where Martin Luther nailed his poster with the 95 Theses on 21 October 1517, which was marked as the beginning of the Reform movement.

and replaced with regular sermons. Since he lived during the same period as Luther, including having conflicts with Luther regarding the meaning of the last supper, Zwingli's role in the Reformation was not greatly expanded beyond his efforts in Zurich. Zwingli died in 1531 during a battle against the Catholics in Kappel.

Johannes Calvin

Calvin, who had only joined the Reformation movement in France in 1530, is considered to have been instrumental in further organizing the Reformation movement to become more focused and evolved with great force. So significant and specific were Calvin's merits that his name was immortalized in the term "Calvinism."[118] Calvin, who studied humanist law, left the Roman Catholic Church after witnessing violence against the Reformation movement in France. In 1536, at the invitation and guidance of Reformed pastor in Geneva William Farel, Calvin became a pastor and settled

---

118. Herman Embuiru, *Geredja Sepanjang Masa*, 195.

there. It was in Geneva that Calvin began building the Protestant church order. Calvin briefly left Geneva and settled in Strasbourg (in 1538–1541) due to a dispute with the city council, but returned to Geneva in 1541 to continue reforming society and the Church.

Calvin founded a high school in Geneva, where he taught the principles of Calvinism, a place to produce cadres of the Reformation. Geneva became a new base for the development of Church reformation, while at the same time the Roman Catholic Church began to counterattack against the Reformation movement. It was Calvin who made the organization of the Reformed Church stronger, an institution that could eagerly fight and nurture cadres to defend themselves from the attacks of the counter-Reformation movement. To this day, Geneva is still a center of the Protestant Church; there also stands the World Council of Churches.

Dutch theologian Enklaar mentions several features of Calvinism: (1) Prioritization of the predestination doctrine, the belief that all events in human life have been predestined by God; (2) the goal of all things, rather than human salvation or the liberation of the world, is only the glory of God; (3) the sanctification of the life of the believers and serving God in all fields of social life; (4) the task of the Church throughout the world and the prioritization of the strong organization of the Church; (5) the demand for full freedom of the Church from the state, in the sense that the state was obliged to obey the word of God as announced by the Church and must protect it, but has no power over it.[119]

Counter-reformation

Failing to prevent and control the development of the Reformation through its political power and religious power, the Roman Catholic Church staged a quite violent counter-Reformation movement with the aim of destroying the Reformation. This counter-Reformation movement ended with fighting between countries supporting the counter-Reformation and those supporting the Reformation.

In order to find a legal basis for the counter-Reformation movement in 1545-1563, a council was convened in Trent. The Council of Trent, which lasted eighteen years, faced many obstacles, including a brief move to Bologna before returning to Trent thanks to the

---

119. I.H. Enklaar, *Sejarah Geredja Ringkas*, 69.

May 25, 1521, Karel V, Emperor of Germany, issued the Worms Edict, which declared Martin Luther as guilty and banned his teachings.

Holy Roman Emperor's protests. The Council of Trent reiterated that the Church's tradition is a source of divine power equal to the Bible. The Church has power over the word of God, and so the Church should not be criticized. As a result, the Church condemned the Lutheran doctrine, justification by faith alone. However, the Catholic Church took several remedial steps due to Luther's criticism, such as stopping the sale of letters of indulgence. In addition, the Council of Trent also launched an index of forbidden books.

To lead the counter-Reformation movement, with the blessing of the Pope, came forward Ignatius Loyola. Known as the founder of the Society of Jesus order in 1540, he was determined to restore power and authority to the Roman Catholic Church by fighting the Reformation as well as heresies and expanding evangelization of the pagan nations of the New World. As it turned out, the Jesuits, who were known to be very disciplined, managed to restore the authority and power of the Roman Catholic Church which had declined due to the Reformation. In fact, in several places in southern Europe, such as Italy and Spain, Jesuits were so influential that the Reformation had difficulty getting into that region.[120]

---

120. *Ibid.*, pp. 60–61.

9

Colonialism Era

At the end of the 15th century, seven hundred years after Thariq ibn Ziyad landed in Gibraltar in 711, the Islamic sovereign of Andalusia for seven centuries was successfully overthrown by King Ferdinand of Aragon and Queen Isabella of Castille. However, the fall of Islamic rule on the Iberian peninsula was not sudden, but in decline since the 11th century, beginning with the fall of Toledo in 1085. The trial of the Inquisition coincided with the downfall of Muslim scientific centers on the Iberian Peninsula, where students from all over Europe studied. The Muslims there had only three choices: leave Andalusia, convert to Christianity or be executed in an Inquisition court.

The discovery of the sea routes by Vasco da Gama (July 9, 1447) and Christopher Columbus (August 3, 1492), was the beginning of a series of attacks, conquests and destruction of Islamic civilizations in their own homelands. Pioneered by the Spanish and Portuguese, then followed by the Dutch, British and French, Muslim countries collapsed. While it is true that initially economic motives were the driving force for the expansion movement, the desire to conquer Islam was undeniably inherent in this conquest and, later, colonialism.

Pope Alexander VI (r. 1492–1503), in the papal bull "Inter Caetera Divinae" issued in 1493, divided the world into two parts, each left to Spain or Portugal. The territory located west of Cape Verde and the Azores, stretching from the North Pole to the South Pole, belonged to Spain, while the area to the east belonged to Portugal. This demarcation line meant Brazil to the east, including the Indonesian archipelago, belonged to Portugal. The papal bull was later affirmed by the Tordesillas Agreement, signed on June 7, 1494, which gave Spain and Portugal privileges to manage the oceans, continents, or islands they discovered through exploration. In addition, the two documents gave Spain and Portugal the right to Christianize the peoples there in the name of His Holiness, as well as to find gold, spices or other valuables.[121]

A church historian, Th. Muller Kruger, noted of the odyssey:

> It's undeniable that it was their desire to Christianize the discovered and conquered areas. It was not in vain that on the sails of their ships the sign of the cross was sewn. They wanted to plant the cross among the unbelievers.

> The Portuguese had entered India with a sword in their right hand and a cross in their left. However, when they found too much gold, the cross was dropped so that their hands could fill their pockets.[122]

Arnold Toynbee described that the discovery of sea routes by da Gama and Columbus was the beginning of the process of conquering the Muslim world, which lasted until the 20th century:

> Indeed, before the end of the sixteenth century, the West, thanks to its conquest of the ocean, had succeeded in throwing a lasso round Islam's neck; but it was not until the nineteenth century that the west ventured to pull the rope tight.[123]

Furthermore, Toynbee argued that the mission of dominating and Christianizing the Muslim world was inherently a conquest by Spain and Portugal, with the blessing of Pope Alexander VI. The efforts of the two countries failed after their power in India was seized by the Dutch in 1601. Likewise, in the Indonesian archipelago, all Portuguese colonies (except Portuguese Timor, which had little economic importance) were taken by the Dutch. Furthermore, Spain and Portugal were forced to withdraw from Japan and Abyssinia in the second quarter of the 17th century.

Although he admits that the influence of Spain and Portugal was quite large, especially in modern South America, Toynbee considers the Netherlands, England and France to be the three European countries to have succeeded in making their mark in the Muslim world from the 17th century to the 20th century.[124] These three countries launched an offensive against India, the Indonesian archipelago, and Africa. The West in general has succeeded in

---

121. O Hashem, Menaklukkan Dunia Islam (Surabaya: Penerbit JAPI, 1968), 11.

122. Th Muller Kruger, Sedjarah Geredja di Indonesia (Jakarta: Badan Penerbit Kristen, 1959), pp. 18–19.

123. Arnold Toynbee, Civilization on Trial, 248.

124. Ibid., 96.

developing its influence on three major civilizations, namely the Orthodox Christian civilization that spread to Russia, the Hindu civilization in South Asia, and the Far East civilizations represented by China and Japan.[125] On the other hand, as the West was starting its offensive in the Muslim world of Asia and Africa, the Ottomans were eyeing Europe (as well as Iraq and Syria in the south), who could only take a defensive stance until the Empire eventually collapsed in Vienna in 1683.

REFORM AND THE RISE OF MODERN CAPITALISM

At the beginning of the 20th century there was a major discourse among economic and social experts about the role of the reform movement, especially Calvinism, in the rise of capitalism. In 1906, Max Weber, a German sociologist, published *The Protestant Ethic and the Spirit of Capitalism*, in which he argues that "the spirit of capitalism" (*der guise des capitalismus*) is a "by-product of the religious ethic of Calvinism."[126]

Weber's thesis certainly spurred criticism and comments across disciplines, especially because Weber applied a sociological view to an economic problem. Weber's views also invited Catholics and Protestants to comment; primarily, his opponents argued that capitalism had grown and developed long before ethical Calvinism was introduced along with the birth and development of Protestantism in the 16th century. Other critics emphasize that Calvinism is considered less progressive than other schools of thought in voicing its views on economic behavior.[127]

However, in 1926, the economist and economic historian R.H. Tawney supported Weber's thesis in *Religion and the Rise of Capitalism*:

> The social history of the sixteenth century which has found acceptance in certain quarters has represented the Reformation as the triumph of commercial spirit over the traditional social ethics of Christendom.[128]

Tawney also argues that Weber's thesis, which only reveals one

---

125. *Ibid.*, 166.

126. Robert W. Green, *Problems in European Civilization: Protestantism and Capitalism* (Boston: DC Heath and Company, 1959), viii.

127. *Ibid.*, x.

128. R.H. Tawney, *Religion and the Rise of Capitalism* (New York: Harcourt, Brace, and Company, 1926), pp. 79–80.

side of the role of Calvinism in the rise of capitalism, is not enough.

Before the emergence of the Renaissance and Reformation, there had been an enabling environment for Calvinism and capitalism due to the advancements of European science and civilization following interactions with the Muslim world during the Crusades and in centers of Islamic civilization such as Baghdad, Cairo, and Al-Andalus. The complete Christianization of Europe in the 11th Century, the discovery of sea routes, the invention of printing machines, etc. also supported the rise of capitalism. Meanwhile, the Renaissance and Reformation were spurred by the rise of humanism, which gave birth to a critical attitude towards the medieval mentality of disrespect for individuals.

The final link in the chain of capitalism is colonialism, which occurred after the Renaissance and Reformation, and was an attempt to expand the reach of cheap natural and local resources. For the case of Indonesia, this is clear in how Magellan came to look for spices in Moluccas, followed by the arrival of Cornelis de Houtman in the bay of Banten in 1596, as well as the formation of the VOC until its dissolution, and then the handover of the Indonesian archipelago to the Dutch colonial government. The series of processes toward this end can be summarized as Renaissance, Reformation, colonization, and finally, the rise of capitalism. Furthermore, Tawney reveals that the link between Calvinism and the rise of capitalism is not only evident in the 16th and 17th centuries, but long after, and includes political, social and economic perspectives.[129] Having said that, Weber's thesis and its critics both offer important analysis and justifications.

THE RISE OF THE WEST AND ITS INVASION OF THE MUSLIM WORLD

Arnold Toynbee mentions several major stages of European history that successively supported the rise of the West and its invasion of the Muslim World.

> *First*, the Christianization of Europe, which is considered to have been completed in the 11th century.
> *Second*, the Renaissance and Reformation from the 14th to 16th century.

---

129. Robert W. Green, *Problems in European Civilization*, ix.

Third, the discovery of sea routes, and the revival of industries that
require raw materials and markets in the 16th and 17th centuries.[130]

In fact, the revival of the West from the Dark Ages and the Middle Ages did not start in southern, western or eastern Europe, the provinces that were once advanced as well as former territories of the Roman Empire. Instead, it began in the north of the Alps, which were backwards provinces. This region developed its own version of Christianity and agrarian culture, followed by the rise of western Europe, which was more stable due to the collapse of the Roman Empire in the fifth century.[131]

Karen Armstrong state that the post-Renaissance and Reformation rise of the West in the 16th century was an event unmatched in history, because it was supported by changes in attitudes such as critical humanism, and the development of an agrarian culture fueled by the development of science, technology and industry, as well as reforms in social, economic, educational, religious, spiritual, political and intellectual structures.[132] Armstrong compares this phenomenal rise of the West with the rise of Islam in the 7th and 8th centuries, although Islam did not hegemonize the world and world civilization at that time.

Meanwhile, Toynbee argues that in fact, the same effort had been initiated by the Ottoman Turks in the 15th to 17th centuries, but that effort was hampered along the eastern European borders due to failure to overthrow Hungary and Vienna. Ottoman energy was depleted by "local border warfare."[133]

Improvements in science and technology gave the West an authentic ability to control a wider area and environment than before. New discoveries in the fields of navigation, agriculture, medicine and industry, which cumulatively drive progress, influenced each other so that the processes of change and progress were inevitable. In the Middle Ages, European society thought that the world could only be governed by eternal laws, but with technological advances and demands for trade developments—supported by a greater investment to seek and control natural resources and markets—Western society entered the industrial revolution era in

---

130. Arnold Toynbee, *Civilization on Trial*, 138.
131. Karen Armstrong, *Islam: A Short History*, 166.
132. *Ibid.*, 166.
133. Arnold Toynbee, *Civilization on Trial*, 166.

the 19th century. The West, in various ways, began to expand its commercial networks in order to source raw materials for export as industrial products. This began the colonization of Muslim countries in Asia and Africa, which at that time were still at the level of an agricultural country. Although the European invasion of the Muslim world was not carried out everywhere in the same manner or amount of time, Europe's growing modernization and industrialization processes in the three hundred years post-Renaissance and Reformation made it still effective.

The 19th century saw further expansion for the colonies of the United Kingdom, France, and the Netherlands. In 1838, the British began to occupy Aden and a number of small islands stretching from Muscat to Bahrain. The French occupied Algeria in 1830, Tunisia in 1881, Lebanon in 1860 and Morocco in 1817. The British occupied Egypt in 1882, and Iraq and Palestine in 1817, while Syria was occupied by France in 1917.

German historian Veit Valentin stated that white supremacy was complete before World War II, as the United Kingdom controlled fifty colonies, France had twenty two colonies, the Netherlands had four colonies, Spain had four colonies, Russia had four colonies, the United States of America had five colonies, Italy had four colonies, Denmark had five colonies, and Germany had eight colonies.[134] Although colonization was originally intended to achieve economic goals, it is recognized that the destruction of Islam ultimately became the foremost goal. Regarding that, the well-known evangelist Samuel M. Zwemer stated that:

> All the savage lands in the world are going to be brought under subjection to the Christian Government of Europe. The sooner the seizure is consummated, the better for the savages.[135]

Zwemer also quotes Scottish evangelist David Livingstone about the European invasion of Muslim countries in Asia and Africa, that:

> The end of the geographical feat is the beginning of the missionary enterprise.[136]

---

134. Veit Valentin, *Kolonialgeschichte der Neuzeit: Ein Abriss* (Tubingen, 1915), pp 224–226.

135. Samuel M. Zwemer, *Arabia: the Cradle of Islam* (Eidenberg and London: F.H. Revell, 1900), 233.

136. *Ibid.*, 29.

COLONIALISM IN THE INDONESIAN ARCHIPELAGO

Colonialism in the Indonesian archipelago began in 1511 with the arrival of the Portuguese in Malacca, a city known as the center of the spice trade in the Indonesian archipelago. After that, the Portuguese also tried to seize the spice islands, Moluccas. At their arrival, the Portuguese were welcomed by Moluccas natives. This can be seen from the spread of Christianity there and also the presence of *keroncong* music. However, this peace would not last, as the Portuguese sought a monopoly in the spice trade.

The arrival of the Portuguese at the Moluccas was followed by the arrival of the Spanish in 1521, who bought spices from the kingdoms of Tidore, Bacan and Jailolo. The success of the Portuguese and Spanish in obtaining spices prompted the British to explore the oceans westward to Moluccas in 1579. The Dutch followed in the footsteps of the Portuguese, Spanish and British by conducting their own exploration into the Indonesian archipelago when their trade relationship with Portugal broke, so they could no longer get spices in Lisbon. Led by Cornelis de Houtman, they landed in Banten in 1596. At that time, Banten served as one of the trading centers in the Indonesian archipelago. The arrival of the Dutch there was the starting point for their colonization of the Indonesian archipelago which lasted three hundred and fifty years.

In the early history of Portuguese and Dutch colonialism in the Indonesian archipelago, two great reactions from Javanese Muslim kings were recorded. The first was an attack launched by Raden Patah of Demak on Malacca in 1513 led by Adipati Unus, which was not successful. The second attack was by Sultan Agung of Mataram Kingdom, who sent 59 ships with 900 warriors from Tegal to attack Dutch Batavia in 1628 and 1629, which also failed due to Dutch naval power. The Dutch gradually solidified their position as major economic and political powers in Java and the Indonesian archipelago. To manage and strengthen control and trade, especially after the collapse of the Mataram Kingdom, the Dutch formed the Dutch East India Company (Vereenigde Oost-Indische Compagnie-VOC). Not only did this Dutch trading company become a major trading force in the Indonesian archipelago, but had been so in many parts of Asia since the 1600's. It was only in the 18th century that the Dutch, through the VOC, began to intervene in the political affairs of Javanese natives in order to increase their grip on the local economy.

Vereenigde Oostindische Compagnie (VOC), or the Dutch East India Company, the first trading company established by the Dutch for their business in their East India colonial territory (which later became Indonesia)

However, due to poor management and intense competition, the VOC went bankrupt and collapsed at the end of the 18th century. It was then nationalized by the Dutch central government, as were all its assets in the Indonesian archipelago. When France occupied the Netherlands (1706–1815), these assets were transferred to the British.

There are two prominent names as architects of the Dutch colonial government in Indonesia. The first is Willem Daendels, who served as governor general in 1808–1811, when the East Indies were ruled by France. The second is Thomas Stamford Raffles, who served as governor general in 1811–1816, when Java was under the rule of the British. Daendels reorganized the central and regional colonial governments by dividing Java into districts (or residencies) led by a European civil servant (resident) as a direct subordinate to the governor general of the Dutch East Indies. Daendels was a pioneer in constructing a cross-Java road known as the "Great Post Road," which stretches across the northern coast to part of the southern coast of Java, and is still functioning today.

The peak of Dutch exploitation in the economic field of the

Dutch East Indies took place during the leadership of Governor General Van den Bosch, who implemented the cultivation system (*cultuurstelsel*) between 1830 and 1870. In this system, the native population was forced to plant crops that were in demand by the world market at that time, such as tea, coffee, sugar cane, and tobacco. Tobacco was a commodity that was not known in Java at that time, and was imported from abroad. Those products were then exported overseas. This cultivation system provided the government of the Dutch East Indies with abundant benefits and wealth, but was protested by Edward Douwes Dekker (also known as Setiabudi Danudirja and Multatuli), assistant resident of Lebak, Banten, through his novel, *Max Havelaar*. This was similar to Harriet Beecher Stowe's *Uncle Tom's Cabin* in America. Dekker depicted the exploitation of "forced" though not enslaved laborers in Java.

In 1901, the Dutch central government began to adopt an ethical policy, or politics of remuneration, which was considered as an investment in human resources through education for the natives. However, behind the ethical policy lies its original mission of colonialism, which was characterized by territorial control and Christianization. It was Governor General Alexander William Frederik Idenburg (who served between 1909 and 1916) who was famous for his Christianization policy (*Kerstening politiek*). Idenburg's measures were based on Queen Wilhelmina of the Netherlands' 1901 state address which stated that:

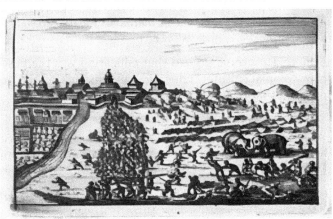

The Mataram Kingdom in Java tried a failed attack on the Dutch / VOC base in Batavia (Jakarta) in 1628.

As a Christian country, the Dutch central government is obliged to better regulate the legal position of the Christian people residing in the Dutch East Indies, strengthen Christian missionaries (zending), [and] continue the policy of Christianization that the Dutch government must fulfill the moral calling of the inhabitants of this colony.[137]

The vehemence of Idenburg's Christianization policy was strengthened by the "Idenburg oath," which says that he "will not leave the Dutch East Indies until this whole country is turned into a Christian country."[138] Colonization and Christianization must go hand in hand; that is the colonial politics of the Dutch East Indies which Idenburg wanted to implement consistently.

This Christianization policy was met with opposition from the Dutch colonial government's advisor for Islamic affairs, Christiaan Snouck Hurgronje (1857–1936). Hurgronje, who once pretended to be a newly converted Muslim and entered Mecca by the name of Abdul Ghafaar in 1885, thought the policy was counterproductive and could potentially trigger resistance from the Muslim population in the Dutch East Indies. Instead, Hurgronje suggested that the colonial government should employ a "cultural association" approach. If Muslims could accept and become close to Dutch or Western culture, they would unconsciously and gradually leave Islam, he suggested. Related to that, Hurgronje said:

Solving the Islamic problem on the strengthening of the relationship between indigenous peoples and Western civilization. The only true problem of Islam lay in the association of Muslims in the Dutch colony to the Netherlands. If this works, the problem of Islam will be over.[139]

Furthermore, Hurgronje argued that education was the best way to instill a colonial culture: "Education and instruction can detach Muslims from Islam."[140]

---

137. *Handelingen der Staten* (*Speech of the Throne, September 18, 1901*), as cited in Deliar Noer, *The Modernist Muslim Movement in Indonesia* (Singapore: Oxford University Press, 1973). See also, F.L. Rutgers, *Idenburg en de Sarekat Islam in 1913* (Utrecht: Drukkerij Ubertas, 1953), 2.

138. Alwi Shihab, *Membendung Arus: respons Gerakan Muhammadiyah terhadap Penetrasi Misi Kristen di Indonesia* (Bandung: Mizan, 1997), pp. 149–150.

139. C. Snouck Hurgronje, *Politique Mussulmane de la Hollande* (Bonn: Kurt Schroeder Verlag, 1911), 291.

140. *Ibid.*, 288.

Colonialism Era

William Alexander Frederick Idenberg, the Dutch Governor General for East India (1909-1916), who inforced the implementation of the Royal Dutch government's Christianization policy for their colonial territory.

PERCEPTIONS OF CHRISTIANITY IN DUTCH EAST INDIES

The colonization by the Western world of the Muslim world had certain differences in each country. Cornelis de Houtman's first visit to the East Indies in 1596 was motivated by trade interests. Although de Houtman, as an individual product of Dark Ages and post-Crusades, was fully aware of the European hatred of Islam, he has no interest in disturbing the lives of Muslims. The Dutch were even worried that any conflicts with Muslims in the East Indies would disrupt and harm their trade.

The relationship between Dutch colonialists and Muslim populations in the Dutch East Indies is of particular interest to Karel Steenbrink, a Dutch theologian of the Radboud University of Nijmegen.[141] Steenbrink has studied Dutch perception, both in the

141. Karel Steenbrink, *Kawan dalam Pertikaian: Kaum Kolonial Belanda dan Islam Indonesia (1596-1942)* (Bandung: Mizan, 1995), pp. 21–22.

VOC era and during the era of the Dutch East Indies government's Christianization policy, and found four patterns:

The first pattern, *curiosity and admiration*

On the one hand, Dutch perception was characterized by a combination of selective attention, curiosity and admiration. However, on the other hand, there appeared to be a significant and emphatic distance from Dutch Christians towards Muslims. Dutch merchants and travelers expressed appreciation of Muslims, especially for their behavior, both with regard to ritual and morality. However, thanks to the prior knowledge which prevailed in their country, they also denounced the contents and doctrine of Islam and condemned it as a heretical religion.

The second pattern, *prejudice about dogma*

This perspective was characterized by an acute prejudice about dogma, so that the Dutch tended to regard Muslims as unwelcome apostates. The earliest Dutch travelers and explorers sailed to the East Indies carrying their prior knowledge and perception about Islam. Dutch theologians believed that Islam was ungodly, synonymous with superstitions and heresy. These theological descriptions were often incompatible with the actual situation of Muslims because they were based only on the skewed perception of Christianity towards others. This pattern was inherited from the medieval period, which combined the aims of the Crusaders with Lutheran politics, which tended to reject Islam due to Ottoman expansion. Meanwhile, Islam was seen as dynamite, a grave danger to the security of the Dutch in the East Indies.

The third pattern, *negative attitude*

This pattern is characterized by hopelessness or lack of positive evaluation on the Dutch part toward Muslims. Even then, when the VOC was less powerful, they had no choice but to live and trade with Muslims who were 'untrustworthy' and fanatical 'in natural enmity.'

The fourth pattern, *superiority of the ruler.*

When the colonial power was so established that worry about revolt had subsided, all that was left was an attitude of superiority as the ruler. The Dutch increasingly saw themselves as teachers and even watchdogs for uneducated Muslims. The colonial government intensified its Christian missionary activities, and at the same time, handed over native education envoys to missionaries as part of the implementation of Idenburg's Christianization policy.

It is no coincidence that the rapid advancement of missionary activities in the Dutch East Indies went together with the spread of the colonial education system.

BETWEEN TOYNBEE AND STEENBRINK

Arnold Toynbee's historical observations on the history of global colonialism, using the lasso rope as an allusion, provide an illustration that is very consistent with Steenbrink's observations about the perception of the relationship between Dutch colonialists and the colonized Muslims of the Dutch East Indies.[142]

The history of colonialism of the Indonesian archipelago records the arrival of the Portuguese in Malacca and Moluccas, as well as the arrival of the Dutch in Banten, both of which occurred in the 16th century. Since the failure of Adipati Unus of Demak in attacking the Portuguese in Malacca in 1513, and the failure of Sultan Agung of Mataram Kingdom to attack Batavia by land and sea in 1628 and 1629, the political position of Muslims in the Indonesian archipelago has been, in Toynbee's words, *"with their back to the wall,"* or, in other words, precarious.[143] That image certainly shows that the Dutch had passed Steenbrink's first pattern successfully.

Steenbrink's second and third pattern occurred at the end of the VOC period and the beginning of the Dutch East Indies government, when the Dutch colonial government, since the time of Daendels' to Van Den Bosch's era, acted with increasing rigor in managing and controlling its colony. The threat of the Dutch colonial government reached its peak with the outbreak of physical resistance, including the rebellion of Prince Diponegoro in the Java War (1825–1830) and the Padri War in West Sumatra (1813–1838), which claimed many victims on both sides.

Steenbrink's fourth pattern, or, in Toynbee's words, tightening the lasso rope, took place at the beginning of the 20th century, starting with the Queen of the Netherlands' state speech that blessed the implementation of Christianization politics as the final goal of a long

---

142. Arnold Toynbee, *Civilization on Trial*, 248.
143. *Ibid.*, 166.

series of conquests in the Muslim World by the Western World that began in the 16th century. The Dutch East Indies, later known as Indonesia, became a complete model of the stages of the Western World's journey in conquering the Muslim World, which is the link between economic interests and evangelism. Thus, the whole process of evangelism can be perceived as an ongoing aspect of colonialism.

The complete model of conquest, economic exploitation and evangelism, apart from the long process of colonialism for four centuries, was a result of the Islamization process of the Dutch East Indies. For the most part, this was evenly distributed, or can be considered nearly finished, when the Portuguese and Dutch set foot on the Indonesian archipelago, especially at the beginning of the 20th century when Islamic sultanates were increasingly divided. That is why Hurgronje thought that it would be too risky if the Dutch colonial government 'teased' Muslims with a vulgar Christianization project, for example, by limiting the pilgrimage and intensifying evangelism, as that would inevitably lead to horizontal resistance from Muslims. Instead, Hurgronje suggested a cultural association approach, especially through education.

10

Orientalism

INACCURACY OF STUDIES

The Church has long realized that missionary activity will only be successful if it is supported by all aspects and branches of science. In accordance with the ability to think critically and the development of science in Europe, especially after the Renaissance and Reformation, missionary measures of the Western-Christian World became increasingly beneficial.

The development of scholarship regarding the East, Orientalism—chiefly in Islamic studies, especially after European colonization gripped Africa and Asia tightly in the 19th century—turned out to be very helpful in facilitating missionary activities. Orientalism includes the study of all things and intricacies related to Islam, such as its history, biographies of Muhammad, various traditions and customs of Islamic society, and, as its main focus, the study of the Qur'an and Muhammad as the messenger of God, which is the backbone of Islamic faith. If these two main sources are destroyed, then Islam will follow, as emphasized by the Indonesian theologian, Reverend Andreas Yewangoe.[144]

However, Orientalism, as a science, is still an impartial science. Science itself is only concerned with facts and falsehoods, depending on users to understand, process, interpret and utilize those facts in accordance with their own objectives. Likewise, regarding Orientalism, Western World insights into Islam are slowly expanding; thanks to scholarship, the Western World has learned to value Muslims and Islam even more. Many studies on the biography of Muhammad, the Qur'an, and prophetic traditions prove that the Western-Christian World was prejudiced toward Islam and did not understand it as a whole. Perceptions of Islam were rather motivated and biased by historical grudges.

---

144. A.A. Yewangoe, *Agama dan Kerukunan*. See Chapter 1.

Slowly, there emerged European figures who appreciated Islam, such as Thomas Carlyle, Voltaire, and Johan Wolfgang von Goethe, who later invited the European community to bury their parochial stance on Islam. Moreover, the Western World has "empirically" recognized and benefited from their interactions with Islamic civilization through various encounters, ranging from cultural interactions with Muslims in Andalusia, Baghdad and Cairo, to the Crusades, as well as Western colonialism in Africa and Asia. In addition, Toynbee has commented positively on the potential of Islam as a force in preventing future racial prejudices, proposing that "if the present situation of mankind were to precipitate a 'race war,' Islam might be moved to play her historical role once again."[145] *The Cambridge Advanced Learner's Dictionary & Thesaurus* defines Orientalism as:

> Western ideas about the Middle East and about East and Southeast Asia, especially ideas that are too simple or not accurate about these societies being mysterious, never changing, or not able to develop in a modern way without Western help.

Although the above-mentioned definition does not specifically mention the hidden agenda and intentions of Orientalism for the Muslim World, some scholars recognize the dishonesty and inaccuracy of the study. This is because Orientalism was marred by dishonesty in its aims and objectives from the beginning.

The above-mentioned definition describes some of the main views of Orientalism: (1) the division of the world into the Western World and the Eastern World, (2) a Western view of the Eastern, (3) that the Eastern World cannot progress without the help of the West, and (4) scholarly inaccuracy. These four points are the essence of Edward Said's criticism and conclusions in his book, *Orientalism*, in which he presents his observations on Orientalism in general, including the approach of the so-called Orientalists.

Orientalism is considered to have been inherent in European civilization and culture. In accordance with the early stages of colonialism, the British and French were the first to develop Orientalism studies, even as early as the 17th century. Since its early development, basic assumptions of Orientalism are based on the ontological and epistemological point of view regarding the Orient

---

145. Arnold Toynbee, *Civilization on Trial*, 187,

and the Occident, i.e., East and West, Asia and Europe. Orientalist academics, including poets, novelists, philosophers, historians, politicians, and economists, all accept some basic premises about the Orient and the Occident, and thus share a similarity of starting points on the character, behavior, traditions, social, economic and political descriptions of the Orient, which distinguishes it from the Occident. At the same time, the Orient, as it is made up of colonies, is itself part of the Occident, bringing the advantages of natural resources to the latter.

Although the British and French have pioneered Orientalism since the late 17th century, Edward Said argues that it was the 18th century that witnessed the consolidation of Orientalism studies, founded by corporate institutions and buttressed by the authority of a central colonial government aimed at dominating, structuring and controlling the Orient. Without the support of the central colonial government, it was impossible for Orientalist policies and views in the social, economic, academic, ideological and even military fields to have any legitimacy. That is why, historically and culturally, there was a fundamental difference between British-French Orientalism and American Orientalism in the post-World War II period, in which the former virtually lost their colonies and the latter took over the role of the former.[146]

THREE DIMENSIONS OF ORIENTALISM

Edward Said describes Orientalism as, inherently, a form of European-centric prejudice against the Arabs and the Muslim World, an instrument of Western supremacy against the East, which has three dimensions.

First, the academic tradition.

In this case, Orientalism is a very diverse discipline, with topics ranging from literature, history, philosophy, economics, and politics, to the military. However, academically, Orientalism is precisely based on dishonesty and discriminatory attitudes on the Western part toward non-European societies for the sake of realizing imperialism. So, it is fitting that *The Cambridge Advanced Learner's Dic-*

---

146. Edward W Said, *Orientalism* (New York: Vintage Books, 1979), pp. 2–5.

tionary & Thesaurus mentions inaccuracy as a defining component of Orientalism. In fact, there were a number of substantively and academically inappropriate works labeled as Orientalism, especially by colonial rulers.[147]

Second, ontology and epistemology.

Related to this, Said argues that:

> "Orientalism is a style of thought based upon an ontological and epistemological distinction made between the Orient and, most of the time, the Occident."[148]

Thus, it is not surprising that the earliest stage in the development of Orientalism methodology was to determine "a point of departure, a beginning principle." And "the European idea of the Orient," what would become the guiding principle of Orientalism, was that the East was not able to develop in the modern day without Western help.[149]

Third, political domination.

> This is grounded in Said's emphasis that Orientalism found its format and strength in the 18th century due to the West's success in further strengthening its grip on its colonies in the East. "Orientalism is a Western style of dominating, restructuring and having authority over the Orient," Said further argues.[150]

Said's analysis and criticism of the development of Orientalism, along with its three dimensions, are historically parallel with the study of the history of colonialism that Toynbee and Steenbrink have extensively described.

PRE-ORIENTALISM

Although Orientalism officially began in the late 17th century and was increasingly structured and supported by the colonial government in the 18th century, even long before that, the Western World and the Church published many works with certain biased perspectives about Islam.

---

147. *Ibid.*, pp. 2–4.
148. *Ibid.*, 2.
149. *Ibid.*, 3.
150. O Hashem, *Menaklukkan Dunia Islam*, pp. 9–49..

O Hashem wrote a long series of descriptions of Western views on various sides of Islam, which include portrayals of the Qur'an and Muhammad as well as the prophetic traditions as bad and brutal. He describes the ugly and brutal picture of Islam during the European Dark Ages, prior to the Crusades, and continuing into the 17ᵗʰ and 18ᵗʰ centuries.

In the era of Islamic sovereignty in Andalusia, Joannis Damacendi (700–749) stated in his book, *the Disputatio Saraceni at Christian* (*The Dispute between the Saracens and Christians*), that Islam is an idolatrous religion. This Greek writer likens Muhammad to a false prophet named Mamet. Later, a Byzantine writer, Theophanes the Confessor (d. 871) slandered Muhammad by claiming that he was a contemporary of Mamet, and stated that "That false prophet of the Saracens was not only poor, but also suffered from epilepsy." Nicotas Bymantius (880), also from Byzantium, mentioned in his *Refutatio Mohammedis* (*Refutation of Muhammad*) that Muhammad was a false prophet, a liar, as well as the child of the devil, in addition to calling the Koran, the book: Muhammad's fairy tales full of lies.

Gilbert de Nogent (d. 1124) said that "the corpse of the Prophet Muhammad, who was sick with epilepsy, was eaten by pigs, that is why it is forbidden for Muslims to eat pork." In other writings it is stated that Muhammad died from drunkenness, which is why Muslims are prohibited from drinking alcohol. In fact, the Father of the Reformation, Martin Luther (1483–1546) in his *Verlegung Alcorans Bruder Ricaldi,* mentions that Muhammad is a robber chieftain, unscrupulous, cowardly, unsuccessful, epileptic, led by Satan and with evil qualities.[151]

In the midst of the Second Crusades (1150), Pierre Maurice, head of the Cluny Monastery, attacked Islam based on his limited knowledge of the Qur'an. Besides calling Islam an idolatrous and cannibalistic religion, Pierre instructed Robert of Retines and Hermann of Dalmatia to translate the Qur'an into Latin. Until the seventeenth century, this Latin translation was the only source used in Europe, and it served to slander Islam. This Latin translation was later translated again into Italian, Dutch and German by Schweigger (1616), into French by Du Ryer (1647), and into Russian (1776). In 1698, Marracio Ludovico translated the Qur'an straight

---

151. *Ibid.*, pp. 33–34.

from Arabic.[152] Marracio, a Franciscan priest, studied the Arabic language specifically for four years in order to be able to translate the Qur'an directly from Arabic. This Maraccio translation sharpens the attack against Islam, because after the translation, Onuphrius Mico published his book *Lex Angelica contra Alcoranum* (*the Bible contra the Qur'an*), which contains sixty-six arguments against the Qur'an, Muhammad and Islam.[153]

On the other hand, Muhammad Hussein Heikal, an Egyptian intellectual, in his *The Life of Muhammad,* wrote about the behavior of Orientalists, beginning with a quote from the *Dictionaire Larousse:*

> "'Muhammad remained in his moral corruption and debauchery a camel thief, a cardinal who failed to reach the throne of the papacy and win it for himself. He therefore invented a new religion with which to avenge himself against his colleagues. Many fanciful and immoral tales dominated his mind and conduct.' (...)

Later on, Heikal writes:

> Hate and prejudice were tenacious of life. From the time of Rudolph de Ludheim (620) until the present, Nicholas de Cuse, Vives, Maracci, Hottinger, Bibliander, Prideaux, etc. present Mohamet as an impostor, Islam as the cluster of all the heresies and the work of the devil, the Mussulmans as brutes, and the Koran as a tissue of absurdities. They declined to treat such a ridiculous subject seriously. However, Pierre le Venerable, author of the first Occidental treatise against Islam, made a Latin translation of the Koran in the twelfth century. Innocent III once called Mahomet the Antichrist, while in the Middle Ages he was nearly always merely looked upon as a heretic. Raymond Lull in the fourteenth century, Guillaume Postel in the sixteenth, Roland and Gagnier in the eighteenth, the Abbe de Broglie and Renan in the nineteenth give rather varied opinions. Voltaire, afterwards, amended in several places the hasty judgment expressed in his famous tragedy. Montesquieu, like Pascal and Malebranche, committed serious blunders on the religion, but his views of the manners and customs of the Mussulmans are well-considered and often reasonable. Le Comte de Boulainvilliers, Scholl, Caussin de Perceval, Dozy, Sprenger, Barthelemy, Saint-Hilaire de Castries, Carlyle, etc., are generally favorable to Islam and its Prophet and sometimes vindicate him.[154]

---

152. Marracio Ludovico, *Alcorani Textus Universus* (Padua: Typographia Seminarii, 1698).

153. O Hashem, *Menaklukkan Dunia Islam*, pp. 35–36.

154. Muhammad Hussein Heikal, *Sejarah Hidup Muhammad* (Jakarta: Pustaka Jaya, 1992), pp. ii–liii.

THE TURNING POINT

It was George Sale (1697–1736) who, in November 1734, translated the Qur'an into English. From then on, several Western scholars began to doubt the criticism of Islam; chiefly among them are Voltaire (1694–1778), Goethe (1749–1832), and Gibbon (1737–1794). Little by little objections to Muhammad and Islam were criticized by some of these Western scholars. Voltaire, in his conversation with Prince Zinzendorf about Martin Luther and John Calvin, commented out of context by saying that "these two men (i.e. Martin Luther and John Calvin) didn't even deserve to be Muhammad's shoemakers." Goethe argued that, when studying Islam, he did not find any rationale to say that Muhammad was a fraud and a liar. In fact, in his *Weststlicher, Divan* Goethe states that "*If Islam means submitting to God, aren't we all alive and going to die in Islam?*".

Meanwhile, Edward Gibbon stated that Muhammad "*possesses courage of both thought and action; bears the stamp of an original and superior genius.*" Apart from Goethe and Gibbon, there are a number of other scholars and leaders who oppose hatred of the Qur'an, Muhammad, and Islam, such as George Bernard Shaw, Napoleon Bonaparte, Thomas Carlyle, Bosworth Smith, and others.[155]

THE ERROR OF THE ORIENTALISM APPROACH

Having discussed Said's view on the Orientalist approach—i.e academic tradition, ontology and epistemology and the dimensions of political domination as Orientalism's points of departure—it is now possible to imagine the direction of orientalist study and how it leads to conclusions supported by each European colonial government. Indonesian scholar Syamsuddin Arif, in his *Orientalist dan Diabolisme Pemikiran* (*Orientalist and Thought Diabolism*), criticized a number of Orientalists' errors.

Criticism of methodology and epistemology

According to Arif, the fragility of Orientalism methodology is not surprising, since its very point of departure was of malintent – to overthrow Islam. This greatly undermined the development of the study's methodology, which was colored by an attitude of willful ignorance, in other words, ignoring data or facts that do not

---

155. O Hashem, *Menaklukkan Dunia Islam*, pp. 36–38.

support its assumptions in order to justify its viewpoint. Consequently, the conclusions are invalid, riddled with hasty generalizations and conjectures.

Furthermore, Arif argues that the methodological confusion shows paradox and ambivalence. On the one hand, Orientalists doubt or even deny the truth of Islamic sources. On the other hand, they use Islamic sources as references (which they unconsciously admit to be true). This paradoxical attitude is the inevitable consequence and methodological dilemma of both believing and not believing. Furthermore, Arif quoted Harald Motzki's view, who stated that:

> On the one hand, it is not possible to write a historical biography of the Prophet without being accused of using the sources uncritically, while, on the other hand, when using such sources critically, it is simply not possible to write such a biography.

In general, from the very beginning, the epistemologies of the Orientalist can be said to be skeptical. They start with doubt and end with doubt too, or, in other words, *doubting the truth and justifying doubt.* As Herbert Berg argues, *"the result of their work is dictated by their presuppositions,"*[156] while *"the data are made to fit the theory."* [157]

Orientalists' misperception about Islam

Syamsuddin Arif considered that the Qur'an, as the Holy Book and the main reference for Muslims and Islam, was the main target of the Orientalists. If Muslim faith in the Qur'an could be broken, then the religion and Muslims would also be broken, even if the Orientalists failed to destroy the history of Muhammad and prophetic traditions. Moreover, Muslims believe that the

---

156. Herbert Berg, *The Development of Exegesis in Early Islam* (Surrey: Curzon Press, 2000), 3.

157. Syamsuddin Arif, *Orientalis dan Diabolisme Pemikiran* (Jakarta: Gema Insani Press, 2008), pp. 40–44. In this regard, Arif pointed out in a footnote which states, "recently an orientalist admirer wrote on the Liberal Islam Network website (Jaringan Islam Liberal or JIL—an Indonesian think-tank organization) that 'what is interesting from this orientalist study is not the conclusion, but how do we arrive at that conclusion. The JIL follower did not understand that the orientalist's conclusion was determined by his methodology. When the methodology is wrong, the conclusion is wrong".

Johan Wolfgang von Goethe (1749-1832) was a great poet, but his writing on West-Oostlicher Divan (Stuttgart 1819), was based on his admiration of the lovely poetry of the Qur'an and his respect for the Prophet Mohammed. People suspected him to be a convert.

Qur'an is a revelation and a miracle from God that was revealed to Muhammad, not only because its contents pertain to all aspects of human life, but also because the Qur'an itself is free from doubt (*la raiba fihi*), so there may be a match (*la ya'tuna bi-mitslihi*) and it is guarded by Allah (*wa inna lahu lahafizun*).

In fact, before Orientalism was developed in the 20th century, the Western World had provided some reckless perspectives on the Qur'an by stating that, among other things, the Qur'an is a fake scripture, plagiarizes the Bible, and contradicts itself. The Orientalists tested the authenticity of the Qur'an as if they wanted to equate it with the authenticity of the Bible, since there are Christian scholars who doubt the Bible's authenticity.

Kurt Aland and Barbara Aland wrote:

> Until the beginning of the fourth century, the text of the New Testament developed freely. The later scribes, for example, allow the parallel passages of the Gospels to differ from one another. They also felt themselves free to make corrections in the text, improving it by their own standard of correctness,

183

whether grammatically, stylistically, or more substantively.[158]

Disappointed by the fact that the narration of the Bible can be altered or changed over time, in 1720 Richard Bentley (1662-1742), the Master of the Trinity College in Cambridge, England, called on Christians to ignore their holy book, the New Testament that was published by Pope Clement in 1592. This exclamation was followed by the publication of the Critical Edition of the New Testament, edited by Brooke Wascott (1825–1903) and Fenton John (1818–1892). Syamsuddin Arif argues that there were three fundamental mistakes the Orientalists made when looking for the weaknesses of the Qur'an:

> *First*, the Qur'an was originally not a writing (*rasm*), but a recitation (*qira'ah*). The process of revelation and delivery, teaching and narration are carried out through oral presentation and memorization, not in writing. Since a long time ago, what is meant by 'reading' the Qur'an is actually recitation from memory (*qara'a 'an zhahri qalbin*). Codification of the Qur'an is merely a supporting function, since the verses of the Qur'an were originally recorded on the surface of tablets, bones, and the wide, flat ends of date palm fronds, etc. all based on the memorization of the memorizer of the Qur'an.

This kind of transmission, with successive *isnads* (*mutawattir*) from generation to generation, is argued to be successful in guaranteeing the integrity and authenticity of the Qur'an, as revealed through Gabriel to Muhammad, then passed on to the companions, until it is finally codified, such as today's Qur'an. This is different from Biblical texts, which consist of manuscript evidence in the form of papyrus, sheets and so on, which become the reference and basis for the Testaments or Gospel. Errors of the Orientalists in evaluating the Qur'an originate from the confusion of text and speech as modes of transmission.

Orientalists such as Arthur Jeffrey, John Wansborough and Gerd Puin, for example, proceeded from an erroneous assumption that the Qur'an is a "written document" or text, not as a rote read or recitation. Because of this, they tried to apply philological methods commonly applied in Bible research, such as historical, source, form and textual criticism. As a result, they regard the Qur'an as a historical

---

158. Kurt Aland and Barbara Aland, *The Text of the New Testament* (Michigan: Grand Rapids, 1995), 69.

product, merely a record of the situation and a reflection of Arab culture in the 7th and 8th centuries. They also argued that the manuscript of the Qur'an found today is incomplete and different from the original (which they themselves do not know for sure).[159]

Second, although in principle it was taught and transmitted orally, the Qur'an was also written in several mediums. Until Muhammad's death, almost all of these early records had the status of being the private properties of the companions of the Prophet, and therefore differed in quality and quantity from one another. Due to personal purposes, many friends wrote additional notes as glosses or commentaries (interpretations) in the margins or in between the verses they write. Only later, when the number of memorizers of the Qur'an shrank because many died on the battlefield, efforts to codify the Qur'an were then carried out at the initiative of Abu Bakr based on first-hand narrations and successive *isnads* since Muhammad. After the death of Abu Bakr (in 634), the manuscript of the Qur'an was kept by Umar ibn Khattab until he died (in 644), then kept by Hafsah, until finally handed over to Uthman ibn Affan. During Uthman's leadership, there was pressure from a number of friends for the establishment of an expert commission to record all existing recitations (*qira'at*) and check and determine the value of validity in order to prevent mistakes and disputes. As a result, the Qur'an was codified into several standard manuscripts, each of which contains consecutive recitations, which are agreed upon as valid narratives from the Prophet.

Thus, historical facts and the codification process are very clear. Orientalists who wish to tweak the Qur'an will usually start by questioning this historical fact while rejecting the results. Instead, they consider that the codification of the Qur'an was only begun in the 9th century. Arthur Jeffrey, for example, recklessly argues, "whether he (i.e. Abu Bakr) *ever made an official recension as the orthodox theory demands is exceedingly doubtful.*"[160] In addition, he claims that "*the text which Uthman canonized was only one out of many rival texts, and we need to investigate what went before the canonical text.*"[161] From his argument, it is clear how Jeffrey did not understand, or perhaps pretended not to know that the history of the Qur'an is not the same as that of the

---

159. Arthur Jeffrey, *Material for the History of the Text of the Qur'an in the Old Codices* (Leiden: E.J. Brill, 1937).

160. *Ibid.*, pp. 6–7.

161. *Ibid.*, x.

Bible; that the Qur'an inherently is by no means merely a manuscript, but that a manuscript was in fact born from the Qur'an.[162]

Third is a misunderstanding of Orientalist scholars regarding the writing (rasm) and recitation (qira'at). As is well known, Arabic writing and characters have developed throughout the ages. At the beginning of Islamic history, the characters used in the codification of the Qur'an were written without the slightest punctuation, while the new vocalization system was introduced later. Even so, this writing style, the so-called Uthmani style, did not cause any problems at all, given that Muslims in that period had learned to memorize the Qur'an directly from the companions of the Prophet, orally, and not through writings. This is what Orientalists like Gerd Puin and Christoph Luxenberg have misunderstood, instead concluding that it is these characters without punctuation that cause variant reading—as is the case for the Bible. They also confuse recitations (qira'at) with readings, since qira'at is "recitation from memory," but not "reading the text" at all. They did not understand that in this case the rule is: writing must follow the recitations narrated from Muhammad (ar-rasmu tabi'un li riwayah), and not the other way around.[163]

MUHAMMADIYAH AND THE RELATIONSHIP BETWEEN ISLAM AND CHRISTIANITY

In the foreword of his book, Karel Steenbrink tells of the reactions of his Dutch colleagues to his book, which 'exposed' the bad practices of the Dutch government and the church during the colonial era in the Dutch East Indies (now Indonesia) (1596-1949), because of the potential to provoke outrage amongst Muslims in Indonesia.[164]

Moreover, the spirit of evangelizing Muslims still lingers in the independence era, as shown by the book *History of the Church with its Summary*-published by the Tomohon Catholic Church Administration in 1949—which states that the Qur'an was composed, and containing falsehoods about Muhammad and Islam. In line with that, the Archdiocese of Semarang, Central Java, published a book

---

162. Syamsuddin Arif, *Orientalis dan Diabolisme Pemikiran*, 12. See also Bukhari, *Al-Jami' al-Sahih*, 3; Abu 'Amr al Dani, *Al-Muqni' fi Rasm Masahif Ahl al-Amsar ma'a Kitab al-Naqt* (Damascus, 1963), pp 124–125.

163. Syamsuddin Arif, *Orientalis dan Diabolisme Pemikiran*, pp. 12–13.

164. Karel Steenbrink, *Kawan dalam Pertikaian,* xv.

of Daily Prayers for Catholics, which contains "Prayers Asking for the Conversion of Muslims" (Sembahyang Nyuwun Mertobatipun Bongso Islam) in pages 195-196.[165] Meanwhile, the Dutch reverend McMuller mentioned in his book, *Rondom het Woord*, that "*Christianity in Indonesia has quadrupled over the twenty years of the independence period, compared to hundreds of years in the colonial period.*"[166] While Steenbrink's colleagues in the Netherlands are concerned about the outrage of Indonesian Muslims, Azyumardi Azra, in the introduction to this book, also mentions the growing outrage among Indonesian Muslims at negative Western-Christian perspectives on the teachings of Islam, Prophet Muhammad and the Qur'an. Thus, the negative perspectives built by the Dutch colonial government and the church not only shocked the Muslims, but also created ambivalent feelings among Indonesian Christians.[167]

However, this ambivalence is something different from the task and intensity of propagating religion. Islam is a missionary religion, but it is not evangelistic in nature, whereas Christianity is a missionary religion that is proactive in carrying out its evangelistic agenda. The Indonesian government has made efforts to enforce a kind of ethical code for religion propagation, although it is not easy to enforce. Christianity has a religious broadcasting machine and infrastructure in the form of human resources and educational institutions, as well as social and health service institutions that have been organized and spread since the colonial period. Meanwhile, Islam, Muhammad and the Qur'an have been portrayed, for centuries, as heretics, a false prophet and false scripture, respectively, and that image cannot simply be erased; in addition, some suggest, the 'Islamic missionary machine' is not evangelistic in nature, is unable to operate properly, lacks quality and is not well coordinated.

The Indonesian government, in the spirit of building the country in line with Pancasila, is trying to contain and reduce friction between Muslims and Christians. However, the ultimate decision must come from Muslims and Christians themselves. As followers of organized religions, both parties must have a 'code of ethics' in propagating the faith.The government also outlines a common

---

165. Sudibyo Markus, *Konsili Vatikan II*, pp 14–15.

166. *Ibid.*, 21.

167. Karel Steenbrink, *Kawan dalam Pertikaian*, xxi.

On August 18, 2016, a group of Muhammadiyah Elementary students in Probolinggo, East Java, were escorted by their teachers to visit the Maria Carmel Mother Church for early tolerance education. Father Hugo O. Carmel welcomed and briefed the students.

code of ethics to not propagate religious doctrines to people who are already religious, even though, again, the choice remains in the hands of each individual.

Finally, efforts to control interreligious relations, marked by the problematic Christianization policy of the Dutch colonial government, found a light when the Second Vatican Council issued a historic decision, Nostra Aetate, a statement on the Church's relationship with non-Christian religions. Through Nostra Aetate, the Church acknowledged for the first time various positive teachings in Islam, as well as the enmity between Christianity and Islam in the past, while inviting both Christians and Muslims to forgive and "promote together for the benefits of all mankind social justice and moral welfare, as well as peace and freedom ."[168]

Pope Paul VI, during his visit to Indonesia in 1970, reinforced the message of the Second Vatican Council by saying:

> Catholicism did not come to Indonesia with a political purpose, Indonesian Christians are not alien among their fellow countrymen.[169]

Pope Paul VI's statement above was certainly valid to put forward in

---

168. "Declaration On The Relation Of The Church To Non-Christian Religions: Nostra Aetate," http://www.vatican.va/archive/hist_councils/ii_vatican_council/documents/vat-ii_decl_19651028_nostra-aetate_en.html.

169. Abdul Mu'ti and Fajar Riza Ul Haq, *Kristen Muhammadiyah: Konvergensi Muslim dan Kristen dalam Pendidikan* (Jakarta: Al-Wasath, 2009), xviii.

the independence period, especially after the Second Vatican Council's decision, although the perspectives and partners that have persisted throughout the history of the Dutch colonial rule over Indonesia cannot possibly be erased from the history of Indonesia.

Fortunately, however, Steenbrink's colleagues' concerns about Muslim outrage did not occur. Indonesian Muslims were able to accept the historical dynamics of national life, including the transition from the colonial period to the independence period. One of these dynamics was the elimination of the phrase "with the obligation to carry out Islamic law for its adherents" from the first point of the Jakarta Charter, which later became Pancasila, the charter and guiding principles of Indonesia at the beginning of the independence period, that is, not doctrinaire. In addition, in his introduction to the book *Christian Muhammadiyah*, Azyumardi Azra reiterates the spread of Islam to Indonesia as "a penetration pacifique, which provides a quite distinctive style for Islam in Indonesia, that it is Islam that is accommodative, tolerant and inclusive."[170]

In fact, Muhammadiyah, the largest modernist Muslim organization in Indonesia—which was founded by Ahmad Dahlan in 1912, during the early years of the Christianization policy in the Dutch East Indies—is an epitome of this distinctive style. Although Alwi Shihab stated that, in its early days, Muhammadiyah had four roles, namely religious reform, social change, political force, as well as a barrier to Christianization, Muhammadiyah never once issued a statement that its stance was to oppose the pace of Christianization in Indonesia. Although Ahmad Dahlan had some discussions with several Dutch pastors, their purpose was not to incite religious upheaval or encourage conversion to Islam, but rather to show that Muslims can talk with Christians, their brothers, to discuss various social issues and relations between religious believers. There was not the slightest aim to conquer one another, for the Qur'an clearly states, in Surah Al-Baqarah verse 256, that "no compulsion is there in religion." As a matter of fact, Muhammadiyah used Surah Al-Ma'un and Ali Imran verses 104 and 110 as its foundations, since these two surah explain the human obliga-

---

170. Alwi Shihab, *Membendung Arus*; On the other hand, if Muhammadiyah was indeed established to hamper the Christianization, it would certainly have used Surah Al-Baqarah verse 120.

tion to help the needy and poor and prevent evil.[171]

Other prominent Muhammadiyah thinkers, Abdul Mu'ti and Riza Ul Haq, argued that Muhammadiyah was never a "rival" Christian mission, but a "competitor."[172] They also emphasized that the research showed that the Muhammadiyah research institute "succeeded in building a culture of religious tolerance and pluralism that paved the way for social cohabitation between Christians and Muslims." [173]

Meanwhile, another Muhammadiyah scholar, Muhadjir Effendy, stated that "the recent development of scientific and intellectual discourse forces us to question the fourth role of Muhammadi-yah, as proposed by Shihab, i.e. its role in hampering the current of Christianization."[174] Mu'ti and Ul Haq's terms of "competitor" and not "rival" are realistic because Muhammadiyah's main pro-grams and activities in the social, education and health fields are very similar to the approach employed by the Christian mission. Thus, this similarity provides Muhammadiyah and Christian orga-nizations with greater opportunities to move further in building humanitarian cooperation, both at home and abroad.

It is clear that the basic attitude of Indonesian Muslims is generally accommodating, cooperative and inclusive, even as they remain in competition with Christian missions in the fields of education, health and social welfare to this day. Thus, it is not an exaggeration to say that this is why Muhammadiyah is the Islamic organization that carries out the most partnerships with Christians, especially in the humanitarian sector. This is evident from the formation of the Communication Forum for Indonesian Public Health Empowerment in the 1970s—spearheaded by a Muhammadiyah medical doctor, Kusnadi, together with the Indonesian Health Service Association (a Catholic organization) and the Indonesian Christian Association for Health Services (a Protestant organization)—and the formation of the Indonesian Humanitarian Forum with Katrina (Catholic), Christian Foundation for Public Health (Protestant), Yayasan Tanggul Bencana PGI (Protestant), Dompet Dhuafa (Islamic), and Pos Keadilan Peduli Umat.

---

171. Abdul Mu'ti and Fajar Riza Ul Haq, *Kristen Muhammadiyah*, pp. xi–xxi.

172. *Ibid*, xi.

173. *Ibid.*, 236.

174. Mudhadjir Effendy, *Masyarakat Equilibrium: meniti perubahan dalam bingkai keseimbangan* (Yogyakarta: Resist and Bentang, 2002), 77.

The Community of Sant'Egidio (Rome) in partnership with Muhammadiyah (Indonesia) and hosted by the Diocese of Cotabato (South Philippines) organized a peace dialogue in support of the establishment of the Bangsamoro Autonomous Regional of the Muslim Mindanao (BARMM), to end the fifty-year regional conflict.

Meanwhile, in the international world, a Muhammadiyah hospital in Jakarta collaborated with Bethesda Hospital-Christian Foundation for Public Health, two Yogyakarta-based Catholic organizations, to dispatch medical personnel to Gaza when Israel bombed the city in December 2008. In addition, Muhammadiyah also collaborated with the Community of Sant'Egidio, a Rome-based Catholic organization, in dealing with the bloody conflict between the Moro Islamic Liberation Front and the Autonomous Region in Muslim Mindanao, in the Philippines. Later, with the *Community of Sant'Egidio*, Muhammadiyah also took care of eight hundred thousand Rohingya refugees at Cox's Bazaar, Bangladesh.

Humanitarian cooperation, chiefly in social services, has played a major role in reducing conflict among Indonesian Christians and Muslims. Now, it is fitting for religious communities in Indonesia, as well as global religious communities, to be more confident in their future, thanks to the Second Vatican Council's Nostra Aetate (1965), the letter of "A Common Word between Us and You" (2008). Furthermore, with the World Humanitarian Summit in Istanbul, May 22-24, 2016, humankind's insights will be more open to the need to respect and uphold dignity and human rights. Indeed, wars and violence continue to occur in various parts of the world for reasons such as politics and natural resources, but at least the bloodshed is no longer as intensely rooted in religious differences.

11

Missionary Adjustment

Father Franciscus Gregorius Josephus van Lith SJ (1863–1926), or simply Father van Lith, was a Dutch Jesuit priest who laid the foundation for a Catholic mission in Java, especially Central Java. He baptized the first Javanese Catholic in Sendangsono, Yogyakarta, founded a teacher's school in Muntilan, Central Java, and fought for the status of education for the indigenous population during the colonial period. He is famous for his ability to harmonize Roman Catholic teachings with Javanese religious tradition (Kejawen), so that it can be accepted by Javanese societies. Thanks to his efforts, Catholicism has become a religion followed by many Javanese and Chinese descendants.

Pope John Paul II, during a speech in Yogyakarta on October 10, 1989, recognized the services of those who had built a foundation of their faith, Father van Lith and two of his students, Albertus Soegijapranata and Igantius Joseph Kasimo.

Van Lith arrived in Semarang, Central Java in 1896. He then studied Javanese culture and customs and was placed in Muntilan in 1897. He settled in Semampir Village, on the Lamat River. On December 14, 1904, van Lith baptized 171 villagers from Kalibawang, Sendangsono, and Yogyakarta. This event is seen as a milestone in the birth of the Church among the Javanese. Today, the location of this baptism is known as the place of pilgrimage in Sendangsono, the Javanese Bethlehem.[175]

For the Church and the Catholic community, van Lith is not only the father of Javanese Catholics, and the pioneer of various public schools and seminaries in Java, but he is synonymous with change. It is easy to imagine what would likely have happened to Catholi-

---

175. http://familycorner-rumahkeluargabahagia.blogspot.com/2017/02/biografi-singkat-rm-van-lith-sj.html.

cism in Java and the Dutch East Indies without him, given that van Lith's policies and measures in Javanizing Catholicism were in fact contrary to the Christian mission at that time and the policies of the Dutch colonial government, which was vigorously implementing its Christianization policy.

The Different Approach

Snouck Hurgronje, Dutch colonial government advisor for Islamic affairs, emphasized that an association of civilizations was needed to enlighten the Javanese people. He was inspired by Thomas Babington Macaulay (1800–1859) who, based on his experience in India, argued that the only appropriate way to advance and civilize Indian society was through education. A version of Macaulay's idea of politics of education by Snouck Hurgronje was described by Indonesian Christian theologian Hardjoko Hardjomardjono O Carm:

> "In that case, the Dutch copied the politics of education created by Macaulay, which attempted to change the Indian under British rule to become 'Indian in blood and color, but English in taste, in opinion, in morals and intellect,' or, in Indonesia's case, 'Indonesian in blood and color, but Dutch in taste, in opinion, in morals and intellect.'"[176]

Hardjomardjono went further by stating that,

> "In reality, the politics of education provides an opportunity for some Indonesian people to pursue knowledge, but, unfortunately, in such a way that they later become worshipers of the colonial culture and civilization."[177] Hardjomardjono also quoted the opinion of a Dutch

---

176. Hardjoko Hardjomardjono, *Penyesuaian Geredja dengan Kepribadian Para Bangsa* (Ende, Flores: Arnoldus, 1962);Stephen Evans, "Macaulay's Minute Revisited: Colonial Language Policy in Nineteenth-century India," *Journal of Multilingual and Multicultural Development* 23(4), September 2002, pp. 260–280.
Original passage:
"Dalam hal itu Belanda menjiplak politik pendidikan yang diciptakan oleh Macaulay, yang mengusahakan perubahan Indian di bawah penjajahan Inggris menjadi 'Indian in blood and colour, but English in tastes, in opinion, in morals and intellect.' Dalam penjiplakan itu, Belanda bermaksud menjadikan kita, 'Indonesian in blood and colour, but Dutch in taste, in opinion, in morals and intellect.'"
177. Hardjoko Hardjomardjono, *Penyesuaian Geredja...*
Original passage:
"Dalam kenyataannya, politik pendidikan itu memberi kesempatan kepada sebagian rakyat Indonesia untuk mengejar pengetahuan, tetapi sayang, sedemikian

Wall relief art of the first ever baptism, for 171 local villagers of Kalibawang in West Yogyakarta on 14 December 1904. The site was officiated as the "Bethlehem of Java" on December 8, 1929, to respect Father Van Lith, who successfully initiated the church's cultural adoption of the Javanese.

historian, whom he called 'Javanicus,' Cornelis Christiaan Berg, that "Macaulay style education enthusiasts are mostly aristocrats who idolize Western culture and civilization, and then underestimate their own people, deeming them old-fashioned, of low quality, the same level as the 'coolies, *jongos* and *babu* (servants),' as demeaned by Javanicus."[178]

In contrast to Hurgronje's Macaulanian approach, Father van Lith instead carried out the Javanization of the Church, opposing the Westernization which was usually carried out by the colonial government and missionaries in general. The Dutch van Lith and his colleagues were completely blind to Eastern things, as were officials of the Society of Jesuits of the Netherlands sent to Indonesia without missionary training. Van Lith's calling at Christ's command prompted him to study for himself what he called 'the secret of the Javanese soul' (*geheim van de Javaansche ziel*), which included Javanese language, culture, morality and customs. Through this learning process, he pioneered in turn what was known as a 'missionary adjustment', something that was initially opposed by the

rupa, hingga mereka kemudian menjadi pemuja-pemuja kebudayaan dan peradaban si penjajah"

178. Cornelis C. Berg, *Djawa*, 8 (1918), 27.

Lord Thomas Babington Macaulay, who pioneered the colonial education policy in India, adopted by the Dutch in Indonesia, in order to make the Indonesian people into "Indonesian blood and color, but Dutch in taste, opinion, morals and intellect."

Church but which was later seen as a strategic and important step. Van Lith's main idea was to enliven Javanization of the Gospel through educational institutions, with young people as the target. Van Lith bravely opposed the political ideas of Macaulanian education, and, consequently, he was disliked by the colonial government, and even by his Jesuit colleagues.

THE DEMANDS OF THE TIMES

In Indonesia (then the Dutch East Indies), the urgent demand for the implementation of missionary adjustments was felt when the Dutch colonial government realized that the colonialism that had lasted for three centuries could no longer be sustained due to movements pressing for the colony to become an independent nation. At that time, the missionaries could no longer hope for support from them. However, the church's policy in implementing missionary adjustments was already well-established. As determined by the Church:

The conformity of evangelists and Catholics with the personalities of non-Christian nations, both in terms of content, and outward appearance of Christianity, was espoused but within certain limits.[179]

According to J. Thauren, the 'personality of nations,' what he called *volktrum in naturlich-kulturellen sinn*, is "all factors that include psychological structure, way of thinking and the entire nation's culture." Pope Pius XII (r. 1939–1958) provides guidelines for the limits of the implementation of missionary adjustments as follows:

> At the meeting point, the Church is dealing with the personality of the nations. At that time superstition and/or falsehood appears, so that the Church is obliged to give up any attempts to conform.[180]

To provide a clearer picture, Thauren explained several terms in connection with missionary adjustments.

1. *Europeism*, an outdated opinion which states that the Church must be guided by Europe wherever it stands.
2. *Syncretism*, which advocates merging religious elements in attempt to unify similar dogmas
3. *Substitution*, namely the replacement of native elements with Christian elements that are similar.
4. *Restoration*, which is to renew and animate infidel regulations that are no longer functioning to their original meaning.

Furthermore, Thauren emphasized that the basis of missionary adjustment is the same as the purpose and essence of the Church, to bridge the supra-nationalism and universality of the Church of Christ. However, in reality, missionary adjustments are still dealing with gray areas in several countries, such as China and Japan, which have distinctive and strong traditions and culture. Missionary adjustments faced obstacles when the Nazis and Adolf Hitler, with their national-socialist ideology, rejected the Church and its supra-nationalism.

Before he reigned as Pope Pius XII, Cardinal Eugenio Pacelli had a lot of experience overcoming vexed relations between the Vatican and several European countries between World War I and World War II. With this background, as papal nuncio, Pacelli had a special task of making concordants, agreements between the Vati-

---

179. Hardjoko Hardjomardjono, *Penyesuaian Geredja...* 9.
180. Ensiklik, "Summi Pontificatus," AAA XXXL, 429.

can and several restive European countries, which aimed to protect Catholics in these countries. As a cardinal, and later as Pope, he was considered quiet and rigid, solving problems silently and avoiding publication. Hence, some people suspected him of being close to the Nazis, despite the fact that he managed to save no less than 860,000 Jews during World War II.

While Pope Pius XII faced the Nazis in World War II, the Queen of the Netherlands' royal speech in 1901 emphasized the moral responsibility of the Dutch colonial government to strengthen Christian missionaries and promote Christianization in the colony.[181] The Dutch central government combined the Christianization policy with its efforts to perpetuate its power in Indonesia— and it was still felt after World War II, when, after the fall of Japan, the Dutch were still very ambitious to re-occupy Indonesia by riding on the backs of the allied force that entered Indonesia.

The strong reaction to the Christianization policy did not come from Muslims, nor Ahmad Dahlan, the founder of Muhammadiyah, but from Ki Hadjar Dewantara, a Javanese syncretic aristocrat and the founder of the Javanese educational organization, Taman Siswa. This figure, who later became the national hero of Indonesia, stated in 1957 that one of the reasons for the establishment of Taman Siswa was that in the colonial period, the authority to manage education was given to the Church.[182]

Compared to the Dutch colonial government, the Church was more able to recognize the colonial government's mistake of adopting Macaulanian politics of education. The Church realized that, in time, the Dutch would have to leave Indonesia, while the Church and its congregations would remain in the country. The Church did not want Christianity to be labeled as a 'religion of the Westerners' (*agama Londo*) when the Dutch rule ended. Pertaining to this, Hardjomardjono commented:

> In addition to the urgency of missionary adjustments based on theological considerations, their firm and consistent implementation today is an era demand that cannot be postponed anymore, namely guidance that applies even more so in Indonesia.[183]

---

181. https://rajvie.wordpress.com/2013/06/03/politik-etis-di-indonesia-pada-masa-kolonial/

182. Sudibyo Markus, *Konsili Vatikan* II, 21.

183. Hardjoko Hardjomardjono, *Penyesuaian Geredja...*, pp. 47–68.

Pope Pius XII (1939-1958) had relations with Nazi Germany during the Second World War. The Pope was suspected to be a pro-Nazi Pope.

Hardjomardjono stated that although the Church had undoubtedly played a role in colonialism, Indonesian hatred towards the West, or the Dutch, must not be attributed to Christianity. Furthermore, Hardjomardjono also quoted Daljono, a representative of the Majelis Syura Muslimin, a Muslim-based Indonesian political party, in a parliamentary session on March 26, 1954:

> The people of Indonesia are the people of Islam, [who] during the colonial period became the target of Christianization. With its teaching systems, cultural systems, societal systems, health systems, the Indonesian people were to be swayed from the religion they profess. Christian teachers are imported from abroad, trained and educated in the country, financed as much as possible. Fathers and *domines* were allowed to enter not for the purposes of Christians, who at that time were still few in number, but to Christianize the Indonesian people with the hidden aim so that the colonial power could last forever.[184]

Original passage:

Di samping urgensi penyesuaian misionaris berdasarkan pertimbangan-pertimbangan teologis, pelaksanaannya secara tegas dan konsekuen dewasa ini merupakan suatu *tuntutan zaman* yang tak dapat ditunda-tunda lagi, yakni tuntunan yang berlaku lebih-lebih di Indonesia.

184. *Ibid.* Original passage:

Rakyat Indonesia adalah rakyat Islam, [yang] dalam periode penjajahan hendak dijadikan Christians. Dengan sistem pengajarannya, sistem kebudayaannya, sistem kesosialannya, sistem kesehatannya, rakyat Indonesia hendak dijahukan dari agama yang mereka anut. Guru-guru Kristen didatangkan dari luar negeri,

Ki Hadjar Dewantara (1889-1959), the Father of Indonesian education and founder of the Taman Siswa movement, was against the Dutch policy in adopting the missionary education system.

According to Azyumardi Azra, the harm the Church had caused for Indonesian Muslims during the colonial period gave birth to their own ambivalence toward Islam. Thus, it is fitting for the Church to thank Father van Lith for having the courage to oppose the Dutch colonial government's politics of education as well as the Church's policy of education, which still had Macaulanian nuances. Thanks to his works and ideas, various seminary schools were established in Indonesia, which later produced Albertus Soegijapranata SJ (1896–1963), the first native Indonesian bishop.[185] Thus, van Lith can not only be regarded as the father of Javanese Catholicism, but also as the father of change, the pioneer of missionary adjustment in Indonesia, without whom the Catholic church in Indonesia would surely be late in anticipating the demands of the times that emerged after Indonesian independence, and without whom Christianity in Indonesia would still be perceived as an alien religion, a "religion of the Westerners".

Now, more than seventy years after Indonesia's independence and fifty years after the Second Vatican Council, missionary

---

dididik dalam negeri, dibiayai sebanyak-banyaknya. Padri-padri dan domine-domine dikasih masuk, [tapi] tidak untuk keperluan Christians yang pada saat itu masih sedikit jumlahnya, akan tetapi untuk mengkristenkan rakyat Indonesia dengan tujuan tersembunyi agar kekuasaan si penjajah dapat berlangsung-selama-lamanya.

185. http://familycorner-rumahkeluargabahagia.blogspot.com/2017/02/bio-grafi-singkat-rm-van-lith-sj.html

adjustments have a clearer direction. The Ad Gentes Decree, concerning the missionary activities of the Second Vatican Council, which strengthened the missionary characteristics of the Church, makes missionary work open to "sincere and patient dialogue" with various cultures in the local context. Moreover, two documents of the Second Vatican Council, the Dignitatis Humanae and Nostra Aetate, also state that the church respects human freedom and recognizes the truth of God in all religions.[186]

---

186. Stephen Bevans, "New Evangelization Or Missionary Church?," 107.

12

The Second Vatican Council

FROM INWARD-LOOKING TO DIALOGUE

On January 25, 1959, three months after being elected, Pope John XXIII (r. 1958–1963) unexpectedly put forward his idea of holding an ecumenical council which is now called the Second Ecumenical Vatican Council, the twenty-first ecumenical council of the Roman Catholic Church. Held by Pope John XXIII on October 11, 1962, the opening was attended by 2,540 bishops of the Roman Catholic Church worldwide, 29 observers from 17 other churches and non-Catholic invitees, before finally being closed by Pope Paul VI on December 8, 1965.

Four sessions were held during the course of the council, with a greater number of bishops from other countries than those present at previous councils. The number of documents it produced was even greater, and the impact on the life of the Catholic Church was greater than any event after the Reformation in the 16th century.

The First Vatican Council was held a century earlier in 1869, which prematurely closed in 1870 due to the Franco-Prussian War; as a result, issues concerning pastoralism and dogma could not be discussed, and this council only had time to produce a dogma regarding papal infallibility.

When Pope John XXIII first put forward his idea of organizing the Second Vatican Council, he expressed his hope of carrying out spiritual renewal, reconciling the Church with modern times, and the ecumenical movement for church reunification. In his first encyclical, Ecclesiam Suam, issued in August, 1964 in the middle of the Second Vatican Council, Pope John XXIII introduced and emphasized the term 'dialogue' in the church. By dialogue, he meant within the Church, as well as outside the Catholic Church with all Christian communities, with non-Christian believers, and even with those who are non-religious.

Afterwards, the language of dialogue was the central theme of the Second Vatican Council, which informed the Council's decisions. Pope John XXIII died on June 3, 1963, and was replaced by Pope Paul VI (r. 1963–1978) who continued the Second Vatican Council until 1965.[187] Pope John XXIII's view was that although the Catholic church still had power in some aspects, it was too inward-looking, unable to keep up with the development of the modern world and too static for four hundred years after the Council of Trent (1545–1563).[188] Although it succeeded in producing a dogma of papal infallibility, The First Vatican Council did not bring changes to the future of the church. The Second Vatican Council is considered a proper response to the Church's freezing and splitting since Martin Luther proposed the ninety-five theses for changes on the gates of All Saints' Church in Wittenberg.

THE RESULT OF THE SECOND VATICAN COUNCIL

Pope John Paul II (r. 1978–2005) reaffirmed Pope John XXIII's statement about the direction of the Second Vatican Council that the results of the Council can be summarized in one word, *dialogue*.[189] This is reflected in its culmination of four constitutions, nine decrees and three declarations.

In their *"Vatican II After Fifty Years"* celebration, held on October 11-12, 2012 in Washington D.C. Georgetown University reiterated the spirit of the Second Vatican Council with the theme "Dialogue and Catholic Identity." Georgetown University considered that the Second Vatican Council was *"the most far-reaching event in the twentieth century for the Catholic church."* The Georgetown University Conference reemphasized the hope of Pope John XXIII in organizing the historical Council:

> *"the hope that it would be a means of spiritual renewal, reconciliation of the church to the modern world, and service to the unity of Christians."*[190]

---

187. http://catholic.resources.org/ChurchDocs/VaticanCouncil2.html

188. This council dimulai pada 1545 oleh Pope Paul III (r. 1534–1549) dan diakhiri oleh Pope Pius IV (r. 1560–1565) in 1563 namun tidak berhasil mengakhiri perpecahan yang timbul akibat Reformasi.

189. Pope John Paul II, "Ut Unum Sint: On commitment to Ecumenism," http://www.vatican.va/content/john-paul-ii/en/encyclicals/documents/hf_jp-ii_enc_25051995_ut-unum-sint.html

190. President.georgetown.edu.vatican-II-dialogue.html

Pope John XXIII officiated Vatican Council II on October 11, 1962. In the midst of the Vatican Council II, the Pope issued the Ecclesiam Suam Encyclical, in which he introduced the term 'dialogue' to the church.

The four constitutions are:

1. *Sacrosanctum Concilium* (Sacred Liturgy) announced in Session II on December 4, 1963;
2. *Lumen Gentium* (The Church) announced at Session III on November 21, 1964;
3. *Dei Verbum* (Divine Revelation) announced at Session IV on November 18, 1965; and
4. *Gaudium et Spes* (The Modern World) announced at Session IV on December 7, 1965.

The nine decrees of the Second Vatican Council are:

1. *Inter Mirifica* (The Media), announced at Session II on December 4, 1963;
2. *Orientalium Ecclesiarum* (The Eastern Rite), announced at Session III on November 21, 1964;
3. *Unitatis Redintegratio* (Ecumenism), announced at Session III on November 21, 1964;
4. *Christus Dominus* (Bishops in the Church), announced at Session IV on October 28, 1965;

The Bishops during the Vatican Council II at the St. Peter's Basilica, Vatican.

5. *Perfectae Caritatis* (Religious Life), announced at Session IV on October 28, 1965;

6. *Optatam Totius* (Priestly Training), announced at Session IV on October 28, 1965;

7. *Apostolicam Actuositatem* (Apostolate of the Laity), announced at the IV session on November 18, 1965;

8. *Ad Gentes* (Mission Activity), announced at Session IV on December 7, 1965; and

9. *Presbyterorum Ordinis* (Priestly Ministry), announced at Session IV on December 7, 1965.

The three declarations of the Second Vatican Council are: (1) Gravissimum Educationis (Education), announced at Session IV on October 28, 1965; (2) Nostra Aetate (Non-Christian Religions), announced at Session IV on October 28, 1965; and (3) Dignitatis Humanae (Religious Freedom), announced at Session IV on December 7, 1965.[191]

Fifty years later, "The Second Vatican Council 50th Anniversary Conference" was confirmed by Georgetown University as the most

---

191. https://en.wikipedia.org/wiki/Second_Vatican_Council

far-reaching event in the 20th century for the Catholic church. At the conference, Pope John XXIII's hopes were again voiced:

> The hope that it would be a means of spiritual renewal, reconciliation of the church to the modern world, and service to the unity of Christians.[192]

THE SECOND VATICAN COUNCIL AND CHURCH RENEWAL

It cannot be denied that the Second Vatican Council is the council that has brought about the most changes compared to the twenty previous ecumenical councils. There were indeed a handful of members of the Roman curia board who opposed the idea of this Church renewal, and when the sixteen decisions of the council were ratified on December 8, 1965, after four hundred years without outward change , Pope Paul VI specifically invited this small group of opponents to "be willing and prepared to give them the service of our thought, action and conduct," that is to say, to implement all the decisions of the Council.[193]

However, in general, it was also reported that the Second Vatican Council brought major changes to ecclesiastical life in its reconciliation with modern times, because "the Roman Catholic Church now believes, sincerely, in human rights in democracy, in freedom of religions, and that antisemitism is a dreadful sin. In theory, at least, the Church even believes in a sort of democracy for itself."[194]

However, each elected Pope has his own leadership style. It was reported that the European Catholics, especially those of middle-class background, were very disappointed when in 1968, three years after the Second Vatican Council ended, Pope Paul VI made the decision to prohibit abortions, contrary to the advice of his own team. Pope John Paul II (elected in 1979) and Cardinal Ratzinger (later reigning as Pope Benedict XVI) denied the accusations that they were the cause of delay in the implementation of the Second Vatican Council and its decisions. Pertaining to that, there was the rebuttal that "it is important that both men claimed to be preserving the true spirit of the Council and argued that its docu-

---

192. "Vatican II After Fifty Years," https://president.georgetown.edu/vatican-ii-dialogue/#

193. "How the second Vatican council responded to the modern world," *The Guardian*, https://www.theguardian.com/commentisfree/andrewbrown/2012/oct/11/second-vatical-council-50-years-catholicism.

194. *Ibid.*

ments had been misinterpreted, not mistaken."[195]

It was also reported that, ten years after the Second Vatican Council, no less than 10,000 pastors resigned worldwide. Many priests have even critically questioned the validity of papal infallibility, the dogma established by the First Vatican Council. It was also reported that the Austrian cardinal and theologist Christoph Schönborn plans to reduce the number of parishes in his area from 660 to 150 due to the limited number of priests. Moreover, all Catholics at this time were not born when the Second Vatican Council was held, and often look to churches outside the Catholic faith. Regarding the role of the lay Catholic community which is getting bigger today, it is clear that without their support, priests could not do much.[196]

THE CHURCH'S MISSION AND DIALOGUE

Following the introduction of dialogue into the language of the Church through Ecclesiam Suam, issued by Pope John XXIII, and later underlined by Pope John Paul II in the encyclical Ut Unum Sint,[197] and in the midst of the spirit of modernization, human rights and democracy, the Church continues to carry out reconciliation through dialogue outside of the Church. In the opening address of the Second Vatican Council, Pope John XXIII called for *aggiornamento*[198] in the church, but not for the benefit of the church, it was for the teaching of the gospel more effectively.[199] Therefore, the Second Vatican Council fundamentally affirms its identity as the missionary church.

The four constitutions of the Second Vatican Council, namely the *Sacrosanctum Concilium* (Sacred Liturgy), *Lumen gentium* (The Church), *Dei verbum* (Divine Revelation) and *Gaudium et spes* (The Modern World), each have a missionary commitment, in addition to the bishops' affirmation of the decree of Ad Gentes.[200] This

---

195. *Ibid.*

196. *Ibid.*

197. Pope John Paul II, "Ut Unum Sint"; "Vatican II After Fifty Years".

198. Etymologically, *aggiornamento* means *a bringing up to date*. B. C. Butler, "The Aggiornamento of Vatican II," https://vatican2voice.org/3butlerwrites/aggiorna.htm/

199. Stephen Bevans and Jeffrey Gros, *Evangelization and Religious Freedom: Ad Gentes, Dignitatis Humanae (Rediscovering Vatican II)* (Mahwah, New Jersey: Paulist Press, 2008), pp. 18–22.

200. Herbert Vorgrimler and Walter Abbott (eds.), *The Documents of Vatican II:*

decree opens with one of the most important statements from the Council, that:

> "The pilgrim Church is missionary by her very nature, since it is from the mission of the Son and the mission of the Holy Spirit that she draws her origin, in accordance with the decree of God the Father."

Furthermore, as stipulated in Ad Gentes, missionaries "should show the people among whom they live, and should converse with them, that they themselves may learn by sincere and patient dialogue what treasures a generous God has distributed among the nations of the earth."[201] The latter statement is closely related to two other declarations of the Council, namely Dignitatis Humanae and Nostra Aetate.[202]

NOSTRA AETATE

Dignitatis Humanae and Nostra Aetate are two important historical decisions for dialogue with non-Christian religions, particularly Islam. It took no less than fourteen centuries for the Church to change its narrow stance on Islam. During those fourteen centuries, the Church regarded the Qur'an as a false scripture that plagiarized the gospel, whose chapters contradict, and whose Prophet Muhammad is a fraud, depicting him in bad illustrations. As a result, the Church considered Islam to be a false religion that is unfit for humanity and which must be conquered by all means necessary; for Indonesia's case, this thought was reflected in the Christianization policy of the Dutch colonial government.

One important thing about the Second Vatican Council is that behind the massive changes—especially the determination to build dialogue with various parties inside and outside the Church, including those with non-Christian religions—the Church did not change various dogmas that have been enforced from the first council to the twenty-first council, that is to say since the Council of Jerusalem to the Second Vatican Council.

With Notes and Comments by Catholic, Protestant, and Orthodox Authorities (New York: Herder and Herder-Association Press, 1966), pp. 710–719.

201. "Decree Ad Gentes: On The Mission Activity Of The Church," http://www. vatican.va/archive/hist_councils/ii_vatican_council/documents/vat-ii-decree_19651207_ad-gentes_en.html.

202. Stephen Bevans, "Revisiting Mission at Vatican II: Theology and Practice for. Today's Missionary Church," Theological Studies 74, no. 2 (June 2013), pp. 263–266.

OUTSIDE THE CHURCH THERE IS NO SALVATION

In "The Second Vatican Council 50th Anniversary Conference" it was reported that "there were no new dogmas proclaimed and none discarded at Vatican II."[203] One of the dogmas that was questioned and initially thought to be removed from the Church (which was not the case, since it symbolizes the narrowness on the Church's part) was *"Extra ecclesiam nulla salus."*

> A mood of hope and reform resulted together with a release from earlier narrowness. That narrowness had included the teaching "extra ecclesiam nulla salus" (outside the church there is no salvation).[204]

Regarding this, in the second paragraph of *Dignitatis Humanae* it is stated:

> We believe that this one true religion subsists in the Catholic and Apostolic Church, to which the Lord Jesus committed the duty of spreading it abroad among all men. Thus He spoke to the Apostles: "Go, therefore, and make disciples of all nations, baptizing them in the name of the Father and of the Son and of the Holy Spirit, teaching them to observe all things whatsoever I have enjoined upon you (Matthew [28]:19-20).[205]

Therefore, the Church does not consider this assertion of exclusive claim an obstacle, as it maintains respect for other religions, as stated in Nostra Aetate. According to Catholic catechism, the dogma *"Extra ecclesiam nulla salus"* purely aims to "affirm the greatness of the faith which the Church lives and celebrates, and does not aim to punish or isolate followers of other religions."[206] In fact, this dogma is an attitude that is normally required by adherents of all religions, so that a person can accept and implement religious teachings in accordance with their respective reasoning. Moreover, it is wise for religious practitioners to develop an "agree to

---

203. "How the second Vatican council responded to the modern world".

204. *Ibid.*

205. "Declaration on Religious Freedom Dignitatis Humanae on the Right of the Person and of Communities to Social and Civil Freedom in Matters Religious; Promulgated By His Holiness Pope Paul VI on December 7, 1965," http://www.vatican.va/archive/hist_councils/ii_vatican_council/documents/vat-ii_decl_19651207_dignitatis-humanae_en.html

206. Carolus Putranto Tri Hidayat, "Extra Ecclesiam Nulla Salus Menurut Katekismus Gereja Katolik," https://proveritas.me/2012/08/16/extra-ecclesia-nulla-salus-menurut-katekismus-gereja-katolik/.

disagree" attitude in today's increasingly plural society.

It is in the context of respecting pluralism of faith, reconciliation with change and modern life, and dialogue with various local cultures that Nostra Aetate operates, so that the Church now respects all non-Christian religions. Although Christianity has been involved in long, and sometimes bloody, conflicts with Islam, the milestones made by the Second Vatican Council, in particular Dignitatis Humanae and Nostra Aetate, remain the Church's historical and monumental resolution to the relationship between the two largest religions in the world. In Nostra Aetate it is further emphasized that:

1. The Church regards with esteem the Muslims. They adore the one God, living and subsisting in Himself; merciful and all-powerful, the Creator of heaven and earth, who has spoken to men;
2. They wholeheartedly surrender to His inscrutable decrees, just as Abraham, with whom the faith of Islam takes pleasure in linking itself, submitted to God.
3. Though they do not acknowledge Jesus as God, they revere Him as a prophet.
4. They also honor Mary, His virgin Mother; at times they even call on her with devotion. In addition,
5. They await the day of judgment when God will render their deserts to all those who have been raised up from the dead. Finally,
6. They value moral life and worship God especially through prayer, almsgiving and fasting.
7. Since in the course of centuries not a few quarrels and hostilities have arisen between Christians and Muslims, this sacred synod urges all to forget the past and to work sincerely for mutual understanding and to preserve as well as to promote together for the benefit of all mankind social justice and moral welfare, as well as peace and freedom.[207]

The attitude of the Church above can be considered a reflection of the attitude of Christians towards Muslims fourteen centuries ago, which was described in the Qur'an, Surah Al-Ma'idah, verse 82:

You will surely find the most intense of the people in animosity

207. "Declaration On The Relation Of The Church To Non-Christian Religions: Nostra Aetate," http://www.vatican.va/archive/hist_councils/ii_vatican_council/documents/vat-ii_decl_19651028_nostra-aetate_en.html; "Declaration on Religious Freedom Dignitatis Humanae..."

toward the believers [to be] the Jews and those who associate others with Allah; and you will find the nearest of them in affection to the believers those who say, "We are Christians." That is because among them are priests and monks and because they are not arrogant.

And it is also mentioned in Surah Al-Baqarah verse 136:

Say, [O believers], "We have believed in Allah and what has been revealed to us and what has been revealed to Abraham and Ishmael and Isaac and Jacob and the Descendants and what was given to Moses and Jesus and what was given to the prophets from their Lord. We make no distinction between any of them, and we are Muslims [in submission] to Him."

The above verses tell about the closeness of Christianity and Islam, two religions that belong to the "fraternity of Abraham." However, in the course of history, this closeness has been torn apart over fourteen centuries by hostilities that have been detrimental to both parties and, more broadly, to the dignity of the human being. The issuance of Nostra Aetate deserves to be welcomed by all. The followers of both religions, who make up more than half of the earth's population, have the ability to greatly influence these relations.

More recently, Nostra Aetate was addressed in "A Common Word between Us and You." The open letter from 138 Muslim scholars and ulamas addressed to Pope Benedict XVI and all top church leaders on October 13, 2007 led to the Vatican periodically holding the Catholic-Muslim Forum to develop this collective agreement into further practical commitments. Now, what is needed is cooperation between Muslims and Christians, as well as followers of other religions, to build and to realize this "common word" into a partnership platform, a vehicle for mutual understanding, mutual respect and sincere cooperation in the field of humanity.

STAGES OF CHURCH TRANSFORMATION

> "Das Abendland war ein anderes Abendland geworden,
> das moderne Abendland,
> und der Islamische Geist war sein Geburtshelfer.
> Das Abendland ist nicht nur Erbe der Kultur Griechenlands und Roms,
> sondern auch der Islamischen Geisteswelt"
> Sigrid Hunke
> *Allahs Sonne über dem Abendland,*
> Stuttgart, 1999.

The Nostra Aetate Declaration was indeed a historical document for the Church, as well as for all religious persons. For the first time after fourteen centuries, the Church recognized and respected Islam as one of the Abrahamic religions, and also extended respect to, and recognized salvation for, non-believers. The question is, why did Europe and the Church, who had had encounters with Islam since the 7th century, need such a long time to understand and pay respect to Islam? One answer for this simple yet fundamental question was given by Wilfred Cantwell Smith, a comparative religion scholar and founder of the Institute of Islamic Studies at McGill University in Quebec, and later the director of Harvard University's Center for the Study of World Religions. In his book, The Meaning and End of Religion (1962), Smith indicates that religious teachings should be standardized and codified, and not the result of actual experiences of individuals and small groups of people. According to Smith, religious traditions should not be continuously changing, nor should rituals be easily replaced by others, but rather, there should be a set of religious doctrines and concepts set forth in the Holy Books.

According to Smith, from the very beginning, Islam was totally different, living side by side with other religious traditions. Al-Qur'an, Al Kafirun 109:6 states "to you your religion, and to me my religion," clearly indicating the clear distinction between Islam and the other Abrahamic traditions. Right from the beginning, the Qur'an provides guidelines for the Muslim on how to behave toward the other Abrahamic as well as non-Abrahamic religions.

Another answer was given by Franz Magnis Suseno SJ, an emeritus professor at the Driyarkara School of Philosophy in Jakarta. He emphasizes that the narrowness of the "Extra Ecclesiam Nulla Salus" dogma is the reason the Church took such a long time to realize the universality of salvation. Frans Magnis also reiterates that within a modern society, the paradigm of "us versus others" has been considerably changed into one which upholds the universality of mankind. He repeatedly underlines that Islam has taught tolerance for 1400 years, while most Christians have taught it since the 19th century, and Catholics only 50 years ago. In a public occasion for discussing the Indonesian State Philosophy of Pancasila, or the Five Principles, Franz Magnis emphasized:

The concept of the Global church, where the church steps into dialogue with Islam and the eastern religions, was discussed at the monthly online religious study for the Indonesian diaspora in Germany at Frankfurt on February 10, 2021, featuring Sudibyo Markus, the author of the book The Western World and Islam, Rev Dr. Martin Lukito Sinaga (Jakarta School of Theology), and Habiburrahman El Shirazy (doctorate student at Leipzig University).

> Over the previous 1400 years, Christians lived in small communities in Egypt, Lebanon, Iraq, Pakistan, etc. Jews lived in the Middle East, where the majority were under Islamic leadership.

Finally, in Karl Rahner's Theological Investigations, he pointed out that the Church only embarked into dialogue with Islam and the Eastern religions in the third stage of the Church's development, "the global church" stage. The first stage was Judaism, as stipulated in the early phase of the New Testament. The second stage is considered to be the Church's integration into Greco-Roman culture, which provided the Church with all of its Christian characteristics today. According to David Pawson, however, the Church has been integrating Western civilization into the rest of the world since the 16th century, through a mixture of imperial colonization and missionary enterprise.

In his book Civilization on Trial and The World and the West, Arnold Toynbee illustrated how the historical pendulum changed in the 16th century as the Islamic world, which had been predominantly influential to Western civilization since the 7th century, was being colonized by Europe. Similar conclusions were demonstrated by Karel Steenbrink's Dutch and Islamic conflict. The Dutch colonial administration wanted to change Indonesian education toward "Indonesian in blood and color, but Dutch in morals and in intellect. These conclusions were applicable to all colonialized countries, especially those with Muslim majorities.

DISTINCTION BETWEEN ISLAM, JUDAISM AND CHRISTIANITY

Judaism is characterized by a belief in one transcendent God who revealed himself to Abraham, Moses, and the Hebrew prophets and by a religious life in accordance with Scriptures and rabbinic traditions. In nearly 4,000 years of historical development, the Jewish people and their religion have displayed remarkable adaptability and continuity. In their encounter with the great civilizations, from ancient Babylonia and Egypt to Western Christendom and modern secular culture, they have assimilated foreign elements and integrated them into their own social and religious systems, thus maintaining an unbroken religious and cultural tradition. The Christian world long believed that until the rise of Christianity the history of Judaism was but a "preparation for the Gospel" (preparatio evangelica) that was followed by the "manifestation of the Gospel" (demonstratio evangelica) as revealed by Christ and the Apostles.

Sigrid Hunke, author of several books on European identity, and especially the relationship between Europe and the Arab World, clearly defined the undeniable contribution of Islamic civilization to Europe. She received her PhD in religious studies from the Friedrich-Wilhelms-University Berlin in 1941. In her writing, she has emphasized that the Europes civilization was not only Greece-Roman, but Islam also played important role in the rebirth of the modern Europe. The Greco-Roman civilization was called the Cradle of Western Civilization. Ancient Greece began from the civilisation of Aegean around 3000 BC - Ancient Rome began around 753 BC on the Italian peninsula. Ancient Rome conquered Greece in 146 BC.

Two historical Muslim letters to Christian leaders, namely the letter to Byzantine Emperor Heraclius (610-641), which was written by the Holy Prophet Mohammed himself in 7th century, and the most recent letter to Pope Benedict XVI and all Church world leaders, "A Common Word between Us and You," both convey the same Qur'anic verse Ali Imran 3:64 started with "Qul yaa ahlal Kitaab" or "Say, O People of the Book," recognizing that Christians, Jews, alongside Muslims are all the followers of the religions of the Fraternity of the Holy Prophet Abraham.

PART 3

A COMMON WORD
BETWEEN US AND YOU

TOWARD A COMMON WORD BETWEEN
MUSLIMS AND CHRISTIANS

The *A Common Word* Initiative is the most significant initiative in Muslim-Christian relations since Nostra Aetate of the Second Vatican Council.

Prof. Miroslav Volf
Yale Divinity School, Yale University

13

From Muhammad's Letter to "A Common Word Between Us and You"

A month after Pope Benedict XVI's speech at the University of Regensburg on September 12, 2006, which was deemed a discredit to Muslims, a total of 38 Muslim scholars sent an open letter to the Pope. The open letter, dated October 13, 2006, contained a request for clarification to the Pope, because in that speech the Pope cited a dialogue that took place in the 14th century between the Emperor of Byzantium and a Persian scholar containing the view that Islam is "*a religion of violence and irrationality.*"

After the request for clarification did not receive an adequate response, and having gained the impression that Pope Benedict XVI was dismissive, exactly a year later, on October 13, 2007, the open letter entitled "A Common Word Between Us and You" was sent again. This time, the letter was not only addressed to Pope Benedict XVI, but to all the leaders of various Churches around the world. The second open letter contained a request for clarification to Pope Benedict XVI as well as a broader invitation to the large population of religious followers worldwide to become pioneers of tolerance and peace for all mankind. This time, the letter, originally signed by 138 Muslim scholars and clerics, received wider support from more Muslim scholars and clerics, and even increased to no less than 300 signatories. Both letters were initiated by Prof. Ghazi bin Muhammad bin Talal, Chairperson of The Royal Aal Al-Bayt Institute for Islamic Thought, Jordan.

While the first open letter did not get an adequate response from Pope Benedict XVI, the second open letter unexpectedly received a spontaneous and positive response from Pope Benedict XVI, as well as Patriarch Alexy II of the Russian Orthodox Church, Dr. Rowan Williams, Archbishop of Canterbury, and Bishop Mark Hanson of the Lutheran World Federation, as well as the World Council of Churches (WCC) in Geneva. In November 2007, just five weeks after the release of "A Common Word," more than 300 prominent pastors in the United States provided their response and support through *The New York Times*. A number of well-known universities with religious studies departments also reacted positively, such as the USA's Yale Divinity School at Yale University, Georgetown University, George Washington University, England's Cambridge University, as well as Eugen Biser Stiftung at the Ludwig Maximilian University in Germany.

Yale University gave its response and support for "A Common Word" on November 18, 2007, five weeks after receiving the document. Following this response, Yale University organized a series of workshops with the theme "Loving God and Neighbor in Word and Deed: Implications for Muslims and Christians." The workshop on July 24–28, 2008 was attended by 60 Muslim and Christian participants and three Jewish participants. This workshop discussed five main points: (1) *love of God*, (2) *love your neighbor*, (3) *love and speech about the other*, (4) *love and world poverty*, and (5) *God is loving*. This limited workshop was immediately followed by a larger conference on July 28–31, 2008, which was attended by 70 Muslim, 70 Christian and 7 Jewish participants, and opened by Senator John Kerry.

"A Common Word" even managed to break through to the General Assembly of the United Nations (UN) in New York, which then gave way to designating the first week of February *"International Interfaith Harmony Week"*[208] following the decision of the Philippine Congress, which passed Law No. 6148 in June 2011, and encouraged the holding of a Symposium on "Love in Abrahamic Religion" at the Oxford University in October 2012.[209]

Furthermore, The Royal Aal Al-Bayt Institute reported widespread support such as the writing of more than 600 special articles on "A Common Word;" no less than 200,000 visits to the "A Common Word" website; and the writing of M.A. theses and Ph.D. dissertations in Islamic Studies at Harvard University, Georgetown University, Tubingen University and Yale University. "A Common Word" was also included in the agenda of the World Economic Forum 2008, the establishment of the three-year Catholic-Muslim

---

208. Mu'assasat Āl al-Bayt lil-Fikr al-Islāmī, *A Common Word between Us and You, 5-Year Anniversary* Edition (Amman: Royal Aal Al-Bayt Institute for Islamic Thought, 2012), pp. 11–50.

209. *Ibid.*, 10.

Forum by the Vatican starting in 2008, and was awarded consecutively by the UK's Association of Muslim Social Scientists' Building Bridge Award, and the Eugen Biser Award at the Ludwig Maximilian University in Germany.[210] Thus, in a span of five years, there were many significant developments, including the initiation of many conferences, seminars, workshops, and training courses at various leading universities, the publication of books, articles, dissertations and various reports; and the commencement of the first Triennial Dialogue agreement between Muslim World and Catholic World in 2008 at the Vatican, and again in 2011 in Jordan and in 2014 in Rome.

THE HOLY PROPHET MUHAMMAD'S LETTERS

Before examining the first open letter, it is important to understand the tradition of communication by means of letters that had been carried out by the Holy Prophet Muhammad, and which were sent directly to the rulers and church leaders via couriers, inviting them to Islam.

Although the background of the first open letter to Pope Benedict XVI and all leaders of world churches was completely different from that of the Prophet Muhammad's letter to rulers and religious leaders during his prophetic period, there are fundamental similarities between the two letters. The basic equation is to use Surah Ali Imran verse 64 as the basic message:

> Say, "O People of the Scripture, come to a word that is equitable between us and you—that we will not worship except Allah and not associate anything with Him and not take one another as lords instead of Allah." But if they turn away, then say, "Bear witness that we are Muslims [submitting to Him]."

In carrying out the mandate to convey the message of Islam, Muhammad delivered it not only verbally to the people around Mecca and Medina, but also in the form of letters to kings and religious leaders in distant places. Since transportation and communications were very limited at that time, the Prophet used couriers to deliver the letters directly to the kings and religious leaders to whom they were addressed.

During his life, the Prophet is recorded to have written 43 let-

---

210. The Royal Aal Al-Bayt Institute for Islamic Thought, *A Common Word between Us and You, 5-Year Anniversary Edition*, 115.

A handwritten letter from the Holy Prophet Muhammad, Peace Be Upon Him, was sent to Heraclius, Emperor of Byzantine (610-641) who was in Jerusalem celebrating the Byzantine victory over the Persian Kingdom.

ters to world leaders such as kings, religious leaders and tribal leaders. Sending the letters to religious leaders and rulers in various parts of the region is understood as a strategic step, because it quickly and peacefully introduced Islam to a wide range of areas.

Among the many religious leaders and rulers recorded to have received letters from Muhammad were:

1. King Najashi of Abyssinia;
2. Muqawqis, the Roman viceroy of Egypt;
3. King Khosrow II of Persia;
4. Emperor Heraclius of the Roman Empire;
5. Bishop Dhughathir of Rome;
6. Governor Munzir ibn Sawa Al-Tamimi of Bahrain;
7. King of Oman;
8. Haudzah, Ruler of Yamamah;
9. Kings of Yemen.

The core and essence of Muhammad's letters sent to these religious leaders and rulers was an invitation to the leaders of the People of the Book, that is the Jews and Christians, to embrace Islam by following and returning to the pure monotheism, *tawhid*, which is the fundamental and most basic essence of the Islamic treatise or Islamic teachings revealed by Allah to Muhammad.

LETTER TO EMPEROR HERACLIUS

Among the many letters Muhammad sent to rulers and religious leaders, one of the most widely known is the letter to Roman Emperor Heraclius, a Roman Catholic. The letter brought by a courier named Dihyah al-Kalbi was delivered to the Emperor in Jerusalem, who was celebrating the victory of the Roman Empire over the Persian Empire. Here is the content of the letter:

In the name of God, the Most Merciful, the Bestower of all Mercy

From Muhammad, Worshiper and Messenger of Allah to Heraclius the Great of the Romans:

Peace be upon he who follows the guidance.

Furthermore, I invite you with the invitation of peace. If you accept then you will find safety and God will double your reward. If you turn away, you will bear the Arians' sins.

"O People of the Scripture! Come to a common word between us and you: that we shall worship none but God, and that we shall ascribe no partner unto Him, and that none of us shall take others for lords beside God. And if they turn away, then say: Bear witness that we are they who have surrendered (unto Him)."[211]

After receiving a letter from the Prophet Muhammad, the Emperor sought information about who the sender really was, he who claimed to be the Prophet. The Emperor sent out orders to bring someone of Arab background before him. Abu Sufyan, who at that time was still an idol-worshiper and a great enemy of the Prophet Muhammad, was in the nearest area for commercial purposes and was immediately presented before the Emperor.

Abu Sufyan was asked to stand at the front as a spokesman since he had the closest lineage to Muhammad. His entourage stood behind him as witnesses. That was the Emperor's strategy to obtain valid information. There was a long dialogue between the Emperor and Abu Sufyan. Emperor Heraclius was an intelligent man with extensive knowledge. He asked tactically and directed his questions to find the truth, whether the writer of the letter was really a prophet or merely someone who claimed to be a prophet. Abu Sufyan, who at that time was hostile to Muhammad and had just signed the Hudaibiyah peace treaty with the Prophet, was also

---

211. Sahih Al-Bukhari 1/4,5

an intelligent man who could read the direction of the Emperor's questions. At the end of the dialogue, the Emperor expressed his opinion that Muhammad possessed the characteristics of a prophet according to the Emperor's views, having read so in the Bible.

Emperor Heraclius had learned about the Prophet Muhammad and confirmed his prophethood completely. However, he was preoccupied by his love for the throne, and hence did not declare adherence to Islam. With his intelligence and breadth of knowledge, the Emperor could see the prophetic truth of the Prophet Muhammad. Even the Emperor declared: "*He (Muhammad) will one day be able to control the territory on which my two feet are standing now.*" At that time the Emperor was on his way to Jerusalem, the Baitul Maqdis.

Abu Sufyan recounted this dialogue after converting to Islam, so that this hadith was accepted. The emperor then honored Dihyah ibn Khalifah Al-Kalby, the courier of the Prophet, by giving him a number of assets and clothes.

SOME RESPONSES TO MUHAMMAD'S LETTER

The reactions of the other rulers and religious leaders who received the letter from the Prophet Muhammad varied. There were religious leaders who accepted the letter well and immediately accepted His invitation to embrace Islam, who understood the prophecies or promises of Allah in their Scriptures to send His messengers in the future. There were also religious leaders who wanted to accept the invitation of the Prophet Muhammad, but did not due to opposition from their followers. There were also religious leaders who wisely tried to dig up accurate information about the sender of the letter claiming to be the messenger of God, before further determining their reaction or answer. Others received the letter with anger.

The following are the different attitudes of some of the recipients:

NAJASHI, KING OF ABYSSINIA. When receiving the letter, Najashi, also known as Ashamah, rushed down from his throne, and upon reading the letter, the King immediately stated that he accepted the Prophet's invitation to embrace Islam through Ja'far ibn Abi Talib. When King Najashi was reported to have died, the Prophet Muhammad performed a distant prayer (*ghaib* prayer) for the late King of Abyssinia.

MUQAWQIS, ROMAN VICEROY OF EGYPT. The Prophet sent his own friend, Habib ibn Abi Balta'ah, to deliver the letter to the viceroy. Muqawqis replied to the Prophet's letter by declaring that he had converted to Islam, and gave the Prophet several gifts, including a horse for his ride.

KHOSROW II, KING OF PERSIA. Muhammad sent Abdullah ibn Hudhafa to bring the letter. Khosrow II was offended by the letter and immediately tore it up. When he received the news about the tearing of the letter, the Prophet Muhammad prayed for the breaking of the Persian empire, and not long after, the Sassanid Empire was defeated by Heraclius' troops at Nineveh in 626. Then, Khosrow II was overthrown by his own son, Sheroe, in 628, until the empire finally collapsed for good after being defeated by the forces of Caliph Umar ibn Khattab.

HERACLIUS, EMPEROR OF ROME. As stated before, the letter to Heraclius was delivered by a courier named Dihyah al-Kalbi, and was received by the Emperor as he was celebrating his victory over the Sassanid Empire. After conducting an in-depth investigation through Abu Sufyan, who at that time was still an enemy of the Prophet, Emperor Heraclius believed in Muhammad's prophethood. Even though Emperor Heraclius was not willing to convert to Islam, the Emperor respected the Messenger of Allah and his initiative to send the letter.

DHUGHATIR, BISHOP OF ROME. The letter to the Bishop of Rome was also delivered by Dihyah al-Khalbi. It was reported that the bishop of Rome declared himself ready to embrace Islam after reading the Prophet's invitation, then took off his black robe, and changed into a white robe. Then Dhughatir met his congregation at the church, but was greeted with anger.

MUNZIR IBN SAWA AL-TAMIMI, Governor of Bahrain. The letter for him was delivered by the Prophet's friend, Al 'Ala ibn Al-Hadrami. Governor Munzir ibn Sawa accepted the Prophet Muhammad's invitation to convert to Islam, and wrote a reply to the Prophet regarding his people, many of whom were willing to embrace Islam. Others refused and wanted to continue to adhere to their religions, Zoroastrianism and Judaism. Rasulullah replied to the letter of Al-Mundzir by saying that those who refused to embrace Islam could pay *jizyah*.[212]

KINGS OF OMAN. The Prophet Muhammad sent his friend, Amru ibn Al-Ash, to deliver a letter to the two kings of Oman, who immediately agreed to embrace Islam.

HAUZAH, RULER OF YAMAMA. The Prophet Muhammad's letter to Haudzah was delivered by Salit ibn 'Amar. Despite respecting Muhammad's invitation, Haudzah of Yamamah, a region east of Mecca, refused to embrace Islam.

FINALLY, THE KING OF YEMEN. This letter to the King of Yemen was sent to Hanitz, Masruh, and Nu'aim ibn Khilal as leaders of the largest group, Himyar, of the Qahtan tribe. Although there were many Jews in the area, the three rulers were willing to embrace Islam. As a token of appreciation, the Prophet sent Mu'adz ibn Jabal as a teacher to teach Islam in Yemen.[213]

BACKGROUND: DEVIATION FROM THE MONOTHEISM PRINCIPLE

Of the many letters sent by Prophet Muhammad, it can be noted that there are three main contents of these letters:

- First, the call was addressed to the People of the Book, namely to Jews and Christians;
- Second, a call or invitation to embrace Islam;
- Third, a call to return to pure monotheism, the oneness of God (*tawhid*).

For the *first* call, this invitation was extended to the People of the Book, Jews and Christians, as fellow adherents of the heavenly religion, part of the fraternity of Abraham.

The *second* call was an invitation to embrace Islam, because the essence of all the teachings that were revealed by all the prophets of God—from Adam, Nuh, Ibrahim (Abraham), Musa (Moses), Daud (David), to Isa (Jesus)—is Islam: to submit to God, with

---

212. The word *jizyah* was derived from Turkish *cizye*, a per capita tax levied upon the non-Muslim population in a Muslim country.

213. Adapted from Wiwik Setiawati, "Saksi Dakwah Rasulullah saw., Ajak Pemimpin Dunia Masuk Islam", www.infoyunik.com/2015/03/surat-surat-ini-saksi-dakwah-rasulullah.html.

pure monotheism as its main doctrine. Therefore, the word of Allah in Surat Ali Imran verse 64 is closed with the sentence: "But if they turn away, then say, 'Bear witness that we are Muslims [submitting to Him]'."

Third, the Prophet Muhammad called upon the people of the Holy Books, the Jews and Christians, to return to the basic religious doctine of *tawhid,* or the Oneness of God. When Muhammad received his revelation, there had been a deviation in the principle of monotheism in the other two religions in the form of "*associating God with others*" and "making a god other than Him."

Philip K. Hitti said of this concept of the Oneness of God (*tawhid*) in Islam:

"In this uncompromising monotheism lies the chief strength of Islam."[214]

The doctrine of *tawhid* is the basic and core principle of Islam, so that even at the beginning of Muhammad's letter, the recipient is called upon to embrace Islam, and the invitation to return to pure monotheism is repeated: *"let's (hold) one sentence (provision) where there is no dispute between us and you, that we have nothing to worship except Allah, and we do not associate Him with anything. Some of us also do not make gods other than Him."*

The reason for this concern is that Christians had adopted the concept of the Trinity, which was decided at the Council of Nicea in 325 concerning the existence of God the Father, God the Son, and Holy Spirit, while the Jews also stated that Uzair was the son of God. It is precisely in the context of this belief that the Qur'an calls on them to return to the common word, the *kalimah sawâ'* (sentence of the oneness of God), which believes that no substance has the right to be worshiped except Allah, and He is God who has no partner, including obeying religious scholars or monks in matters that deviate from Allah's commands and prohibitions.

Pertaining to that, Rev. C. F. Andrews underlined the existence of deviations from the pure monotheism (*tawhid*):

One of the greatest blessings which Islam has brought to East and West alike has been the emphasis which at a crucial period in human history it placed upon the Divine Unity. For during those Dark Ages both in East and

---

214. Philip K. Hitti, *History of the Arabs,* pp. 98–99.

West, from 400 to 1000 A.D., this doctrine was in danger of being overlaid and obscured in Hinduism and in Christianity itself, owing to the immense accretions and subsidiary worship of countless demi-gods and heroes. Islam has been, both to Europe and India, in their dark hour of aberration from the sovereign truth of God Unity, an invaluable corrective and deterrent. Indeed, without the final emphasis on this truth, which Islam gave from its central position—facing India and facing Europe—it is doubtful whether this idea of God as one could have obtained that established place in human thought which is uncontested in the intellectual world today.[215]

That is what was meant by the invitation to return to "the common word," or the *kalimah sawa*—as stated in Surah Ali Imran verse 64—a return to monotheistic teachings. Monotheism is the most central and fundamental teaching, and therefore Islam considers that "associating partners with God" or equating Him with substances other than Him is the greatest sin. This is contained in the Qur'an, Surah An-Nisaa verse 48:

Indeed, Allah does not forgive association with Him, but He forgives what is less than that for whom He wills. And he who associates others with Allah has certainly fabricated a tremendous sin.

The invitation to embrace Islam, a return to the religion of pure monotheism, is very relevant in the context of the continuity of the evolution of revelation. Ahmad Ghalwash describes the importance of a basic understanding of the nature of Islam in the context of the continuous evolution of Allah's revelation as follows:

It must be again and again reiterated until the basis of the religion of Islam is well understood, that this religion doesn't profess to be a new religion formulated by the Prophet Muhammad, but it is a continuation of the true religious principles established by God through His revelations, from Adam, Noah, Abraham, and the other inspired Messengers of God.[216]

Thus, in general it can be emphasized that, inherently, the letters of the Prophet Muhammad to the rulers and religious leaders were invitations to embrace the doctrine of pure monotheism as the final form of the evolution of revelation, revealed by Allah to the prophets and messengers of Allah, Adam, Noah, Abraham and all the prophets sent by Allah to the Prophet Muhammad, the ultimate messenger of Allah.

---

215. Syed Abdul Latif, *The Mind Al-Qur'an Built* (Singapore: Genuine Islam, 1936).
216. Ahmed A. Ghalwash, *The Religion of Islam* (Alexandria: 1958), 192.

It is undeniable that the letters of the Prophet Muhammad sent to so many religious leaders and rulers in several regions has played an important role in the successful dissemination of Islamic teachings to a wide area in a relatively short time. Muhammad Husein Heikal wrote and acknowledged the role of the Prophet Muhammad's letters as a "basis for dissemination" in his first edition of the Foreword of *The Life of Muhammad*:

> *Muhammad did not have to wait long for his religion to become known, or for his dominion to spread. God has seen fit to complete the religion of Islam even before his death. It was he who laid down the plans for the propagation of this religion. He had sent to Chosroes, to Heraclius and other princes and kings of the world inviting them to join the new faith. No more than a hundred and fifty years passed from then until the flags of Islam were flying high between Spain in the west and India, Turkestan and indeed China in the east. Thus by joining Islam, the territories of al-Sham Iraq, Persia, and Afghanistan have linked the Arabian Peninsula with the kingdom of "the Son of Heaven" (i.e. China).*[217]

---

217. Muhammad Hussein Heikal, *Sejarah Hidup Muhammad*, pp. xvi–xvii.

14

A Common Word:
From Pure Monotheism to Peace

THE GENESIS OF "A COMMON WORD"

On April 19, 2005, Cardinal Joseph Ratzinger was elected Pope to succeed the late Pope John Paul II and took the name Benedict XVI as his papal name. Before being appointed Bishop of Munich in 1977, Joseph Ratzinger spent most of his career teaching at several universities in Germany. Shortly after being appointed Archbishop of Munich, he was ordained a Cardinal and received a special assignment from Pope John Paul II to direct the affairs of publishing and church doctrine at the Vatican.

The idea for a number of Muslim scholars to write the open letter "A Common Word between Us and You" to Pope Benedict XVI and all church leaders worldwide came after his controversial speech at Regensburg University on September 12, 2006, which drew widespread criticism from the Muslim World. In his speech, he quoted the words of Manuel II Paleologus—the Byzantine Emperor who in 1391 had a dialogue with a Persian scholar about the concepts of the Bible and the Qur'an—which described Islam as "a religion of violence and irrationality." Although the Pope maintained that the quote was by no means a papal statement, it was still widely criticized by Muslims and others as an insensitive speech, especially in the post-Vatican II era.[218]

On October 13, 2006, a month after the speech, at the initiative of Prince Ghazi bin Muhammad bin Talal, 38 Muslim scholars sent the open letter to Pope Benedict XVI asking for clarification on his speech. However, the Vatican did not immediately respond to this letter, and was also unwilling to apologize for the Pope's speech. The Vatican's response came in December 2006, two months after

---

218. The Royal Aal Al-Bayt Institute for Islamic Thought, *A Common Word between Us and You, 5-Year Anniversary Edition*, pp 16 and 47.

Prince Prof. Ghazi bin Muhammad bin Talal, Advisor to King Abdullah II and President of The Royal Aal Al-Bayt Institute for Islamic Thought, the one who initiated the open letter, "A Common Word Between Us and You."

the open letter was sent. The Vatican commissioned the Vatican Ambassador to go to Jordan with Archbishop Pier Luigi Celata and a pastor to carry out a perfunctory courtesy visit to Prince Ghazi bin Muhammad bin Talal, who requested clarification at his home in Amman.

The Vatican's special envoy to Prince Ghazi bin Muhammad did not provide any clarification on the main issue of the Pope's speech. The Vatican Ambassador only said that if Muslims want to have a special dialogue with the Pope, it is advisable for them to write a letter to the Vatican through the Vatican Secretary of State. Prince Ghazi felt uncomfortable with the Vatican's seemingly dismissive response.

Meanwhile, Cardinal Jean-Louis Tauran, head of the Pontifical Council for Interreligious Dialogue, maintained that "dialogue with Muslims is difficult to carry out," since:

> Muslims don't accept one question to the Qur'an, because it was written, they say, by the dictation from God. With such an absolute interpretation, it is difficult to discuss the contents of faith.[219]

---

219. *Ibid.*, 16.

He further doubted the seriousness and spirit of the invitation to dialogue from "A Common Word," especially the use of the term 'love' in the Love of God and Love of neighbors. He stated that:

"... But some questions remain when we speak of the Love of God, are we speaking about the same love ?"[220]

THE HISTORICAL STRATEGIC SIGNIFICANCE
OF THE POPE'S VISIT TO ISTANBUL

Amid the disappointment of the 38 Muslim scholars who sent the first open letter, in November 2006, two months after the speech at Regensburg University, Pope Benedict XVI suddenly made a visit to the Turkish capital, Istanbul, which was formerly Constantinople.

On this occasion, Pope Benedict XVI visited the Blue Mosque,[221] and allegedly aimed, following a mandate from the Decree of the Second Vatican Council on Nostra Aetate, to forget the past hostility of the Church to Muslims, and quell the disappointment of Muslims that had been a result of his speech in Regensburg.

At first, it appeared that his papal visit to Istanbul had no connection with the first open letter, since papal visits to various parts of the world regularly occur. Moreover, in his various explanations about the background and history of the letter, Prince Ghazi bin Muhammad bin Talal never linked the Pope's visit to Istanbul with the first or second open letter.

However, it is clear that Pope Benedict XVI's visit was definitely not just a regular papacy visit.

---

220. *Ibid.*

221. This mosque was built from 1609 to 1616, and is opposite and only a few hundred meters from Hagia Sofia, a former Byzantine Empire church built in 537 but later converted into a mosque after the defeat of the Byzantines by the Ottoman Empire, and converted into a museum by Mustapha Kemal Attaturk who overthrew the Ottoman empire and turned Turkey into a secular republic in 1923.

It should be noted that Turkey, Istanbul and the Hagia Sophia are eternal symbols of the encounter between the West and Islam, with all their long history. Especially after the conquest of Constantinople in 1453, the Turks tried to besiege Vienna in 1529 and 1683 but failed. In fact, long before that, the Crusaders' departure through the command of Pope Urban in Clermont on November 25, 1095, in addition to aiming to seize the holy city of Jerusalem, also intended to help the Byzantine Emperor in Constantinople, which at that time was already being disturbed by the Seljuk Turkish troops.

Pope Benedict XVI was escorted by the Imam of the Blue Mosque in Istanbul during his strategic visit to Istanbul on November 30, 2006, only two months after his controversial speech at the Regensburg University.

It should be noted that the Pope's visit to Turkey could also be considered a state visit, given his position as the Holy Seer. There seemed to be a strategic agenda of state politics behind the visit. The first question is, why two months after Regensburg? The second question is, why to Istanbul? Why did he not, for example, visit Indonesia, a country with the largest Muslim population in the world?

To answer the first question, the strategic reason is that Pope Benedict XVI firmly argued that in his speech in Regensburg, when he quoted the Byzantine Emperor in the fourteenth century that Islam is "a religion of violence and irrationality," it was just a quote, not at all a papal declaration.

Therefore, the Pope thought there was no reason for him to explain it at length, let alone apologize to Muslims for a speech from the fourteenth century.

However, Pope Benedict XVI certainly did not want the criticism to damage the relationship between Muslims and Christians, especially the Catholic church. Moreover, there was an opinion that this controversy was caused by carelessness, since he said something contrary to the spirit of reform by the Second Vatican Council.

It seems that Pope Benedict XVI preferred to use the language of diplomacy to diminish the disappointment of Muslims, which is why the papal visit to the Islamic state of Turkey was carried out relatively soon, two months after the Regensburg speech.

As for the second question, why to Turkey and not to Indonesia - this is similar to the first tactical move by United States President Barack Obama who, once elected, directly visited and delivered a speech addressed to the entire Islamic world from Cairo, Egypt. Of course, Cairo and Egypt were chosen due to their position as one of the oldest centers of Islamic culture. Cairo has played a big role in the history of religious life. Barack Obama thought that his *'assalamu'alaikum'* speech to the Islamic world delivered in Cairo would have some added value, reach more people, and provide stronger and faster effects on the rest of the Muslim World than if it had been delivered elsewhere. Obama, who lived in Indonesia as a child, understood that Indonesia has the largest Muslim population in the world. However, delivering his *'assalamu'alaikum'* speech in Indonesia would not have the same significance as in Cairo, Egypt.

Likewise, Pope Benedict XVI preferred to visit Turkey in the midst of his unfavorable relationship with the Muslim world in order to quickly reduce Muslim disapproval. To prevent a counterproductive situation, Pope Benedict XVI deliberately did not visit the Hagia Sophia. He instead visited the sultanate mosque, the Sultan Ahmed mosque, which is known as the Blue Mosque. The historical strategic significance of Turkey is in the framework of implementing the recommendations of the Second Vatican Council on Nostra Aetate to forget the "few quarrels and hostilities that have arisen between Christians and Muslims."[222] Pope Benedict XVI, who spent nearly twenty years teaching at several universities in Germany, was well aware of the meaning of the West's historical resentment toward Turkey which had, in 1453, seized Constantinople, and thus overthrew the Byzantine Empire. This is also true for the Ottoman Empire which had attempted twice to capture Vienna in 1529 and 1683, but failed.

History records that, when the Islamic sovereignty in Spain fell in 1492, the Seljuk Sultanate, under Sultan Murad I, succeeded in expanding its territory to Hungary in mainland Europe. Sultan

---

222. "Declaration On The Relation Of The Church To Non-Christian Religions: Nostra Aetate".

Mehmed II, his successor who was only 23 years old, later managed to conquer Constantinople in 1453 in a legendary attack, then changed the name of Constantinople to Istanbul, and converted the Hagia Sophia church into a mosque. Historical analysts note that if the attack of the Islamic Kingdom of Spain on Paris had not been thwarted by Charles Martel in Poitiers, which is only 70 km from Paris, in 732, and if the Ottomans succeeded in capturing Vienna in 1529 or 1683, the course of European history would have been very different.

This insistent threat of the Muslim World on the West, especially from Turkey, has been used as an excuse by Huntington in developing the clash of civilizations theory.

AGAINST HUNTINGTON'S THEORY

Pope Benedict XVI's visit to Istanbul, Turkey, was indeed a very smart move. The visit tactically suppressed the unrest of Muslims caused by the Regensburg speech, and encouraged the forgiveness of the long history of the West's hostility, hatred and historical grudges toward Islam, as mandated by the Second Vatican Council. It also challenged the truth and value of Huntington's clash of civilizations.

Indeed, ideologies of conflict, as in the theory of the clash of civilizations (said to occur after the collapse of the Soviet Union in 1990) are still happening, as mentioned by Ghazi in his honorary speech when he received the Eugen Biser Award in Munich, Germany on November 22, 2008.[223] According to Ghazi, the idea of "A Common Word" was precisely based on the pure desire to end the hostility of Muslims and Christians which has persisted for centuries. In other words, the visit of Pope Benedict XVI brought a mission of peace as mandated by one of the decrees of the Second Vatican Council, Nostra Aetate, to end the hostile relationship between Muslims and Christians which has prevailed for fourteen centuries. Moreover, in January 2011, the Abu Dhabi Gallup Center

---

223. Prince Ghazi bin Muhammad, *"A Common Word between Us and You,"* 269. Prince Ghazi bin Muhammad mentioned several examples of cases of "clash of civilizations" that still occur, including (1) the case of Jerusalem and Palestine, (2) American foreign policy against Iraq, (3) terrorism, (4) fundamentalism and fundamentalist propaganda, (5)) missionary activities from both sides, (6) historical, cultural, racial roots, misunderstanding and suspicion.

reported the results of its study, "Measuring the State of Muslim-West Relations, Assessing the New Beginning." The study was conducted over four years (2006–2010), with 100,000 respondents in 55 countries. The Gallup poll firmly rebutes Huntington's "Clash of Civilizations," reporting that the majority of the population surveyed view Muslim-West interactions as an advantage rather than a threat.[224]

Despite Pope Benedict XVI's visit to Istanbul, as well as the positive results of the Gallup poll, the hatred of the West against the Muslim World still exists. However, an Indonesian theologian, Frans Magnis-Suseno, argues that the animosity between Muslims and Christians throughout history, especially in the case of Indonesia, was by no means based on religious factors.[225]

HISTORICAL EVENTS AFTER THE SECOND VATICAN COUNCIL

Facing a dismissive Vatican, the new open letter aimed to not only ask for clarification of the Pope's speech, but highlight a more substantial and central issue in Christian-Islamic relations. It was later discovered that the initiative taken by Prince Ghazi was inseparable from an order by King Abdullah II, given the former's position as an adviser to the latter, to take the necessary measures to control the unhealthy Christian-Muslim relations caused by the Pope's speech in Regensburg. Thus, Prince Ghazi immediately took quick steps by drafting an open letter, written in English, and consulting with several major Jordanian scholars, including Grand Mufti Jordan Shaykh Nuh Al-Qu-da, and even with Seyyed Hossein Nasr, a professor of Islamic Studies at the George Washington University in Washington DC. Finally, on October 13, 2007, coinciding with Eid al-Fitr 1428 AH and a year after the delivery of the first open letter (13 October 2006), 138 Muslim scholars from many countries sent an open letter to Pope Benedict XVI and all the leaders of the Church worldwide, entitled "A Common Word Between Us and You.

In Chapter 10 of *A Common Word Between Us and You: 5-Year Anniversary Edition*,[226] Prince Ghazi bin Muhammad recounts his spe-

---

224. Gallup Inc., *"Measuring the State of Muslim-West Relations..."*

225. *www.citizenjournalism.online/2017/05/06/prof-dr-magnis-suseno-islam-adalah-agama-pertama-yang-menerapkan-toleransi*

226. The Royal Aal Al-Bayt Institute for Islamic Thought, *A Common Word be-*

cific and deep involvement in writing the draft of a second, more substantive, open letter entitled "A Common Word Between Us and You" (later shortened as "A Common Word"). The writing of "A Common Word," with notions such as 'love of God' and 'love your neighbor' as main motives, turned out to be very much inspired by his doctoral dissertation at Cambridge University (1988–1993). Professor Miroslav Volf of Yale Divinity School, Yale University—which provided much support for the letter—argued that the letter had very high and important historical momentum.

In fact, the first paragraph of the second open letter to Pope Benedict XVI, dated October 13, 2007, highlights the importance of the role of religious communities, especially Muslims and Christians, as pioneers of peace on earth, stating that:

> Muslims and Christians together make up well over half of the world population. Without peace and justice between these two religious communities, there can be no meaningful peace in the world. The future of the world depends on peace between Muslims and Christians.

Given the history of the relationship between the Muslim and Christian worlds during the fourteen centuries after the death of the Prophet Muhammad, this situation in 2007 was very different - the motive behind the common essence of the Prophet Muhammad's letters and "A Common Word," shifted from *an invitation to accept Islam and return to pure monotheism* to the need *to end centuries of bloody conflict* between religious believers and build peace.

Meanwhile, two major world religions, Islam and Christianity, are both missionary religions. Simply due to the competition to increase followers, friction is inevitable between these two religious communities. Still in every victory of Islamic rulers over new territories—from the Prophet Muhammad's conquering of Mecca to times of Islamic souvereignty in Spain—there was no forced conversion of the local population. Islam is indeed a preaching religion, yet it does so peaceably.[227]

Friction and conflict between Islam and Christianity, initially individual in nature, are now susceptible to national and international scales because of their relevance to the realm of wider pub-

---

tween Us and You, 5-Year Anniversary Edition, pp. 131–133.

227. Azyumardi Azra in his "Introduction" to Abdul Mu'ti and Fajar Riza Ul Haq, *Kristen Muhammadiyah*, xxi.

lic interests such as regional issues, natural resources, politics and power. History records that for fourteen centuries, Muslims and Christians have instigated and been involved in various humanitarian conflicts. It was precisely this fact that urged David Cordis to conclude that "religion has created more problems than providing solutions in human life."[228]

"A Common Word between Us and You" acknowledges that it is time to end the hostility and conflict between Muslims and Christians, and that Muslims and Christians must become the backbones and even the pioneers of the world peace process. Volf's opinion is correct that this open letter was an important historical milestone in the Islam-Christianity relationship after the Second Vatican Council.

FROM A CALL FOR MONOTHEISM TO A CALL FOR PEACE

Although the idea to write "A Common Word between Us and You" did originate from Muslim scholars' concerns over the papal speech at the University of Regensburg on September 12, 2006, the ideas in the open letter are ideas that were previously developed by Prince Ghazi. The central idea was derived from the 2005 Amman Message Declaration, which was an initiative of the King of Jordan, Abdullah II, and the result of a study by The Royal Aal Al-Bayt Institute for Islamic Thought, contained an agreement between various Islamic sects on issues of Islam and global humanity. The 2005 Amman Message Declaration, which was originally entitled "Love in the Qur'an," was finalized in an open letter format in September, 2007. The Amman Declaration emphasized that the relationship between Islam and Christianity must be more advanced than merel *polite theological dialogues, which will lead to a pseudo relationship*. Prince Ghazi further asserted:

> We had honestly ... only one motive: peace. We were aiming to try to spread peace and harmony between Christians and Muslims all over the world, not through governments and treaties but on the all-important popular and mass level, through the world's most influential popular leaders precisely— that is to say through the leaders of the two religions.[229]

---

228. David M. Cordis, "The Role of Religion in History," in David M. Cordis, George B. Grose and Muzammil H. Siddiqi (eds.), *The Abraham Connection*.

229. Prince Ghazi bin Muhammad, "A Common Word between Us and You," pp. 5–6.

The 2005 Amman Message contains an affirmation of the core values of Islam; chief among those values are caring, respect, tolerance, openness and freedom of religion, an agreement between Muslims that has been sustained for thousands of years. Given the historical and universal content of this agreement, the 2005 Amman Message was not only accepted by the Organization of Islamic Countries (OIC), but was also welcomed by nations at large. The "Three Key Points of 2005 Amman Message" gained further momentum when King Abdullah II ordered Ghazi bin Muhammad, his adviser, to take concrete steps, so that he took the initiative himself to write the initial draft of "A Common Word," combining the spirit of the 2005 Amman Message with his doctoral dissertation at Cambridge University.[230] The draft was then discussed with the Grand Mufti of Jordan, Shaykh Nuh Al-Quda, and several other major Jordanian scholars, and later with Professors Seyyed Hossein Nasr and David Ford, the supervisor of Professor Nasr's doctoral studies in 1988–1993.

SURAH ALI IMRAN VERSE 64 IS NOT A DIALOGUE REFERENCE

Some do not agree with the use of Surah Ali Imran verse 64, which was used as a reference in "A Common Word Between Us and You." Hafidz Abdulrahman maintains that this surah is not a justification for interreligious dialogue:

---

230. The Amman Message 2005, stems from King Abdullah II bin Al-Hussein's request to answer three basic questions about Islam, namely (1) What is Islam and what is not Islam, (2) Is it justified to declare one's disbelief or apostasy, and (3) Who has the authority to issue fatwas? On the advice of three major scholars, Shaykh Al-Azhar, Ayatollah Sistani and Sheikh Qaradawi, in July 2005 King Abdullah II held a Conference in Amman which was attended by 200 major scholars from 50 countries, which succeeded in formulating the 2005 Amman Message consisting of "Three Points of Amman Message", hence answers the three basic questions of King Abdullah II.

The Amman Message 2005 is a large historical and universal agreement between various sects in Islam, or *ijma 'ulama*, which has not been achieved for thousands of years, where for the first time the plurality of religious understanding was agreed, not only among Muslims, but also by non-Muslim communities. That is because the Amman Message 2005 opens a new universal understanding of various global humanitarian issues which include human rights, women's rights, religious freedom, Muslim life in non-Muslim countries, democratic governance and wrong views of radicalism and terrorism.

The above verse is often used as an argument by certain groups who try to justify Interreligious Dialogue, with the assumption that what the three religions—Islam, Christianity and Judaism—have in common is that all are divine religions. In fact, there is not a single word or phrase in the text above that can be used as an argument for the idea, both the phrase "kalimat[in] sawâ '[in] bainanâ wa bainakum" and the phrase "faqûlu isyhadû biannâ muslimûn.".[231]

Indeed, as admitted by Ghazi, "A Common Word" can be used as a basis for cooperation and humanitarian dialogue, but in itself is hardly able to bring about this kind of progress.

Moreover, Cardinal Jeane-Louis Tauran has stated that "*a theological dialogue with Islam is impossible; Muslims don't accept one question to the Qur'an, because it was written, they say, by the dictation from God.*"[232] In addition, the Archbishop of Canterbury, The Most Reverend Rowan Williams, argues that the theological differences between Islam and Christianity are "so serious" that it is impossible to resolve them through dialogue.[233] Seyyed Hossein Nasr, during the Catholic-Muslim Dialogue at the Vatican on 4–6 November 2008 (a follow-up to the open letter "A Common Word"), argued that:

with so many profound similarities, why then have we had such a long history of confrontation and opposition? The answer is that we of course also have our differences which have providentially kept Christianity and Islam distinct and separate.[234]

THE MOMENTUM FOR PEACE

The guidance of Allah and the choice to accept Islam or not, remain with each personAccording to Surah Al-Maaidah verse 48:

And We have revealed to you, (O Muhammad), the Book in truth, confirming that which preceded it of the Scripture and as a criterion over it. So judge between them by what Allah has revealed and do not follow their inclinations away from what has come to you of the truth. To each of you We prescribed a law and a method. Had Allah willed, He would have made you one nation (united in religion), but (He intended) to test

231. Hafidz Abdulrahman, "Tafsir Surah Ali Imran (3) Ayat 64: Kalimat Sawa," www.globalmuslim.web.id/2011/05/tafsir-surat-ali-imran-63.html

232. *A Common Word between Us and You* (Amman, Jordan: the Royal Aal al-Bayt Institute for Islamic Thought, 2009), 132.

233. *Ibid.*

234. *Ibid.*, 243.

Franz Magnis Suseno, a Jesuit Father and emeritus Professor at the Jakarta Dri-yarkara School of Philosophy, emphasized that Islam began practicing tolerance of others 1400 years ago. Most Christians implemented tolerance in the nineteenth century, while the Catholic Church only did so 50 years ago.

you in what He has given you; so race to (all that is) good. To Allah is your return all together, and He will (then) inform you concerning that over which you used to differ.

In addition, Allah also emphasizes that the acceptance of a religion cannot be forced, as stated in Surah Al-Baqarah verse 256:

There shall be no compulsion in (acceptance of) the religion. The right course has become clear from the wrong. So whoever disbelieves in Taghut and believes in Allah has grasped the most trustworthy handhold with no break in it. And Allah is Hearing and Knowing.

Now, fourteen centuries after the revelation was bestowed and the Prophet Muhammad sent a number of letters to religious leaders and regional rulers, humankind is still free to continue and choose their respective beliefs. Humans live in a plurality of religions, in which there has been friction in the course of life between religious believers, even among communities of faith.

Indeed, peace cannot be realized by one party, but requires commitment from both parties. "A Common Word" is a new initiative for peace in the form of helping hands from Muslims, and welcome support from the Christian world – truly a historic moment.

ISLAM AND THE WEST

However, it is important to realize that efforts to achieve peace can only be carried out if there is support from all related parties. Now, "A Common Word" is expected to foster a new momentum for a more structured, institutionalized, and sustainable peace movement between religious believers.

SUPPORT FOR "A COMMON WORD"

So serious and exhaustive were Prince Ghazi's measures[235] in preparing "A Common Word" that he not only consulted with Muslim scholars inside Jordan, but with several parties outside Jordan who are believed to have been of great help in spreading the letter and conditioning it in order to receive a quick and broad response. Consultations were also carried out with Christian figures, including Professor David Ford from Cambridge University and Bishop of London Richard Chartres, who enthusiastically supported the open letter idea from the start.

The response from Professor David Ford was, in fact, issued on the very same day as the delivery date of "A Common Word," October 13, 2007. This was because David Ford, who has institutional and personal connection with Ghazi bin Muhammad, was actively involved in helping the preparation of the substance to his dissemination of the "A Common Word" document. Professor Ford and Bishop Richard Chartres of London were prepared to provide a statement of support, once "A Common Word" was sent publicly. The Bishop of the Lutheran Church in America, Revd. Mark S. Hanson, gave his support on October 12, 2007, after receiving this letter from one of the Muslim scholars who signed the open letter, a day before "A Common Word" was officially sent.

In his spontaneous response, Prof. David Ford noted that the document "A Common Word" contains profound contents that emerge from the heart of the signatories, and that "A Common Word" seems to give "*an answer to the quiet times of the Islamic world*" after the World Trade Building attack, New York, September 11, 2001.[236]

In addition, Prince Ghazi was preparing for wide social media

---

235. The Royal Aal Al-Bayt Institute for Islamic Thought, *A Common Word between Us and You, 5-Year Anniversary Edition*, 133.

236. The Royal Aal Al-Bayt Institute for Islamic Thought, *A Common Word between Us and You*, pp. 77–80.

support. A well-known London-based public relations firm, Bell Portinger, contracted a special low cost for 3 months to support the dissemination of the open letter. The King of Jordan himself, Abdullah II, paid the fees for the public relations company. Realizing the importance of electronic media to expand and accelerate these new ideas, a website, *www.acommonword.com*, was opened before the open letter was sent.

The First Catholic – Muslim Forum, November 4, 2008, conducted by the Vatican. Pope Benedict XVI underlined that "religions are the instruments of peace."

The Second Catholic – Muslim Forum, November 13, 2011, took place at the baptism site in Jordan.

15

Contents of and Responses to
"A Common Word Between Us and You"

THE FIRST PART: THE RECIPIENTS OF THE LETTER

The open letter to Pope Benedict XVI and all church leaders world-wide, "A Common Word between Us and You,"[237] consists of several sections. It begins with an introduction stating the date of delivery, coinciding with Eid al-Fitri 1426 H/October 13, 2007, as well as the date of the previous letter, October 13, 2006. It then addresses the recipients, Pope Benedict XVI, followed by 26 names of leaders of other churches worldwide:

1. His All-Holiness Bartholomew I, Patriarch of Constantinople, New Rome;
2. His Beatitude Theodoros II, Pope and Patriarch of Alexandria and All Africa;
3. His Beatitude Ignatius IV, Patriarch of Antioch and All the East;
4. His Beatitude Theophilos III, Patriarch of the Holy City of Jerusalem;
5. His Beatitude Alexy II, Patriarch of Moscow and All Russia;
6. His Beatitude Pavle, Patriarch of Belgrade and Serbia;
7. His Beatitude Daniel, Patriarch of Romania;
8. His Beatitude Maxim, Patriarch of Bulgaria;
9. His Beatitude Ilia II, Archbishop of Mtskheta-Tbilisi, Catholicos-Patriarch of All Georgia;
10. His Beatitude Chrisostomos, Archbishop of Cyprus;
11. His Beatitude Christodoulos, Archbishop of Athens and All Greece;
12. His Beatitude Sawa, Metropolitan of Warsaw and All Poland;
13. His Beatitude Anastasios, Archbishop of Tirana, Durres and All Albania;
14. His Beatitude Christoforos, Metropolitan of the Czech and Slovak Republics;
15. His Holiness Pope Shenouda III, Pope of Alexandria and Patriarch of All Africa on the Apostolic Throne of St. Mark;

---

237. See Appendix.

16. His Beatitude Karekin II, Supreme Patriarch and Catholicos of All Armenians;
17. His Beatitude Ignatius Zakka I, Patriarch of Antioch and All the East, Supreme Head of the Universal Syrian Orthodox Church;
18. His Holiness MarThoma Didymos I, Catholicos of the East on the Apostolic Throne of St. Thomas and the Malankara Metropolitan;
19. His Holiness Abune Paulos, Fifth Patriarch and Catholicos of Ethiopia, Echege of the See of St. Tekle Haymanot, Archbishop of Axium;
20. His Beatitude Mar Dinkha IV, Patriarch of the Holy Apostolic Catholic Assyrian Church of the East;
21. The Most Rev. Rowan Williams, Archbishop of Canterbury;
22. Rev. Mark S. Hanson, Presiding Bishop of the Evangelical Lutheran Church in America, and President of the Lutheran World Federation;
23. Rev. George H. Freeman, General Secretary, World Methodist Council;
24. Rev. David Coffey, President of the Baptist World Alliance;
25. Rev. Setri Nyomi, General Secretary of the World Alliance of Reformed Churches;
26. Rev. Dr. Samuel Kobia, General Secretary, World Council of Churches,

And leaders of Christian Churches, everywhere...

THE SECOND PART: SUMMARY AND ABRIDGEMENT

The second part is a summary and abridgement of the scriptural review of the two religions, and explains why the 138 Muslim scholars felt the need to send the open letter. The first paragraph calls on Christians to realize their role as followers of the world's largest religion, and Muslims as adherents of the world's second largest religion, to join in bringing about peace in the world, stating:

> *Muslims and Christians together make up well over half of the world's population. Without peace and justice between these two religious communities, there can be no meaningful peace in the world. The future of the world depends on peace between Muslims and Christians.*[238]

The second paragraph, which is the core of the letter, contains an invitation to return to the two main commandments of both Islam

---

238. The Royal Aal Al-Bayt Institute for Islamic Thought, *A Common Word between Us and You* (Amman: The Royal Aal Al-Bayt Institute for Islamic Thought, 2009), 6.

and Christianity, namely love of the One God and love of one's neighbors (hereinafter referred to as 'a common word,' or the *kalimatun sawa*). In Islam, the love and relationship between humans and God is called *hablunminallah,* while love for neighbors, or fellow human beings, is called *hablunminanass.* This part cites Surah Ali Imran verse 64 as the main basis for the Muslim faith, and the Gospel of Mark 12:29–31 as the main basis for the Christian faith. The second paragraph of "A Common Word" states:

> The basis for this peace and understanding already exists. It is part of the very foundational principles of both faiths: love of the One God, and love of the neighbor. These principles are found over and over again in the sacred texts of Islam and Christianity. The Unity of God, the necessity of love for Him, and the necessity of love of the neighbour is thus the common ground between Islam and Christianity.[239]

Furthermore, several verses are quoted from the Holy Qur'an and the Bible relating to the Oneness of God and love for God, as well as several verses on love for fellow humans, including, among others: Of God's Unity, God says in the Holy Qur'an:

> "Say: He is God, the One! / God, the Self-Sufficient Besought of all! (Al-Ikhlas verses 1–2).

Of the necessity of love for God, God says in the Holy Qur'an:

> "So invoke the Name of thy Lord and devote thyself to Him with a complete devotion (Al-Muzzammil verse 8).

Of the necessity of love for the neighbour, Prophet Muhammad said:

> "None of you has faith until you love for your neighbor what you love for yourself."[240]

In the New Testament, Jesus Christ says:

> "The most important one," answered Jesus, "is this: 'Hear, O Israel: The Lord our God, the Lord is one. Love the Lord your God with all your heart and with all your soul and with all your mind and with all your strength. The second is this: 'Love your neighbor as yourself.' There is no commandment greater than these" (Mark, 12:29-31).

---

239. *Ibid.*
240. *Ibid.*, 6.

In the Qur'an, God commands Muslims to call upon Christians and Jews who hold a noble title, as the People of the Book:

> *Say, "O People of the Scripture, come to a word that is equitable between us and you—that we will not worship except Allah and not associate anything with Him and not take one another as lords instead of Allah." But if they turn away, then say, "Bear witness that we are Muslims (submitting to Him)"* (Ali Imran verse 64).

The closing paragraph of this second part of "A Common Word" contains the following concluding remarks:

> *The words: "we shall ascribe no partner unto Him" relate to the Unity of God, and the words: "worship none but God, relate to being totally devoted to God." Hence they all relate to the First and Greatest Commandment. According to one of the oldest and most authoritative commentaries on the Holy Qur'an the words: "that none of us shall take others for lords beside God," mean that none of us should obey the other in disobedience to what God has commanded. This relates to the Second Commandment because justice and freedom of religion are a crucial part of love of the neighbor. Thus in obedience to the Holy Qur'an, we as Muslims invite Christians to come together with us on the basis of what is common to us, which is also what is most essential to our faith and practice: the Two Commandments of love.*[241]

THE THIRD PART: DETAILED COMMENTARY

The third part contains a detailed commentary based on the Qur'an and the Bible concerning love of the One God and love of one's neighbors:

1. Love of God in the review of the Islamic Scriptures and Christian teachings;
2. Love of neighbors in the review of the Islamic and Christian Scriptures;
3. Come to a Common Word between Us and You.

It begins with a quote from Surah An-Nahl verse 125:

> *Invite to the way of your Lord with wisdom and good instruction, and argue with them in a way that is best. Indeed, your Lord is most knowing of who has strayed from His way, and He is most knowing of who is (rightly) guided.*

This Word of God teaches that, in seeking the way of God, one

---

241. *Ibid.*, 7.

should be virtuous and avoid actions such as force and violence, scolding and cursing, and harsh words.

The initiators of "A Common Word" understand this. In fact, the basic concept of "A Common Word" was developed from the 2005 Amman Message, a declaration from the Amman Conference on "The International Islamic Conference: True Islam and its Role in Modern Society," which focused on fighting the label of extremism in Islam. This negative impression of Islam had become especially strong after the collapse of the Twin Towers of the World Trade Center in New York on September 11th, 2001, which became the justification for George W. Bush's policy of "the war on terror." Newsweek columnist Fareed Zakaria praised the 2005 Amman Message as a step forward in changing this view, calling it the "the first of its kind" in which Muslim scholars and Islamic clerics united to oppose extremism, radicalism and call for interfaith peace.[242]

Ghazi discussed the draft of "A Common Word" with muftis and Muslim scholars from several countries, as well as Christian scholars Professor David F. Ford, Director of the Cambridge Interfaith Program at the University of Cambridge, and Richard Chartres, Bishop of London, who assessed the validity of the letter from a Christian point of view and helped to disseminate it. The last draft of the open letter was still being developed in a seminar on love in the Qur'an in September 2007. The seminar, organized by The Royal Aal Al-The Bayt Institute for Islamic Thought, was even attended by King Abdullah II, who commented:

> *Never before have the Muslims delivered this kind of definitive consensus statement on Christianity. Rather than engage in polemic, the signatories have adopted the traditional and mainstream Islamic position of respecting the Christian scriptures and calling Christians to be more, not less, faithful to it.*[243]

---

242. Fareed Zakaria, "How Can We Prevail. New Hope: Defeating terror requires Muslim help and much more than force of arms", *Newsweek*, July 18, 2005, US Edition, <http://www.fareedzakaria.com/articles/newsweek/071805.html>.

243. The Royal Aal Al-Bayt Institute for Islamic Thought, *A Common Word between Us and You, 5-Year Anniversary Edition*, 19.

LOVE OF GOD

Love of God in Islam

The Love of God must be understood as reciprocal; it means two things: First is God's love for humans, created as the most noble creatures on earth, and the heavens and the earth to be used by humans. Second is humans' love for God, the attitude of surrendering and serving God in accordance with the purpose of human creation. In Surah Ar-Rahmaan verses 1–78, it is stated how great is Allah's gift to humans, who are good at speaking, and who are blessed with the sun and moon that circulate according to calculations, plants, sky, fruits, sea, and so many other things, many which can be used by man and each of His creations. In verse 21, Allah says: *"fa bi ayyi aalla-i rabbikumaa tukadziban,"* or *"So which of the favors of your Lord would you deny?"*

Apart from Surah Ar-Rahman verses 1–78, the Qur'an contains many other messages about God's love for humankind, and humans' love for God. All 114 chapters in the Qur'an, from *Surah Al-Fatihah* to *Surah An Naas*, begin with the sentence, *"In the Name of Allah—the Most Compassionate, Most Merciful."*

The shahada

Part III of "A Common Word" begins with the *shahada* (testimony of faith): *"There is no God but Allah and Muhammad is the Messenger of Allah,"* a *conditio sine qua non* (essential requirement) for Muslims. Anyone who rejects the shahada cannot be a Muslim. The *shahada* is the basis for upholding Islamic law, and is where the Love of God begins.

It follows with a quote from the Prophet Muhammad:

> *The best that I have said—myself, and the prophets that came before me—is: There is no god but God. He alone, He hath no associate, His is the sovereignty and His is the praise and He hath power over all things.*[244]

Furthermore, "A Common Word" provides further explanation of this quote on the *love of God* and devotion to Him.

---

244. The Royal Aal Al-Bayt Institute for Islamic Thought, *A Common Word between Us and You*, 10.

The Prophet's verses on the love of God

In the quote, the words, "He Alone" refers to Surah Al-Ahzaab verse 4, when Allah says: *"Allah has not made for a man two hearts in his interior,"* that is, a person's love for God cannot be ambiguous.

The phrase *"He hath no associate"* is explained in Surah Al-Baqarah verse 165: "And [yet], among the people are those who take other than Allah as equals [to Him]. They love them as they (should) love Allah." Also, the word of Allah in Surah Az-Zumar verse 23: "Their skins and their hearts relax at the remembrance of Allah."

The phrase "His is the sovereignty" is explained by the words of Allah in Surah Al-Mulk verse 1: "Blessed is He in whose hand is dominion, and He is over all things competent."

The sentence "His is the praise and He hath power over all things" is in accordance with the word of Allah in Surah Al-'Ankabut verses 61–63:

> "If you asked them, 'Who created the heavens and earth and subjected the sun and the moon?' they would surely say, 'Allah.' Then how are they deluded? Allah extends provision for whom He wills of His servants and restricts for him. Indeed Allah is, of all things, Knowing. And if you asked them, 'Who sends down rain from the sky and gives life thereby to the earth after its lifelessness?' they would surely say 'Allah.' Say, 'Praise to Allah', but most of them do not reason."

So it can be concluded that the Prophet's assertion that there is no god but Allah, He is the only one, He has no partner, He is the only Ruler and He is praiseworthy and He is the one who rules over all, following the *shahada* sentence, "there is no god but Allah," reminds all that every Muslim must surrender both body and soul to fully serve God.

Thus, Allah said to the Prophet Muhammad in Surah Al-An'am verses 162–164:

> *Say, "Indeed, my prayer, my rites of sacrifice, my living and my dying are for Allah, Lord of the worlds. No partner has He. And this I have been commanded, and I am the first (among you) of the Muslims."* [245] *Say, "Is it other than Allah I should desire as a lord while He is the Lord of all things? And every soul earns not [blame] except against itself, and no bearer of burdens*

---

245. What is meant by phrase "The first (among you) of the Muslims," is the first Muslim among the people of Mecca.

248

will bear the burden of another. Then to your Lord is your return, and He will inform you concerning that over which you used to differ."

The Word of Allah in Surah Al-An'am verse 162 above— *"Indeed, my prayer, my rites of sacrifice, my living and my dying are for Allah, Lord of the worlds"* or *"inna shalaati wa nusukii wa mahyaaya wa mamaatii lil-laahi rabbil 'aalmin"*—describes how comprehensive the attitude of a Muslim is in surrendering and loving Allah.

Love of God as the first and greatest commandment of God in the Bible

A discussion of the love of God from the Bible review begins by quoting the Shema[246] in Deuteronomy, 6:4–5, of the Old Testament and the Jewish liturgy, which says:

> *"Hear, O Israel: The Lord our God, the Lord is one. Love the Lord your God with all your heart and with all your soul and with all your strength."*

Then, in the New Testament, there is a passage detailing when Jesus Christ was asked about the Greatest Commandment:

> *"Hearing that Jesus had silenced the Sadducees, the Pharisees got together. One of them, an expert in the law, tested him with this question: 'Teacher, which is the greatest commandment in the Law?' Jesus replied: 'Love the Lord your God with all your heart and with all your soul and with all your mind.' This is the first and greatest commandment. And the second is like it: 'Love your neighbor as yourself.' All the Law and the Prophets depend on these two commandments"* (Matthew, 22:34-40).

Both the Old Testament Scriptures and the New Testament mention that the first and greatest commandment is loving God, and it is widely found in the Old and New Testaments, such as in Mark, 12:28–31; Deuteronomy 4:29, 10:12 , 11:13 (also in parts of the Shema), 13: 3, 26:16, 30: 2, 30: 6, 20:10; Joshua 22: 5; Mark 12:32–33; and Luke 10:27– 28.

Between the Gospels, there are different versions and languages – for example, the Old Testament is in Hebrew, and the original statement of Jesus in the New Testament is in Aramaic, which was later

---

246.   www.hebrew4christians.com/scriptures/Torah/The_shema/theshema. html. The shema is the central prayer in the Jewish prayer book (Siddur). The complete shema consists of three parts that are connected to each other and constitute one unit, which consists of (1) Shema (Deuteronomy 6:4–5), (2) Vehayah (Deuteronomy 11:13–21) and (3) Vaiyomer (Deuteronomy 15:37–41).

transcribed into Greek – but the command to love God, or love of God, is still equally regarded as the first and greatest commandment.

Teachings about the love of God, which were revealed by Allah and written in the Qur'an, in the words of the Prophet Muhammad, and in the teachings in the Old and New Testaments, differ in versions and contexts; however, all emphasize the absolute importance of loving and serving God.[247]

LOVE OF THE NEIGHBOR

Love of Neighbors in Islam

In Islam, loving neighbors is a very essential and integral part of trusting and loving God. Being Muslim without love for neighbors is tantamount to weak love for God. Pertaining to that, the Prophet Muhammad said:

> "None of you has faith until you love for your brother what you love for yourself."[248] And: "None of you has faith until you love for your neighbor what you love for yourself."[249]

However, as Allah says in Surah Al-Baqarah verse 177, empathy and sympathy for neighbors, even in the form of prayer, is not enough. Loving neighbors must also be in the form of good deeds and even sacrifices:

> Righteousness is not that you turn your faces toward the east or the west, but (true) righteousness is (in) one who believes in Allah, the Last Day, the angels, the Book, and the prophets and gives wealth, in spite of love for it, to relatives, orphans, the needy, the traveler, those who ask (for help), and for freeing slaves; (and who) establishes prayer and gives zakah; (those who) fulfill their promise when they promise; and (those who) are patient in poverty and hardship and during battle. Those are the ones who have been true, and it is those who are the righteous.

Likewise, the word of Allah in Ali Imran verse 92 states:

> Never will you attain the good (reward) until you spend (in the way of Allah) from that which you love. And whatever you spend—indeed, Allah is Knowing of it.

---

247. The grammatical word 'common' (*sawa*) a common word between us and you also means just or fair.

248. Shahih Al-Bukhori, Kitab al-Iman, Hadith no. 13.

249. Sahih Muslim, Kitab al-Iman, 67-1, Hadith no. 45.

Love of Neighbors in the Gospel

In Christianity, the words of Jesus Christ affirm that loving one's neighbors is the second greatest commandment of God after the Love of God. As stated in Matthew 22:38-40: "This is the first and greatest commandment. And the second is like it: 'Love your neighbor as yourself.' All the Law and the Prophets depend on these two commandments."

The commandment to love your neighbor, as well as the commandment to love God, is also found in the Old Testament, Leviticus 19:17-18:

> "Do not hate a fellow Israelite in your heart. Rebuke your neighbor frankly so you will not share in their guilt. Do not seek revenge or bear a grudge against anyone among your people, but love your neighbor as yourself. I am the Lord".

Thus, the first commandment to love God and the second commandment to love our neighbors require magnanimity and sacrifice. These two laws depend on the entire law and the Prophets.

COME TO A COMMON WORD BETWEEN US AND YOU

"A Common Word"

This document realizes that there are many differences in the teachings of Islam and Christianity, and these differences cannot be overlooked. Yet, the similarities between the two in the two greatest commandments are a true *common ground, kalimatun sawa,* between the Qur'an, the Torah and the Bible. God for the Shema in the Torah, starting with Deuteronomy 6:4, states:

> "Hear, O Israel: The Lord our God, the Lord is one."

Meanwhile, Allah says in Surah Al-Iklhas 112, verses 1-2:

> "Say, 'He is Allah, the One. Allah is the All-embracing.'"

Such is the importance of the meaning of the two commandments of God, that Jesus Christ said in the Gospel of Matthew 22:40,

> *"All the Law and the Prophets hang on these two commandments."*

The words of Jesus are reinforced by Surah Fussilat verse 43:

> *"Nothing is said to you, (O Muhammad), except what was already said to the*

messengers before you."

This is confirmed again by the word of Allah in Surah Al-Ahqaaf verse 9:

> *"Say, I am not a novelty among the Apostles, nor do I know what will be done with me or with you, I just follow whatever is revealed to me, and I am just a manifest warner."*

The Qur'an also affirms the importance of the Oneness of God, the need for submission to God, and the importance of loving God and fellow human beings in the following chapters:

> *And We certainly sent into every nation a messenger, (saying), "Worship Allah and avoid Taghut."*[250] *And among them were those whom Allah guided, and among them were those upon whom error was (deservedly) decreed. So proceed through the earth and observe how was the end of the deniers* (An-Nahl, verse 36).

> *We have already sent Our messengers with clear evidences and sent down with them the Scripture and the balance that the people may maintain (their affairs) in justice. And We sent down iron, wherein is great military might and benefits for the people, and so that Allah may make evident those who support Him and His messengers unseen. Indeed, Allah is Powerful and Exalted in Might* (Al-Hadiid, verse 25).

"Between Us and You"

Before getting into the core of the call or invitation for dialogue "between us and you," or between Muslims and Christians (through the Pope and leaders of all denominations of the Christian church), "A Common Word" again quotes Surah Al-Baqarah verses 136–137, which confirm the existence of a common ground between the two major world religions:

> Say, (O believers), "We have believed in Allah and what has been revealed to us and what has been revealed to Abraham and Ishmael and Isaac and Jacob and the Descendants and what was given to Moses and Jesus and what was given to the prophets from their Lord. We make no distinction between any of them, and we are Muslims (in submission) to Him".

> So if they believe in the same as you believe in, then they have been

---

250. Thagut are those who worship other than Allah.

(rightly) guided; but if they turn away, they are only in dissension, and Allah will be sufficient for you against them. And He is the Hearing, the Knowing.

The third part ends with an invitation: "A Common Word" should not only become the basis of ecumenical dialogue between religious leaders, but a dialogue for peace between religious believers, to prevent interreligious conflicts that occurred in the past from being repeated, and encouraging religious practitioners to become pioneers and activators of peace. The rapid development of military technology means the stakes are even higher in conflicts between religious believers. Christians make up one-third, and Muslims make up one-fifth of the earth's population, so that the total number of adherents to these two major religions is no less than 55% of the earth's population. If an understanding between them can be realized, then this would be a major step toward world peace.

Finally, "A Common Word" closed with Al-Maa'idah 5, verse 48,

And We have revealed to you, (O Muhammad), the Book in truth, confirming that which preceded it of the Scripture and as a criterion over it. So judge between them by what Allah has revealed and do not follow their inclinations away from what has come to you of the truth. To each of you We prescribed a law and a method. Had Allah willed, He would have made you one nation (united in religion), but (He intended) to test you in what He has given you; so race to (all that is) good. To Allah is your return all together, and He will (then) inform you concerning that over which you used to differ.

NOTABLE RESPONSES FROM RELIGIOUS FIGURES AND GROUPS

As noted, the second open letter, "A Common Word between Us and You," received overwhelming responses from all around the world, including the Catholic Church, religious leaders and several well-known universities. The response and support entitled "Loving God and Neighbor Together: A Christian Response to A Common Word between Us and You," which was widely published by The Yale Center for Faith and Culture, greatly influenced the Vatican's attitude. Just two days after the publication of the Yale University document, the Vatican's Secretary of State, Cardinal Tarcisio Bertone, on behalf of Pope Benedict XVI, sent a reply letter to Prince Ghazi bin Muhammad. Since then, the Vatican has taken concrete measures to build a Muslim-Christian dialogue by forming the Catholic-Muslim Forum.

The Catholic-Muslim Vatican Forum held the Catholic-Muslim Dialogue I at the Vatican on November 4–6, 2008. This was followed by the Catholic-Muslim Dialogue II on November 21–24, 2011, at the Baptism Site in Jordan, and later by the Catholic-Muslim Dialogue III in Rome on November 11–13, 2014. The Catholic-Muslim Dialogue I, which was attended by 24 participants and 5 advisers, took the theme "Love of God, Love of Neighbor: the Dignity of the Human Person and Mutual Respect." At the end of his remarks at the Catholic-Muslim Dialogue I, Pope Benedict XVI further asserted:

> "Let us resolve to overcome past prejudices and to correct the often-distorted images of the other which even today can create difficulties in our relations; let us work with one another to educate all people, especially the young, to build a common future."[251]

The Catholic-Muslim Dialogue I was held in a warm and friendly gathering, full of brotherhood. It discussed two main themes, "Theological and Spiritual Foundations" and "Human Dignity and Mutual Respect." The Catholic-Muslim Dialogue I produced 15 Points of Recommendation, of which the 11th point emphasizes:

> We profess that Catholics and Muslims are called to be the instruments of love and harmony among believers, and for humanity as a whole, renouncing any oppression, aggressive violence and terrorism, especially that committed in the name of religion, and upholding the principle of justice for all.[252]

The Muslim Catholic Dialogue II was attended by 24 delegations, discussing three themes: reason, faith and the human person. The Catholic-Muslim Dialogue III, under the theme of "Working Together to Serve Others," discussed three main topics: working together to serve young people, enhancing interreligious dialogue, and service to society. In this third Dialogue, various forms of Catholic-Muslim cooperation that have been carried out in the field of education and various other forms of philanthropic activities were highlighted. The entire Catholic-Muslim Dialogue III delegation agreed on the need:

---

251. *Ibid.*, pp. 37–38.
252. *Ibid.*, 247.

to work together to face various tensions and conflicts in the world. Furthermore, the dialogue condemns all forms of terror, violence and persecution against innocent people, and the destruction of holy places and historical or cultural heritage. Moreover, it is absolutely unjustified that such violent and destructive acts are carried out in the name of religion.[253]

The Royal Aal Al-Bayt Institute has specifically reported several key responses received shortly after the submission of the document "A Common Word" in its *5-Year Anniversary Edition A Common World*, including:

1. Bishop Rev. Mark S. Hanson, Presiding Bishop of the Evangelical Lutheran Church in America, on October 12, 2007;
2. Prof. John Esposito, Professor of Religion and International Affairs, Georgetown University, on October 22, 2007;
3. H.E. Cardinal Angelo Scola, Patriarch of Venice, on October 24, 2007;
4. The Yale Response signed by over 300 leading Christian scholars, on November 18, 2007
5. H.H. Pope Benedict XVI's Response From the Vatican, on November 19, 2007
6. Daniel Madigan SJ, The Vatican's Commission for Religious Relations with Muslims, on January 18, 2008
7. Rev. Dr. Samuel Kobia, World Council of Churches (WCC), on March 18, 2008
8. His Holiness Patriarch Alexy II, Patriarch of Moscow and all Russia, on April 14, 2008
9. The Most Revd. and Rt. Hon. Rowan Williams, The Archbishop of Canterbury, on July 14, 2008
10. Extended response from the Baptist World Alliance, The Revd. David Coffey, The Revd. Neville Callam, The Revd. Prof. Paul S. Fiddes and The Revd. Regina Claas, on December 26, 2008

The responses from leaders of the prominent churches mentioned above are very representative of the majority of Catholics and Christians around the world. Below are more notable responses:

Pope Benedict XVI

In his response to "A Common Word" through the Vatican's Secretary of State, Cardinal Tarcisio Bertone, dated November 19, 2007—a day after Yale University's response—Pope Benedict XVI,

---

253. *Ibid.*

among others, said:

> *"I am profoundly convinced that we must not yield to the negative pressures in our midst, but must affirm the values of mutual respect, solidarity and peace. The life of every human being is sacred, both for Christians and for Muslims. There is plenty of scope for us to act together in the service of fundamental moral values."*[254]

Prof. John S. Esposito

In his response on October 22, 2007, Professor John S. Esposito, professor of Religion and International Relations at Georgetown University, wrote:

> *"This is really the first time in history that we have an initiative where Muslims have collectively come together and agreed on the fundamental principles that bind them to Christians, love of the One God and neighbor. This historic document is a crystal-clear message of peace and tolerance from 138 Muslim leaders from across the Islamic world."*[255]

Request for forgiveness from Yale University

Yale University after quickly holding a large Seminar in response to "A Common Word", then sent a letter of support signed by 300 Christian pastors and theologians on November 18, 2007, apologizing first and acknowledging their *guilt* for past actions towards Muslims by stating:

> We want to begin by acknowledging that in the past (e.g. in the Crusades) and in the present (e.g in excesses of the 'war on terror') many Christians have been guilty of sinning against our Muslim neighbors.

> Before we 'shake your hand' in responding to your letter, we ask forgiveness of the All-Merciful One and of the other Muslim communities around the world. We share the sentiment of the Muslim signatories expressed in the opening line of the open letter.

> *Peaceful relations between Muslims and Christians stand as one of the central challenges of this century. Though tensions, conflicts and even wars in which Christians and Muslims stand against each other are not primarily*

---

254. The Royal Aal Al-Bayt Institute for Islamic Thought, *A Common Word between Us and You, 5-Year Anniversary Edition*, pp. 163–164.

255. *Ibid.*, 139.

religious in character, they possess undeniable religious dimensions.[256]

The response from Yale University further supports the sentiment that the 'war on terror' was a mistake, and Samuel Huntington's *clash of civilizations* theory. Between this and the Crusades, Muslims endured long centuries of persecution and oppression under the name of colonialism, which until now, according to Franz Magnis-Suseno, *"left scars in the collective memory of Muslims."* In return, some argue, Islamic-based groups such as the Taliban commit acts of terrorism. But again, such conflict is exactly the reason why the Nostra Aetate Declaration from the Second Vatican Council and "A Common Word" emerged, to forget the past and build a human future that is free from the violence and radicalism that only bring prolonged suffering. Therefore, if the efforts to bring about peace are not yet deemed fruitful, the spirit of that peace found within "A Common Word" is at the very least a good place to start.

THE POWER OF "A COMMON WORD BETWEEN US AND YOU"

"A Common Word," other than being a very significant measure on the part of Muslims to improve their relationships with Christians after the Second Vatican Council, is also a major step in the custom of communication by letter, following the traditions of the Prophet Muhammad SAW.

While the Prophet Muhammad and the 138 Muslim scholars both used Surah Ali Imran verse 64 as their central theme, their situations were very different, and hence Surah Ali Imran verse 64 in the two letters should be interpreted differently. "A Common Word" takes into account theological differences, especially the concept of pure monotheism as one of the most fundamental tenets in the Abrahamic religions. In fact, without this tenet, it would be difficult to propose a basis of cooperation between Christianity and Islam. The concept of oneness of God, or tawhid, in Islam is very contrary to the concept of the Trinity in Catholic and Christian teachings. Nevertheless, Islam respects Prophet Isa as the Messiah, or Al-Masih. In the spirit of religious freedom and mutual respect, cooperation between Islam and Christianity can still be built, even though, for example, Muslims still oppose the

---

256. *Ibid.*, 144.

practice of aggressive proselytization by some churces.[257]

It is hoped and strongly believed that the cordial relationship between Muslims and Christians will end fourteen centuries of hostility, which inflicted loss of life and property to both parties, but even worse, tainted the image of religious communities, since engaging in enmity can only prove that both groups of religious believers have denied the true purposes of their respective religion while at the same time denying human rights in the name of religion. It cannot be denied that violence in the name of religion is not a monopoly of any one religious adherent, but occurs among all followers of religion.

Hate speech against Islam was certainly employed by Pope Urban II to ignite the embers of hatred against Islam in his agitating speech in Clermont on November, 25, 1095. Among the consequences of this is "Crusades syndrome," or stigmatization of Islam which consciously or subconsciously still haunts the Western world and Christian society in the post-Vatican II Council era. The massacre in Srebrenica in Bosnia, right after the breakup of Yugoslavia, is an example of the syndrome's persistence. It is why, according to Edward W. Said, Western emotions regarding Islam are so easily ignited. Said further argues that culture is not static, but develops dynamically, as does the relationship between cultures, and maintains that Huntington was overly influenced by a history of prolonged hostility between Islam and Christianity in Europe.[258]

Ghazi bin Muhammad bin Talal, in his speech on the occasion of the Eigen Biser Award in Munich on November 22, 2008, expressed his view that, in addition to the World Trade bomb tragedy on September 11, 2001, there were a number of incidents between Islamic civilization and the Western-Christian World which were employed to justify the clash of civilizations theory. Such incidents included: (1) the question of Jerusalem and Palestine, (2) discontentment with US Foreign Policy (especially the war in Iraq), (3) terrorism, (4) fundamentalism and fundamentalist propaganda (on both sides), (5) missionary activity (also on both sides), and

---

257. The Royal Aal Al-Bayt Institute for Islamic Thought, *A Common Word between Us and You, 5-Year Anniversary Edition*, 243.

258. Dr. Zainal Abidin in discussion "Great Thinkers," <Crcs.ugm.ac/id/artikel/339/menguji-the-clash-of-civilization-samuel-p-huntington-2.html>

(6) deeply rooted, historical, cultural and racial misunderstanding, suspicion, and even loathing.[259] It is strange and sad, yet understandable how Islam, as "the first religion that teaches the first tolerance," according to Magnis-Suseno, is now accused of being anti-peaceful and anti-peace instead.[260]

Ghazi also cited Georgetown University's comprehensive international survey of religious history published by John Esposito and Dahia Mogahed, which stated that "60% of Christians worldwide harbor prejudice against Muslims and 30% of Muslims harbor prejudice against Christians,"[261] especially regarding war and genocide based on religion. The Bosnian Grand Mufti, Dr. Mustafa Ceric, who also received the Eigen Biser, experienced genocide firsthand in Yugoslavia, a country which was initially considered solid and united when it was under President Joseph Broz Tito. John Esposito, in his response to the letter dated October 22, 2007, argued that "A Common Word" truly answers the question, "where are the voices of moderate Muslims?" Thus, one can say that "A Common Word" was sent at the right time. In the end—in the midst of the threat of various forms of violence and war, from religion and politics, as well as the world's ever-increasing population—an awareness and demand for peace is absolutely necessary.

259. The Royal Aal Al-Bayt Institute for Islamic Thought, *A Common Word between Us and You*, 260.

260. www.citizenjournalism.online/2017/05/06/prof-dr-magnis-suseno-islam-adalah-agama-pertama-yang-menerapkan-toleransi

261. The Royal Aal Al-Bayt Institute for Islamic Thought, *A Common Word between Us and You, 5-Year Anniversary Edition*, 251.

PART 4

THE WAY FORWARD TOWARD
THE AGENDA FOR HUMANITY

In modern society, the paradigm of "us versus others" has been changing gradually into the paradigm of a "universal mankind."

Franz Magnis Suseno SJ

16

Toward the Agenda for Humanity

WORLD INTERFAITH HARMONY WEEK

After receiving extensive support from Christian and Catholic communities worldwide, on October 20, 2010, Ghazi bin Muhammad bin Talal, advisor to Radja Jordan, Abdullah II, submitted a proposal before the United Nations General Assembly in New York. The proposal was put forward by Jordan and supported by 29 co-sponsoring countries, including Albania, Azerbaijan, Bahrain, Bangladesh, Costa Rica, the Dominican Republic, Egypt, El-Salvador, Georgia, Guatemala, Guyana, Honduras, Kazakhstan, Kuwait, Liberia, Libya, Mauritius, Morocco, Oman, Paraguay, Qatar, the Russian Federation, Saudi Arabia, Tanzania, Tunisia, Turkey, the United Arab Emirates, Uruguay, and Yemen.[262]

This effort brought positive results. The United Nations General Assembly issued a draft Resolution No. A/ 65/5 entitled "The World Interfaith Harmony Week," which was unanimously passed after receiving proposals and diplomatic lobbying from Arab Muslim countries, Central American countries, and Russia. The 2010 resolution contains, among others, the following proposals:

1. Reaffirms that mutual understanding and interreligious dialogue constitute important dimensions of a culture of peace;
2. Proclaims the first week of February every year the World Interfaith Harmony Week between all religions, faiths and beliefs;
3. Encourages all States to support, on a voluntary basis, the spread of the message of interfaith harmony and goodwill in the world's churches, mosques, synagogues, temples and other places of worship during that week, based on love of God and love of one's neighbor or on love of the good and love of one's neighbor, each according to their own religious traditions or convictions;
4. Requests the Secretary-General to keep the General Assembly informed of the implementation of the present resolution.

---

262. https://en.wikipedia.org/wiki/World_Interfaith_Harmony_Week

An Interfaith session of the United Nations in New York was conducted on July 17, 2017

WORLD HUMANITARIAN SUMMIT

The increasing humanitarian role of religious communities is evident in the United Nations' holding of the "World Humanitarian Summit" on May 23-24, 2016, in Istanbul. In his opening speech, Ban Ki-Moon, then the Secretary General of the United Nations, stated: "The aspirations of the World Humanitarian Summit are to stand up for our common humanity and take action to prevent and reduce human suffering."[263] In his report, "The Road to Istanbul," Ban Ki-Moon observes the dramatic escalation of the humanitarian crisis in the post-World War II era, illustrating the international community's frustration at the multiplicity of humanitarian crises and the enormous costs involved in overcoming them, marked by a lack of unity and solidarity.

Furthermore, Ban Ki-Moon states that efforts to overcome these crises require a unified vision. It must be inclusive and universal, involving all countries and various communities, and accepting of various cultural, political and religious differences. Humanity must become grounded in a set of common values, 'One Humanity' of various ethnic differences, national identities, religious beliefs and customs, and cultures.[264]

---

263. The Royal Aal Al-Bayt Institute for Islamic Thought, *A Common Word between Us and You, 5-Year Anniversary Edition*, 125.

264. The United Nations, "Secretary-General Urges Reaffirmation of 'Our Common Humanity', at World Humanitarian Summit Round Table on Political Leadership," https://www.un.org/press/en/2016/sgsm17777.doc.htm

Ban Ki-Moon also calls on all nations, civil society and world leaders to build a global effort, to jointly prevent the erosion of humanity and international human rights. Moreover, he argues that the Istanbul World Humanitarian Summit is an initial test for the commitment of the international community in raising global humanitarian solidarity which is truly based on the spirit of 'no one left behind' for those who bear various humanitarian risks caused by natural disasters, conflicts, and violence.

According to Ban Ki-Moon's report, patterns of displacement have changed over time. More than half of the 19.4 million refugees and 38 million internally displaced persons currently live outside of refugee camps. In 2014 alone, everyday conflict and violence caused 42,000 people to leave their homelands to seek safety, both nearby and abroad. Also, in 2014, it was estimated that "the average length of displacement owing to war and persecution is 17 years," while only one percent of the refugees have managed to return to their home communities.[265]

ONE HUMANITY, SHARED RESPONSIBILITY

The World Humanitarian Summit is the beginning and peak of the UN agenda in the field of peace and humanity. There has perhaps never been a UN agenda prepared in such detail and extending over so long a time that also involves so many agencies within the UN itself, member states, international humanitarian agencies, and participants.

Initiated by UN Secretary General Ban Ki-Moon in January, 2012, the summit, under the theme of "One Humanity, Shared Responsibility," involved consultations with 23,000 people in 153 countries, and was attended by 9,000 participants from 173 countries and 55 heads of government. Eight regional consultations had also been held before ideas were further discussed at the Global Consultation in Geneva on October 14–16, 2015. The results of the summit were submitted to one of the United Nations agencies in the humanitarian sector, the Geneva-based United Nations Office

---

265. The United Nations General Assembly, "One humanity: shared responsibility Report of the Secretary-General for the World Humanitarian Summit," https://agendaforhumanity.org/sites/default/files/Secretary-General%27s%20 Report%20for%20WHS.pdf

Fifty Five Heads of State attended the Inauguration of the World Humanitarian Summit in Istanbul, May 23-24 2016.

for the Coordination Humanitarian Affairs (UNOCHA).[266]

The World Humanitarian Summit in Istanbul, as reported in the "2017 Annual Synthesis Report," created an Agenda for Humanity consisting of 3,700 commitments divided into five main commitments or five core responsibilities:

THE FIRST CORE RESPONSIBILITY: Global leadership to prevent and end conflict. Preventing conflicts and finding political solutions to resolve them is our first and foremost responsibility to humanity;

THE SECOND CORE RESPONSIBILITY: Uphold the norms that safeguard humanity. Every day, civilians are deliberately or indiscriminately killed in wars. We are witnessing the erosion of 150 years of international humanitarian law;

THE THIRD RESPONSIBILITY: Leave no one behind. The World Humanitarian Summit is the first test of our commitment to transform the lives of those most at risk of being left behind;

THE FOURTH RESPONSIBILITY: Change people's lives—from delivering aid to ending need. Success must now be measured by how all people's vulnerability and risk are reduced, not by how needs are met year after year. Ending need will require three

---

266. *http://www.worldhumanitariansummit.org/*

fundamental shifts in the way we work: Reinforce, don't replace national systems; Anticipate, don't wait for crises; Transcend the humanitarian-development divide;

THE FIFTH RESPONSIBILITY: Invest in Humanity. Accepting and acting upon our shared responsibilities for humanity requires political, institutional and financial investment.[267]

Criticisms were conveyed, especially regarding how to ensure that the 3,700 commitments would actually be carried out by all stakeholders or interested parties. The main concern is the lack of a binding agreement. However, the major supporters of the World Summit expressed their optimism, stating that "as a non-intergovernmental process,"[268] in that non-international organizations have never considered that every decision must be binding, for it is realized that the characteristics of independence and self-sufficiency of civil society organizations will consistently carry out all these commitments, with or without the 'binding' clause.

Although there is still a long way to go to solidify the consolidation of the agreement between Christians and Muslims in responding to the various Humanitarian Agendas, at least "A Common Word"—with various follow-ups at various levels, from international, regional to local levels—has confirmed the agreement to unite the vision of humanity between Christians and Muslims. Religious communities must unite and ground their shared vision, in One Humanity.

COMMITMENT TO ACTIONS

The UN Secretary General's report on the World Humanitarian Summit ended with "Commitments to Action." This document further outlines many of the global commitments of all nations to the Agenda for Humanity, which is the central essence of the Istanbul World Humanitarian Summit agreement. "Commitments to Action" is a point of departure, including all collective hopes to see radical progress for refugees and other victims of crises. "Commitments to Action" is an elaboration of the Five Core Responsibilities of the Agenda for Humanity.

In addition to the growing development of humanitarian ser-

---

267. https://sgreport.worldhumanitariansummit.org/
268. *Ibid.*

vice institutions at various levels in the world—ranging from international, regional, national and local levels that provide direct or
supporting services – and along with the increasing and widening
of various humanitarian problems that must be answered, several
humanitarian study centers are now emerging and growing. The
missions of humanitarian study centers are to explore the development of humanitarian challenges and trends, as well as predict
new challenges that must be faced and answered by the humanitarian service agency. Catastrophic challenges in the future may
very well occur due to complex causes, such as population den-
sity, seizure of territories and natural resources, extreme climate
change and water stress, nuclear accidents, mega tsunamis, failed
states and so on.

   The founders of humanitarian study center The Humanitarian
Futures Programme, Dr. Randolph Kent[269] of King's College, London, noted that most of the humanitarian missions carried out in
humanitarian crisis centers worldwide—to address various conflicts and humanitarian crises in various parts of the world—are
carried out by various humanitarian organizations, including non-
governmental organizations (NGOs), at various levels. However,
these humanitarian NGOs have to face various internal and external obstacles that limit their movement. Kent further argued:

> Civil society delivers some 70% of the last mile of international
> humanitarian assistance. An NGO crisis would mean a crisis of the
> entire humanitarian system... The humanitarian system may already
> be different than the traditional actors perceive.[270]

Kent further asserted that humanitarian organizations from the
international, local to community levels must jointly seek new
formulations on how to build a system of cooperation and collabo-

---

269. In July 2007, at the Mahakam Hotel, Jakarta, I was introduced by Jamilah
Mahmood, Director of Mercy Malaysia / Secretary General of the International
Federation of the Red Cross / Crescent (IFRC) in Geneva, to Dr. Randolph Kent of
King's College London, to be interviewed on the development of The Humanitar-
ian Future Programme. So on, until now Dr. Randolph Kent always updates the
development of The Humanitarian Future to the author via a mailing list.

270. The Humanitarian Futures Programme, "The Future of Non-Governmental Organizations in the Humanitarian Sector: Global transformations and their
consequences," *https://reliefweb.int/sites/reliefweb.int/files/resources/The-Future-of-
Humanitarian-NGOs-HFP-Discussion-Paper-Aug2013-copy.pdf*

rate and criticize their new roles. This assertion derives from his studies carried out intensively for ten years in various disciplines from social sciences, to the government, military circles, and various humanitarian organizations and religious organizations, from global to local levels. The Humanitarian Futures Programme explores several key issues related to the trend of the threat of future humanitarian crises. In general, there are several challenges that humanitarian organizations have to face, based on different concepts of risk, which include:

1. The changing nature of humanitarian crisis threats
2. Political and socio-economic changes in a post-Western hegemonic age
3. A new vulnerability paradigm cutting across all sectors of society
4. Emerging opportunities to offset even some of the most extreme crisis drivers
5. Institutional constraints that will have to be overcome to ensure effective means for dealing with ever-more complex crisis drivers.[271]

---

271. The Humanitarian Futures Programme, "The Virtuous Triangle and the Fourth Dimension: The Humanitarian, Private and Military Sectors in a Fragile World," *https://www.humanitarianfutures.org/wp-content/uploads/2014/06/Virtuous-Triangle-the-Fourth-Dimension-web.pdf*

17

The Shrinking of Humanitarian Space

THE SHRINKING OF HUMANITARIAN SPACE AND ITS IMPACT

The shrinking of humanitarian space is the result of the escalating conflicts occuring in various parts of the world. This has an increasingly complex impact, and requires a new paradigm. Logistical assistance alone—without touching the basic causes of conflict and various approaches to organizing humanitarian movements (such as synergy between Islamic and Christian humanitarian agencies)—will never be able to solve the problem. In his preparatory report for the implementation of the Istanbul World Humanitarian Summit, Ban Ki-Moon asserted that the escalation of conflict and resulting humanitarian crises are due to the limited scale of humanitarian efforts, which require international collaboration from all cultural, political, and religious groups. This shrinking of humanitarian space is a rising concern for various global humanitarian agencies.

In that regard, Sarah Collinson and Samir Elhawary of the Humanitarian Policy Group, Overseas Development Institute (HPG, ODI, London), conducted a study in 2012 entitled "Humanitarian space: a review of trends and issues." In this study, HPG ODI provides an overview of the meaning, history, and trends of humanitarian space, how its decline affects the international humanitarian system, and how humanitarian actors should respond. They list several definitions of humanitarian space, in terms of:

First, humanitarian agencies: "The humanitarian agency is at the center of this definition, with humanitarian space delineating the agency's ability to operate freely and meet humanitarian needs in accordance with the principles of humanitarian action."
Second, the impact on society: "The affected community is at the center of this definition, with humanitarian space delineating their ability to uphold their rights to relief and protection. The

Water distribution at the Darfur refugee camp, West Sudan. There is no hope or imagination when to go home.

humanitarian agency is still essential; however, it recognizes the role that other actors play, including the affected community themselves, in meeting humanitarian needs."

Third, international humanitarian law: "Humanitarian space is analogous with respect for international humanitarian law under this definition, and therefore focuses on the actions of warring parties with regard to their responsibilities in upholding the law. This includes their responsibilities to meet humanitarian needs or allow impartial humanitarian organizations to provide relief and protection of civilians."

Fourth, military, political and legal complex: "The definition put forward by this HPG study highlights the context in which humanitarian action takes place. It highlights the highly political nature of the task humanitarian agencies seek to achieve and that humanitarian needs (and their relief) are a product of the dynamic and complex interplay of political, military and legal actors, interests, institutions and processes."[272]

Furthermore, it is emphasized that the current humanitarian system approach is in the form of a network of partners, but what is more important to emphasize is the humanitarian system as a form of network-based governance, in order to build a synergy between various humanitarian agencies.

---

272. *https://cdn.odi.org/media/documents/7643.pdf*

Nevertheless, it must be emphasized again that the humanitarian agenda is "to prevent and alleviate human suffering wherever it may be found ... to protect life and health and to ensure respect for the human being," as declared in the International Humanitarian Law (IHL) and upheld by various codes of conduct in the International Red Cross and the International Red Crescent.

Kristalina Georgieva, Commissioner for International Cooperation, Humanitarian Aid and Crisis Response from the European Union, also expressed her concern for the murder or kidnapping of humanitarian workers that are increasingly occurring as a result of shrinking humanitarian space: "It is paramount that we understand and respect the core principles of humanitarian aid: humanity, impartiality, neutrality and independence. We must stop the shooting of humanitarian workers — when they are hurt, so is the hope in the future of our children."

The Humanitarian Aid of the European Commission reports that, on average, a humanitarian worker is killed every three days. On August 19, 2003, the United Nations humanitarian affairs office in Baghdad was hit by a bomb attack that killed 22 humanitarian workers. That day is now designated World Humanitarian Day. In 2008 alone, 260 humanitarian workers were killed, not to mention the kidnapping and injury of many others. In most countries, this figure is getting worse each year (except for Sudan (Darfur), Somalia and Afghanistan). The shrinking of humanitarian activities mostly occurs in countries with high levels of conflict, and *The Journal of Humanitarian Assistance,* 2012, emphasized that this is difficult to stop. UNHCR expressed the need for intensive cooperation from the government, including the military, in Cameroon, Chad and Nigeria, to assist refugees from conflict in Nigeria, especially in northeast Nigeria. Opportunities for assistance are lessening, especially in conflict-affected regions and in the disaster-affected areas in general, as too often social workers or volunteers, including those working on behalf of the International Red Cross and religious institutions, are killed. Andreas Kamm, General Secretary, the Danish Refugee Council stated that:

> We see a huge gap between the increasing humanitarian needs in the world ... while at the same time, the risk linked to helping people in need is also increasing. From 1997 to 2016, the number of humanitarian aid workers killed on duty doubled. We need to remember that

humanitarians should never be a target. It must never cost lives to save lives.

The safety of humanitarian workers is one of the main measures of the humanitarian space, in addition to the respect for International Humanitarian Law (IHL) and the access given to humanitarian workers to crisis victims.

The International Council of Voluntary Organizations (ICVA), a Geneva-based international NGO network (the largest of its kind), has made humanitarian space part of their annual meeting agenda. In November, 2018, ICVA published an in-depth survey report that aims to map out the problem and provide suggestions for solutions so that humanitarian actors from civil society can continue to play an effective role in the field. The ICVA survey identified six levels of shrinkage:

1. Increased substantially 53%
2. Increased a small amount 19%
3. Remained at a similar level 9%
4. Reduced a small amount 6%
5. Reduced substantially 9%
6. Don't know or not applicable 4%

The ICVA survey, conducted by Andrew Cunningham and Steve Tibbett, shows that the existence of the shrinking of humanitarian space was confirmed by 72% of respondents, otherwise interpreted as 72% of countries or conflict areas. This confirms the studies of other humanitarian agencies such as UNHCR and ODI that the level of shrinkage has not only occurred, but is increasing, varying from region to region.

The higher and sharper the level of the conflict, the greater the shrinkage. In order to get a more complete and more specific picture of the intensity and typology of this, the ICVA survey recommends (1) the full mapping of the involvement of civil society in the humanitarian field, and (2) the full mapping of the various problems facing every country/region.

ICVA also recommends holding more advocacy and empowerment agendas for civil society to overcome barriers to humanitarian services, including building cooperation between civil society and government, donor agencies, the private sector, and philanthropic organizations.

THE VIRTUOUS TRIANGLE AND THE FOURTH DIMENSION

According to the Journal of the Humanitarian Policy Group (HPG) from the Overseas Development Institute (ODI), the issue of *"the shrinking of humanitarian space"* is correlated with the higher conflict intensity in countries all over the world. However, Collinson and Elhawary noted that the phrase 'the shrinking of humanitarian space,' first introduced by Rony Brauman of Medicins Sans Frontiers in 1990, is somewhat misleading. The term, therefore, must be seen from the perspective of the humanitarian system at large, as well as from the side of International Humanitarian Law (IHL).

The Humanitarian Futures Program mentioned the virtuous triangle as the main actor in handling various humanitarian crises: the humanitarian actor, the private sector, and the military. Collaboration between these three elements is so important that it is considered a fourth dimension, and must exist as a whole as well as between pairs: humanitarian actor to private sector, humanitarian actor to military, and private sector to military. Collaboration can only be truly effective if it can create synergy, carried out properly by functional coordination agencies such as UN OCHA, ASEAN, European Union, World Economic Forum, and others, each finding a place in the virtuous triangle with their respective comparative advantages. Such humanitarian actors include humanitarian agencies, with an average contribution of 70%, the private sector, with a contribution of 15–30%, and the military with its facilitating capacity.

THE BEKAA VALLEY INCIDENT: COOPERATION WITH THE MILITARY

One can easily study *"the shrinking of humanitarian space"* in humanitarian services in the Middle East, whose countries have been torn apart by civil war since 2011. Afghanistan, Iran, Iraq, Syria, Lebanon, Jordan and Turkey are now increasingly becoming 'borderless countries' due to the influx of civil war refugees who must cross national borders to seek safety for their families. At the same time, humanitarian actors, humanitarian service agencies, and especially humanitarian NGOs also have limited space due to the strict regulations imposed by local governments, especially by the national security or military.

In addition to the regular militaries of each country and their allies, there are also 'splinter groups' who are often identified as

274

Sr. Agnes Mariam, the Founder of St. James monastery in Qara, Syria, takes care of a hundred thousand refugees in Lebanon. She has to promote good connections with the military in order to repatriate the refugees to their home lands in Syria.

terrorists, such as ISIS and Jubhat al-Nosra. The number of refugees of these groups have not only reached tens or hundreds of thousands, but over nine million scattered in many areas. The Bekaa Valley, Homs, Aleppo, Darra and Hama are considered hellish, not only for the refugees, but for the volunteers and humanitarian workers. This is exactly where the fourth dimension of the *virtuous triangle* is needed, in the form of collaboration between humanitarian actors, the private sector and the military.

Sister Mother Agnes Mariam, a nun and the daughter of a Palestinian father and a Lebanese mother, is the founder and chair of the Monastery of St. James in the city of Qara, Syria. The Monastery, with the help of others, runs several refugee camps for Syria. One camp in Arsal near the Bekaa Valley has over 100,000 refugees. Apart from providing education and health services for the refugees, Mother Agnes Mariam has also promoted harmony between Muslim and Christian refugees. The main principle of her social service is to return the refugees to their hometowns as soon as possible to minimize their exposure to unexpected changes in the political climate.

In fact, the activity of helping refugee victims during the civil war in Syria was completely outside the plans and expectations of Mother Agnes Mariam when she established the Monastery of

St. James at Qara, Syria in 2000. The Monastery was established under the Archbishop of the Greek Catholic Church Homs, Hama and Yabroud, decision no. 914/2000 VIII on September 14, 2000. The objectives of the establishment of the monastery were *(1) to provide services to local Catholics; (2) to restore and maintain several old monasteries (heritage), which were founded in the third, fourth and fifth centuries scattered in the region;* and (3) *build harmony between Muslims and Christians.*

Mother Agnes Mariam began her ministry in the Bekaa valley and around Beirut in 2012, providing assistance in the form of food and clothing and opening schools and clinics. Refugees not only need food, education and medical treatment, but a place that is safe from the attacks of all warring factions, even from third parties who ignore International Humanitarian Law (IHL), such as the ISIS group.

In order to realize the hope of repatriating all refugees to their hometowns in Syria, Mother Mariam conducted intensive coordination with the military authorities in Lebanon and Syria. Returning 100,000 refugees from Arsal in Lebanon to their hometowns in Syria is not an easy task, which included guiding pregnant women, parents, and children up and down the inhospitable barren hills, many of whom still require sufficient health and logistical support. On the way from the Bekaa valley, they had to travel through difficult terrain in the form of a (sometimes barren) desert plateau. While moving in the middle of the desert, all the refugees must move under one command. On the way back to Syria, despite the approval of the Lebanese and Syrian militaries, the refugees were still shot by the Syrian military, because some of the refugees were carrying weapons. Finally, Mother Agnes asked permission directly from the President of Syria, so that the 'high-risk safari' in the civil war arena could finally arrive safely at its destination. The case of the leadership quality of Mother Agnes Mariam from the St. James monastery at Qara is quite complex and massive in the midst of the escalating civil war in the Middle East, whose impacts are penetrating national borders.

DIALOGUE WITH ATHEISM: CHINA

Apart from carrying out dialogue with people of other faiths, especially with Jews and Muslims of its fellow Abrahamic religions,

A Catholic church in Jingshou, China, under tight control of the Communist government, who restricts religious life. The Vatican has limited influence on the Chinese Church.

and even Hindus, Buddhists and Confucianists, the Church must also engage in dialogue with those who do not believe in God. If the Church has a long historical relationship and interaction with Islam and has certain foundations or commonalities for dialogue, it is an entirely different challenge to engage in a dialogue with atheist persons or entities, such as the communist government of China. However, as it happens within the People's Republic of China, this may accompany freedom of religious choice. At the same time, it is apparent that all regulations concerning Catholic livelihoods, including the daily activities of the Church, are under the control of the communist government.

Some International news agencies, the Associated Press (AP) and Reuter, recently reported on the agreement between the Chinese Communist government and the Vatican on the procedures for the appointment of Catholic bishops in China. The Chinese government officially prohibits the Vatican from directly appointing bishops in China, as it is done in other countries, and instead requires approval from the government. The spokesman for the Vatican Holy See, Greg Burke, on September 22, 2018, announced that an agreement was reached between the Vatican and the Chinese government regarding the appointment of bishops. This agreement was not political in nature, but pastoral; it began with the Vatican's recognition of the seven bishops previously appointed by the Chinese government as a 'bridge' to cover past wounds. Furthermore, it was agreed that the appointment of bishops by the Vatican will be based on a proposal from the Chinese Government. Therefore, the Chinese government recognizes the Vatican, but the two have no diplomatic relations.

The agreement was signed by Wang Chao, Deputy Minister of Foreign Affairs of China, and Mgr. Antoine Camilleri, Head of Council on Foreign Relation of the Vatican, who received a lot of protest from Chinese Catholics, and who argued that the agreement was unfair and that the church and Catholics had been persecuted by the Chinese government. Even Cardinal Joseph Zen, the Bishop of Hong Kong, urged Cardinal Pietro Parolin, the Vatican Foreign Minister, to resign. This was due to his role as head of negotiations on the Vatican side. Joseph Zen said, "I am afraid he is not a man with real faith. He is just a secular diplomat who prioritizes worldly affairs. They gave sheep to wolves. This is a great betrayal."

The agreement between the Vatican and the Chinese government is expected to end their decades-long dispute in the appointment of bishops in China. As a result of this dispute, there was a split in the Chinese Catholic church, in which one church is now recognized by the Vatican while the other is recognized by the Chinese communist government. The Chinese government considers the church recognized by the Vatican an unofficial church. The Chinese Catholic Church serves about twelve million Catholics.

Problems for Muslims

Religious life in China has not only been difficult for Catholics, but Muslims, especially Uighur Muslims, who constitute the majority in the Special Autonomous Region of Xinjiang, the largest province in China. In that regard, on February 17–24, 2019, a number of representatives from the largest Islamic organization in Indonesia, the Muhammadiyah, Nahdlatul Ulama (NU) and Indonesian Ulama Council (MUI) visited Xinjiang upon invitation from the Chinese Government. During the visit, Muhyiddin Junaidy, Deputy Chairperson of the MUI for Foreign Relations, said that the visit was not for the purpose of investigating the many media reports on persecutions and restrictions in the practice of worship against Uighur Muslims, but for building friendship with fellow Muslims in Xinjiang. Johari Oratmangun, the Indonesian Ambassador to the PRC, expressed his utmost support for the friendship between the

Abudurekefu Tumunijazi, Chair of the Chinese Muslim Association in Xinjiang, briefed the Indonesian Muslim visitors. The Xinjiang Muslims have limited accsess to perform their religious teachings. They have to join the indoor compulsory training on state ideology, Mandarin language, and vocational skills.

Indonesian Muslim community and Uighur Muslims in Xinjiang, hoping that cooperation between the peoples of the two countries will strengthen cooperation between the Indonesian Government and the Chinese Government.

It was also reported that the Deputy Chairman of the Chinese Muslim Association, Abdul Amin Jin Rubin, denied the reports of persecution and restriction on religious freedom in China. Rather, what is happening is the prevention of various forms of radicalism, extremism and terrorism that have started to bloom due to the impact of radical ISIS infiltration from the Middle East since the 1990s. Whatever is happening to Catholics and Muslims in China at this time cannot be separated from the background of the current communist government, which allows religious freedom.

Arnold Toynbee points out that the Chinese civilization, with its strong background of Confucianism, Taoism and Buddhism, is one of the five remaining world civilizations from the original nineteen civilizations—in addition to Western Christian civilizations that spread through Europe; the Christian Orthodox civilization that spread from Eastern Europe to the East coast of Russia; the Islamic civilization as the 'half-sister civilization' of Christian civilization; as well as Hindu and Far Eastern civilizations. The silk route that stretches from Europe to mainland China has brought European-Christian and Muslim civilization together with Chinese civilization in the East since the seventh century. The process of civilizational dialogue between Christian European civilizations and Islam and Chinese civilization will continue, both in the form of natural dialogue and 'induced dialogue.' This is because, although China does not promote belief in God, as far as humanitarian issues are concerned, the door is always open to carry out dialogue and cooperate in the humanitarian and social sector, as stated by the Indonesian Ambassador to China.

The decline in the number of adherents of traditional religions in China

According to the National Geographic Society's World Religion Database, the decline in the number of adherents of traditional Chinese religions is the largest compared to that of other religions in the world. It was reported that between 1900 and 2010, the number of adherents of traditional Chinese religions shrank from 23.5% to 6.6%. In comparison, the number of Christians in China decreased from only 34.5% to 33%, the decline in Buddhists from 7.8% to 6.7%, the decline in adherents of ethnic religions from 7.3% to 3.9%, The only increase was in Islam, from 12.3% to 22.5%. The decline is likely due in part to the Chinese government's control over religious institutions. As this is the case, the international community cannot easily intervene, as the situation is related to the constitution of the communist state. The only way to affect it is through cultural dialogue by, from and for the people, as part of a greater and long-term civilizational dialogue. Even then, a cautious approach must be made with the Chinese communist government, so that all goodwill in carrying out the civilizational dialogue is not considered an interference with the PRC's Constitution.

18

Toward a New "Religion of Humanity"

Author's Note: In mid-June 2006, at the Muhammadiyah humanitarian post for tsunami victims at the Aceh Muhammadiyah University campus mosque, Professor Sirajuddin "Din" Syamsuddin, then the General Chairman of the Muhammadiyah Central Board in Jakarta, called briefly to ask if I could go to London the week after to attend a meeting with Dr. Hanny El Banna, Director of Birmingham-based Islamic Relief Worldwide. Immediately I replied, "God willing, I can." At first, I thought that the meeting was only an ordinary seminar, but it turned out that this particular meeting was a meeting to establish a new institution for international humanitarian cooperation that requires broad support from the East and West.

Less than 15 minutes after receiving Pak Din Syamsuddin from Jakarta, Dr. Hanny El Banna called me from London. "This is a kind of an East and West humanitarian forum," said Dr. Hanny at the end of the phone. "Alhamdulillah, within a week you can get a British visa, but tickets are only one-way from Jakarta to London, because it's the peak season of summer holiday in Europe, so European tickets to Asia are all full. Tickets back to Jakarta will only be available one month later." It's not easy to get a ticket back to Jakarta. Finally, for the hard work of the Indonesian Embassy in London, I got a ticket that cost 18 million Rupiahs. Since I didn't bring enough money (and my credit cards were just declined due to insufficient funds), I borrowed personal money from Mr. Pribadi, the Head of the Political Function of the Indonesian Embassy, which I paid back when he happened to go to Jakarta the week after. This is the art of Muhammadiyah's 'diplomats.'

HUMANITARIAN FORUM, LONDON

This particular meeting for the establishment of the Humanitarian Forum was attended by a number of Islamic humanitarian organizations, namely Qatari Red Crescent, Kuwaiti International Charitable Organization, Jeddah-based Muslim World Youth Assembly, Istanbul-based IHH, Islamic Relief Worldwide, Iranian Sheikh Khomeini Foundation, and Indonesian Muhammadiyah. Western partners in attendance included Great Britain's Oxfam, the British Red Cross, Norwegian Refugee Council, Geneva-based International Council on Voluntary Agency (ICVA), observers from the International Federation of Red Cross and Red Crescent Societies (IFRC) and United Nations Office for the Coordination of Humanitarian Affairs (UN OCHA).

AGAINST GEORGE W. BUSH'S WAR ON TERROR

The meeting, which took place at the Charity Commission of UK & Wales offices in London on June 22–23, 2006, turned out to be a follow-up to a meeting in Geneva which was held at the initiative of the Swiss Permanent Mission at the United Nations' office in Geneva three months earlier. From several initial documents, it is clear that the idea of establishing the Humanitarian Forum has two backgrounds. *First*, it seeks to understand how the humanitarian communities must unite in facing the escalation of the problem of the growing humanitarian crisis. *Second*, it underlines the objection of the Islamic humanitarian organization and its Western counterparts to George W. Bush's policy on "the war on terror" after the attack on the World Trade Twin Towers in New York on September 11, 2001.

George W. Bush's "war on terror" is a dangerous generalization, very incompatible with the reality of the field, and actually detrimental to humanitarian service activities at large. It is the source of much international friction leading to the shrinking of humanitarian space, and the reason why these Eastern and Western humanitarian organizations came together: to oppose the negative image of Islamic humanitarian organizations and to coordinate and promote various forms of cooperation or collaboration by establishing the East & West Humanitarian Forum.

However, in the fourth meeting to finalize the establishment of the Humanitarian Forum, held in March 2007 in Qatar, Barrister Mr. Ahmad Thompson from the United Kingdom was invited in order to officially process the registration of this new institution at the Charity Commission of UK & Wales in London. However, the sentence against "the war on terror" was abolished due to being uncommon in legal language. An observer from the International Federation of Red Cross and Red Crescent Societies commented, "It's up to you if you want to erase this historic sentence. What

The third preparatory meeting in Istanbul on November 9, 2006 to establish the Humanitarian Forum. Dr. Hany al- Banna sits in front, right between the MWYA Jeddah and IFRC Geneva representatives. Author Sudibyo Markus stands on the right corner. The next meetings were in Qatar, Jakarta and Sana'a to finalize the processes.

is clear is that we support you because of that spirit, because the policy of 'war on terror' is not in accordance with the spirit and code of ethics of humanity."

The fifth meeting was held in October, 2007 in Jakarta at the Sari Pan Pacific Hotel, was fully attended by the entire board of trustees, daily administrators and the founders. This meeting standardized the Humanitarian Forum's future strategic agenda. Attempts by representatives of the British Red Cross from London to invite Dr. Mar'ie Muhammad, then the Chairman of the Indonesian Red Cross (IRC), did not succeed, since the latter was determined to prevent the IRC from becoming a faith-based humanitarian actor, who was strongly represented in the Humanitarian Forum.

HUMANITARIAN PRINCIPLES

It cannot be denied that the spirit against the "war on terror"—which has also targeted Islamic humanitarian organizations from the United Kingdom, the Middle East and Asia—does involve these faith-based institutions, because they are all active in humanitarian activities in many parts of the world and always in cooperation with one another. They carry out these humanitarian tasks based on universal humanitarian principles, embracing the differences in ethnicities, religions, races and political flow and power. They consistently agree upon these humanitarian principles:

a. Humanity: equal rights to receive humanitarian assistance;
b. neutrality as aid providers are neutral;
c. impartiality: assistance is provided regardless of race, nationality, religion, and so on;
d. Transparency;
e. Independence: to avoid becoming part of political tools or interests, foreign policy and so on.[273]

At the previous meeting in Qatar, it was agreed that the priority for initial activities, developed into three pilot projects, was namely countries with conflict intensity and serious disaster threat levels. Initially, the three selected countries were Indonesia, Yemen and Somalia. However, since Indonesia was then deemed to be in less of an emergency compared to the conflict or natural disasters experienced by several countries in Africa and Central Asia, Indonesia no longer became the target for priority service of the London-based Humanitarian Forum. It was also considered to have the ability to independently solve its problems, not to mention that later Indonesia also succeeded in establishing the Indonesian Humanitarian Forum (IHF).

PARTNERSHIP PRINCIPLES

Following the establishment of the Humanitarian Forum in 2006 was the initiative of Dr. Randolph Kent of King's College London to develop The Humanitarian Future Program in 2007, and then on July 1–2, 2008, the initiative by the Geneva-based ICVA to develop a collaborative partnership. ICVA is the largest humanitarian NGO network, supported by over 100 humanitarian NGOs, such as Oxfam GB, World Vision International, Plan International, Islamic Relief Worldwide, IHH and so on. Due to its position in Geneva, ICVA was able to gain first access to United Nations Agencies in Geneva, for the development of various international humanitarian issues. It was ICVA who also had the idea of developing the Humanitarian Forum, and held the pilot meeting at the Swiss Permanent Mission

273. United Nations General Assembly, "One Humanity: Shared responsibility. Report of the Secretary General for the World Humanitarian Summit," 15, https://reliefweb.int/sites/reliefweb.int/files/resources/Secretary-General%27s%20Report%20for%20WHS%202016%20%28Advance%20Unedited%20Draft%29.pdf

Office in March 2006 with Islamic Relief Worldwide and Oxfam GB.

After the Humanitarian Forum was established, on July 1-2, 2008, ICVA, together with Oxfam GB and UN OCHA, held an International Conference in Geneva entitled "Strengthening Partnership to Improve Humanitarian Action".[274] This conference, which was opened at the office of the World Council of Churches in Geneva emphasized the urgency of partnership and collaboration in response to the escalation of the global humanitarian crisis, which cannot be handled individually, even by large and strong humanitarian agencies like the UN OCHA.

The meeting, which was initiated by ICVA, Oxfam GB and UN OCHA in Geneva, produced a partnership with principles consisting of (1) equity, (2) result-oriented, (3) responsibility, (4) complementarity and (5) transparency.[275]

FROM LONDON TO JAKARTA

On February 8, 2008, at the Muhammadiyah Da'wah Center, Jakarta, a number of representatives from several faith-based humanitarian organizations were gathered – namely Muhammadiyah, the Christian Foundation for People's Welfare (YAKKUM), Caritas Indonesia (Karina), representing the Indonesian Church Trustees Conference, Tanggul Bencana Foundation, representing the Indonesian Church Fellowship, and Dompet Dhuafa. The meeting was specifically on the establishment of the Humanitarian Forum Indonesia, and was also attended by Dr. Hany El Banna, then the CEO of Humanitarian Forum, and Dr. Din Syamsuddin, then the General Chairman of the Muhammadiyah Central Board. The Humanitarian Forum of Indonesia was established with Arifin Purwakananta from Dompet Dhuafa as its first chairman.

In opening the historical meeting for the establishment of the Humanitarian Forum Indonesia, Din Syamsuddin—then the General Chairman of the Muhammadiyah Central Board and one of the founders of the Center for Dialog of Culture and Civilization (CDCC) in Jakarta—said that in this global era, religious communities are increasingly called to work together to overcome various

---

274. Thanks to Jamillah Mahmood, the then Director of Mercy Malaysia, I was also invited to the Conference.

275. 5 ICVA, Global Humanitarian Platform, Strengthening Partnerships to Improve Humanitarian Action, July 1–2 , 2008, Geneva.

Dr. Hany Al Banna, CEO of the Humanitarian Forum (London), visited Jakarta on February 8, 2008 for a meeting to establish the Humanitarian Forum Indonesia (HFI). The meeting, which took place at the Muhammadiyah Central Office, was attended mostly by faith-based humanitarian NGOs.

humanitarian problems. The barriers between religious beliefs are disappearing, where religions are increasingly working together to overcome humanitarian problems.

In the Humanitarian Forum Indonesia's statute, it is stated that the aim of the Humanitarian Forum is "to create an environmental situation that is conducive to the implementation of the principles of humanitarian activities," which can be implemented through:

a. providing a platform for dialogue;
b. promoting mutual understanding;
c. supporting capacity building and development of NGOs and charities;
d. advocating for a legal framework for greater transparency and accountability;
e. promoting humanitarian principles and standards;
f. improving communication and cooperation.[276]

The Humanitarian Forum, as a network of humanitarian organizations, is actively carrying out its humanitarian activities in several parts of the world, such as Yemen, Ethiopia, Somalia, Syria and

276. www.humanitarianforum.org

several other African countries, which are still being ripped apart by bloody conflicts. Likewise, the Humanitarian Forum Indonesia continues to carry out humanitarian service activities for disaster victims, both domestically and internationally. At the international stage, Humanitarian Forum Indonesia carried out humanitarian services in Gaza (2009), Central Philippines when it was hit by Typhoon Hyan (2013) and helped the earthquake victims in Nepal (2015). Furthermore, since 2017, in cooperation with the Indonesian government and other humanitarian agencies, it provides humanitarian services in Rakhine, Myanmar, and monitors the exodus of Rohingya refugees to Cox's Bazaar, Bangladesh. The medical team from the Muhammadiyah General Hospital—under the coordination of Muhammadiyah Aid / Muhammadiyah Disaster Management Center (MDMC) and in collaboration with The Dreamer, the Bangladeshi medical association—was sent to work at Cox's Bazaar until the end of 2018. Furthermore, the medical team will accompany the return of the refugees to Myanmar when an agreement between the Bangladesh government and the Myanmar government has been reached.

The Humanitarian Forum Indonesia's visit to Gaza managed to make a phenomenal breakthrough, led by Ardiansyah, M.D., a surgeon from Cempaka Putih Islamic Hospital of Jakarta, and Djoko Murdiyanto, M.D., an anesthesiologist from the Muhammadi-

The joint medical team of Muhammadiyah and a Christian hospital arrived at Gaza on February 6, 2009, and conducted an emergency meeting in the darkness.

yah General Hospital of Yogyakarta, along with nurses from the Bethesda General Hospital-Yakkum and the Muhammadiyah General Hospital of Yogyakarta. Due to the precarious situation, the Egyptian government closed the Rafah crossing, the only gate on the Egyptian border with Gaza, and consequently all humanitarian teams from all over the world failed to enter Gaza; even those in Gaza were ordered to leave.

The Indonesian Ministry of Health's Humanitarian Team, released by the Minister of Health, Siti Fadhilah Supari, M.D. at Soekarno Hatta Airport, also only made it to Cairo. However, the Humanitarian Team of Muhammadiyah and Yakkum managed to enter Gaza via the Erez crossing at the Gaza-Israel border in the north. Armed with a visa on arrival (obtained at the Israeli Embassy in Amman), the team broke into Gaza following the route of Indonesian pilgrims to the Al-Aqsa Mosque, through the King Hussein bridge which is on the Jordan-Israel border. After carrying out the pilgrimage, the team continued to Erez, crossing on the north side of the Gaza-Israel border. As reported by the Yakkum Journal 2009, a little past sunset, they arrived at Erez crossing, and were picked up by Dr. Mohammad Soussy, staff of Islamic Relief Worldwide in Gaza who was specifically assigned by Dr. Hanny El Banna to receive and pick up the arriving team at the Erez crossing.[277]

---

277. Ardiansyah, M.D.—a surgeon at the Jakarta Islamic Hospital who led the Muhammadiyah-Yakkum Humanitarian Team, who had been waiting in vain for several days in Amman, and who had no hope of continuing the journey since Gaza was declared closed by the Egyptian government—sent a short message to me while I was in Perth, Australia. He asked my permission for the Humanitarian Team detained in Amman to be allowed to return to Jakarta. At that time, I was a Chairman of PP Muhammadiyah for Health & Humanity (2005–2010), and felt that he had a responsibility for the success of the team, trying to find a breakthrough through Muhammadiyah's humanitarian network. For two hours I sent a short message to six international partners: (1) Dr. Iyang Iskandar. Secretary General of IRC, (2) Dr. Jounis Al Khatib, Chair of the Palestinian Red Crescent, (3) Dr. Hanny Al Banna, Director of the Islamic Relief Worldwide and CEO of the Humanitarian Forum, (4) Dr. Moh Soussy, Islamic Relief Worldwide staff in the Gaza strip, (v) Prof. Al Hadid, Secretary General of IFRC Geneva and Humanitarian Adviser of Queen of Jordan who lives in Amman, and most recently (5) Mr. Steve Stein, Special Staff of Magen David Adom (MDA), the Israeli Red Cross. Finally, after waiting for two hours, with the help of Steve Stein, the Muhammadiyah-Yakkum Humanitarian Team was allowed to enter Gaza through the Erez crossing, and the next day headed to the Erez crossing on the northern Gaza border, and was picked up by

Imam Muhammad Ashafa and Pastor James Wuye, who were trying to kill each other during the 90's, are now sharing their campaign to promote interfaith partnership and peace.

THE IMAM AND THE PASTOR IN NIGERIA

Imam Muhammad Ashafa and Pastor James Wuye are two prominent leaders of the militia groups that fought each other in Nigeria in 1990 in the name of religious 'vocation.' "My hatred toward Muslims was limitless," said Father James, whose group killed Imam Ashafa's teacher and two of his cousins. Three years later, Imam Ashafa planned a retaliation, and was bent on killing Pastor James, until one day a Friday sermon about the act of forgiveness by Prophet Muhammad changed his life.

The priest and pastor then met, forgave each other, and worked together to resolve conflicts over religious and ethnic nuances. Through the Interfaith Mediation Center, the institution they founded, both of them have contributed to developing peace-building and inclusive governance, not only in Nigeria or Africa, but worldwide.

In October 2017, Imam Muhammad Ashafa and Pastor James came to Indonesia, at the invitation of the Paramadina Center for

---

Dr. Moh Soussy of Islamic Relief Worldwide.

In the next communication, Steve Stein emphasized that the main concern when he sought the departure of the Muhammadiyah-Yakkum Humanitarian Team to Gaza through Israeli territory, through the Erez crossing, was the safety of the Team, given the precarious situation. For that, he assigned MDA officers to monitor the security of the Muhammadiyah-Yakkum Humanitarian Team for 24 hours. "Imagine what happens if your team gets into an accident," said Steve Stein.

Religion and Democracy Studies (PUSAD), the Maluku Inter-Faith Institute, Gadjah Mada University's Religious and Cross-Cultural Studies Program (CRCS) and Master of Peace and Conflict Resolution Program (MPRK), the Tanenbaum Foundation, and the Tifa Foundation. The two previously hostile figures gave several public lectures in Jakarta and Yogyakarta. There was no visible resentment between the two, since in the past the hostility between them and their militias was motivated by a limited understanding of their religion at that time. Now both are friends and unite to build peace among religious communities, having found a common ground between their respective religions.[278]

---

278. CRCS UGM, "Ketika Agama Membawa Damai, Bukan Perang: Belajar dari 'The Imam and The Pastor,'" https://crcs.ugm.ac.id/kuliah-umum-belajar-dari-the-imam-and-the-pastor/.

19
Human Fraternity, Abu Dhabi

POPE FRANCIS' VISIT TO ABU DHABI

Besides official responses from the various church leaders world-wide, who represent a large proportion of Catholics and Christians around the world, further studies of "A Common Word" took the form of conferences, courses and publications conducted by a number of universities and religious institutions. These studies on the "A Common Word" are no longer in the realm of theory and philosophy, but practical life.

A conference on "A Common Word," organized by Yale University on July 24–28, 2008, for example, discussed the theme "Love and World Poverty." The symposium on "Theory & Application on A Common Word," jointly organized by the University of South Carolina and Zayed University of the United Arab Emirates, discussed the environment, human rights, and development issues in the perspectives of Islam and Christianity. Meanwhile, Georgetown University collaborated with Prince Al-Alwal in holding a seminar on "A Common Word and a Global Agenda for Change," which discussed five themes, including:

1. Islamic-Christian Relations in the 21st Century,
2. Religion and Plurality in the 21st Century,
3. Religion-Violence and Peace Building,
4. The Role of International NGOs in a Plural World, and
5. Future Plans at the Center and the Royal Aal Al-Bayt Institute, a two-day conference in October 2009 to discuss future plans.[279]

It seems that the spirit of "A Common Word," as a commitment to global interfaith dialogue and partnership, is spreading. Zayed University's involvement is strong; Prince Mohammed bin Zayed

---

279. The Royal Aal Al-Bayt Institute for Islamic Thought, *A Common Word between Us and You, 5-Year Anniversary Edition*, pp. 111–114.

al-Nahyan, the Crown Prince and Commander of the UAE Armed Forces, invited Pope Francis to the UAE, which finally commenced on February 3–5, 2019.

Pope Francis' three-days visit, the first visit of a Pope to the Arabian Peninsula, was truly productive. There, His Holiness attended an interfaith conference, participated in laying the foundation stone of the mosque and church in neighboring Abu Dhabi, held a large mass at the Zayed Sport City stadium, which was attended by 130,000 participants, and most importantly, signed the Declaration of Human Fraternity together with Sheikh Ahmed el-Thayeb, the Grand Imam of Al Azhar, Cairo. As someone who has been involved in several forums related to the follow-up to "A Common Word," Prince Zayed has long invited and expected the presence of the Pope.

Pope Francis' visit to the UAE shocked human rights observers. The surprise of human rights activists from Human Rights Watch (HRW) was not without reason. The United Arab Emirates has been involved in various wars and human rights violations, along with Saudi Arabia, including attacks on Houthi rebels in Yemen, as well as wars in Syria and Libya. In fact, the UAE, along with Saudi Arabia, Bahrain and Egypt, since June 2017, have also isolated Qatar. Quoting Reuter, the UAE is still practicing restrictions for Christians to worship openly.[280]

THE ROLE OF THE CROWN PRINCE OF UAE

Prince Sheikh Mohammed bin Zayed al-Nahyan, Crown Prince and Commander of the UAE Armed Forces, is also behind the modernization of the UAE, and contributed to its development as a center of international business. To support this, the UAE has had to partner with both Muslim and non-Muslim communities and countries. Therefore, the UAE needs various 'bridging' efforts between cultures. In 2017, the Grand Mosque of Abu Dhabi, which was originally named the Sheikh Mohammed bin Zayed Grand Mosque, was renamed Mary, Mother of Jesus Mosque. This was well received in the UAE, As Muslims really respect Maryam, the mother of Prophet Isa, and even in the Qur'an, there is Surah Maryam, the 19th chapter.

---

280. Tempo, "4 Fakta Menarik dari Kunjungan Paus Fransiskus ke Uni Emirat Arab," https://dunia.tempo.co/read/1172714/4-fakta-menarik-dari-kunjungan-paus-fransiskus-ke-uni-emirat-arab.

Pope Francis leads a mass at the Zayed Sport City of Abu Dhabi, attended by 130,000 Catholics from Arab and Middle East countries. (Aljazeera.com).

Meanwhile, the Arab Spring has been exacerbated in several countries, especially Syria and Libya. Therefore, Prince Moham-med bin Zayed, as the Crown Prince, was inclined to continue the modernization of the Arabian Peninsula and build civilizational dialogue. He understands the UAE's image in human rights abuses and its involvement in various wars, which may very well hinder the modernization of the UAE and the Arabian Peninsula, which is why the UAE needs to build a bridge of civilization to provide support for the modernization process, not to mention business.

CONTINUATION OF THE SPIRIT OF NOSTRA AETATE AND A COMMON WORD

Pope Francis's historic and monumental visit to the UAE cannot be separated from the implementation of the spirit of the Statement of Nostra Aetate from the Second Vatican Council (1962–1965), as well as the continuing commitment to implement the five themes of "A Common Word and Global Agenda for Change."

The Document on Human Fraternity for World Peace and Living, signed together by Pope Francis with Sheikh Ahmed el-Thayeb, the Grand Imam of Al-Azhar, in Abu Dhabi on February 4, 2019, describes the spirit of the Nostra Aetate and "A Common Word." It emphasizes the importance of the concept of full citizenship, which strives to equally empower minority groups, as well as the importance of partnership between the West and the East.

The first ever visit of Pope Francis to the Arab Countries, welcomed by the Crown Prince Mohammed bin Zayed Al-Nahyan, and the Grand Imam of Al Azhar Sheikh Ahmed al-Thayeb.

The Declaration of Human Fraternity and Pope Francis' visit to the Arabian Peninsula provided a win-win solution for both parties. In general, the past grudges between the West and the East (Islam) were agreed to be forgotten. Meanwhile, the Vatican and Christian world benefit in two ways, *first*, the provision of a better climate of worship in the Arab world for Christian migrants, and *second*, the consolidation of the Christian minority which has been living in safety, peace and protection within the government and the local Muslim majority for fourteen centuries. The fate of traditional Christian communities across the Arabian Peninsula is still at risk, however, and has been since the Western invasion of Iraq and other peninsula countries in 2002.

In addition, the UAE and Arab countries on the peninsula are now valuable partners for the control of radicalism and terrorism, which is also expected to be a good investment for the modernization of the area. At the very least, it can temporarily counter their involvement in various wars and various forms of human rights violations, as highlighted by Human Rights Watch.

However, economic competition and various political conflicts outside of religious cooperation are still very real. That is the challenge behind the Human Fraternity declarations and documents. To address this, The Pope, at an interfaith gathering in Abu Dhabi

Pope Francis and Sheikh Ahmad al-Thayib, the Grand Imam of Al Azhar, Cairo greeting each other right after the signing of the Declaration on Human Fraternity at Abu Dhabi on February 4, 2019.

attended by hundreds of people of various faith backgrounds, candidly and emphatically expressed his objection to a number of wars in which several Gulf states were involved:

> War cannot create anything but misery, weapons bring nothing but death... I am thinking in particular of Yemen, Syria, Iraq and Libya... Every form of violence must be condemned without hesitation... No violence can be justified in the name of religion.[281]

In fact, this interfaith gathering in Abu Dhabi was not only attended by Sheikh Ahmed Thayeb and Pope Francis, but an Indonesian envoy, Professor Quraish Shihab. In his remarks, Quraish Shihab expressed his appreciation for the statement of the Second Vatican Council Nostra Aetate for challenging the barrier between Islam and Christianity, and for Sheikh Ahmed Thayeb and Pope Francis, who had initiated the Document on Human Fraternity. Therefore, the spirit of building humanitarian brotherhood between religions does not only apply to the Arabian Peninsula, but universally.[282]

281. Al-Jazeera, "Pope in UAE: Reject wars in Yemen, Syria, Iraq and Libya," https://www.aljazeera.com/news/2019/2/4/pope-in-uae-reject-wars-in-yemen-syria-iraq-and-libya.

282. Alif.id, "Naskah Lengkap Pidato M. Quraish Shihab di Depan Pemimpin Agama-Agama," https://alif.id/read/redaksi/naskah-lengkap-pidato-m-quraish-shihab-di-depan-pemimpin-agama-agama-b215226p/.

The breakthroughs made by Pope Francis together with Prince Mohammed bin Zajed al-Nahyan and Sheikh Ahmed al-Thayeb have eloquently demonstrated that the commitment to strengthen cooperation between religious communities has never subsided or stopped, even in the middle of various external and internal obstacles, including the shrinking of humanitarian space. The spirit of Nostra Aetate from the Second Vatican Council and the spirit of Love of God and Love Your Neighbor continue, even at the level of action, in the global commitment of the Agenda for Humanity.

THE ZAYED AWARD FOR HUMAN FRATERNITY

The award is named in honor of Sheikh Zayed bin Sultan al Nahyan, the late ruler of Abu Dhabi and founder of the United Arab Emirates, whose values of humility, humanitarianism and respect epitomize the ideals celebrated by this award. The Zayed Award for Human Fraternity recognizes profound contributions to the facilitation of peaceful coexistence and human progress. The award is for individuals or entities anywhere in the world who lead by example, creating breakthroughs by collaborating selflessly and tirelessly across divides to drive real, conviction-led progress.

The award was established in February, 2019, to mark the historic meeting in Abu Dhabi between the head of the Catholic Church, His Holiness Pope Francis, and His Eminence the Grand Imam Dr Ahmed Al-Tayeb, to co-sign the Document on Human Fraternity.

The Zayed Award for Human Fraternity is awarded by the Higher Committee for Human Fraternity and includes a prize of one million dollars. The Document on Human Fraternity contains a powerful call for all people to put aside their differences in pursuit of progress through understanding, reconciliation and peace

In 2019, Pope Francis and the Grand Imam Dr Ahmed Al-Tayeb were the first honorary recipients of the Zayed Award for Human Fraternity. On February 4, 2020, during a ceremony in Abu Dhabi marking the first anniversary of the signing of the Document on Human Fraternity, Sheik Abdullah bin Zayed Al Nahyan announced that the Zayed Award for Human Fraternity would become an annual event.

HIGHER COMMITTEE

A Higher Committee for Human Fraternity (HCHF) was established in the United Arab Emirates in August 2019 in order to launch a worldwide search for persons embodying the "values of humility, humanitarianism and respect." This Committee was tasked with developing a framework to ensure the objectives of the global Declaration of Human Fraternity are realized, and to prepare the necessary plans to implement the document, follow up on its implementation at regional and international levels, and hold meetings with religious leaders, heads of international organizations, and others to support and spread the idea behind this historic document.

Mr. Muhammad Jusuf Kalla, former Vice President of the Republic of Indonesia (2004-2009 and 2014-2019), along with all the Selection Committee Members, meeting Pope Francis in Vatican City, October 23rd, 2020.

The HCHF selected five individuals to select the recipient(s) for the 2021 Award, including: Catherine Samba-Panza, former President of the Central African Republic; Muhammad Jusuf Kalla, former Vice-president of Indonesia; Michaelle Jean, the 27th Governor-General and Commander-in-Chief of Canada; Cardinal Dominique Mamberti, serving in the Vatican's Supreme Tribunal; and Adama Dieng, a former UN Special Adviser on the Prevention of Genocide.

Regarding his appointment to the selection committee, Adama

Dieng said, "We are delighted to invite nominations for the 2021 Zayed Award for Human Fraternity. The award is an opportunity to recognize people around the world who are deeply committed to initiatives that bring people together and promote peaceful co-existence. The judging committee will consider people or entities anywhere in the world who are leading by example by collaborating selflessly and tirelessly, across divides, to deliver real and positive change."

Mr. Muhammad Jusuf Kalla, the former Vice President of the Republic of Indonesia (2004-2009 and 2015-2019), was noted for his success in initiating the Helsinki Accord, a Peace Agreement between the Government of Indonesia with the Gerakan Aceh Merdeka (The GAM or Aceh Freedom Movement).Since December 2020, upon the request of the two conflicting parties, the Thaliban movement and the government of Afghanistan, he also initiated a similar mission in Afghanistan.

Pope Francis had the opportunity to meet with all of the selection committee members at his personal library in the Vatican on October 23, 2020, where he reemphasized his hopes of "encouraging all virtuous exemplars of men and women who in this world embody love through actions and sacrifices made for the good of others, no matter how different they may be in religion, or ethnic and cultural affiliation."[283]

THE 2021 ZAYED AWARD HONOREES[284]

It was officially revealed on February 4, 2021, that Antonio Guterres, UN Secretary-General, and Latifa Ibn Ziaten, Moroccan-French activist, are the two honorees of the 2021 award.

As Secretary-General of the UN since 2017, António Guterres has embarked on a dedicated mandate to address issues relating to world peace and security. Among some of the key initiatives he has spearheaded during his time in office, are "countering hate speech and violence; modernizing UN peacekeeping practices; and the Global Cease Fire Appeal and Initiative during the Covid-19 pandemic – resulting in 170 member and observer states heeding

---

283. *https://www.vaticannews.va/en/world/news/2020-10/nominations-zayed-award-human-fraternity-document.html*

284. https://www.vaticannews.va/en/world/news/2021-02/zayed-award-human-fraternity-latifah-ibn-ziaten-antonio-guterres.html

Antonio Guterres, Secretary General of the United Nations. As former Director General of UNHCR, he has devoted most of his life for global peace.

the call to sign up."[285]

Prior to receiving his award, Guterres said:

"It is with humility and deep gratitude that I feel honored to receive the Zayed Award for Human Fraternity. I see it also as recognition of the work the United Nation is doing every day, everywhere, to promote peace and human dignity.

"We live in challenging times. We see the threats coming from the pandemic, from the climate, threats from war and conflict in different parts of the world. Therefore, it is fantastic to see the enormous leadership of His Holiness the Pope and His Eminence the Grand Imam of Al-Azhar, pushing humankind to come together, in unity, in dialogue, to promote peace, to promote fraternity, and to promote the unity that is necessary to address all the challenges to defeat hate and ensure that human solidarity wins the battles we are facing."

Latifa Ibn Ziaten is "a mother and Moroccan-French activist,

---

285. https://www.prnewswire.com/news-releases/zayed-award-for-human-fraternity-announces-un-secretary-general-and-moroccan-french-activist-as-its-2021-honorees-301221355.html

Latifa Ibn Ziaten, a Moroccan-French activist who devoted her life for peace to commemorate her son who was assasinated by terrorist attack

dedicated to raising awareness against escalating religious extremism, following her own personal tragedy of losing her son, Imad, to a terrorist attack, in 2012. Since then, Latifa has become a well-known civil society activist, in France and beyond; working with families and communities to prevent youth radicalization and spreading the message of peace, dialogue, and mutual respect.

Upon her accepting her award, Ms. Latifa said:

'It is a great honor, and indeed humbling, to have been recognized by the Zayed Award for Human Fraternity for the work I and many others do, each day, in addressing extremism through dialogue, mutual respect, and peaceful co-existence. Most importantly, I hope this award helps raise awareness among a wider audience about the need to continue these efforts.

"The situation in France and Europe has often presented many challenges due to a sense of exclusion and marginalization that affects so many young hearts. That said, I feel progress is being made, and we continue to work with families and communities to prevent youth radicalization and to understand how we can create opportunities for more open dialogue and advocacy; making co-operation and mutual understanding the norm - not the exception,' Latifa concluded."[286]

---

286. https://www.prnewswire.com/news-releases/zayed-award-for-human-fraternity-announces-un-secretary-general-and-moroccan-french-activist-as-its-2021-honorees-301221355.html

20

Toward a Base Community

Because of efforts like the Humanitarian Forum, the spirit of interfaith cooperation is growing. In fact, collaboration that is 'South-South' in nature is also increasing at the regional level, which responds to regional issues, such as victims of the bloody conflict against the Rohingya minority in Rakhine State, Myanmar; victims of the conflict in Southern Thailand; and victims of the conflict between the Moro Islamic Liberation Front (MILF) and other splinter groups (e.g. the Maute group and the Abu Sayyaf group). In fact, in November 2017, a delegation from the High-Level Interfaith Council of Afghanistan asked for assistance from the government and the Indonesian people to overcome the sectarian conflicts there.

Since December 9th, 2009, Indonesians in Muhammadiyah have participated in the International Contact Group (ICG) for peace negotiation assistance between the Philippine government and the Moro Islamic Liberation Front, together with the Swiss Centre for Humanitarian Dialogue (or the Henry Dunant Centre), the English Conciliation Resource, the Cambodian Center for Peace and Conflict Studies (CPCS), and the Rome-based Community of Sant'Egidio, the largest Catholic association in the world, which has a special focus on interfaith cooperation. Moreover, the involvement of Muslim-Catholic humanitarian agencies in handling conflict is very prominent in the half-century-old conflict in Mindanao, which began with Portuguese colonialism against the background of the Muslim-Catholic conflict in 7th century Europe. Muhammadiyah's cooperation with the Community of Sant'Egidio was carried out at Cox's Bazar, Bangladesh, to help its 650,000 Rohingya refugees. Initially, the Muhammadiyah medical and humanitarian team was assigned to Cox's Bazar for only three months, but then it was extended to six months, and finally to one year until December 2018, while also tasked with the plan to escort

Members of the International Contact Group (ICG) consisted of representatives from Muhammadiyah (Indonesia), the Asia Foundation (Manila), Conciliation Resource (UK), Center for Humanitarian Dialogue (Switzerland), and Center for Peace and Conflict Studies (CPCS, Cambodia), a supporting team to the negotiation between the Govt of the Philippines and the Moro Islamic Liberation Front (MILF)

the refugees back to Rakhine, Myanmar.

THE AWAKENING OF BASE COMMUNITY

"A Common Word" and the Agenda for Humanity's mission is most effectively implemented at the level of base communities, to build a foundation for its implementation regionally, nationally and internationally. For the commitment to be upheld at the local level, a basic vehicle is needed in the form of a network of basic community groups that possess high dynamism.

Ashutosh Varshney from Yale University, in his study of the bloody conflict between Hindus and Muslims in India, divides networks or community ties related to the conflict into two 'bond' groups: *First*, associational civic engagement, or the relationship between residents in a certain locality through various associations (e.g. for women, youth, sports, farmers, teachers, religious study (*majlis taklim*), etc.) where the interaction between members of different associations form a 'web' or strong network. *Second*, everyday civic engagement, or a routine pattern of individual relationships such as those between neighbors, without any involvement in formal associations.[287]

Varshney concluded that the solid web or network of the first bond group is a strong deterrent to conflict. Conversely, a bond group with loose ties is weak and does not have a mechanism of prevention of internal or external conflict. Varshney further concluded that cases of conflict rarely occurred in Hindu-Muslim communities with associational ties, while in environments with loose ties, cases of Hindu-Muslim conflict were more common.

'OUT THERE' AND 'IN HERE' PHENOMENA

The process of globalization does not run linearly, like an endless road. Rather, the globalization process will culminate and end in the hometown or local base community. The base community is the locale of various impacts in social, economic and cultural fields, and it is in that base community that responses, feedback and protective mechanisms from the impact of globalization will emerge.

Initially, people thought that the process of globalization was like a vortex of a centrifugal movement, in the form of a whirlwind that would immediately uproot the cultural roots of communities. But what actually happened was that in the middle of that centrifugal pull – meaning the local community – there was also a defense mechanism which was centripetal,[288] strengthening the self in the base community. Therefore, there is a need to build balance between the "out there" centrifugal pull, and the "in here" centripetal pull and self-defense process.

The understanding that globalization is an 'out there phenomenon' balanced by the strengthening of basic communities or "in here" phenomena was supported by Prof. Lester Salamon, Director of the Center for Civil Society Studies at the John Hopkins University. Salamon stated that "the awakening of the citizenry at the grassroots is a global revolution of associations, which has proved as significant as the rise of the nation state."[289]

---

287. Ashutosh Varshney, *Ethnic conflict and civil life: Hindus and Muslims in India* (New Haven: Yale University Press, 2002).

288. While centrifugal means 'moving or directed away from a center or axis,' centripetal means 'moving toward a center or axis of rotation.' See, *American Heritage Dictionary: Third Edition* (New York: Dell Publishing, 1976), 119.

289. Lester Salamon, Center for Civil Society Studies, John Hopkins University,

Salamon observes that the development of grassroots societies in the second millennium, in the era of globalization, is as phenomenal as the rise of civil society in the era of the world's first city-state (polis), the city of Athens (508 BC–322 BC).

It is necessary to understand civil society through its operational definition and qualifications. According to Helmut K. Anheier, the operational definition of civil society is "the sphere of institutions, organizations, and individuals located between the family, the state and the market in which people associate voluntarily to advance common interest."[290] Meanwhile, Edwards, Foley and Diani argued that citizens should strive for a "strong and vibrant civil society characterized by social infrastructures of dense networks of face-to-face relationships that cross-cut existing social cleavages such as race, ethnicity, class, sexual orientation, and gender that will underpin strong and responsive democratic government."[291]

It is precisely the associative nature and characteristics of inter-citizen ties, which Varshney calls associational civic engagement, that form the network needed of a committed base community. This is the 'in here' format of civil society, which due to the dynamic interaction between its citizens, has a strong resistance to outside threats such as radicalism and intolerance.

There is a fundamental difference between the function of the revival of civil society at the time of the rise of the city-state of Athens between 508 BC and 322 BC and the revival in the present. At the time of the birth of the nation-state, the rise of civil society was intended to challenge the hegemony of authoritarian government. The rise of civil society in the second millennium has a very different role and function: namely, as a critical partner for the government and the market. This position is clear from the inclusion of civil society as one of the four pillars of the UN's global sustainable development goals (SDGs), in addition to government, business/philanthropy, and intellectualism.

Christian Science Monitor, February 3, 2000

290. Helmut K. Anheier, *Civil Society Measurement, Evaluation, Policy* (London: Earthscan, 2004), 22.

291. Edwards, Foley and Diani, *Beyond Tocqueville: Civil Society and the Social Capital Debate in Comparative Perspective* (Hanover: University Press of New England, 2001).

Berkeley Center for Religious, Peace and World Affairs, Georgetown University in Washington, is one of the most active centers in studying and promoting peace.

G20 INTERFAITH FORUM, BOLIVIA, AND WORLD INTERFAITH HARMONY WEEK, INDONESIA

On September 26–28, the G20 2018 Conference in Bolivia scheduled the G20 Interfaith Forum for the fifth time. All forum participants–religious leaders from the G20 countries–discussed what they have done and what they plan to do in the future to deal with various issues in the fields of job opportunities, education and food security. The G20 Interfaith Forum started before the commencement of the official session of the G20, and was expected to contribute to the official recommendations of the G20 Conference.

The G20 Interfaith Forum also discussed various 'non-traditional' issues, such as radicalism and extremism, violence, slavery, corruption, the impact of displacement on children, and other forms of global inequality. The Berkley Center for Religion, Peace and World Affairs at Georgetown University, Washington, has pro-actively held preliminary discussions as a form of contribution to the success of The G20 Interfaith Forum in Bolivia.

On February 8–10, 2018, World Interfaith Harmony Week was held in Indonesia for the first time. It was attended by nearly 400,000 representatives of religious communities from all over the country, spearheaded by the Special Envoy of the President of Indonesia, Din Syamsuddin, for Dialogue and Cooperation between Religions and Civilizations. The goal of World Interfaith Harmony Week in Indonesia is to spread the spirit of cooperation between religious believers and cooperation in the field of interfaith humanity, in order to build a base for best practices in Indonesia.[292]

SINGAPORE AND MINAHASA: STUDY CASES

People's Association Singapore[293]

In 1960, when Singapore detached from the Malaysian Federation, the state of the country was not so different from Indonesia. The city-state had numerous poor and slum pockets, and was also plagued by communist subversion. Faced with these two pressing issues, a young Lee Kuan Yew established the People's Association (PA). The PA started out as an association at the basic community level, which drives various daily mutual cooperation activities, such as youth activities, sports, various cultural arts, religious activities, and so on.

To support these activities, the residents, with government subsidies, set up a kind of community center. It included a sports room, cultural arts opportunities, and training center which offered courses for various business skills. Later, PA rose to the district level, and then the national level. Indeed, in the end the PA became the vehicle for Lee Kuan Yew's political activism, but its success as a vehicle for social development for citizens cannot be denied.

In 1970, ten years later, Singapore's economy was improving, and communist subversion was slowly but surely losing its footing. In that year, 150 PAs (community centers) had grown in the city-state, staffed by 1,500 managers, 450 volunteers and 2,000 management committees. Furthermore, in 1980, the PA was able to raise 20.9 million Singaporean dollars. The PA used the Singapore government subsidies to develop a community center with various prevention and development programs against various community afflictions. The PA in Singapore is indeed more homogeneous than the social association network in Minahasa and Bitung (both in Indonesia), It is more of a grassroots-level civil society movement, which is resilient to conflict and a vehicle for community development.

---

292. *https://nasional.sindonews.com/berita/1281229/15/din-syamsuddin-jika-hewan-bisa-mengapa-manusia-tidak-bisa-bersatu*

293. Lee Khoon Choy, "A Better Community of Life, if Best Leaders Come Forward," *The Straits Times, Singapore*, November 26, 1980, 6.

Perhaps, in a very limited spatial area, communication and interrelations between groups of citizens is easier than larger areas. However, what is important is not the small size of the country, but the commitment of the state's leadership and society. To this day, this is still prominent in the People's Association of Singapore, scattered across many parts of the island nation.

Community forum in Minahasa

Located at the northern tip of the province of North Sulawesi, Indonesia, the Minahasa district is famous for its community harmony. Conflicts between religious followers are rare. When building the community mosque, local Christians helped, and when building the local church, Muslims helped. In fact, at the General Assembly of the Minahasa Evangelical Church Council (GMIM), the board was a combination of Muslims and Christians.

North Sulawesi, especially Minahasa, is flanked by three conflict-prone areas: North Maluku, Maluku, and Central Sulawesi. At a bloody conflict in Ternate in 2000, as many as 50,000 refugees (internal displaced persons) took refuge along the northern coast of Minahasa and Bitung. There were efforts by the refugees to provoke friction between local Christians and Muslim residents, but it never worked. Up to 50,000 refugees returned to Ternate, and the conflict never occurred in Minahasa and Bitung. Efforts to break the peaceful harmony of life in the society (*kawanua*) have not succeeded.

Village general association

The villages in Minahasa have a strong community infrastructure. All villagers are members of the general village association, and at the community association level (*rukun warga*), they are members of the community association unit. They are very friendly with one another and pay dues in an orderly manner. When misfortune occurs, the family receives a donation to buy a coffin and a garland. In 2000, the donation for the coffin amounted to 250,000 Rupiahs and 75,000 Rupiahs for flower bouquets.

In addition to 'structural' community associations at the village level and those which function as vehicles for mutual cooperation, each villager is also an active member of various other cooperative associations. For example, every 25 GMIM members are tied to a congregation group called a *colon*. There is also a religious study group (*majlis taklim*) from the residents of 'Javanese-Tondano' descent, or Jaton. There are women's and youth associations, savings and loan cooperatives, associations for sports activities, etc. Every citizen can concurrently be a member in various associations; hence, the dynamic interaction between residents is also an interaction between community cooperative institutions.

This kind of bond is what Varsney called associational civic engagement, which is indeed capable of realizing solid cohesion between citizens, who have the power to resist threats or potential conflicts.[294]

THE DECISION-MAKING PROCESS FOR ACTION

The development of the People's Association in Singapore and the harmony between residents in Minahasa show that at the grass-roots community network, especially one supported by a network of various solid local associations, is truly a reliable medium for social interaction and solidarity, including in communities with the potential for inter-religious conflict. This platform for social interaction at the grassroots community level not only functions to carry out activities that are social in nature, but to promote interrelation and interdependence between citizens, both individually and as a group, in various fields: social, economic, educational, cultural, and so on.

This is especially so because the process of globalization is not just driven and carried out for mere economic motivations, but for inter-religious, social and cultural interdependence. Thus, the various processes of realizing best practices in "A Common Word" and the Agenda for Humanity are at the level of the base community.

According to Norman Uphoff, the decision-making process for action occurs at ten levels, moving from smaller to larger: (1) personal, (2) family, (3) primary group, (4) community group, (5) locality, (6) sub-district level, or the equivalent of sub-districts, (7) districts, (8) regional or provincial, (9) national, and (10) global or international. The decision-making process for the best course of action occurs most effectively at a level where face-to-face and interpersonal relationship communication still occurs. This com-

---

294. rofil Wahana Kesejahteraan Sosial Berbasis Masyarakat (WKSBM), Indonesian Ministry of Social Affairs, Jakarta 2004.

munication happens at the level of primary groups, community groups and localities.[295]

The primary group level can have different domiciles in the community, different ages, education levels, and beliefs, but is made up of a small group of people with a common idea in a particular community. The community group level is a group of residents in a particular community unit or neighborhood, including a neighborhood association (*rukun tetangga*), community association (*rukun warga*), or hamlet. The locality level is a group of people in a wider village or sub-district, who are accustomed to and tied to a certain social life together; for example, members usually share markets, schools, mosques or churches, or joint crop cultivation activities, all of which associate them with a small culture.

According to Norman Uphoff, the personal and family levels have their own ideas, but they are not yet significant in the decision-making process for collective action. At the community group level, contributions to decision-making for collective action are also minimal, due to factors such as the low level of face-to-face contact and interpersonal relationships, or because of their stronger personal interests.

Meanwhile, at the locality level, short, medium and long-term program planning is used to outline policies, strategies and programs at the global and national 'macro' level, as well as at the regional 'meso' level. Thus, empirically as well as academically, it is agreed that basic community groups are indeed the single best environment in which to realize various best practices in implementing "A Common Word" and One Humanity, at the local, regional, and global level. Again, as Magnis Suseno stated, "In modern society, the paradigm of 'us versus others' is increasingly being replaced by the universal humanistic paradigm."

This is also what Randolph Kent calls the 'globalization paradox,' which has both an operational and practical meaning in addressing whether or not a particular need for assistance is needed to overcome a crisis:

The more globalized the world becomes, the more localized it will

---

295. Norman Uphoff, *Local Institutions And Participation For Sustainable Development*, Gatekeeper Series No. 31 (New York: Cornell International Institute for Food, Agriculture and Development at Cornell University, 1986), 11.

also be. External assistance will be driven less by supply and more by demands.[296]

What Kent calls the 'globalization paradox' is the core responsibility of the Istanbul World Humanitarian Summit's decision, that "Success must now be measured by how people's vulnerability and risk are reduced, not by how needs are met year after year."

This is where the importance of the principle and spirit of no one left behind which was echoed in the World Humanitarian Summit, also in the Sustainable Development Goals (SDGs), then also adopted by Christians and Muslims as the spirit and value of a calling in implementing 'A Common Word' and the Agenda for Humanity.

In the end, all of the facets of implementing of 'A Common Word' and the Global Agenda for Change[297] will only be carried out well when there is strong collective action at the community level. This cannot be an exclusive activity or program, but must be part of the daily life of the community; interfaith groups especially are in the mainstream of regional and local development.

---

296. Randolph Kent, Justin Armstrong and Alice Obrecht, "The Future of Non-Governmental Organizations in the Humanitarian Sector: Global transformations and their consequences," *https://reliefweb.int/sites/reliefweb.int/files/resources/The-Future-of-Humanitarian-NGOs-HFP-Discussion-Paper-Aug2013-copy.pdf*

297. Covers five main agendas: Islamic-Christian Relations in the 21st Century, Religion and Plurality in the 21st Century, Religion-Violence and Peace Building, The Role of International NGOs in a Plural World, and Future Plans. The Royal Aal Al-Bayt Institute for Islamic Thought, *A Common Word between Us and You*, 5-Year Anniversary Edition, pp. 111–114.

PART 5

TOWARD A UNIVERSAL HUMANITY

O mankind, indeed We have created you from male and female and made you peoples and tribes that you may know one another. Indeed, the most noble of you in the sight of Allah is the most righteous of you. Indeed, Allah is Knowing and Acquainted.

Al-Qur'an Surah Al-Hujuraat, verse 13

21

Between Dialogue and
The Clash of Civilizations

DIALOGUE AMONG CIVILIZATIONS

The long journey of mankind has found its humanistic path again. The experience of life for two millennia, now entering the third millennium, has flowed in a direction of awareness and hope for the global community, through respect for humanity and the need for cooperation and togetherness. The history of ignorance, hatred, and resentment between religious communities, especially Christians and Muslims, has driven them into long hostilities, from the Crusades to colonialism. After Pope John XXIII initiated the Second Vatican Council in 1962, tearing down 400 years of Vatican traditionalism and extinguishing the church's hostility to non-Christian religions, the relationship between Muslims and Christians was at a turning point. At the same time, the twentieth century showed decline and underdevelopment for the Muslim World, crippled by colonialism and humiliated despite having contributed to the birth of 'a new Europe' through the dissemination of knowledge from cultural centers in Baghdad, Cairo and Cordoba up to the 15th century. The very positive initiative of certain leaders of the Muslim community through "A Common Word between Us and You" has offered a step forward in the revitalization of the Islamic world that is eagerly awaited by the peace-loving community.

The end of bloody hostilities between members of the Abrahamic fraternity is within reach, supported by the Declaration of Nostra Aetate of the Second Vatican Council and "A Common Word between Us and You," and further and later the World Humanitarian Summit's Agenda for Humanity in Istanbul, 2016, which provided a structural, operational, framework for how to move forward. Conflicts are still ongoing for various political reasons, especially conflicts over

The meeting of juries for the selection of the Arab Gulf Fund for Development (AGFUND) Award for Evaluation of Refugee Camps in some major conflicting countries, Geneva, March 2017. The AGFUND Panel was chaired by Queen Sofia (Spain) and Prof. Muhammad Junus (Banglades Nobel Prize winner).

natural resources, but at least religious communities are less and less involved in igniting and exacerbating these conflicts with religious sentiments. Now, religious communities are empowered to become humanitarian actors who can help reduce and overcome the sufferings inflicted by these conflicts.

Following the spirit of dialogue between churches and non-Christian religions, as well as those who have no religion, Austrian philosopher Hans Kochler, following his lecture at the University of Innsbruck in 1972,[298] wrote a letter to the Director General of The United Nations Educational, Scientific and Cultural Organization (UNESCO) echoing the Second Vatican Council regarding the importance of dialogue between different civilizations (or *dialogue entre les différentes civilizations*).[299] In 2001, the President of Iran, Mohammad Khatami, put forward both the Vatican's views and Hans Kochler's ideas to the United Nations. The idea for 'dialogue among civilizations' was accepted by the United Nations and became the basis of the resolution, which named 2001 the United

298. Innsbruck: Arbeitsgemeinschaft für Wissenschaft und Politik, 1973, 75-78.
299. Letter dated 26 September 1972, addressed to the Division of Philosophy of UNESCO. *http://www.i-p-o.org/Koechler-letter-UNESCO-26Sep1972.jpg*

Rahim Yaran, the Grand Imam of the Blue Mosque, Istanbul, explained relevant Qur'an verses to Pope Francis, who visited Istanbul on November 29, 2017, eleven years after the visit of his predecessor Pope Benedict XVI.

Nations' Year of Dialogue among Civilizations.[300] Follow-up dialogue included the three-year Catholic-Muslim Dialogue, which began at the Vatican in 2008, and the United Nations' Resolution No. A / Res / 65/5 regarding World Interfaith Harmony Week.

THE CLASH OF CIVILIZATIONS

In a lecture at The American Enterprise Institute in 1992, political scientist Samuel P. Huntington introduced his Clash of Civilizations theory. He argued that the fundamental source of future conflict, - post-cold war conflict – was neither ideological or economic, nor a conflict between countries, but a war between cultures, with extreme Islam the greatest threat to world peace. Before being officially published as a book in 1996, Huntington's views appeared in the *Foreign Affairs Journal* in 1993. In this journal, Huntington argues that:

> It is my hypothesis that the fundamental source of conflict in this new world will not be primarily ideological or primarily economics. The great divisions among humankind and the dominating source of conflict will be cultural. Nation states will remain the most powerful actors in world affairs, but the principal conflicts of global politics will occur between nations and groups of different civilizations.

---

300. *https://unesdoc.unesco.org/ark:/48223/pf0000123890*

The clash of civilizations will dominate global politics. The fault lines between civilizations will be the battle lines of the future.

Furthermore, Huntington considers that different civilizations, which manifest the cultural identities of populations, are considered very important in analyzing various potential conflicts. For this reason, Huntington divides the world's population into nine major groups of civilizations, which include:

1. Western civilization (United States, Canada, Central and Western Europe, Australia and Oceania).
2. Latin American civilization (Central and South America, Cuba and the Dominican Republic).
3. Orthodox civilization (the former Soviet Union, former Yugoslavia (except Croatia and Slovenia), Bulgaria, Greece and Southern Cyprus).
4. Eastern civilization (China and Japan).
5. Buddhist civilization (Bhutan, Cambodia, Laos, Mongolia, Myanmar, Sri Lanka and Thailand).
6. Confucian civilization (China, Korea, Singapore, Taiwan, and Vietnam. This also includes the Chinese diaspora which is scattered throughout Southeast Asia).
7. Hindu civilization (India, Bhutan and Nepal, including the Indian diaspora).
8. The Muslim world (Greater Middle East (including Armenia, North Cyprus, Ethiopia, Georgia, Israel, Malta and South Sudan), North Africa, Albania, Bangladesh, Bosnia Herzegovina, Brunei, Comoros, Indonesia, Malaysia and the Maldives).
9. Sub-Saharan African civilization (Southern Africa, Central Africa (except Chad), East Africa (except Ethiopia, Comoros, Mauritius, Swahili coast of Kenya and Tanzania), Cape Verde, Ghana, the Ivory Coast, Liberia, and Sierra Leone).[301]

Huntington also identifies six reasons why civilizational conflicts can occur:

1. Civilizations can be easily distinguished from another by their basic differences, which include history, language, culture, tradition, and religion. These differences have grown and developed over centuries, and will remain part of a population's identity for a long period of time.

---

301. Baylis J., Smith S., Owens P. (eds.), *The Globalization of World Politics*, 5th ed (New York: Oxford University Press; 2011), 416–426.

2. The world is becoming smaller. The interactions between peoples of different civilizations are increasing; these increasing interactions intensify "civilization consciousness" and awareness of differences between civilizations and commonalities within civilizations.

3. As a result of economic modernization and social changes, the world's population has been increasingly isolated from "long standing local identities." Religion replaced the role of local identity, and grew as the basis for a new commitment to breaking through national borders and unifying civilizations.

4. "Civilization consciousness" is fueled by the dual role of the Western world. While the Western World has reached the peak of its power, the non-Western world is experiencing a "return-to-the-roots phenomenon." A conflict may occur as Western civilization encounters a non-Western world with its own power and ability to influence the world. .

5. Because of their longstanding history, cultural differences and characteristics are difficult to change, and so compromises and resolutions are not reached as easily as in political and economic disputes.[302]

6. Economic regionalism, or institutional arrangements that facilitate trade within a region, is increasing, but this may only reinforce "civilization-consciousness" if the trade is within a common civilization.

THE CLASH OF CIVILIZATIONS IS NOT AN ACADEMIC THEORY

While Huntington felt that his theory gained momentum after the attack on the twin towers of the World Trade Center in New York on September 11, 2001, important scholars and historians oppose it. British historian Arnold Toynbee has emphasized that civilization is a dynamic process that continues to develop, and that civilizations continue to influence each other. Furthermore, Toynbee also emphasizes that, of the twenty-one great civilizations that have existed in the world, there are only six left.[303] Toynbee's opinion is supported by Edward Said, who counters Huntington's theory with the article "The Clash of Ignorance." Said emphasizes the dynamism and interdependence of cultures, including religions, rather than viewing each civilization as a fixed and frozen entity.

History clearly describes the dynamics of interaction, exchange

---

302. Samuel P. Huntington, *"The Clash of Civilizations?"*.
303. *Ibid.*

and borrowing between civilizations. Thus, Huntington's paradigm does not provide an explanation of the existing reality, just one concrete and practical perspective. Said noted that Huntington's perspective on Islam was strongly influenced by the old memory of warring Muslims and Europeans, especially competition among fellow Abrahamic religions. According to him, the 'clash of civilizations' is nothing more than a new term for an old perspective that cultures have, ignoring the interdependence that continues to this day.[304]

Various polls conducted by the Pew Research Institute and the Gallup Center Abu Dhabi, with 100,000 respondents over 4 years (2006–2010), show that the process of dialogue, or interaction, between civilizations and cultures is a necessity, and provides more benefits than disadvantages. The West's historical resentment against attacks from the Islamic world—in the form of the failed attack on Paris by Muslim troops, which was thwarted by Charles Martel in Poitiers in 732, the seizure of Constantinople by the Ottoman Turks in 1453, and the two failed Sieges of Vienna by The Ottoman Turks in 1529 and 1683—which Samuel P. Huntington used to support his theory, has lost its significance since the Second Vatican Council issued the Nostra Aetate Declaration. It is questionable why Huntington pointed a finger toward the attacks of the Umayyad Caliphate against the Gauls of France in 732 and the two failed Sieges of Vienna in 1529 and 1683, but conveniently forgot the colonization and exploitation of Islamic nations in Africa and Asia by European nations over a period of 400 years. Not to mention that, when the West gripped the Muslim World in the east for 400 years, the church actually considered its self-instated Christianization policy as the 'white man's burden.' Moreover, Huntington's theory is increasingly irrelevant after Pope Benedict XVI's historic friendly visit to Istanbul in November 2006, given that Huntington deemed Turkey as an entity that has threatened Europe several times since the 15th and 16th centuries.[305]

---

304. Dr. Zainal Abidin in discussion "Great Thinkers," https://crcs.ugm.ac.id/menguji-the-clash-of-civilizations-samuel-p-huntington/

305. Pope Benedict XVI's visit to Istanbul, including a visit to the Sultan Ahmed Mosque, known as the Blue Mosque, in November 2006, is a historic first visit of a top leader of the Catholic Church, given that Turkey had a special historical relationship with the Catholic Church, from the pre-Crusade period to its conquest

Between Dialogue and The Clash of Civilizations

The Nobel Prize winner in economics, Amartya Sen, gave the below response to Huntington's thesis:

Diversity is a feature of most cultures in the world. Western civilization is no exception. The practice of democracy that has won out in the modern West is largely a result of a consensus that has emerged since the Enlightenment and the Industrial Revolution, and particularly in the last century or so. To read in this a historical commitment of the West—over the millennia—to democracy, and then to contrast it with non-Western traditions (treating each as monolithic) would be a great mistake.[306]

Huntington's clash of civilizations is increasingly losing its historical and academic significance, especially when Huntington himself, who was a political scientist at Harvard University, admitted

of Constantinople in 1453, and the two failed sieges of Vienna in 1529 and 1683. Pope Urban's agitated speech to instigate the Crusades in the city of Clermont on November 25, 1095, was actually on the side to reclaim the holy city of Jerusalem, and also to fulfill requests for help from the Emperor of Constantinople, Alexios I Komnenos whose territory, Anatolia and Asia Minor, had been encroached by the Seljuks since the early eleventh century.

Meanwhile, Pope Benedict XVI made his decision to carry out the Papal visit to Istanbul in November 2006, only two months after the Pope's controversial speech at the University of Regensburg on September 12, 2006—which drew protests and requests for clarification from 38 Muslim scholars led by Prof. Prince Ghazi bin Muhammad, Adviser to the King of Jordan on October 13, 2006. In his speech at the University of Regensburg, Pope Benedict XVI quoted a dialogue between the Emperor of Constantinople and a Persian scholar in the fourteenth century, where there was talk that "Islam is a religion of violence and backwardness." Pope Benedict XVI did not feel the need to respond to the request for clarification by the 38 Muslim scholars, since what was said was not a Papal statement. But the Pope's attitude disappointed some Muslim scholars, and urged them to write a letter, requesting clarification. Surprisingly, the Pope was on a state visit to Istanbul, Turkey, the only country that, according to Samuel P. Huntington, is historically associated with a threat to the Western World. Pope Benedict XVI's visit to Istanbul was actually a smart choice, rather than having to answer in writing the request for clarification, which it was feared would cause further polemic. But the Papal visit to Istanbul is precisely diplomatic in nature, in the commitment of the Second Vatican Council to forget the past Christian-Muslim animosity. In a similar vein, Pope Benedict XVI's visit to Istanbul is a testimony of how insignificant Huntington's clash of civilizations theory is.

306. Amartya Sen, "Democracy as a Universal Value," *Journal of Democracy*, 10.3 (1999), pp. 3-17 *https://www.unicef.org/socialpolicy/files/Democracy_as_a_Universal_Value.pdf.*

that his thesis is not academic. It is rather an interpretation of the post-cold war global political evolution. In the introduction to his book, he stated that the theory is "highly simplified" in order to provide a framework for looking at global politics that will benefit experts as well as policy makers when thinking about the world. That is why there have been so many criticisms conveyed by academics, because much of Huntington's thesis is based on an outdated structure and narrow approach to civilization.

While global politics has certain interests and political policy lines in fighting for hegemony, the exaltation of humanity has its own urgent need for commitment. Pope Benedict XVI's consecutive visits to Istanbul in 2006 followed by Pope Francis in 2017 are a testimony to the fact that interactions between the West and Islam today are more beneficial than detrimental, and the actions of these leaders as well as the global community continue to disprove of Huntington's theory of grudges and fear.

22

The Struggles of European Muslims

CHALLENGES FOR MUSLIM MIGRANTS

Tariq Ramadan, a Swiss philosopher of Egyptian descent who teaches at the Collège de Saussure, in Lancy, Switzerland, wrote a book about the struggle of Muslim immigrants in Europe in their quest to become both good Muslims and good European citizens. This struggle is related to many things, ranging from social relations in the community, to education of children, employment and economic opportunities, various socio-cultural relations, and awareness of the law as citizens in the country where they live. The story of these struggles is titled *To be a European Muslim: A Study of Islamic Sources in the European Context*.[307]

The early migration of Muslims to Europe, especially in France, Britain and Germany, was organized after World War II, especially in the 1960s, after Europe became more stable and increasingly advanced in terms of social, educational, economic and political life. Muslim migrants flocked to Europe for education and job opportunities, especially to the countries that had previously colonized their homes. Their numbers increased from year to year, and in 1970 the number of Muslim migrants into Europe had reached 15 million people. Tariq Ramadan, who has lived in Paris and calls himself an early generation Muslim migrant, feels the need to remind young Muslim migrants to prepare themselves for the process of interaction and dialogue with the communities and countries they are now living in.

However, it should be noted that there is a wide gap between Muslim migrants—who vary even among themselves in their educational, social, economic and even Islamic beliefs—and Europeans whose culture is more Westernized. What must not be forgotten

---

307. Tariq Ramadan, *To Be a European Muslim: a Study of Islamic Sources in the European Context* (Leicester, UK: Islamic Foundation, 1999).

Sir Muhammad Iqbal (February 22, 1873-April 21, 1938), was highly respected in the UK and got his royal family title for his contribution in promoting the philosophy of the country.

is that the 'Crusades Syndrome' and other misunderstandings of Islam were still very strong in Europe at the time of the early arrival of Muslim migrants. Naturally, this migrant influx aroused suspicion and fear among non-Muslims; this would not turn out well for Muslim migrants, whose hopes for a better life in Europe would turn out to be "an Islamic ideal which does not exist in reality."[308] The situation was exacerbated by the unclear yet fast-spreading image of Islam as a radical religion, which some considered to be a threat to the Western World.

In dealing with this situation, caution needed to be developed so that civilizational dialogue between Muslim migrants and the European non-Muslim population could be realized. Thus, the early generation of immigrant Muslims tried hard to make 'double adjustments' to transform themselves and their groups into 'European Muslims' – not just Muslims living in Europe. This double adjustment entails two main things: *first*, building and strengthening one's identity as a Muslim, and, *second*, adapting to new conditions and European progress in the fields of education, social interaction, and economics, while also adjusting to various laws

---

308. *Ibid.*, 215.

in a new country. Not just as temporary migrants, Muslim immigrants have a permanent presence in Europe and must deal with the acculturation process through a cultural dialogue, from the micro level of basic community to the macro level of responsibility and life order, rights and obligations as citizens.

MUSLIMS' IDENTITIES

Every individual becomes part of the environment, both physical and psychosocial, socio-cultural, economic, political and legal. The individual can be influenced as part of their environment, or, conversely, to have an effect on their environment. The latter option is the goal: to be strong and dynamic in dialogue with the physical and social environment, in which each individual has a strong self-identity, so that he or she will be able to assimilate changes and then rise to meet those changes; the other option would be to to surrender, disappear and dissolve into the assimilation seemingly demanded by the environment. For this reason, Sir Muhammad Iqbal, English-educated Punjabi poet and philosopher, uses the term "ego (*khudi*) in which the individual becomes a self-contained exclusive center."[309] According to Iqbal, a Muslim with a strong *khudi* must be able to absorb and cultivate the attributes of God or divine nature within oneself, which is in accordance with the prophetic tradition: "Cultivate in yourselves the attributes of Allah."[310] With a strong *khudi*, a Muslim, as a caliph and messenger of Allah on earth, will be able to dialogue with his or her environment in Europe, so that he or she will be able to become a European Muslim – not just a Muslim who

---

309. Muhammad Iqbal, *Secrets of the Self (Asrar-i khudi): A philosophical poem by Sheikh Muhammad Iqbal*, trans. Reynold A. Nicholson (London: Macmillan and Co., 1920), xix.

310. "Ego (*khudi*) in which the individual becomes a self contained exclusive center." The self no longer exists in time, but time itself has become a personal dynamism. The self, or *khudi*, is an action of life and life is personal. God incarnates his characteristics not in this realm perfectly but in the individual so that approaching God means cultivating His attributes in oneself. So, seeking God is not by humbling oneself or begging, but by means of a burning energy, manifesting divine (*uluhiyyah*) qualities in us and in the general public. Strictly speaking to God is to perfect the human person, strengthen his will (*irada*). Therefore, according to Iqbal, the true self is not the one who controls the natural world but the self who is covered by God into his own ego (*khudi*). See, Sanusi Batubara, "Muhammad Iqbal: filsafat tentang Tuhan dan Khudi," https://www.anekamakalah.com/2012/04/muhammad-iqbal-filsafat-tentang-tuhan.html

lives in Europe, nor even a Westernized Muslim. In short, according to Iqbal, to assimilate change, the essence of life must be motion-guided and determined by the ego (khudi).

Furthermore, Ramadan maintained that there are at least five elements that must be strengthened to build an identity as a European Muslim:

1. Faith and Islamic spirituality. This is the perfect manifestation of faith that every Muslim should uphold.
2. Worship. This is carrying out the prayers and commands of Allah as a logical consequence and manifestation of the faith and spirituality of a Muslim.
3. Freedom. The duty of a Muslim is to testify to the truth of Islam that was sent down by Allah to the earth through the Qur'an, which was revealed through the Prophet Muhammad. The duty of a Muslim is limited to conveying messages or messages of Islamic truth through preaching, and not attracting or compelling non-Muslims to convert to Islam. As in Azyumardi Azra's statement: "A believer is a person who already knows and then accepts, while an infidel is someone who already knows but then rejects and denies it." The concept of Islamic propagation (da'wah) is clear, that "there is no compulsion in religious matters."[311]

---

311. Azyumardi Azra, in his foreword to the writings of Abdul Mu'ti and Fajar Riza ul Haq, Christian Muhammadiyah, wrote "This book also shows that Muhammadiyah is not an evangelical missionary organization. In its missionary activities, Islamization, in the sense of forcing others to embrace Islam and formalizing Islam in state life, was never a Muhammadiyah's agenda. Although the Muhammadiyah movement has often been argued as 'anti-Christian' in several studies, Muhammadiyah schools in the three study areas not only accommodate Christian students (both Catholic and Protestant), but also recognize the basic rights of students (Christians) to obtain religious education in accordance with the mandate of Indonesia's National Education System Law No. 20 of 2003. Muhammadiyah schools in the three regions, except in Putussibau, facilitate Christian Religious Education (PAK) which is taught by Christian teachers. Author's note:

1. Muhammadiyah "anti-Christian"? The study of Muhammadiyah's Opinion as an "anti-Christian" movement has been widely denied by Muhammadiyah academics and leaders. What is clear is that there is not a single official Muhammadiyah document which depicts an anti-Christian bias. This includes the Statute of Muhammadiyah, Matan, Keyakinan, dan Cita-cita Hidup Muhammadiyah (the Character, Personality, Meaning and the Ideals of Muhammadiyah), Pedoman Hidup Islami Warga Muhammadiyah (Islamic Life Guidelines for Muhammadiyah Communities) and various Muhammadiyah

4. Protection. In addition to freedom of religion and worship, a Muslim also needs protection of social, political and economic rights, three main elements necessary for true recognition of human dignity and integrity.
5. Participation. In fact, Islamic spirituality will increasingly develop through participation in various charitable and social activities, on the local, national and international level. Charitable participation in activities in various fields, besides being an effective medium for community dialogue, is also a means to fill and perfect their faith and the essential message of their religion.[312]

Furthermore, Tariq Ramadan shows the complex reality that is currently being faced by all Muslim migrants in Europe: whether they will continue to think of themselves as Muslim, or to some degree identify as European despite their cultural background. Behind these simple questions is a reality in which Muslims must endure the concern, doubts and suspicions of European non-Muslims towards these new citizens.

The dichotomy between European Muslims and Muslims living in Europe, according to Ramadan, sounds logical. Nevertheless, the constitutional framework in the era of industrialization today does not see conflict between "European" and "Muslim." If anything, there is a conflict of perception, but not at all a conflict of substance. Being a Muslim means upholding the mandate that makes life meaningful, which can only be fully understood through the conception of life, death, and destiny as part of one's faith. Mean-

---

fatwas, especially the latest document, *Negara Indonesia sebagai Dar al-'Ahd wa al-Shahadah* (the Republic of Indonesia as State of Agreement). In fact, Muhammadiyah is now the Islamic organization that is most involved in partnerships with the Christian world, ranging from the charity activities in local communities to the realm of international interfaith peace.

2. Muhammadiyah is not an evangelical missionary movement. In the case of the subject of Al-Islam and Kemuhammadiyahan (Islamic and Muhammadiyah studies) taught in Muhammadiyah schools and colleges, this is only as part of the official curriculum to meet the semester credit target of each student, and in no way an instrument of proselytization. My late sister—an English teacher at the Pangudi Luhur Catholic College in South Jakarta and considered a lay Catholic figure who contributed to building the Cilandak Marinir Catholic Church—Caterina Suwarni Budiman, actually studied and graduated from the Muhammadiyah University Prof. HAMKA, and got a score of 8 for the Al Islam course exam.

312. Tariq Ramadan, *To Be a European Muslim.*

while, the concept of nationality, as understood in industrialized countries, emphasizes something completely different: namely, how to relate to fellow citizens of other countries. Neither of these sentiments are exclusive to the identity of 'European' or 'Muslim; thus, the effort to compare and contrast European Muslims and Muslims living in Europe is an effort that is complex.

23
Reënvisioning a Global Humanity

THE ENABLING ENVIRONMENT

The struggle of European Muslims, as described by Tariq Ramadan, is a model of an 'in situ' struggle, or one that takes place within a European sphere and environment, as well as a fourteen-century-long context of Muslim-European relations. Europe was a special place for early Muslim migrants, the 'pioneers' of the civilizational dialogue between the Western World and the Muslim World, and is an environment that must be paid close attention to, so that the format of this 'in situ' dialogue can proceed naturally and properly.

Apart from Europe's historical background, it has distinctive social, economic and cultural conditions, and it is believed that this continent will provide a more conducive environment for several key factors in building civilizational dialogue toward realizing a global humanity, as mentioned in Surah Hujuraat verse 13 of the Qur'an:

> O mankind, indeed We have created you from male and female and made you peoples and tribes that you may know one another. Indeed, the most noble of you in the sight of Allah is the most righteous of you. Indeed, Allah is Knowing and Acquainted.

Various civilizational dialogue efforts between the West and Islam have occured 'in situ,' or as well as 'ex situ' in various parts of the world outside Europe. Enabling environments to increase the implementation of civilizational dialogue between the Western World and the Muslim World is happening more frequently and can be carried out more effectively.

REËNVISIONING A GLOBAL HUMANITY

The Second Vatican Council, "A Common Word Between Us and You," and the Agenda for Humanity are three historical mile-stones that have provided opportunities for the successful dia-

Mr. Andrew Sisson, USAID Country Director in Indonesia, witnessed the MOU between Catholic, Christian and Muhammadiyah hospitals in Yogyakarta, August 21, 2013, for combating the maternal and neonatal or infant mortality in Indonesia.

logue between the Western World and Muslim World, as well as the Church and Islam.

First, the Second Vatican Council

The Nostra Aetate Declaration of the Second Vatican Council (1965) was a breakthrough in reforming the Church's attitudes towards Islam. This was the era where the Church embarked to its third transformational stage as a *'global church,'* because it recognized universal human salvation. Salvation was no longer only for the baptized, but those who do good things in their lives.

The German Jesuit priest, Karl Rahner, summarized that the Second Vatican Council was the beginning of an evolution toward the *'global church.'* This 3rd stage of the Church transformation is preceded by the Judaism era, the 1st stage, as stipulated within the New Testament, and the Greco Roman and European era, the 2nd stage. The *'global church'* is the stage where the church began dialoguing with Islam and the Eastern religions.[313]

---

313. Rahner, Karl, *Theological Investigations,* Volume 5, Baltimore, 1966

Franz Magnis Suseno SJ, emeritus professor at the Driyarkara School of Philosophy in Jakarta, has reiterated that the Second Vatican Council now supports the salvation of all virtuous persons regardless of their religious traditions. However, the New Testament doesn't provide any speculation on the fate of those who are not baptized, and so the church has required a long time to get to this point. Frans Magnis has also reflected on the notion that within modern societies, the paradigm of "us versus others" has been considerably replaced by the paradigm of the universality of mankind.[314] Indeed, the Second Vatican Council was the beginning and turning point of the Church's transformation toward new values on global humanity, leaving behind centuries of spiritual chauvinism.

Second, "A Common Word between Us and You"

Although it is widely understood that Islam, as a religion of peace, has taught tolerance since fourteen centuries ago, the call for peace on the part of Muslims to Christians in the form of "A Common Word," sent nearly fifty years after the Second Vatican Council, is still regarded by John L Esposito, as *"the first time in history that we have an initiative where Muslims have collectively come together and agreed on the fundamental principles that bind them to Christians."*[315]

Third, the Agenda for Humanity

The World Humanitarian Summit, held in Istanbul on October 22–24, 2016, is the culmination of the United Nations' commitment to realizing the Agenda for Humanity. The Catholic-Muslim Forum I was held at the Vatican on November 4–6, 2008, in which the leaders declared, "We profess that Catholics and Muslims are called to be instruments of love and harmony among believers, and for humanity as a whole, renouncing any oppression, aggression, violence and terrorism."[316] This is expected to become the reference for the global development of humanitarian efforts among religious communities in carrying out the Agenda for Humanity.

---

314. Franz Magnis *Suseno SJ, Katolik itu Apa?* (What is Catholic), PT Kanisius, 2017. p. 140
315. The Royal Aal Al-Bayt Institute for Islamic Thought, *A Common Word between Us and You, 5-Year Anniversary Edition*, 139.
316. https://www.ncronline.org/news/christians-muslims-call-religious-freedom

"Pope Francis wants Fratelli Tutti to move us to action"
www.americanamagazine.org October 5, 2020

POPE FRANCIS' ENCYCLICAL: FRATELLI TUTTI

The issuance of the Nostra Aetate by the Second Vatican Council, "A Common Word," and the warm acceptance by Church leaders didn't automatically solve all the physical and psychological impacts of the fourteen centuries of bloody and painful conflict between the Abrahamic traditions. Continued, structured measures have to be built by all parties in order for trauma healing, communication, dialogue, and partnership to occur. Eventually, this will create "the art of encounter" between peoples of different faiths, as stipulated in Chapter Six of Pope Francis' third social Encyclical, "Fratelli Tutti" ("All Brothers") which was released on October 3, 2020. This immediately followed the signing of the Declaration of Human Fraternity by Pope Francis and Sheikh Ahmed al-Thayeb, Grand Imam of Al-Azhar Cairo, in Abu Dhabi on February 4, 2019. Both are strategic efforts to 'ground' or put the ideas of all the great milestones into action at the community, national and global levels.

The Encyclical Fratelli Tutti, which consists of eight chapters focusing on building human fraternity and friendship, are encouraged by the Pontiff in order to create a more just and peaceful world, with the contribution of all people and institutions.[317]

---

317. https://www.vaticannews.va/en/pope/news/2020-10/fratelli-tutti-pope-fraternity-social-friendship-short-summary.html

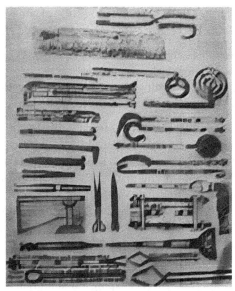

Surgery equipment of the Muslim doctors in the eleventh century, as illustrated by Abu al-Qasim As-Zahrawi (936-1013), the great surgeon who influenced medical science. *Rom Landau*, p. 46

"Fratelli Tutti" clearly stated that in addition to the worldwide crisis of the COVID-19 pandemic, it was also inspired by the Declaration of Human Fraternity.

The Document on "Human Fraternity for World Peace and Living Together" along with the social Encyclical "Fratelli Tutti," are both stronger outcomes of the previous three historical milestones. "Fratelli Tutti" encourages the world to seek an 'art of encounter' with others through "dialogue and friendship."

INTERNATIONAL HUMANITARIAN LAW

In his report as a result of regional consultations on February 9, 2016, the then-Secretary General of the United Nations, Ban Ki-Moon, stated that for 150 years, humanity has neglected the commitment to implementing International Humanitarian Law (IHL), which was initiated by Henry Dunant at the Geneva Conference in 1863. The World Humanitarian Summit in Istanbul has reaffirmed the commitment of the international community to the International Humanitarian Law, as well as to human rights as the foundation of recognition and respect for human dignity.

In point 18 of the UN Report on the results of the World Humanitarian Summit, the Secretary-General of the United Nations stated:

> The World Summit affirmed that compliance with international humanitarian and human rights law is critical to saving lives, reducing suffering and safeguarding human dignity during and after conflict and in other situations of violence.[318]

International Humanitarian Law is in part due to the long civilizational dialogue between the West and Islam; it is rather on a par with the Geneva Conference (1863) that gave birth to the Committee of the Red Cross after the great battle of Solferino on June 24, 1859. James Cockayne, an Australian senior legal officer in International Crime, even stated that the civilizational dialogue between the West and Islam in realizing IHL started with the Crusades. Cockayne said that:

> The modern interaction between Islamic and Western civilizations has played an important part in shaping humanitarian law as we now know it. The innovative influence of Islam on European laws and customs of war stretches back at least as far as the Crusades.[319]

While, the influence of Islamic innovation in the positive and customary laws of European warfare started at least as early as the Crusades, the second influence of Islamic civilization is its strong orientation toward humanism at the beginning of the Renaissance movement. The influence of Islamic civilization emerged strongly at the battle of Solferino itself, where Muslim forces allied with French and Sardinian forces under the command of Napoleon III, while showing sympathy for their Austrian adversaries, who were eventually defeated in the battle. Official Islamic influence came from the Ottoman Empire, which sent representatives to attend the Conference on Maritime Law in Paris, April 16, 1856, as well as the ratification by the Ottomans in 1864 of the outcome of the 1863 Geneva Conference, which was followed by Persia (Iran) in 1874.[320]

---

318. The United Nations General Assembly, "Outcome of the World Humanitarian Summit," https://agendaforhumanity.org/sites/default/files/A-71-353%20-%20SG%20Report%20on%20the%20Outcome%20of%20the%20WHS.pdf

319. James Cockayne, "Islam and international humanitarian law: From a clash to a conversation between civilizations," *International Review of the Red Cross*, No. 847, 30-09-2002, pp. 597–598.

320. *Ibid.*, 601.

Thus, International Humanitarian Law, as a joint code of conduct between religious believers, as well as the result of a long civilizational dialogue between the West and Islam, deserves to be used as a reference again in mobilizing various humanitarian efforts to create peace and honor humans as the most noble creature of God, according to Islam.[321]

The similarity of this Qur'anic concept with the Geneva Convention is not limited to the principle of honor and respect for humans as the most noble creatures of God; both the Qur'an and the Geneva Conventions explain the positive outcomes of this principle, namely a number of obligations which can be reduced to two:

First, respect for oneself, in the form of an obligation to maintain one's self-respect and dignity, so as not to fall into decadence.
Second, the honoring of others, in the form of what each person must do to express his respect for others.[322]

CONCLUSION

The success of Tariq ibn Ziyad in crossing the Strait of Gibraltar and taking control of the Iberian Peninsula in 711, nearly a century after the fall of Jerusalem in 638, was due to the weakness of the Roman Empire, which practically fell in 476. That is why – as stated by Karen Armstrong – as the Crusades, in addition to aiming to reclaim the Holy city of Jerusalem and assisting the Eastern Roman Emperor in Constantinople with interference from the Seljuks, were also an attempt to raise the dignity of the European community after its downturn and defeat. Europe practically slumped with the fall of the Roman Empire, and then entered the Dark Ages, a period that, according to Edward Gibbon, spanned from the fall of the Roman Empire in 476 to the fall of Constantinople in 1453. The Crusades, especially the First Crusade's defeat and capture of Jerusalem, have been termed by historians Guilbert of Nogent, Robert the Monk, and Baldric of Bourgeuil, *"full scale of Biblical war"* and *"the greatest event of world history."*[323]

Despite Pope Urban's success in mobilizing the Crusaders with

---

321. Surah At-Tin, verses 1–4.

322. Muhammad Irqsusi, *Martabat Manusia dalam Perspektif Al-Qur'an dan Konvensi Jenewa: Islam dan Hukum Humaniter Internasional* (Bandung: ICRC Mizan and 2012), pp. 1–20.

323. Karen Armstrong, *Holy War: The Crusade and Their Impact on Today's World* (New York: Anchor Books, 2001), 183.

the support of France, England and Germany, the two-century war has left many records and lessons learned, both for Christians and Muslims, both past and present. The German-born Indonesian pastor, Frans Magnis Suseno, considers the Crusades a "shameful heresy, which until now has left scars in the collective memory of Muslims."

Praise God, the long drama of the fourteen-centuries-old conflicts between religious followers of the Prophet Abraham is nearing a close, due to the Nostra Aetate of the Second Vatican Council, and the open letter "A Common Word between Us and You," which Professor David F. Ford, Regius professor of Divinity and Director, Cambridge Interfaith Programme, University of Cambridge has called "*the single most important initiative ever taken by Muslim scholars and authorities towards Christians.*"[324]

All religious leaders are responsible for learning from this costly and long history and for leading the implementation of the commitments to humanitarian efforts that have been agreed upon. With respect to this, and in accordance with the spirit of 'no one left behind,' in the end, humanity depends on religious and other leaders and individuals to implement change at the community level. The challenge after challenge facing humanity at large, at both the local and global stage, is the golden thread that is open to weave individually and collectively. The Agenda for Change—the operational follow-up to the three milestones: the Nostra Aetate, "A Common Word," and the Agenda for Humanity—requires quick answers from all parties. Globalization is not a dead end, but rather will return to each locality and community. Globalization does not only produce *centripetal forces* that attract and uproot local communities through regional and global dialogue, but it creates *centrifugal forces*, engendering a defense mechanism for local communities to protect themselves, their existence, identity, and 'egos' (or *khudi*). Globalization will create a balance between the 'out there' and 'in here' phenomena. The existing religious communities must play their roles at both ends of the dialogue of culture and civilization within their respective local communities in the widest possible scopes, working through obstacles in the form of the "shrinking of humanitarian space."

---

324. Ford, David F. A Common Word between Us and You, 5-Year Anniversary Edition, MABDA, English Monograph Series, 2012, The Royal Aa-ayt Institute for Islamic Thought, Amman, 11195, Jordan. P.8

The Indonesian Consul General in Frankfurt, Dr. Acep Somantri: "In support to the re-envisioning of the global humanity, the Indonesian students in Europe have to make any necessary cultural adjustments required, to absorb Europe's scientific and developmental spirit to build up their personal identity and integrity."

The commitment to carry out the spirit of the Nostra Aetate of the Second Vatican Council, the spirit of "A Common Word between Us and You,", and the passion for embracing and realizing the Agenda for Humanity of The World Humanitarian Summit, are undoubtedly the golden threads, or the collective 'Light on the Horizon,' in Father Franz Magnis-Suseno's words.

The Abu Dhabi Human Fraternity Declaration and the "Fratelli Tutti" are examples of how these commitments can be continuously renewed and developed, always seeking breakthrough partnerships between religions down to the level of base communities in various parts of the world. In the end, it is at the community level that the mutual commitment between religious believers is realized, both in the form of human relations with God (*hablun minallah*) and those in the nature of human relations with fellow humans (*hablum minannas*). Religious people, especially Muslims and Christians, who constitute more than half of the entire population of the earth, must be able to carry out their function as instruments of peace, individually and collectively.

All the religious commitments, the Nostra Aetate of the *Second Vatican Council* and *"A Common Word,"* which was renewed and consolidated by Abu Dhabi's declaration on *"Human Fraternity"* and the Papal Encyclical *Fratelli Tutti*, along with the United Nations'

Agenda for Humanity or Istanbul Declaration are now on the ground. The current agenda is re-envisioning the global humanity we have agreed upon, and at the same time changing the agenda for all humanity into one of action and best practices at the community level.

Let us hold firm to all wise words of our religions, which have been part of our daily lives, cultures, and histories. Let the Muslim hold firm to and implement the Divine guidance that Islam is "rahmatan lil alamin" or "a blessing to the Universe." Let the Christians share worldwide the spirit of the greatest commandment, to "love thy neighbor as thyself." The framework for achieving peace and civilizational dialogue between religious followers has been laid out already, and just needs the support of communities, countries and religious institutions to make the vision of a Global Humanity a reality.

APPENDIX I

[AR - BE - CS - DE - EN - ES - FR - IT - HE - HU - LA - PT - SW - ZH]

DECLARATION ON THE RELATION OF THE CHURCH
TO NON-CHRISTIAN RELIGIONS

NOSTRA AETATE

PROCLAIMED BY HIS HOLINESS POPE PAUL VI
ON OCTOBER 28, 1965

1. In our time, when day by day mankind is being drawn closer together, and the ties between different peoples are becoming stronger, the Church examines more closely her relationship to non-Christian religions. In her task of promoting unity and love among men, indeed among nations, she considers above all in this declaration what men have in common and what draws them to fellowship.

One is the community of all peoples, one their origin, for God made the whole human race to live over the face of the earth.(1) One also is their final goal, God. His providence, His manifestations of goodness, His saving design extend to all men,(2) until that time when the elect will be united in the Holy City, the city ablaze with the glory of God, where the nations will walk in His light.(3)

Men expect from the various religions answers to the unsolved riddles of the human condition, which today, even as in former times, deeply stir the hearts of men: What is man? What is the meaning, the aim of our life? What is moral good, what is sin? Whence suffering and what purpose does it serve? Which is the road to true happiness? What are death, judgment and retribution after death? What, finally, is that ultimate inexpressible mystery which encompasses our existence: whence do we come, and where are we going?

2. From ancient times down to the present, there is found among various peoples a certain perception of that hidden power which hovers over the course of things and over the events of human history; at times some indeed have come to the recognition of a Supreme Being, or even of a Father. This perception and recognition penetrates their lives with a profound religious sense.

Religions, however, that are bound up with an advanced culture have struggled to answer the same questions by means of more refined concepts and a more developed language. Thus in Hinduism, men contemplate the divine mystery and express it through an inexhaustible abundance of myths and through searching philosophical inquiry. They seek freedom from the anguish of our human condition either through ascetical practices or profound meditation or a flight to God with love and trust. Again, Buddhism, in its various forms, realizes the radical insufficiency of this changeable world; it teaches a way by which men, in a devout and confident spirit, may be able either to acquire the state of perfect liberation, or attain, by their own efforts or through higher help, supreme illumination. Likewise, other religions found everywhere try to counter the restlessness of the human heart, each in its own manner, by proposing "ways," comprising teachings, rules of life, and sacred rites. The Catholic Church rejects nothing that is true and holy in these religions. She regards with sincere reverence those ways of conduct and of life, those precepts and teachings which, though differing in many aspects from the ones she holds and sets forth, nonetheless often reflect a ray of that Truth which enlightens all men. Indeed, she proclaims, and ever must proclaim Christ "the way, the truth, and the life" (John 14:6), in whom men may find the fullness of religious life, in whom God has reconciled all things to Himself.(4)

The Church, therefore, exhorts her sons, that through dialogue and collaboration with the followers of other religions, carried out with prudence and love and in witness to the Christian faith and life, they recognize, preserve and promote the good things, spiritual and moral, as well as the sociocultural values found among these men.

3. The Church regards with esteem also the Moslems. They adore the one God, living and subsisting in Himself; merciful and all- powerful, the Creator of heaven and earth,(5) who has spoken to men; they take pains to submit wholeheartedly to even His inscrutable decrees, just as Abraham, with whom the faith of Islam takes pleasure in linking itself, submitted to God. Though they do not acknowledge Jesus as God, they revere Him as a prophet. They also honor Mary, His virgin Mother; at times they even call on her with devotion. In addition, they await the day of judgment when God will render their deserts to all those who have been raised up from the dead. Finally, they value the moral life and worship God especially through prayer, almsgiving and fasting.

Since in the course of centuries not a few quarrels and hostilities have arisen between Christians and Moslems, this sacred synod urges all to forget the past and to work sincerely for mutual understanding and to preserve as well as to promote together for the benefit of all mankind social justice and moral welfare, as well as peace and freedom.

4. As the sacred synod searches into the mystery of the Church, it remembers the bond that spiritually ties the people of the New Covenant to Abraham's stock.

Thus the Church of Christ acknowledges that, according to God's saving design, the beginnings of her faith and her election are found already among the Patriarchs, Moses and the prophets. She professes that all who believe in Christ-Abraham's sons according to faith (6)-are included in the same Patriarch's call, and likewise that the salvation of the Church is mysteriously foreshadowed by the chosen people's exodus from the land of bondage. The Church, therefore, cannot forget that she received the revelation of the Old Testament through the people with whom God in His inexpressible mercy concluded the Ancient Covenant. Nor can she forget that she draws sustenance from the root of that well-cultivated olive tree onto which have been grafted the wild shoots, the Gentiles.(7) Indeed, the Church believes that by His cross Christ, Our Peace, reconciled Jews and Gentiles. making both one in Himself.(8)

The Church keeps ever in mind the words of the Apostle about his kinsmen: "theirs is the sonship and the glory and the covenants and the law and the worship and the promises; theirs are the fathers and from them is the Christ according to the flesh" (Rom. 9:4-5), the Son of the Virgin Mary. She also recalls that the Apostles, the Church's main-stay and pillars, as well as most of the early disciples who proclaimed Christ's Gospel to the world, sprang from the Jewish people.

As Holy Scripture testifies, Jerusalem did not recognize the time of her visitation,(9) nor did the Jews in large number, accept the Gospel; indeed not a few opposed its spreading.(10) Nevertheless, God holds the Jews most dear for the sake of their Fathers; He does not repent of the gifts He makes or of the calls He issues-such is the witness of the Apostle.(11) In company with the Prophets and the same Apostle, the Church awaits that day, known to God alone, on which all peoples will address the Lord in a single voice and "serve him shoulder to shoulder" (Soph. 3:9).(12)

Since the spiritual patrimony common to Christians and Jews is thus so great, this sacred synod wants to foster and recommend that mutual understanding and respect which is the fruit, above all, of biblical and theological studies as well as of fraternal dialogues.

True, the Jewish authorities and those who followed their lead pressed for the death of Christ;(13) still, what happened in His passion cannot be charged against all the Jews, without distinction, then alive, nor against the Jews of today. Although the Church is the new people of God, the Jews should not be presented as rejected or accursed by God, as if this followed from the Holy Scriptures. All should see to it, then, that in catechetical work or in the preaching of the word of God they do not teach anything that does not conform to the truth of the Gospel and the spirit of Christ.

Furthermore, in her rejection of every persecution against any man, the Church, mindful of the patrimony she shares with the Jews and moved not by political reasons but by the Gospel's spiritual love, decries hatred, persecutions, displays of anti-Semitism, directed against Jews at any time and by anyone.

Besides, as the Church has always held and holds now, Christ underwent His passion and death freely, because of the sins of men and out of infinite love, in order that all may reach salvation. It is, therefore, the burden of the Church's preaching to proclaim the cross of Christ as the sign of God's all-embracing love and as the fountain from which every grace flows.

5. We cannot truly call on God, the Father of all, if we refuse to treat in a brotherly way any man, created as he is in the image of God. Man's relation to God the Father and his relation to men his brothers are so linked together that Scripture says: "He who does not love does not know God" (1 John 4:8).

No foundation therefore remains for any theory or practice that leads to discrimination between man and man or people and people, so far as their human dignity and the rights flowing from it are concerned.

The Church reproves, as foreign to the mind of Christ, any discrimination against men or harassment of them because of their race, color, condition of life, or religion. On the contrary, following in the footsteps of the holy Apostles Peter and Paul, this sacred synod ardently implores the Christian faithful to "maintain good fellowship among the nations" (1 Peter 2:12), and, if possible, to live for their part in peace with all men,(14) so that they may truly be sons of the Father who is in heaven.(15)

NOTES

1. Cf. Acts 17:26
2. Cf. Wis. 8:1; Acts 14:17; Rom. 2:6-7; 1 Tim. 2:4
3. Cf. Apoc. 21:23f.
4. Cf. 2 Cor. 5:18-19
5. Cf .St. Gregory VII, letter XXI to Anzir (Nacir), King of Mauritania (Pl. 148, col. 450f.)
6. Cf. Gal. 3:7
7. Cf. Rom. 11:17-24
8. Cf. Eph. 2:14-16
9. Cf. Lk. 19:44
10. Cf. Rom. 11:28
11. Cf. Rom. 11:28-29; cf. dogmatic Constitution, Lumen Gentium (Light of nations) AAS, 57 (1965) pag. 20
12. Cf. Is. 66:23; Ps. 65:4; Rom. 11:11-32
13. Cf. John. 19:6
14. Cf. Rom. 12:18
15. Cf. Matt. 5:45

https://www.vatican.va/archive/hist_councils/ii_vatican_council/documents/vat-ii_decl_19651028_nostra-aetate_en.html

APPENDIX II

THE 'A COMMON WORD' TEXT

A COMMON WORD BETWEEN US AND YOU

IN THE NAME OF GOD, THE COMPASSIONATE, THE MERCIFUL

On the Occasion of the *Eid al-Fitr al-Mubarak* 1428 A.H. / October 13th 2007 C.E., and on the One Year Anniversary of the Open Letter of 38 Muslim Scholars to H.H. Pope Benedict XVI,

An Open Letter and Call from Muslim Religious Leaders to:

His Holiness Pope Benedict XVI,
His All-Holiness Bartholomew I, Patriarch of Constantinople, New Rome,
His Beatitude Theodoros II, Pope and Patriarch of Alexandria and All Africa,
His Beatitude Ignatius IV, Patriarch of Antioch and All the East,
His Beatitude Theophilos III, Patriarch of the Holy City of Jerusalem,
His Beatitude Alexy II, Patriarch of Moscow and All Russia,
His Beatitude Pavle, Patriarch of Belgrade and Serbia,
His Beatitude Daniel, Patriarch of Romania,
His Beatitude Maxim, Patriarch of Bulgaria,
His Beatitude Ilia II, Archbishop of Mtskheta-Tbilisi, Catholicos- Patriarch of All Georgia,
His Beatitude Chrisostomos, Archbishop of Cyprus,
His Beatitude Christodoulos, Archbishop of Athens and All Greece,
His Beatitude Sawa, Metropolitan of Warsaw and All Poland,
His Beatitude Anastasios, Archbishop of Tirana, Duerres and All Albania,
His Beatitude Christoforos, Metropolitan of the Czech and Slovak Republics,
His Holiness Pope Shenouda III, Pope of Alexandria and Patriarch of All Africa on the Apostolic Throne of St. Mark,
His Beatitude Karekin II, Supreme Patriarch and Catholicos of All Armenians,
His Beatitude Ignatius Zakka I, Patriarch of Antioch and All the East, Supreme Head of the Universal Syrian Orthodox Church,
His Holiness Marthoma Didymos I, Catholicos of the East on the Apostolic Throne of St. Thomas and the Malankara Metropolitan,
His Holiness Abune Paulos, Fifth Patriarch and Catholicos of Ethiopia, Tekle Haymanot, Archbishop of Axium,
His Beatitude Mar Dinkha IV, Patriarch of the Holy Apostolic Catholic Assyrian Church of the East,
The Most Rev. Rowan Williams, Archbishop of Canterbury,
Rev. Mark S. Hanson, Presiding Bishop of the Evangelical Lutheran Church in America, and President of the Lutheran World Federation,

Rev. George H. Freeman, General Secretary, World Methodist Council,
Rev. David Coffey, President of the Baptist World Alliance,
Rev. Setri Nyomi, General Secretary of the World Alliance of Reformed Churches,
Rev. Dr Samuel Kobia, General Secretary, World Council of Churches,
And Leaders of Christian Churches, everywhere.

***

IN THE NAME OF GOD, THE COMPASSIONATE, THE MERCIFUL

A COMMON WORD BETWEEN US AND YOU

SUMMARY AND ABRIDGEMENT

Muslims and Christians together make up well over half of the world's population. Without peace and justice between these two religious communities, there can be no meaningful peace in the world. The future of the world depends on peace between Muslims and Christians.

The basis for this peace and understanding already exists. It is part of the very foundational principles of both faiths: love of the One God, and love of the neighbour. These principles are found over and over again in the sacred texts of Islam and Christianity. The Unity of God, the necessity of love for Him, and the necessity of love of the neighbour is thus the common ground between Islam and Christianity. The following are only a few examples:

Of God's Unity, God says in the Holy Qur'an: *Say: He is God, the One! / God, the Self-Sufficient Besought of all! (Al-Ikhlas,* 112:1-2). Of the necessity of love for God, God says in the Holy Qur'an: *So invoke the Name of thy Lord and devote thyself to Him with a complete devotion (Al-Muzzammil,* 73:8). Of the necessity of love for the neighbour, the Prophet Muhammad said: *None of you has faith until you love for your neighbour what you love for yourself.*

In the New Testament, Jesus Christ said:

> *'Hear, O Israel, the Lord our God, the Lord is One. / And you shall love the Lord your God with all your heart, with all your soul, with all your mind, and with all your strength.' This is the first commandment. / And the second, like it, is this: 'You shall love your neighbour as yourself.'*
>
> *There is no other commandment greater than these.* (Mark, 12:29-31)

In the Holy Qur'an, God Most High enjoins Muslims to issue the following call to Christians and Jews—the People of the Scripture:

> *Say: O People of the Scripture! Come to A Common Word between us and you: that we shall worship none but God, and that we shall ascribe no partner unto Him, and that none of us shall take others for lords beside God. And if they turn away, then say: Bear witness that we are they who have surrendered (unto Him).* (Ali Imran, 3:64)

342

The words: *we shall ascribe no partner unto Him* relate to the Unity of God, and the words: *worship none but God*, relate to being totally devoted to God. Hence they all relate to the *First and Greatest Commandment.* According to one of the oldest and most authoritative commentaries on the Holy Qur'an the words: that *none of us shall take others for lords beside God*, mean 'that none of us should obey the other in disobedience to what God has commanded'. This relates to the Second Commandment because justice and freedom of religion are a crucial part of love of the neighbor.

Thus in obedience to the Holy Qur'an, we as Muslims invite Christians to come together with us on the basis of what is common to us, which is also what is most essential to our faith and practice: the *Two Commandments* of love.

***

IN THE NAME OF GOD, THE COMPASSIONATE, THE MERCIFUL
AND MAY PEACE AND BLESSINGS BE UPON THE PROPHET MUHAMMAD

A COMMON WORD BETWEEN US AND YOU

In the Name of God, the Compassionate, the Merciful, Call unto the way of thy Lord with wisdom and fair exhortation, and contend with them in the fairest way. Lo! thy Lord is Best Aware of him who strayeth from His way, and He is Best Aware of those who go aright. (The Holy Qur'an, Al-Nahl, 16:125)

(I) LOVE OF GOD

LOVE OF GOD IN ISLAM

The Testimonies of Faith

The central creed of Islam consists of the two testimonies of faith or *Sha-hadahs*,[1] which state that: *There is no god but God, Muhammad is the messenger of God.* These Two Testimonies are the *sine qua non* of Islam. He or she who testifies to them is a Muslim; he or she who denies them is not a Muslim. Moreover, the Prophet Muhammad said: The best remembrance is: '*There is no god but God*' ...[2]

The Best that All the Prophets Have Said

Expanding on the best remembrance, the Prophet Muhammad also said:

The best that I have said—myself, and the prophets that came before me—is: 'There is no god but God, He Alone,

He hath no associate, His is the sovereignty and His is the praise and He hath power over all things'.[3]

The phrases which follow the First Testimony of faith are all from the Holy Qur'an; each describes a mode of love of God, and devotion to Him.

343

The words: *He Alone,* remind Muslims that their hearts[4] must be devoted to God Alone, since God says in the Holy Qur'an: *God hath not assigned unto any man two hearts within his body* (Al- Ahzab, 33:4). God is Absolute and therefore devotion to Him must be totally sincere.

The words: *He hath no associate,* remind Muslims that they must love God uniquely, without rivals within their souls, since God says in the Holy Qur'an:

> *Yet there are men who take rivals unto God: they love them as they should love God. But those of faith are more intense in their love for God ...* (Al-Baqarah, 2:165)

Indeed, *[T]heir flesh and their hearts soften unto the remembrance of God ...* (Al-Zumar, 39:23)

The words: *His is the sovereignty,* remind Muslims that their minds or their understandings must be totally devoted to God, for *the sovereignty* is precisely everything in creation or existence and everything that the mind can know. And all is in God's Hand, since God says in the Holy Qur'an: *Blessed is He in Whose Hand is the sovereignty, and, He is Able to do all things.* (Al-Mulk, 67:1)

The words: *His is the praise* remind Muslims that they must be grateful to God and trust Him with all their sentiments and emotions. God says in the Holy Qur'an:

> *And if thou were to ask them: Who created the heavens and the earth, and constrained the sun and the moon (to their appointed work)? they would say: God. How then are they turned away? / God maketh the provision wide for whom He will of His servants, and straiteneth it for whom (He will). Lo! God is Aware of all things. / And if thou were to ask them: Who causeth water to come down from the sky, and therewith reviveth the earth after its death? they verily would say: God. Say: Praise be to God! But most of them have no sense.* (Al- 'Ankabut, 29:61–63)[5]

For all these bounties and more, human beings must always be truly grateful:

> *God is He Who created the heavens and the earth, and causeth water to descend from the sky, thereby producing fruits as food for you, and maketh the ships to be of service unto you, that they may run upon the sea at His command, and hath made of service unto you the rivers; / And maketh the sun and the moon, constant in their courses, to be of service unto you, and hath made of service unto you the night and the day. / And He giveth you of all ye ask of Him, and if ye would count the graces of God ye cannot reckon them. Lo! man is verily a wrong- doer, an ingrate.* (Ibrahim, 14:32–34)[6]

Indeed, the *Fatihah*—which is the greatest chapter in the Holy Qur'an[7]—starts with praise to God:

> In the Name of God, the Infinitely Good, the All- Merciful. / Praise be to God, the Lord of the worlds. / The Infinitely Good, the All-Merciful. / Owner of the Day of Judgement. / Thee we worship, and Thee we

ask for help. / Guide us upon the straight path. / The path of those on whom is Thy Grace, not those who deserve anger nor those who are astray. (Al-Fatihah, 1:1–7)

The *Fatihah*, recited at least seventeen times daily by Muslims in the canonical prayers, reminds us of the praise and gratitude due to God for His Attributes of Infinite Goodness and All-Mercifulness, not merely for His Goodness and Mercy to us in this life but ultimately, on the Day of Judgement[8] when it matters the most and when we hope to be forgiven for our sins. It thus ends with prayers for grace and guidance, so that we might attain—through what begins with praise and gratitude— salvation and love, for God says in the Holy Qur'an: *Lo! those who believe and do good works, the Infinitely Good will appoint for them love.* (Maryam, 19:96)

The words: *and He hath power over all things,* remind Muslims that they must be mindful of God's Omnipotence and thus fear God.[9] God says in the Holy Qur'an:

And fear God, and know that God is with the God-fearing. / Spend your wealth for the cause of God, and be not cast by your own hands to ruin; and do good. Lo! God loveth the virtuous. (Al-Baqarah, 2:194–5)

And fear God, and know that God is severe in punishment. (Al-Baqarah, 2:196)

Through fear of God, the actions, might and strength of Muslims should be totally devoted to God. God says in the Holy Qur'an:

... And know that God is with those who fear Him. (Al-Tawbah, 9:36)

O ye who believe! What aileth you that when it is said unto you: Go forth in the way of God, ye are bowed down to the ground with heaviness. Take ye pleasure in the life of the world rather than in the Hereafter? The comfort of the life of the world is but little in the Hereafter. / If ye go not forth He will afflict you with a painful doom, and will choose instead of you a folk other than you. Ye cannot harm Him at all. God is Able to do all things. (Al-Tawbah, 9:38–39)

The words: *His is the sovereignty and His is the praise and He hath power over all things,* when taken all together, remind Muslims that just as everything in creation glorifies God, everything that is in their souls must be devoted to God:

All that is in the heavens and all that is in the earth glorifieth God; His is the sovereignty and His is the praise and He hath power over all things. (Al-Taghabun, 64:1)

For indeed, all that is in people's souls is known, and accountable, to God:

He knoweth all that is in the heavens and the earth, and He knoweth what ye conceal and what ye publish. And God is Aware of what is in the breasts (of men). (Al-Taghabun, 64:4)

As we can see from all the passages quoted above, souls are depicted in the

Holy Qur'an as having three main faculties: the mind or the intelligence, which is made for comprehending the truth; the will which is made for freedom of choice, and sentiment which is made for loving the good and the beautiful.[10] Put in another way, we could say that man's soul knows through *understanding* the truth, through *willing* the good, and through virtuous emotions and *feeling* love for God. Continuing in the same chapter of the Holy Qur'an (as that quoted above), God orders people to fear Him as much as possible, and to listen (and thus to understand the truth); to obey (and thus to will the good), and to spend (and thus to exercise love and virtue), which, He says, is better for our souls.

By engaging everything in our souls—the faculties of knowledge, will, and love—we may come to be purified and attain ultimate success:

> *So fear God as best ye can, and listen, and obey, and spend; that is better for your souls. And those who are saved from the pettiness of their own souls, such are the successful.* (Al-Taghabun, 64:16)

In summary then, when the entire phrase *He Alone, He hath no associate, His is the sovereignty and His is the praise and He hath power over all things* is added to the testimony of faith—*There is no god but God*—it reminds Muslims that their hearts, their individual souls and all the faculties and powers of their souls (or simply their *entire* hearts and souls) must be totally devoted and attached to God. Thus, God says to the Prophet Muhammad in the Holy Qur'an:

> *Say: Lo! my worship and my sacrifice and my living and my dying are for God, Lord of the Worlds. / He hath no partner. This am I commanded, and I am first of those who surrender (unto Him). / Say: Shall I seek another than God for Lord, when He is Lord of all things? Each soul earneth only on its own account, nor doth any laden bear another's load ...* (Al-An'am, 6:162–164)

These verses epitomize the Prophet Muhammad's complete and utter devotion to God. Thus in the Holy Qur'an God enjoins Muslims who truly love God to follow this example[11], in order in turn to be loved[12] by God:

> *Say, (O Muhammad, to mankind): If ye love God, follow me; God will love you and forgive you your sins. God is Forgiving, Merciful.* (Ali Imran, 3:31)

Love of God in Islam is thus part of complete and total devotion to God; it is not a mere fleeting, partial emotion. As seen above, God commands in the Holy Qur'an: *Say: Lo! my worship and my sacrifice and my living and my dying are for God, Lord of the Worlds. / He hath no partner.* The call to be totally devoted and attached to God, heart and soul, far from being a call for a mere emotion or for a mood, is in fact an injunction requiring all-embracing, constant and active love of God. It demands a love in which the innermost spiritual heart and the whole of the soul—with its intelligence, will and feeling—participate through devotion.

346

APPENDIX II

NONE COMES WITH ANYTHING BETTER

We have seen how the blessed phrase: *There is no god but God, He Alone, He hath no associate, His is the sovereignty and His is the praise and He hath power over all things*—which is the best that all the prophets have said—makes explicit what is implicit in *the best remembrance (There is no god but God)* by showing what it requires and entails, by way of devotion. It remains to be said that this blessed formula is also in itself a sacred invocation—a kind of extension of the First Testimony of faith (*There is no god but God*)—the ritual repetition of which can bring about, through God's grace, some of the devotional attitudes it demands, namely, loving and being devoted to God with all one's heart, all one's soul, all one's mind, all one's will or strength, and all one's sentiment. Hence the Prophet Muhammad commended this remembrance by saying:

> He who says: 'There is no god but God, He Alone, He hath no associate, His is the sovereignty and His is the praise and He hath power over all things' one hundred times in a day, it is for them equal to setting ten slaves free, and one hundred good deeds are written for them and one hundred bad deeds are effaced, and it is for them a protection from the devil for that day until the evening. And none offers anything better than that, save one who does more than that.[13]

In other words, the blessed remembrance, *There is no god but God, He Alone, He hath no associate, His is the sovereignty and His is the praise and He hath power over all things*, not only re- quires and implies that Muslims must be totally devoted to God and love Him with their whole hearts and their whole souls and all that is in them, but provides a way, like its beginning (the testimony of faith)—through its frequent repetition[14]—for them to realize this love with everything they are.

God says in one of the very first revelations in the Holy Qur'an:

> So invoke the Name of thy Lord and devote thyself to Him with a complete devotion. (Al-Muzzammil, 73:8)

LOVE OF GOD AS THE FIRST AND
GREATEST COMMANDMENT IN THE BILE

The *Shema* in the Book of Deuteronomy, 6:4–5, a centrepiece of the Old Testament and of Jewish liturgy, says:

> Hear, O Israel: The LORD our God, the LORD is one! / You shall love the LORD your God with all your heart, and with all your soul, and with all your strength.[15]

Likewise, in the New Testament, when Jesus Christ the Messiah is asked about the Greatest Commandment, he answers:

> But when the Pharisees heard that he had silenced the Sadducees, they gathered together. / Then one of them, a lawyer, asked Him a question, testing Him, and saying, / "Teacher, which is the great commandment in the law?"

> Jesus said to him, "'You shall love the LORD your God with all your heart, with

*all your soul, and with all your mind.' / This is the first and greatest command-
ment. / And the second is like it: 'You shall love your neighbour as yourself.' /
On these two commandments hang all the Law and the Prophets."* (Matthew,
22:34–40)

And also:

*Then one of the scribes came, and having heard them reasoning together, per-
ceiving that he had answered them well, asked him, "Which is the first commandment of all?" / Jesus answered him, "The first of all the commandments
is: 'Hear, O Israel, the LORD our God, the LORD is one. / And you shall love the
LORD your God with all your heart, with all your soul, with all your mind, and
with all your strength.' This is the first commandment. / And the second, like
it, is this: 'You shall love your neighbour as yourself.' There is no other commandment greater than these."* (Mark, 12:28–31)

The commandment to love God fully is thus the First and Greatest Commandment of the Bible. Indeed, it is to be found in a number of other places
throughout the Bible including: Deuteronomy, 4:29, 10:12, 11:13 (also part of
the *Shema*), 13:3, 26:16, 30:2, 30:6, 30:10; Joshua, 22:5; Mark, 12:32–33 and Luke,
10:27–28.

However, in various places throughout the Bible, it occurs in slightly different forms and versions. For instance, in Matthew 22:37 (*You shall love the
lord your God with all your heart, with all your soul, and with all your mind*), the
Greek word for "heart" is *kardia*, the word for "soul" is psyche, and the word
for "mind" is *dianoia*. In the version from Mark, 12:30 (*And you shall love the
lord your God with all your heart, with all your soul, with all your mind, and with
all your strength*) the word "strength" is added to the aforementioned three,
translating the Greek word *ischus*.

The words of the lawyer in Luke, 10:27 (which are confirmed by Jesus
Christ in Luke, 10:28) contain the same four terms as Mark, 12:30. The words
of the scribe in Mark, 12:32 (which are approved of by Jesus Christ in Mark,
12:34) contain the three terms *kardia* ("heart"), *dianoia* ("mind"), and *ischus*
("strength").

In the *Shema* of Deuteronomy, 6:4–5

*(Hear, O Israel: The LORD our God, the LORD is one! / You shall love the
LORD your God with all your heart, and with all your soul, and with all your
strength).*

In Hebrew the word for "heart" is *lev*, the word for "soul" is *nefesh*, and the
word for "strength" is *me'od*.

In Joshua, 22:5 the Israelites are commanded by Joshua to love God and be
devoted to Him as follows:

*But take careful heed to do the commandment and the law which Moses the
servant of the LORD commanded you, to love the LORD your God, to walk in*

all His ways, to keep His commandments, to hold fast to Him, and to serve Him with all your heart and with all your soul. (Joshua, 22:5)

What all these versions thus have in common—despite the language differences between the Hebrew Old Testament, the original words of Jesus Christ in Aramaic, and the actual transmitted Greek of the New Testament—is the command to love God fully with one's heart and soul and to be fully devoted to Him. This is the First and Greatest Commandment for human beings.

In the light of what we have seen to be necessarily implied and evoked by the Prophet Muhammad's blessed saying:

The best that I have said—myself, and the prophets that came before me—is: 'There is no god but God, He Alone, He hath no associate, His is the sovereignty and His is the praise and He hath power over all things',[16] we can now perhaps understand the words *'The best that I have said—myself, and the prophets that came before me'* as equating the blessed formula *'There is no god but God, He Alone, He hath no associate, His is the sovereignty and His is the praise and He hath power over all things'* precisely with the 'First and Greatest Commandment' to love God, with all one's heart and soul, as found in various places in the Bible. That is to say, in other words, that the Prophet Muhammad was perhaps, through inspiration, restating and alluding to the Bible's First Commandment. God knows best, but certainly we have seen their effective similarity in meaning. Moreover, we also do know (as can be seen in the endnotes), that both formulas have another remarkable parallel: the way they arise in a number of slightly differing versions and forms in different contexts, all of which, nevertheless, emphasize the primacy of total love and devotion to God.[17]

***

(II) LOVE OF THE NEIGHBOUR

LOVE OF THE NEIGHBOUR IN ISLAM

There are numerous injunctions in Islam about the necessity and paramount importance of love for—and mercy towards—the neighbour. Love of the neighbour is an essential and integral part of faith in God and love of God because in Islam without love of the neighbour there is no true faith in God and no righteousness. The Prophet Muhammad said: *None of you has faith until you love for your brother what you love for yourself.*[18] And: *None of you has faith until you love for your neighbour what you love for yourself.*[19]

However, empathy and sympathy for the neighbour—and even formal prayers— are not enough. They must be accompanied by generosity and self-sacrifice. God says in the Holy Qur'an:

It is not righteousness that ye turn your faces[20] *to the East and the West; but righteous is he who believeth in God and the Last Day and the angels and the Scripture and the prophets; and giveth wealth, for love of Him, to kinsfolk and to orphans and the needy and the wayfarer and to those who ask, and to set slaves free; and observeth proper worship and payeth the poor-due. And those who keep their treaty when they make one, and the patient in tribulation and adversity and time of stress. Such are they who are sincere. Such are the pious.* (Al-Baqarah, 2:177)

And also:

Ye will not attain unto righteousness until ye expend of that which ye love. And whatsoever ye expend, God is Aware thereof. (Ali Imran, 3:92)

Without giving the neighbour what we ourselves love, we do not truly love God or the neighbour.

LOVE OF THE NEIGHBOUR IN THE BIBLE

We have already cited the words of the Messiah, Jesus Christ, about the paramount importance, second only to the love of God, of the love of the neighbour:

This is the first and greatest commandment. / And the second is like it: 'You shall love your neighbour as yourself.' / On these two commandments hang all the Law and the Prophets. (Matthew, 22:38–40)

And:

And the second, like it, is this: 'You shall love your neighbour as yourself.' There is no other commandment greater than these. (Mark, 12:31)

It remains only to be noted that this commandment is also to be found in the Old Testament:

You shall not hate your brother in your heart. You shall surely rebuke your neighbour, and not bear sin because of him. / You shall not take vengeance, nor bear any grudge against the children of your people, but you shall love your neighbour as yourself: I am the LORD. (Leviticus, 19:17–18)

Thus, the Second Commandment, like the First Commandment, demands generosity and self-sacrifice, and *On these two commandments hang all the Law and the Prophets.*

***

(III) COME TO A COMMON WORD BETWEEN US AND YOU

A COMMON WORD

Whilst Islam and Christianity are obviously different religions—and whilst there is no minimizing some of their formal differences—it is clear that the *Two Greatest Commandments* are an area of common ground and a link between the Qur'an, the Torah and the New Testament. What prefaces the Two Commandments in the Torah and the New Testament, and what they arise out of, is the Unity of God—that there is only one God. For the *Shema* in the Torah, starts: (Deuteronomy, 6:4) *Hear, O Israel: The LORD our God, the LORD is one!* Likewise, Jesus said: (Mark, 12:29) *The first of all the commandments is: 'Hear, O Israel, the LORD our God, the LORD is one'.* Likewise, God says in the Holy Qur'an: *Say: He, God, is One. / God, the Self-Sufficient Besought of all.* (Al-Ikhlas, 112:1–2) Thus the Unity of God, love of Him, and love of the neighbour form a common ground upon which Islam and Christianity (and Judaism) are founded.

This could not be otherwise since Jesus said: (Matthew, 22:40) *On these two commandments hang all the Law and the Prophets.* Moreover, God confirms in the Holy Qur'an that the Prophet Muhammad brought nothing fundamentally or essentially new: *Naught is said to thee (Muhammad) but what already was said to the messengers before thee.* (Fussilat, 41:43)

And:

> *Say (Muhammad): I am no new thing among the messengers (of God), nor know I what will be done with me or with you. I do but follow that which is Revealed to me, and I am but a plain warner.* (Al-Ahqaf, 46:9)

Thus, also God in the Holy Qur'an confirms that the same eternal truths of the Unity of God, of the necessity for total love and devotion to God (and thus shunning false gods), and of the necessity for love of fellow human beings (and thus justice), underlie all true religion:

> *And verily We have raised in every nation a messenger, (proclaiming): Worship God and shun false gods. Then some of them (there were) whom God guided, and some of them (there were) upon whom error had just hold. Do but travel in the land and see the nature of the consequence for the deniers!* (Al-Nahl, 16:36)

> *We verily sent Our messengers with clear proofs, and revealed with them the Scripture and the Balance, that mankind may stand forth in justice...* (Al-Hadid, 57:25)

COME TO A COMMON WORD

In the Holy Qur'an, God Most High tells Muslims to issue the following call to Christians and Jews—the *People of the Scripture*:

> *Say: O People of the Scripture! Come to A Common Word between us and you: that we shall worship none but God, and that we shall ascribe no partner unto Him, and that none of us shall take others for lords beside God. And if they turn away, then say: Bear witness that we are they who have surrendered (unto Him).* (Ali Imran, 3:64)

Clearly, the blessed words: *we shall ascribe no partner unto Him* relate to the Unity of God. Clearly also, worshipping *none but God*, relates to being totally devoted to God and hence to the *First and Greatest Commandment*. According to one of the oldest and most authoritative commentaries (*tafsir*) on the Holy Qur'an—the *Jami' Al-Bayan fi Ta'wil Al-Qur'an* of Abu Ja'far Muhammad bin Jarir Al-Tabari (d. 310 A.H. / 923 C.E.)—*that none of us shall take others for lords beside God*, means 'that none of us should obey in disobedience to what God has commanded, nor glorify them by prostrating to them in the same way as they prostrate to God'. In other words, that Muslims, Christians and Jews should be free to each follow what God commanded them, and not have 'to prostrate before kings and the like';[21] for God says elsewhere in the Holy Qur'an: *Let there be no compulsion in religion....* (Al-Baqarah, 2:256) This clearly relates to the Second Commandment and to love of the neighbour of which justice[22] and freedom of religion are a crucial part. God says in the Holy Qur'an:

> *God forbiddeth you not those who warred not against you on account of religion and drove you not out from your homes, that ye should show them kindness and deal justly with them. Lo! God loveth the just dealers.* (Al-Mumtahinah, 60:8)

We thus as Muslims invite Christians to remember Jesus' words in the Gospel (Mark, 12:29–31):

> *... the LORD our God, the LORD is one. / And you shall love the LORD your God with all your heart, with all your soul, with all your mind, and with all your strength.' This is the first commandment. / And the second, like it, is this: 'You shall love your neighbour as yourself.' There is no other commandment greater than these.*

As Muslims, we say to Christians that we are not against them and that Islam is not against them—so long as they do not wage war against Muslims on account of their religion, oppress them and drive them out of their homes, (in accordance with the verse of the Holy Qur'an (*Al-Mumtahinah*, 60:8) quoted above). Moreover, God says in the Holy Qur'an:

> *They are not all alike. Of the People of the Scripture there is a staunch community who recite the revelations of God in the night season, falling prostrate (before Him). / They believe in God and the Last Day, and enjoin right conduct and forbid indecency, and vie one with another in good works. These are of the righteous. / And whatever good they do, nothing will be rejected of them. God is Aware of those who ward off (evil).* (Ali Imran, 3:113–115)

Is Christianity necessarily against Muslims? In the Gospel Jesus Christ says:

> *He who is not with me is against me, and he who does not gather with me scatters abroad.* (Matthew, 12:30)

> *For he who is not against us is on our side.* (Mark, 9:40) *... for he who is not against us is on our side.* (Luke, 9:50)

According to the *Blessed Theophylact's*[23] *Explanation of the New Testament*, these statements are not contradictions because the first statement (in the actual

Greek text of the New Testament) refers to demons, whereas the second and third statements refer to people who recognised Jesus, but were not Christians. Muslims recognize Jesus Christ as the Messiah, not in the same way Christians do (but Christians themselves anyway have never all agreed with each other on Jesus Christ's nature), but in the following way: ... *the Messiah Jesus son of Mary is a Messenger of God and His Word which he cast unto Mary and a Spirit from Him ...* (Al- Nisa', 4:171). We therefore invite Christians to consider Muslims *not against,* and thus *with them,* in accordance with Jesus Christ's words here.

Finally, as Muslims, and in obedience to the Holy Qur'an, we ask Christians to come together with us on the common essentials of our two religions

That we shall worship none but God, and that we shall ascribe no partner unto Him, and that none of us shall take others for lords beside God ... (Ali Imran, 3:64)

Let this common ground be the basis of all future interfaith dialogue between us, for our common ground is that on which hangs *all the Law and the Prophets* (Matthew, 22:40). God says in the Holy Qur'an:

Say (O Muslims): We believe in God and that which is revealed unto us and that which was revealed unto Abraham, and Ishmael, and Isaac, and Jacob, and the tribes, and that which Moses and Jesus received, and that which the prophets received from their Lord. We make no distinction between any of them, and unto Him we have surrendered. / And if they believe in the like of that which ye believe, then are they rightly guided. But if they turn away, then are they in schism, and God will suffice thee against them. He is the Hearer, the Knower. (Al-Baqarah, 2:136–137)

BETWEEN US AND YOU

Finding common ground between Muslims and Christians is not simply a matter for polite ecumenical dialogue between selected religious leaders. Christianity and Islam are, respectively, the largest and second largest religions in the world and in history. Christians and Muslims reportedly make up over a third and over a fifth of humanity respectively. Together they make up more than 55% of the world's population, making the relationship between these two religious communities the most important factor in contributing to meaningful peace around the world. If Muslims and Christians are not at peace, the world cannot be at peace. With the terrible weaponry of the modern world; with Muslims and Christians intertwined everywhere as never before, no side can unilaterally win a conflict between more than half of the world's inhabitants. Thus our common future is at stake. The very survival of the world itself is perhaps at stake.

And to those who nevertheless relish conflict and destruction for their own sake or reckon that ultimately they stand to gain through them, we say that our very eternal souls are all also at stake if we fail to sincerely make every effort to make peace and come together in harmony. God says in the Holy Qur'an:

Lo! God enjoineth justice and kindness, and giving to kinsfolk, and forbiddeth lewdness and abomination and wickedness. He exhorteth you in order that ye may take heed. (Al-Nahl, 16:90)

Jesus Christ said: *Blessed are the peacemakers ...* (Matthew, 5:9), and also: *For what profit is it to a man if he gains the whole world and loses his soul?* (Matthew, 16:26).

So let our differences not cause hatred and strife between us. Let us vie with each other only in righteousness and good works. Let us respect each other, be fair, just and kind to one another and live in sincere peace, harmony and mutual goodwill. God says in the Holy Qur'an:

And unto thee have We revealed the Scripture with the truth, confirming whatever Scripture was before it, and a watcher over it. So judge between them by that which God hath revealed, and follow not their desires away from the truth which hath come unto thee. For each We have appointed a law and a way. Had God willed He could have made you one community. But that He may try you by that which He hath given you (He hath made you as ye are). So vie one with another in good works. Unto God ye will all return, and He will then inform you of that wherein ye differ. (Al-Ma'idah, 5:48)

WAL-SALAAMU 'ALAYKUM, PAX VOBISCUM.

NOTES

1. In Arabic: *La illaha illa Allah, Muhammad Rasul Allah.* The two *Shahadahs* actually both occur (albeit separately) as phrases in the Holy Qur'an (in Muhammad, 47:19, and Al-Fath, 48:29, respectively).
2. *Sunan Al-Tirmidhi, Kitab Al-Da'awat*, 462/5, no. 3383; *Sunan Ibn Majah*, 1249/2.
3. *Sunan Al-Tirmidhi, Kitab Al-Da'awat, Bab al-Du'a fi Yawm 'Arafah*, Hadith no. 3934. It is important to note that the additional phrases, *He Alone, He hath no associate, His is the sovereignty and His is the praise and He hath power over all things*, all come from the Holy Qur'an, in exactly those forms, albeit in different passages. *He Alone*—referring to God—is found at least six times in the Holy Qur'an (7:70; 14:40; 39:45; 40:12; 40:84 and 60:4). *He hath no associate*, is found in exactly that form at least once (Al-An'am, 6:173). *His is the sovereignty and His is the praise and He hath power over all things*, is found in exactly this form once in the Holy Qur'an (Al-Taghabun, 64:1), and parts of it are found a number of other times (for instance, the words, *He hath power over all things*, are found at least five times: 5:120; 11:4; 30:50; 42:9 and 57:2).
4. The Heart: In Islam the (spiritual, not physical) heart is the organ of perception of spiritual and metaphysical knowledge. Of one of the Prophet Muhammad's greatest visions God says in the Holy Qur'an: *The inner heart lied not (in seeing) what it saw.* (Al-Najm, 53:11) Indeed, elsewhere in the Holy Qur'an, God says: *[F]or indeed it is not the eyes that grow blind, but it is the hearts, which are within the bosoms, that grow blind.* (Al-Hajj, 22:46; see whole verse and also: 2:9–10; 2:74; 8:24; 26:88–89; 48:4; 83:14 et al. ... There are in fact over a hundred mentions of

354

the heart and its synonyms in the Holy Qur'an.)

Now there are different understandings amongst Muslims as regards the direct Vision of God (as opposed to spiritual realities as such) be it in this life or the next—God says in the Holy Qur'an (of the Day of Judgement): *That day will faces be resplendent, / Looking toward their Lord;* (Al-Qiyamah, 75:22–23)

Yet God also says in the Holy Qur'an:

Such is God, your Lord. There is no God save Him, the Creator of all things, so worship Him. And He taketh care of all things. / Vision comprehendeth Him not, but He comprehendeth (all) vision. He is the Subtle, the Aware. / Proofs have come unto you from your Lord, so whoso seeth, it is for his own good, and whoso is blind is blind to his own hurt. And I am not a keeper over you. (Al-An'am, 6:102–104)

Howbeit, it is evident that the Muslim conception of the (spiritual) heart is not very different from the Christian conception of the (spiritual) heart, as seen in Jesus's words in the New Testament: *Blessed are the pure in heart, for they shall see God.* (Matthew, 5:8); and Paul's words: *For now we see in a mirror, dimly, but then face to face. Now I know in part, but then I shall know just as I am known.* (1 Corinthians, 13:12)

5. See also: *Luqman, 31:25.*

6. See also: *Al-Nahl,* 16:3–18.

7. *Sahih Bukhari, Kitab Tafsir Al-Qur'an, Bab ma Ja'a fi Fatihat Al-Kitab* (Hadith no. 1); also: *Sahih Bukhari, Kitab Fada'il Al-Qur'an, Bab Fadl Fatihat Al-Kitab* (Hadith no. 9), no. 5006.

8. The Prophet Muhammad said:

God has one hundred mercies. He has sent down one of them between genii and human beings and beasts and animals and because of it they feel with each other; and through it they have mercy on each other; and through it, the wild animal feels for its offspring. And God has delayed ninety-nine mercies through which he will have mercy on his servants on the Day of Judgement. (Sahih Muslim, Kitab Al-Tawbah; 2109/4; no. 2752; see also Sahih Bukhari, Kitab Al-Riqaq, no. 6469).

9. Fear of God is the Beginning of Wisdom: The Prophet Muhammad is reported to have said: *The chief part of wisdom is fear of God—be He exalted (Musnad al-Shahab,* 100/1; *Al-Dulaymi, Musnad Al-Firdaws,* 270/2; *Al-Tirmidhi, Nawadir Al-Usul;* 84/3; *Al-Bayhaqi, Al-Dala'il* and *Al-Bayhaqi, Al-Shu'ab; Ibn Lal, Al-Makarim; Al-Ash'ari, Al-Amthal,* et al.) This evidently is similar to the Prophet Solomon's words in the Bible: *The fear of the lord is the beginning of Wisdom ...* (Proverbs, 9:10); and: *The fear of the lord is the beginning of knowledge.* (Proverbs, 1:7)

10. The Intelligence, the Will and Sentiment in the Holy Qur'an: Thus God in the Holy Qur'an tells human beings to believe in Him and call on Him (thereby using the intelligence) with fear (which motivates the will) and with hope (and thus with sentiment):

Only those believe in Our revelations who, when they are reminded of them, fall down prostrate and hymn the praise of their Lord, and they are not scornful, / Who forsake their beds to cry unto their Lord in fear and hope, and spend of that We have bestowed on them. / No soul knoweth what is kept hid for them of joy, as a reward for what they used to do. (Al-Sajdah, 32:15–17)

*(O mankind!) Call upon your Lord humbly and in secret. Lo! He loveth not aggressors.
/ Work not confusion in the earth after the fair ordering (thereof), and call on Him
in fear and hope. Lo! the mercy of God is near unto the virtuous.* (Al-A'raf, 7:55–56)

Likewise, the Prophet Muhammad himself is described in terms which
manifest knowledge (and hence the intelligence), eliciting hope (and hence
sentiment) and instilling fear (and hence motivating the will):

*O Prophet! Lo! We have sent thee as a witness and a bringer of good tidings and a
warner. (Al-Ahzab, 33:45)*

*Lo! We have sent thee (O Muhammad) as a witness and a bearer of good tidings
and a warner,* (Al-Fath, 48:8)

11. A Goodly Example: The love and total devotion of the Prophet Muhammad to God
is for Muslims the model that they seek to imitate. God says in the Holy Qur'an:

*Verily in the messenger of God ye have a goodly example for him who hopeth for
God and the Last Day, and remembereth God much.* (Al-Ahzab, 33:21)

The totality of this love excludes worldliness and egotism, and is itself
beautiful and loveable to Muslims. Love of God is itself loveable to Muslims.
God says in the Holy Qur'an:

*And know that the messenger of God is among you. If he were to obey you in many
matters, ye would surely fall into misfortune; but God hath made the faith loveable to you and hath beautified it in your hearts, and hath made disbelief and
lewdness and rebellion hateful unto you. Such are they who are the rightly guided.*
(Al-Hujurat, 49:7)

12. This 'particular love' is in addition to God's universal Mercy *which embraceth all
things (Al-A'raf, 7:156);* but God knows best.

13. *Sahih Al-Bukhari, Kitab Bad' al-Khalq, Bab Sifat Iblis wa Junudihi;* Hadith no. 3329.
Other Versions of the Blessed Saying: This blessed saying of the Prophet Muhammad's, is found in dozens of hadith (sayings of the Prophet Muhammad)
in differing contexts in slightly varying versions.

The one we have quoted throughout in the text (*There is no god but God,
He alone. He hath no associate. His is the sovereignty, and His is the praise, and He
hath power over all things*) is in fact the shortest version. It is to be found in
Sahih al-Bukhari: Kitab al-Adhan (no. 852); *Kitab al-Tahajjud* (no. 1163); *Kitab al-
'Umrah* (no. 1825); *Kitab Bad' al-Khalq* (no. 3329); *Kitab al-Da'awat* (nos. 6404,
6458, 6477); *Kitab al-Riqaq* (no. 6551); *Kitab al-I'tisam bi'l-Kitab* (no. 7378); in
Sahih Muslim: Kitab al-Masajid (nos. 1366, 1368, 1370, 1371, 1380); *Kitab al-Hajj*
(nos. 3009, 3343); *Kitab al-Dhikr wa'l-Du'a'* (nos. 7018, 7020, 7082, 7084); in *Sunan Abu Dawud: Kitab al-Witr* (nos. 1506, 1507, 1508); *Kitab al-Jihad* (no. 2772);
Kitab al-Kharaj (no. 2989); *Kitab al-Adab* (nos. 5062, 5073, 5079); in *Sunan al-Tirmidhi: Kitab al-Hajj* (no. 965); *Kitab al-Da'awat* (nos. 3718, 3743, 3984); in *Sunan
al-Nasa'i: Kitab al-Sahw* (nos. 1347, 1348, 1349, 1350, 1351); *Kitab Manasik al-Hajj*
(nos. 2985, 2997); *Kitab al-Iman wa'l-Nudhur* (no. 3793); in *Sunan Ibn Majah: Kitab
al-Adab* (no. 3930); *Kitab al-Du'a'* (nos. 4000, 4011); and in *Muwatta' Malik: Kitab*

APPENDIX II

al-Qur'an (nos. 492, 494); *Kitab al-Hajj* (no. 831).

A longer version including the words *yuhyi wa yumit*—(There is no god but God, He alone. He hath no associate. His is the sovereignty, and His is the praise. He giveth life, and He giveth death, and He hath power over all things.)—is to be found in *Sunan Abu Dawud: Kitab al-Manasik* (no. 1907); in *Sunan al-Tirmidhi: Kitab al-Salah* (no. 300); *Kitab al-Da'awat* (nos. 3804, 3811, 3877, 3901); and in *Sunan al-Nasa'i: Kitab Manasik al-Hajj* (nos. 2974, 2987, 2998); *Sunan Ibn Majah: Kitab al-Manasik* (no. 3190).

Another longer version including the words *bi yadihi al-khayr*—(There is no god but God, He alone. He hath no associate. His is the sovereignty, and His is the praise. In His Hand is the good, and He hath power over all things.)—is to be found in *Sunan Ibn Majah: Kitab al-Adab* (no. 3931); *Kitab al-Du'a'* (no. 3994).

The longest version, which includes the words *yuhyi wa yumit wa Huwa Hayyun la yamut bi yadihi al-khayr*—(There is no god but God, He alone. He hath no associate. His is the sovereignty, and His is the praise. He giveth life, and He giveth death. He is the Living, who dieth not. In His Hand is the good, and He hath power over all things.)—is to be found in *Sunan al-Tirmidhi: Kitab al-Da'awat* (no. 3756) and in *Sunan Ibn Majah: Kitab al-Tijarat* (no. 2320), with the difference that this latter hadith reads: *bi yadihi al-khayr kuluhu* (in His Hand is *all* good).

It is important to note, however, that the Prophet Muhammad, only described the first (shortest) version as: *the best that I have said—myself, and the prophets that came before me,* and only of that version did the Prophet say: *And none comes with anything better than that, save one who does more than that.*

(These citations refer to the numbering system of *The Sunna Project's Encyclopaedia of Hadith (Jam' Jawami' al-Ahadith wa'l-Asanid)*, prepared in cooperation with the scholars of al-Azhar, which includes *Sahih al-Bukhari, Sahih Muslim, Sunan Abu Dawud, Sunan al-Tirmidhi, Sunan al-Nasa'i, Sunan Ibn Majah, and Muwatta' Malik.*).

14. Frequent Remembrance of God in the Holy Qur'an: The Holy Qur'an is full of injunctions to invoke or remember God frequently:

Remember the name of thy Lord at morn and evening. (Al-Insan, 76:25)

So remember God, standing, sitting and [lying] down on your sides. (Al-Nisa, 4:103)

And do thou (O Muhammad) remember thy Lord within thyself humbly and with awe, below thy breath, at morn and evening. And be not thou of the neglectful. (Al-'Araf, 7:205)

... Remember thy Lord much, and praise (Him) in the early hours of night and morning. (Ali Imran, 3:41)

O ye who believe! Remember God with much remembrance. / And glorify Him early and late. (Al-Ahzab, 33:41–42)

See also: 2:198–200; 2:203; 2:238–239; 3:190–191; 6:91; 7:55; 7:180; 8:45; 17:110; 22:27–41; 24:35–38; 26:227; 62:9–10; 87:1–17, et al.

Similarly, the Holy Qur'an is full of verses that emphasize the paramount importance of the Remembrance of God (see: 2:151–7; 5:4; 6:118; 7:201; 8:2–4;

13:26–28; 14:24–27; 20:14; 20:33–34; 24:1; 29:45; 33:35; 35:10; 39:9; 50:37; 51:55–58; and 33:2; 39:22–23 and 73:8–9 as already quoted, et al.), and the dire consequences of not practising it (see: 2:114; 4:142; 7:179–180; 18:28; 18:100–101; 20:99–101; 20:124–127; 25:18; 25:29; 43:36; 53:29; 58:19; 63:9; 72:17 et al.; see also 107:4–6). Hence God ultimately says in the Holy Qur'an:

Has not the time arrived for the believers that their hearts in all humility should engage in the remembrance of God .... ? (Al-Hadid, 57:16)

... [S]lacken not in remembrance of Me. (Taha, 20:42)

15. Herein all Biblical Scripture is taken from the New King James Version. Copyright © 1982 by Thomas Nelson, Inc. Used with permission. All rights reserved.
16. *Sunan Al-Tirmithi, Kitab Al-Da'wat, Bab al-Du'a fi Yawm 'Arafah, Hadith no. 3934.* Op. cit.
17. In the Best Stature: Christianity and Islam have comparable conceptions of man being created in the best stature and from God's own breath. The Book of Genesis says:

Remember your Lord whenever you forget. (Al-Kahf, 18:24)

So God created man in His own image; in the image of God He created him; male and female He created them. (Genesis, 1:27)

And:

And the lord God formed man of the dust of the ground, and breathed into his nostrils the breath of life; and man became a living being. (Genesis, 2:7)

And the Prophet Muhammad said:

Verily God created Adam in His own image (Sahih Al- Bukhari, Kitab Al-Isti'than, 1; Sahih Muslim, Kitab Al-Birr 115; Musnad Ibn Hanbal, 2: 244, 251, 315, 323 etc. et al.).

And We created you, then fashioned you, then told the angels: Fall ye prostrate before Adam! And they fell prostrate, all save Iblis, who was not of those who make prostration. (Al-A'raf, 7:11)

By the fig and the olive / By Mount Sinai, / And by this land made safe / Surely We created man of the best stature / Then We reduced him to the lowest of the low, / Save those who believe and do good works, and theirs is a reward unfailing. / So who henceforth will give the lie to the about the judgment? / Is not God the wisest of all judges? (Al-Tin, 95:1–8)

God it is Who appointed for you the earth for a dwelling-place and the sky for a canopy, and fashioned you and perfected your shapes, and hath provided you with good things. Such is God, your Lord. Then blessed be God, the Lord of the Worlds! (Al-Ghafir, 40:64)

Nay, but those who do wrong follow their own lusts without knowledge. Who is able to guide him whom God hath sent astray ? For such there are no helpers. / So set thy purpose (O Muhammad) for religion as a man by nature upright - the nature (framed) of God, in which He hath created man. There is no altering (the laws of) God's creation. That is the right religion, but most men know not—/ (Al-Rum, 30:29–30)

And when I have fashioned him and breathed into him of My Spirit, then fall down before him prostrate. (Sad, 38:72)

And when thy Lord said unto the angels: Lo! I am about to place a viceroy in the earth, they said: Wilt thou place therein one who will do harm therein and will shed blood, while we, we hymn Thy praise and sanctify Thee ? He said: Surely I know that which ye know not. / And He taught Adam all the names, then showed them to the angels, saying: Inform Me of the names of these, if ye are truthful ./ They said: Be glorified! We have no knowledge saving that which Thou hast taught us. Lo! Thou, only Thou, art the Knower, the Wise. / He said: O Adam! Inform them of their names, and when he had informed them of their names, He said: Did I not tell you that I know the secret of the heavens and the earth ? And I know that which ye disclose and which ye hide. / And when We said unto the angels: Prostrate yourselves before Adam, they fell prostrate, all save Iblis. He demurred through pride, and so became a disbeliever... / And We said: O Adam! Dwell thou and thy wife in the Garden, and eat ye freely (of the fruits) thereof where ye will; but come not nigh this tree lest ye become wrong-doers. (Al-Baqarah, 2:30–35)

18. *Sahih Al-Bukhari, Kitab al-Iman,* Hadith no. 13.
19. *Sahih Muslim, Kitab al-Iman,* 67–1, Hadith no. 45.
20. The classical commentators on the Holy Qur'an (see: *Tafsir Ibn Kathir, Tafsir Al-Jalalayn*) generally agree that this is a reference to (the last movements of) the Muslim prayer.
21. *Abu Ja'far Muhammad Bin Jarir Al-Tabari, Jami' al-Bayan fi Ta'wil al-Qur'an, (Dar al-Kutub al-'Ilmiyyah, Beirut, Lebanon,* 1st ed, 1992/1412,) tafsir of Ali Imran, 3:64; Volume 3, pp. 299–302.
22. According to grammarians cited by Tabari (op cit.) the word 'common' (*sawa'*) in ' *A Common Word* between us' also means 'just', 'fair' (*adl*).
23. The Blessed Theophylact (1055–1108 C.E.) was the Orthodox Archbishop of Ochrid and Bulgaria (1090–1108 C.E.). His native language was the Greek of the New Testament. His *Commentary* is currently available in English from Chrysostom Press.

LIST OF SIGNATORIES TO 'A COMMON WORD'

The following is a list of the original 138 signatories to the *A Common Word* (ACW) Open Letter. It is followed by a list of those who have endorsed ACW after its publication.

LIST OF SIGNATORIES

(in alphabetical order)

1. His Royal Eminence Sultan Muhammadu Sa'ad Ababakar The 20th Sultan of Sokoto; Leader of the Muslims of Nigeria
2. H.E. Shaykh Dr Hussein Hasan Abakar Imam of the Muslims, Chad; President, Higher Council for Islamic Affairs, Chad
3. H.E. Prof. Dr Abdul-Salam Al-Abbadi President of Aal al-Bayt University; Former Minister of Religious Affairs, Jordan
4. Prof. Dr Taha Abd Al-Rahman President of the Wisdom Circle for Thinkers and Researchers, Morocco; Director of Al-Umma Al-Wasat Magazine, International Union of Muslim Scholars
5. Imam Feisal Abdul Rauf Co-founder and Chairman of the Board of the Cordoba Initiative; Founder of the ASMA Society (American Society for Muslim Advancement); Imam of Masjid Al-Farah, NY, NY, USA
6. Sheikh Muhammad Nur Abdullah Vice President of the Fiqh Council of North America, USA
7. Dr Shaykh Abd Al-Quddus Abu Salah President of the International League for Islamic Ethics; Editor of the Journal for Islamic Ethics, Riyadh, Saudi Arabia
8. H.E. Prof. Dr Abd Al-Wahhab bin Ibrahim Abu Solaiman Member of the Committee of Senior Ulama, Saudi Arabia
9. Dr Lateef Oladimeji Adegbite Acting Secretary and Legal Adviser, Nigerian Supreme Council for Islamic Affairs
10. H.E. Amb. Prof. Dr Akbar Ahmed Ibn Khaldun Chair of Islamic Studies, American University in Washington DC, USA
11. H.E. Judge Prince Bola Ajibola Former International High Court Judge; Former Minister of Justice of Nigeria; Former Attorney-General of Nigeria; Founder of the Crescent University and Founder of the Islamic Movement of Africa (IMA)
12. H.E. Prof. Dr Kamil Al-Ajlouni Head of National Centre for Diabetes; Founder of the Jordanian University of Science and Technology (JUST), Former Minister and Former Senator, Jordan
13. Shaykh Dr Mohammed Salim Al-'Awa Secretary General of the International Union of Muslim Scholars; Head of the Egyptian Association for Culture and Dialogue
14. Mr. Nihad Awad National Executive Director and Co-founder of the Council on American-Islamic Relations (CAIR), USA
15. H.E. Prof. Dr Al-Hadi Al-Bakkoush Former Prime Minister of Tunisia, Author

360

16. H.E. Shaykh Al-Islam Dr Allah-Shakur bin Hemmat Bashazada Grand Mufti of Azerbaijan and Head of the Muslim Administration of the Caucasus
17. H.E. Dr Issam El-Bashir Secretary General of the International Moderation Centre, Kuwait; Former Minister of Religious Affairs, Sudan
18. H.E. Prof. Dr Allamah Shaykh Abd Allah bin Mahfuz bin Bayyah Professor, King Abdul Aziz University, Saudi Arabia; Former Minister of Justice, Former Minister of Education and Former Minister of Religious Affairs, Mauritania; Vice President of the International Union of Muslim Scholars; Founder and President, Global Center for Renewal and Guidance
19. Dr Mohamed Bechari President, Federal Society for Muslims in France; General Secretary of the European Islamic Conference (EIC), France; Member of the International Fiqh Academy
20. Prof. Dr Ahmad Shawqi Benbin Director of the Hasaniyya Library, Morocco
21. Prof. Dr Allamah Shaykh Muhammad Sa'id Ramadan Al-Buti Dean, Dept. of Religion, University of Damascus, Syria
22. Prof. Dr Mustafa Çagrıcı Mufti of Istanbul, Turkey
23. H.E. Shaykh Prof. Dr Mustafa Ceric Grand Mufti and Head of Ulema of Bosnia and Herzegovina
24. Professor Ibrahim Chabbuh Director General of the Royal Aal al-Bayt Institute for Islamic Thought, Jordan; President of the Association for the Safeguarding of the City of Qayrawan, Tunisia
25. H.E. Prof. Dr Mustafa Cherif Muslim Intellectual; Former Minister of Higher Education and Former Ambassador, Algeria
26. Dr Caner Dagli Assistant Professor, Roanoke College, USA
27. Ayatollah Prof. Dr Seyyed Mostafa Mohaghegh Damad Dean of Department of Islamic Studies, The Academy of Sciences of Iran; Professor of Law and Islamic Philosophy, Tehran University; Fellow, The Iranian Academy of Sciences, Iran; Former Inspector General of Iran
28. Ayatollah Seyyed Abu Al-Qasim Al-Deebaji Imam Zayn Al-Abideen Mosque, Kuwait
29. H.E. Prof. Dr Shakir Al-Fahham Head of the Arabic Language Academy, Damascus; Former Minister of Education, Syria
30. Shaykh Seyyed Hani Fahs Member of Supreme Shia Committee, Lebanon; Founding Member of the Arab Committee for the Islamic-Christian Dialogue, and the Permanent Committee for the Lebanese Dialogue
31. H.E. Shaykh Salim Falahat Director General of the Muslim Brotherhood, Jordan
32. Chief Abdul Wahab Iyanda Folawiyo Member, Supreme Council for Islamic Affairs of Nigeria; Vice President, Jamaat Nasril Islam
33. H.E. Shaykh Ravil Gainutdin Grand Mufti of Russia
34. Justice Ibrahim Kolapo Sulu Gambari Justice of Nigerian Court of Appeal; National Vice Chairman, Nigerian Football Association (NFA)

35. Prof. Dr Abd Al-Karim Gharaybeh Historian and Senator, Jordan
36. H.E. Prof. Dr Abdullah Yusuf Al-Ghoneim Director of the Kuwaiti Centre for Research and Studies on Kuwait; Former Minister of Education, Kuwait
37. H.E. Prof. Dr Bu Abd Allah bin al-Hajj Muhammad Al Ghulam Allah Minister of Religious Affairs, Algeria
38. Prof. Dr Alan Godlas Co-Chair, Islamic Studies, University of Georgia, USA; Editor-in- Chief, Sufi News and Sufism World Report; Director, Sufis Without Borders
39. H.E. Shaykh Nezdad Grabus Grand Mufti of Slovenia
40. H.E. Shaykh Dr Al-Habib Ahmad bin Abd Al-Aziz Al-Haddad Chief Mufti of Dubai, UAE
41. Al-Habib Ali Mashhour bin Muhammad bin Salim bin Hafeeth Imam of the Tarim Mosque; Head of Fatwa Council, Tarim, Yemen
42. Al-Habib Umar bin Muhammad bin Salim bin Hafeeth Dean, Dar Al-Mustafa, Tarim, Yemen
43. Professor Dr Farouq Hamadah Professor of the Sciences of Tradition, Mohammad V University, Morocco
44. Shaykh Hamza Yusuf Hanson Founder and Director, Zaytuna Institute, CA, USA
45. H.E. Shaykh Dr Ahmad Badr Al-Din Hassoun Grand Mufti of the Republic of Syria
46. H.E. Shaykh. Sayyed Ali bin Abd Al-Rahman Al-Hashimi Advisor to the President for Judiciary and Religious Affairs, UAE
47. Prof. Dr Hasan Hanafi Muslim Intellectual, Department of Philosophy, Cairo University
48. Shaykh Kabir Helminski Shaykh of the Mevlevi Tariqah; Co-Director of the Book Foundation, USA
49. H.E. Shaykh Sa'id Hijjawi Chief Scholar, The Royal Aal al-Bayt Institute for Islamic Thought; Former Grand Mufti of Jordan
50. H.E. Prof. Dr Shaykh Ahmad Hlayyel Chief Islamic Justice of Jordan; Imam of the Hashemite Court; Former Minister of Religious Affairs
51. H.E. Amb. Dr Murad Hofmann Author and Muslim Intellectual, Germany
52. H.E. Dr Anwar Ibrahim Former Deputy Prime Minister of Malaysia; Honorary President of AccountAbility
53. H.E. Shaykh Dr Izz Al-Din Ibrahim Advisor for Cultural Affairs, Prime Ministry, UAE
54. H.E. Prof. Dr Ekmeleddin Ihsanoglu Secretary-General, Organization of the Islamic Conference (OIC)
55. H.E. Prof. Dr Omar Jah Secretary of the Muslim Scholars Council, Gambia; Professor of Islamic Civilization and Thought, University of Gambia
56. H.E. Prof. Dr Abbas Al-Jarari Advisor to Hm the King, Morocco
57. Al-Habib Ali Zain Al-Abidin Al-Jifri Founder and Director, Taba Institute, United Arab Emirates

58. H.E. Shaykh Prof. Dr Ali Jum'a Grand Mufti of the Republic of Egypt
59. Prof. Dr Yahya Mahmud bin Junayd Secretary General, King Faisal Centre for Research and Islamic Studies, Saudi Arabia
60. Dr Ibrahim Kalin Director, SETA Foundation, Ankara, Turkey; Asst. Prof. Georgetown University, USA
61. H.E. Amb. Aref Kamal Muslim Intellectual, Pakistan
62. Professor Dr 'Abla Mohammed Kahlawi Dean of Islamic and Arabic Studies, Al-Azhar University (Women's College), Egypt
63. Prof. Dr Said Hibatullah Kamilev Director, Moscow Institute of Islamic Civilisation, Russian Federation
64. Prof. Dr Hafiz Yusuf Z. Kavakci Resident Scholar, Islamic Association of North Texas, Founder & Instructor of IaNt Qur'anic Academy; Founding Dean of Suffa Islamic Seminary, Dallas, Texas, USA
65. Shaykh Dr Nuh Ha Mim Keller Shaykh in the Shadhili Order, USA
66. Prof. Dr Mohammad Hashim Kamali Dean and Professor, International Institute of Islamic Thought and Civilization (ISTAC), International Islamic University, Malaysia
67. Shaykh Amr Khaled Islamic Missionary, Preacher and Broadcaster, Egypt; Founder and Chairman, Right Start Foundation International
68. Prof. Dr Abd Al-Karim Khalifah President of the Jordanian Arabic Language Academy; Former President of Jordan University
69. H.E. Shaykh Ahmad Al-Khalili Grand Mufti of the Sultanate of Oman
70. Seyyed Jawad Al-Khoei Secretary-General, Al-Khoei International Foundation
71. Shaykh Dr Ahmad Kubaisi Founder of the 'Ulema Organization, Iraq
72. Mr. M. Ali Lakhani Founder and Editor of Sacred Web: A Journal of Tradition and Modernity, Canada
73. Dr Joseph Lumbard Assistant Professor, Brandeis University, USA
74. H.E. Shaykh Mahmood A. Madani Secretary General, Jamiat Ulama-i-Hind; Member of Parliament, India
75. H.E. Prof. Dr Abdel-Kabeer Al-Alawi Al-Madghari Director General of Bayt Mal Al-Quds Agency (Al-Quds Fund); Former Minister of Religious Affairs, Morocco
76. H.E. Imam Sayyed Al-Sadiq Al-Mahdi Former Prime Minister of Sudan; Head of Ansar Movement, Sudan
77. H.E. Prof. Dr Rusmir Mahmutcehajic Professor, Sarajevo University; President of the International Forum Bosnia; Former V.P. of the Government of Bosnia and Herzegovina
78. Allamah Shaykh Sayyed Muhammad bin Muhammad Al-Mansour High Authority (Marja') of Zeidi Muslims, Yemen
79. Prof. Dr Bashshar Awwad Marouf Former Rector of the Islamic University, Iraq
80. H.E. Prof. Dr Ahmad Matloub Former Minister of Culture; Acting President of the Iraqi Academy of Sciences, Iraq
81. Prof. Dr Ingrid Mattson Professor of Islamic Studies and Christian-Mus-

lim Relations and Director, Islamic Chaplaincy Program, Hartford Seminary; President of the Islamic Society of North America (ISNA), USA
82. Dr Yousef Meri Special Scholar-in-Residence, Royal Aal al-Bayt Institute for Islamic Thought, Jordan
83. Dr Jean-Louis Michon Author; Muslim Scholar; Architect; Former UNESCO expert, Switzerland
84. Shaykh Abu Bakr Ahmad Al-Milibari Secretary-General of the Ahl Al-Sunna Association, India
85. Pehin Dato Haj Suhaili bin Haj Mohiddin Deputy Grand Mufti, Brunei
86. Ayatollah Sheikh Hussein Muayad President and Founder, Knowledge Forum, Baghdad, Iraq
87. Prof. Dr Izzedine Umar Musa Professor of Islamic History, King Sa'ud University, Saudi Arabia
88. Prof. Dr Mohammad Farouk Al-Nabhan Former Director of Dar Al-Hadith Al-Hasaniya, Morocco
89. Prof. Dr Zaghloul El-Naggar Professor, King Abd Al-Aziz University, Jeddah, Saudi Arabia; Head, Committee on Scientific Facts in the Glorious Qur'an, Supreme Council on Islamic Affairs, Egypt
90. Mr. Sohail Nakhooda Editor-in-Chief, Islamica Magazine, Jordan
91. Prof. Dr Hisham Nashabeh Chairman of the Board of Higher Education; Dean of Education at Makassed Association, Lebanon
92. H.E. Professor Dr Seyyed Hossein Nasr University Professor of Islamic Studies, George Washington University, Washington DC, USA
93. Prof. Dr Aref Ali Nayed Former Professor at the Pontifical Institute for Arabic and Islamic Studies (Rome); Former Professor at the International Institute for Islamic Thought and Civilization (ISTAC, Malaysia); Senior Advisor to the Cambridge Interfaith Program at the Faculty of Divinity in Cambridge, UK
94. H.E. Shaykh Sevki Omarbasic Grand Mufti of Croatia
95. Dato Dr Abdul Hamid Othman Advisor to the H.E. the Prime Minister of Malaysia
96. Prof. Dr Ali Ozek Head of the Endowment for Islamic Scientific Studies, Istanbul, Turkey
97. Imam Yahya Sergio Yahe Pallavicini Vice President of co.re.Is., Italy, Chairman of Isesco Council for Education and Culture in the West, Advisor for Islamic Affairs of the Italian Minister of Interior
98. H.E. Shaykh Dr Nuh Ali Salman Al-Qudah Grand Mufti of the Hashemite Kingdom of Jordan
99. H.E. Shaykh Dr Ikrima Said Sabri Former Grand Mufti of Jerusalem and All of Palestine, Imam of the Blessed Al-Aqsa Mosque, and President of the Islamic Higher Council, Palestine
100. Ayatollah Al-Faqih Seyyed Hussein Ismail Al-Sadr Baghdad, Iraq
101. Mr. Muhammad Al-Sammak Secretary-General of the National Council

for Islamic-Christian Dialogue; Secretary-General for the Islamic Spiritual Summit, Lebanon

102. Shaykh Seyyed Hasan Al-Saqqaf Director of Dar Al-Imam Al-Nawawi, Jordan
103. Dr Ayman Fuad Sayyid Historian and Manuscript Expert, Former Secretary General of Dar al-Kutub Al-Misriyya, Cairo, Egypt
104. Prof. Dr Suleiman Abdallah Schleifer Professor Emeritus, The American University in Cairo
105. Dr Seyyed Reza Shah-Kazemi Author and Muslim Scholar, UK
106. Dr Anas Al-Shaikh-Ali Chair, Association of Muslim Social Scientists, UK; Chair, Forum Against Islamophobia and Racism, UK; Academic Advisor, IIIt, UK
107. Imam Zaid Shakir Lecturer and Scholar-in-Residence, Zaytuna Institute, CA,USA
108. H.E. Prof. Dr Ali Abdullah Al-Shamlan Director General of the Kuwait Foundation for the Advancement of Sciences (Kfas); Former Minister of Higher Education, Kuwait
109. Eng. Seyyed Hasan Shariatmadari Leader of the Iranian National Republican Party (INr)
110. Sharif Muhammad al-Alwini Head of the European Academy of Islamic Culture and Sciences, Brussels, Belgium
111. H.E. Dr Mohammad Abd Al-Ghaffar Al-Sharif Secretary-General of the Ministry of Religious Affairs, Kuwait
112. Dr Tayba Hassan Al-Sharif International Protection Officer, The United Nations High Commissioner for Refugees, Darfur, Sudan
113. Prof. Dr Muhammad bin Sharifa Former Rector of Wajda University; Morocco; Fellow of the Royal Moroccan Academy
114. Prof. Dr Muzammil H. Siddiqui / on behalf of the whole Fiqh Council of North America Islamic Scholar and Theologian; Chairman of the Fiqh Council of North America, USA
115. Shaykh Ahmad bin Sa'ud Al-Siyabi Secretary General of the Directorate of the Grand Mufti, Oman
116. Al-Haji Yusuf Maitama Sule Former Nigerian Permanent Representative to the United Nations; Former Nigerian Minister of National Guidance
117. Prof. Dr Muhammad Abd Al-Rahim Sultan-al-Ulama Deputy-Dean of Scientific Research Affairs, United Arab Emirates University, UAE
118. Shaykh Dr Tariq Sweidan Director-General of the Risalah Satellite Channel
119. H.E. Shaykh Ahmad Muhammad Muti'i Tamim The Head of the Religious Administration of Ukrainian Muslims, and Mufti of Ukraine
120. H.E. Shaykh Izz Al-Din Al-Tamimi Senator; Former Chief Islamic Justice, Minister of Religious Affairs and Grand Mufti of Jordan
121. H.E. Shaykh Dr Tayseer Rajab Al-Tamimi Chief Islamic Justice of Palestine; Head of the Palestinian Center for Religion and Civilization Dialogue
122. Prof. Dr H.R.H. Prince Ghazi bin Muhammad bin Talal Personal Envoy

and Special Advisor of H.M. King Abdullah II; Chairman of the Board of the Royal Aal al-Bayt Institute for Islamic Thought, Jordan

123. Prof. Dr Ammar Al-Talibi Former Member of Parliament, Professor of Philosophy, University of Algeria

124. Ayatollah Shaykh Muhammad Ali Taskhiri Secretary General of the World Assembly for Proximity of Islamic Schools of Thought, Iran

125. H.E. Prof. Dr Shaykh Ahmad Muhammad Al-Tayeb President of Al-Azhar University, Former Grand Mufti of Egypt

126. Prof. Dr Muddathir Abdel-Rahim Al-Tayib Professor of Political Science and Islamic Studies, International Institute of Islamic Thought and Civilization (ISTAC), Malaysia

127. H.E. Amb. Prof. Dr Abdel-Hadi Al-Tazi Fellow of the Royal Moroccan Academy

128. H.E. Shaykh Naim Trnava Grand Mufti of Kosovo

129. H.E. Dr Abd Al-Aziz bin 'Uthman Al-Tweijiri Director-General of the Islamic Educational, Scientific and Cultural Organization (IESCO)

130. H.E. Prof. Dr Nasaruddin Umar Rector of the Institute for Advanced Qur'anic Studies; Secretary General of the Nahdhatul Ulama Consultative Council; Lecturer at the State Islamic University Syarif Hidayatullah, Jakarta, Indonesia

131. Shaykh Muhammad Hasan 'Usayran Jafari Mufti of Sidon and Al-Zahrani, Lebanon

132. Allamah Justice Mufti Muhammad Taqi Usmani Vice President, Darul Uloom Karachi, Pakistan

133. Prof. Dr Akhtarul Wasey Director, Zakir Husain Institute of Islamic Studies, Jamia Milla Islamiya University, India

134. Shaykh Dr Abdal Hakim Murad Winter Shaykh Zayed Lecturer in Islamic Studies, Divinity School, University of Cambridge; Director of the Muslim Academic Trust, UK

135. Prof. Dr Mohammed El-Mokhtar Ould Bah President, Chinguitt Modern University, Mauritania

136. H.E. Shaykh Muhammad Sodiq Mohammad Yusuf Former Grand Mufti of the Muslim Spiritual Administration of Central Asia, Uzbekistan; Translator and Commentator of the Holy Qur'an

137. Prof. Dr Shaykh Wahba Mustafa Al-Zuhayli Dean, Department of Islamic Jurisprudence, University of Damas- cus, Syria

138. H.E. Shaykh Mu'ammar Zukoulic Mufti of Sanjak, Bosnia.

ADDITIONAL SIGNATORIES / SUSULAN PENANDATANGAN.

A number of prominent Muslim figures have also endorsed the ACW document after its publication:

139. Shaikh Ahmad Kutty Toronto, Canada

140. Dr M. Saud Anwar Co-Chair, American Muslim Peace Initiative.

141. Amir Hussain, PhD Associate Professor of Theological Studies, Loyola Marymount University, Los Angeles
142. Dr Hisham A. Hellyer Senior Research Fellow, University of Warwick, UK
143. Mehrézia Labidi-Maiza International Co-ordinator of Religious Women for Peace Network, and Member of the Inter-Religious Council leading the RfP organization
144. Professor Tariq Ramadan European Muslim Network
145. Shaykh Faraz RabbaniHanafi Scholar, SunniPath.com
146. Imam Abdul Malik Mujahid Chairman of the Council of Islamic Organizations of Greater Chicago
147. Prof. Dr Najib al-Hsadi Professor of Philosophy, Gar Yunis University, Benghazi Libya
148. Prof. Dr Basit Koshul Lahore University of Management Sciences, Pakistan
149. Dr Muhammad Suheyl Umar Director, Iqbal Academy, Pakistan
150. Prof. Dr Muhammad Fathullah Al-Ziadi Dean Islamic Call College, Tripoli Libya
151. Prof. Dr Muhammad Ahmed al-Sharif Director World Islamic Call Society, Tripoli Lybia
152. Dr Zumer Saleh Religious Leader of Albanian Community in London Albani
153. Shaykha Yasmin Mahmud Al-Husary Head of Husary Islamic Foundation, Egypt
154. Shaykh Dr Usama Al-Rifaei Mufti of Akkar, Lebanon
155. Sayyed Umar Ibn Hamed Al-Jailani Chief Jurist and Scholar, Yemen
156. Dr Umar Abdul-Kafi Prominent Caller to Islamic Faith, Egypt
157. Shaykh Sayyed Smajkic Mufti of Mostar, Bosnia
158. H.H. Shaikh Salem Ibn Mohammad Al-Qasimi Chairman of Islamic Forum, Sharjah, UAE
159. Dr Saleha Al-Rahooti Professor & Researcher, Faculty of Arts, Rabat, Morocco
160. Dr Salah Al-Din Kuftaro Chairman of 'Shaykh Ahmad Kuftaro' Foundation, Damascus, Syria
161. Shaykh Salah Al-Din Fakhri Director of 'Azhar of Lebanon', Lebanon
162. Shaykh Saad Allah Al-Barzanji Prominent Scholar, Iraq
163. Shaykh Rifat Vesic Chairman of Islamic Chaplaincy in Montenegro, Montenegro
164. Dr Ramez Zakai General Director, Albanian Center for Islamic Thought & Culture; Chairman of Supreme Council for Education & Culture in the West, Albania
165. Dr Qais ibn Mohammad Aal Mubarak Associate Professor of Jurisprudence, Faculty of Education, Al-Ahsa, Saudi Arabia
166. Shaykh Nasrat Abdibigovic Mufti of Travnik, Bosnia
167. Prof. Dr Nasr Aref Head of Islamic Studies' Department, Zayed University, Abu Dhabi, UAE

168. Prof. Dr Najib al-Hsadi Professor of Philosophy, Gar Yunis University, Benghazi, Libya
169. Shaykh Nafiullah Ashirov Mufti of the Asian Part of Russia, Russia
170. Dr Mullay Al-Hussein Alhyan Professor at Al-Qurawiyyin University, Morocco
171. Shaykh Muhammad Abdullah B. Qarachay Deputy Mufti of Russia, Russia
172. Dr Mohammad Rashid Qabbani Grand Mufti of Lebanon, Lebanon
173. Dr Mohammad Rabi'e Al-Nadawi Chairman of Nadwat Al Ulama, India
174. Dr Mohammad Mattar Al-Qa'bi Director, Abu Dhabi Religious Affairs Authority, UAE
175. Dr Mohammad Kharobat Professor at Qadi Iyadh University, Marrakesh, Morocco
176. Dr Mohammad Hasan Shurahbili Professor at Al-Qurawiyyin University, Morocco
177. Dr Mohammad Binkiran Professor at Ibn Tofayl University in Qunaytira, Morocco
178. Dr Milooda Shamm Professor at the Law College in Rabat, Morocco
179. Dr Maymoon Barish Professor at Qadi Iyadh University, Marrakesh, Morocco
180. Dr Larbi Kachat Director of Dawah Mosque and Head of the Islamic Cultural Center, Paris, France
181. Shaykh Khaled Al-Sulh Mufti of Baalbek, Lebanon
182. Shaykh Jihad Hashim Brown Director of Research, Tabah Foundation, USA
183. Prof. Dr Jassem Ali Al-Shamsi Dean, Shariah College, U.A.E. University, UAE
184. Dr Jamal Farouk Professor of Faiths and Schools, College of Da'wah, Azhar University, Egypt
185. Shaykh Ismael Smajlovic Mufti of the Armed Forces, Bosnia
186. Dr Ibrahim Bumilha Head of Organizing Committee of Holy Quran Dubai International Award, UAE
187. Shaykh Hussein Smajic Mufti of Sarajevo, Bosnia
188. Shaykh Hussein Kvasovic Mufti of Tuzla, Bosnia
189. Shaykh Hasan Makjic Mufti of Bihac, Bosnia
190. Prof. Dr Hani Sulayman Al-Tu'aymat Dean, Shariah and Islamic Studies, UAE University, Jordan
191. Prof. Dr Hamed Ahmad Al-Refaie President of World Islamic Forum for Dialogue, Saudi Arabia
192. Shaykh Hamed Afandic Mufti of Gorazde, Bosnia
193. Dr Hamdan M. Al-Mazroui Chairman of Abu Dhabi Religious Affairs Authority, UAE
194. Dr Buthayna Al-Galbzuri Professor & Researcher, Faculty of Arts, Rabat, Morocco
195. Dr Bassem H. Itani Director, Dar Iqra for Islmaic Sciences; Member of the Admin Body of Guidance and Reform Trust, Beirut, Lebanon

APPENDIX II

196. Shaykh Asmat Sebahic Deputy Head of 'Ulama of Bosnia and Herzegovina, Bosnia
197. Dr Asmat Mojaddedi Chairman of the Muslim Council of Denmark (MFR), Denmark
198. Dr Al-Jilani Al-Murini Professor at Sidi Mohammad ibn Abdullah, Fes, Morocco
199. Dr Ali Binbraik Professor at Avenzoar University in Aghadir, Morocco
200. Dr Al-Batul Binali Professor & Researcher, Faculty of Arts, Rabat, Morocco
201. Dr Al-Arabi Busilham Professor at Mohammad V University in Rabat, Morocco
202. Dr Al-Arabi Al-Buhali Professor at Qadi Iyadh University, Marrakesh, Morocco
203. Shaykh Ajoob Dawtovic Mufti of Zenica, Bosnia
204. Dr Aisha Y. Al-Manna'ie Dean, Shariah and Islamic Studies College, Qatar
205. Dr Ahmad Omar Hashim Former President, Azhar University; Head of Religious Committee, Egyptian People's Council, Egypt
206. Dr Ahmad Mihrizi Al-Alawi Professor at Qadi Iyadh University, Marrakesh, Morocco
207. Dr Ahmad Fakir Professor at Avenzoar University, Agadir, Morocco
208. Shaykh Adham Samcic Mufti of Banja Luka, Bosnia
209. Dr Abdul-Razzaq Hirmas Professor at Avenzoar University in Aghadir, Morocco
210. Dr Abdul-Rafi'e Al-Ilj Professor at 'Wali Ismael' University in Meknes, Morocco
211. Dr Abdul-Nasser Jabri Dean, Islamic Call College, Beirut, Lebanon
212. Dr Abdul-Mu'ti Bayyoumi Member of the Islamic Body for Research, Azhar University, Egypt
213. Sayyed Abdullah ibn Mohammad Fad'aq Caller to the Faith, Mecca, Saudi Arabia
214. Dr Abdul-Hakim Ikaiwi Professor at Avenzoar University in Aghadir, Morocco
215. Dr Abdul-Fattah Al-Bizm Mufti of Damascus; Director of Al-Fath Islamic Institute, Syria
216. Dr Abdul-Aziz Al-Hafadhi Research Professor at Muhammad V University, Wajda, Morocco
217. Dr Agel Elmeri WICS
218. Prof. Dr Marcia Hermansen Professor of Islamic Studies, Loyola, Illinois, USA
219. Prof. Fadel Abdullah Lecturer in Arabic
220. Dr Ghada Talhami Professor of Politics. Lake Furest College, Illinois, USA
221. Dr Assad Busoil Professor and Chairman: Arabic Department. American Islamic College, Chicago, USA
222. Prof. Dr Mahmoud Abul-Futouh al-Sayyid Ex-Chairman, Department of Religions and Madhahib, Islamic Da'wa School, Azhar University, Cairo

369

223. Prof. Dr Mohammad Mahmoud Mitwalli Abdul-Birr Professor, Islamic Culture Department, Islamic Da'wa School, Azhar University, Cairo, Egypt
224. Prof. Dr Mohammad Abdul-Hadi Imam Professor, Department of Religions and Madhahib, Islamic Da'wa School, Azhar University, Cairo
225. Prof. Dr Abdul-Basit al-Sayyid al-Mursi Professor, Islamic Culture Department, Islamic Da'wa School, Azhar University, Cairo, Egypt
226. Prof. Dr Mohammad Ibrahim al-Juyuoshi Ex-Dean of Islamic Da'wa School, Azhar University, Cairo, Egypt
227. Prof. Dr Tal'at Mohammad Afifi Ex-Dean of Islamic Da'wa School, Azhar University, Cairo, Egypt
228. Prof. Dr Adil Mohammad Mohammad Darwish Professor, Department of Religions and Madhahib, Islamic Da'wa School, Azhar University, Cairo, Egypt
229. Prof. Dr Adil Mahmoud Abdul-Khaliq Professor, Islamic Culture Department, Islamic Da'wa School, Azhar University, Cairo, Egypt
230. Prof. Dr Hasan Jabr Hasan Shuqair Dean of Islamic Da'wa School, Azhar University, Cairo, Egypt·
231. Prof. Dr Abdullah Abdul-Hameed Samak Chairman, Department of Religions and Madhahib, Islamic Da'wa School, Azhar University, Cairo, Egypt
232. Prof. Dr Ahmed Mohammad Ibrahim Shihatah Professor, Islamic Culture Department, Islamic Da'wa School, Azhar University, Cairo, Egypt
233. Prof. Dr Ahmed Rabi' Ahmed Yousef Dean of Islamic Da'wa [Call] School, Azhar University, Cairo, Egypt
234. Prof. Dr Din Syamsuddin President, Central Board of Muhammadiyah, Indonesia.
235. Maher Hathout Senior Advisor, Muslim Public Affair Council, Los Angeles, CA, USA
236. Salam Al-Marayati Executive Director, Muslim Public Affairs Council, Los Angeles, CA, USA
237. Amina Rasul Lead Convenor, Philippine Council for Islam and Democracy, Mandaluyong City, Philippines
238. Latifa Al. Al-Busseir Executive Manager, H.R.H. Prince Alwaleed bin Talal Bin Abdulaziz Al-Saud's Kingdom Foundation, Saudi Arabia
239. Muna AbuSulayman Executive Director, H.R.H. Prince Alwaleed bin Talal Bin Abdulaziz Al-Saud's Kingdom Foundation, Saudi Arabia
240. Prof Dr Shahrzad Houshmand Zadeh Professor of Islamic Studies and Muslim-Christian Relations, The Institute for Studies on Religions and Cultures, The Pontifical Gregorian University, Rome, Italy
241. Prof. Dr Adnane Mokrani Professor of Isalmic Studies and Muslim-Christian Relations, The Institute for Studies on Religions and Cultures, The Pontifical Gregorian University, Rome, Italy
242. Congressman Keith Ellison The Fifth Congressional District of Minnesota, United States House of Representatives, USA
243. Prof. Dr Hmida Ennaifer Professor of Islamic Theology, al-Zaytuna Univer-

370

sity, Tunis. Muslim Co-President of the Muslim-Christian Research Group (GRIC). Founder of 15/21, Magazine of Intercultural Dialogue (Tunis)

244. Anwar N. Haddam Elected-Member to the Algerian Parliament (FLS list, Dec. 1991), President, Movement for Liberty and Social Justice, Algeria

245. Dr Naveed S. Sheikh Lecturer in International Relations, Keele University, UK

246. Professor M.A.S. Abdel Haleem Director Centre of Islamic Studies, School of Oriental and African Studies, UK

247. Dr Fareeha Khan Assistant Professor of Islam, Department of Religion, Georgia State University, USA

248. Ayesha Siddiqua Chaudhry Dept. of Middle Eastern and Islamic Studies, New York University, USA

249. H.R.H. Princess Dr Areej Ghazi Founder and Director, The School of Life, Jordan

250. Mr. Mohamed Ali CEO, Islam Channel, London, UK

251. Dr Musharraf Hussain Al Azhar Director, Karimia Institute, Nottingham, UK

252. Mr. Salah Elgafrawi Secretary General Assistant for Islamic European Conference, Germay

253. Dr Ejaz Akram Associate Professor (Religion & Politics), Humanities and Social Sciences, Lahore University of Management Sciences, Lahore, Pakistan

254. Zainul Abidin Rasheed Senior Minister of State for Foreign Affairs, and Mayor of North- East District, Singapore

255. Mr. Ahmed Ali M. al-Mukhaini Co-Founder and Inter-Faith Activist, Christian Muslim Majlis, Oman

256. Qaiser Shahzad Lecturer/Research Associate, Philosophy and Science Unit, Islamic Research Institute, International Islamic University, Islamabad, Pakistan

257. Professor Dr AbdelHaq Azzouzi President of c.m.I.e.s.I., Morocco

258. Prof. Sallama Shaker Deputy Foreign Minister of Egypt

259. Prof. Mona Hassan Assistant Professor of Islamic Studies (starting Fall 2009), Departments of Religion and History, Duke University, USA

260. Dr Samir Kreidie Chairman, Inma Foundation. Managing Director Rabya Trading & Agriculture Co. Ltd., Saudi Arabia

261. Ayatollah Prof. Dr Ahmad Iravani Director of Islamic Studies and Dialogue Center for the Study of Culture and Values, Catholic University of America, USA

262. Dr Sayyid Muhammad Syeed National Director Office of Interfaith & Community Alliance, Islamic Society of North America, Usa

263. Dr Mahmoud Ayoub Faculty Associate in Shi'ite Islam and Christian-Muslim Relations, Hartford Seminary, USA

264. Imam Suhaib Webb American Islamic activist, speaker, and religious scholar, USA

265. Mr. Shabbir Mansuri Founding Director Institute on Religion & Civic Values (IRCV), USA

266. Mr. Yasir Qadhi Dean of Academic Affairs, AlMaghrib Institute, USA
267. Prof. Dr Yahya Michot Lecturer in Islamic Theology, Oxford University, UK
268. Dr Hussam S. Timani Professor of Religious Studies, Christopher Newport University, USA
269. Dr Syed Ali Wasif President, Society For International Reforms And Research, USA
270. Dr Noureddine Laftouhi Professor, Cadi Ayyad University, Morocco
271. Sara Shroff Senior Director, Changing Our World. USA
272. Dr Fuad Nahdi Editor-in-Chief, Q-News International, UK
273. Shaikh Saleh bin Muhammad bin Hasan Al-Asmari Director of the Institute for Juristic Studies & General Director of the Al-Manarah Network, Saudi Arabia
274. Prof. Abdul Ali Hamid Principal, The Muslim College, London, UK
275. Dr Ataullah Siddiqui Director, Markfield Institute of Higher Education, Leicester, UK
276. Dr.Ahmed Mirza (M.D., FACP, FACG) Secretary, Naqshbandiya Foundation For Islamic Education (NfIe), USA
277. Assoc. Prof. Dr Ozcan Hidir The Dean of the Faculty of Islamic Sciences at the Islamic University of Rotterdam, Netherlands
278. Allama Abulfateh G R Chishti President Modern Islamic Studies Centre, Jamia Masjid Mai Saleem Akhtar New Sohan Capital Dist. Islamabad, Pakistan
279. Dr Abdalaziz Eddebbarh Director of Ibn Asheer Institute of Islamic Studies, Imam of Taha Mosque, President of the Santa Fe Interfaith Leadership Alliance, USA
280. Habib Faisal El-Kef Caller to Allah, Saudi Arabia
281. Dr Qamar-ul Huda Islamic studies scholar, Religion & Peacemaking, U.S. Institute of Peace, USA
282. Professor Ahmad Gianpiero Vincenzo Johns Hopkins University in Bologna, President of Society of Italian Muslim Intellectuals. Italy
283. Dr Sadig Malki Visiting Scholar, Center for Muslim-Christian Understanding, USA
284. Dr Yassin Ali al-Makusi Professor at the World Islamic Sciences and Education University, Jordan
285. Engineer Marwan Awwad al-Fa'ouri Secretary General, International Moderation Assembly
286. Ms. 'Aysha Nour Soulaq Assistant–Justice and Development Party at Istanbul Municipality, Turkey
287. Mr. Amr al-Shobaki Director of the United Arab European Studies at al-Ahram, Egypt
288. Mr. Muhammad al-Hamddayi President of the Movement for Tawhid and Reform
289. Mr. Muhammad Zahid Ghol Turkish Writer and Researcher, Turkey

290. Mr. Anwar Yugil Owner of Bukhjashahr University
291. Dr Bakr Karliga University Professor
292. Dr Abu Bakr Muhammad Ahmed Muhammad Ibrahim Deputy Dean – Institute for Islamization of Knowledge
293. Sheikh Tajuddin Hamid al-Hilali Mufti of Australia, Australia
294. Dr Yousef al-Koudah President of the Sudanese Center Party, Sudan
295. Dr Al-Akhdar Shareet Professor at the University of Algeria, Algeria
296. Mr. Muntasser al-Zayyat Secretary General of the Egyptian Bar Association, Egypt
297. Prof. Muhammad al-'Aadil President of the Turkish-Arabic Society in Ankara, Turkey
298. Dr Sa'duddin al-Uthmani Former Secretary General in the Justice and Development Party
299. Prof. Dr Azmi Taha al-Sayyid Ahmed Editor-in-Chief of the Jordanian Journal for Islamic Studies, Jordan
300. Prof. Dr Burhan Kuruglu Professor at the University of Bukhjashahr – Director of the Center for Civilization Studies
301. Imam Abu Eesa Niamatullah Imam of the Cheadle Mosque, Cheshire; Lecturer and Resident-Scholar of the Cheadle Muslim Association (CMA), UK
302. Khalid al-Anani Senior Analyst, Expert on Political Islam and Democratization, Middle East, Al-Ahram Foundation, Egypt
303. Waleed El-Ansary Assistant Professor of Islamic Studies, Department of Religious Studies, University of South Carolina, Columbia, SC, USA
304. Abdool Magid Abdool Karim Vakil Founder and President of the Islamic Community, Co-Founder and President of the Abrahamic Forum of Portugal and Member of the Committee for Religious Freedom (Ministry of Justice), Portugal
305. Prof. Dr Azzedine Gaci President of the Regional Council of the Muslim Faith (CRCM). Lyon, France
306. Sarah Joseph OBE Editor & CEO, EMEL Magazine, UK
307. Prof. Asma Afsaruddin Professor of Islamic Studies, Department of Near Eastern Languages and Cultures, Bloomington, Indiana University, UK
308. Dr Munawar A. Anees University of Management and Technology, Lahore: Director, Center for Global Dialog Director, Institute of Islamic Banking Editor-in- Chief, Islamic Banking and Finance Review (Quarterly) Editor-in- Chief, Convivencia: Islam in Global Affairs, Pakistan

Chapter 4 THE 'A COMMON WORD' TEXT, A Common Word Between Us and You, 5-Year Anniversary Edition. pp 51-101, MABDA English Monograph Series No. 20 @2012 The Royal Aal Al-Bayt Institute for Islamic Thought, 10 Sa'ed Bino Road, Dabuq, PO Box 950361, Amman 1195, Jordan. Legal Deposit Number, The Hashemite Kingdom of Jordan National Library 2012/9/3632

APPENDIX III

A DOCUMENT ON HUMAN FRATERNITY FOR
WORLD PEACE AND LIVING TOGETHER

INTRODUCTION

Faith leads a believer to see in the other a brother or sister to be supported and loved. Through faith in God, who has created the universe, creatures and all human beings (equal on account of his mercy), believers are called to express this human fraternity by safeguarding creation and the entire universe and supporting all persons, especially the poorest and those most in need.

This transcendental value served as the starting point for several meetings characterized by a friendly and fraternal atmosphere where we shared the joys, sorrows and problems of our contemporary world. We did this by considering scientific and technical progress, therapeutic achievements, the digital era, the mass media and communications. We reflected also on the level of poverty, conflict and suffering of so many brothers and sisters in different parts of the world as a consequence of the arms race, social injustice, corruption, inequality, moral decline, terrorism, discrimination, extremism and many other causes.

From our fraternal and open discussions, and from the meeting that expressed profound hope in a bright future for all human beings, the idea of this Document on Human Fraternity was conceived. It is a text that has been given honest and serious thought so as to be a joint declaration of good and heartfelt aspirations. It is a document that invites all persons who have faith in God and faith in human fraternity to unite and work together so that it may serve as a guide for future generations to advance a culture of mutual respect in the awareness of the great divine grace that makes all human beings brothers and sisters.

DOCUMENT

In the name of God who has created all human beings equal in rights, duties and dignity, and who has called them to live together as brothers and sisters, to fill the earth and make known the values of goodness, love and peace;

In the name of innocent human life that God has forbidden to kill, affirming that whoever kills a person is like one who kills the whole of humanity, and that whoever saves a person is like one who saves the whole of humanity;

In the name of the poor, the destitute, the marginalized and those most in

374

need whom God has commanded us to help as a duty required of all persons, especially the wealthy and of means;

In the name of orphans, widows, refugees and those exiled from their homes and their countries; in the name of all victims of wars, persecution and injustice; in the name of the weak, those who live in fear, prisoners of war and those tortured in any part of the world, without distinction;

In the name of peoples who have lost their security, peace, and the possibility of living together, becoming victims of destruction, calamity and war;

In the name of human fraternity that embraces all human beings, unites them and renders them equal;

In the name of this fraternity torn apart by policies of extremism and division, by systems of unrestrained profit or by hateful ideological tendencies that manipulate the actions and the future of men and women;

In the name of freedom, that God has given to all human beings creating them free and distinguishing them by this gift;

In the name of justice and mercy, the foundations of prosperity and the cornerstone of faith;

In the name of all persons of good will present in every part of the world;

In the name of God and of everything stated thus far; Al-Azhar al-Sharif and the Muslims of the East and West, together with the Catholic Church and the Catholics of the East and West, declare the adoption of a culture of dialogue as the path; mutual cooperation as the code of conduct; reciprocal understanding as the method and standard.

We, who believe in God and in the final meeting with Him and His judgment, on the basis of our religious and moral responsibility, and through this Document, call upon ourselves, upon the leaders of the world as well as the architects of international policy and world economy, to work strenuously to spread the culture of tolerance and of living together in peace; to intervene at the earliest opportunity to stop the shedding of innocent blood and bring an end to wars, conflicts, environmental decay and the moral and cultural decline that the world is presently experiencing.

We call upon intellectuals, philosophers, religious figures, artists, media professionals and men and women of culture in every part of the world, to rediscover the values of peace, justice, goodness, beauty, human fraternity and coexistence in order to confirm the importance of these values as anchors of salvation for all, and to promote them everywhere.

This Declaration, setting out from a profound consideration of our contemporary reality, valuing its successes and in solidarity with its suffering, disasters and calamities, believes firmly that among the most important causes of the crises of the modern world are a desensitized human conscience, a distancing from religious values and a prevailing individualism accompanied by materialistic philosophies that deify the human person and introduce worldly and material values in place of supreme and transcendental principles.

While recognizing the positive steps taken by our modern civilization in the fields of science, technology, medicine, industry and welfare, especially in developed countries, we wish to emphasize that, associated with such historic advancements, great and valued as they are, there exists both a moral deterioration that influences international action and a weakening of spiritual values and responsibility. All this contributes to a general feeling of frustration, isolation and desperation leading many to fall either into a vortex of atheistic, agnostic or religious extremism, or into blind and fanatic extremism, which ultimately encourage forms of dependency and individual or collective self-destruction.

History shows that religious extremism, national extremism and also intolerance have produced in the world, be it in the East or West, what might be referred to as signs of a "third world war being fought piecemeal". In several parts of the world and in many tragic circumstances these signs have begun to be painfully apparent, as in those situations where the precise number of victims, widows and orphans is unknown. We see, in addition, other regions preparing to become theatres of new conflicts, with outbreaks of tension and a build-up of arms and ammunition, and all this in a global context overshadowed by uncertainty, disillusionment, fear of the future, and controlled by narrow-minded economic interests.

We likewise affirm that major political crises, situations of injustice and lack of equitable distribution of natural resources – which only a rich minority benefit from, to the detriment of the majority of the peoples of the earth – have generated, and continue to generate, vast numbers of poor, infirm and deceased persons. This leads to catastrophic crises that various countries have fallen victim to despite their natural resources and the resourcefulness of young people which characterize these nations. In the face of such crises that result in the deaths of millions of children – wasted away from poverty and hunger – there is an unacceptable silence on the international level.

It is clear in this context how the family as the fundamental nucleus of society and humanity is essential in bringing children into the world, raising them, educating them, and providing them with solid moral formation and domestic security. To attack the institution of the family, to regard it with contempt or to doubt its important role, is one of the most threatening evils of our era.

We affirm also the importance of awakening religious awareness and the need to revive this awareness in the hearts of new generations through sound education and an adherence to moral values and upright religious teachings. In this way we can confront tendencies that are individualistic, selfish, conflicting, and also address radicalism and blind extremism in all its forms and expressions.

The first and most important aim of religions is to believe in God, to honour Him and to invite all men and women to believe that this universe

376

depends on a God who governs it. He is the Creator who has formed us with His divine wisdom and has granted us the gift of life to protect it. It is a gift that no one has the right to take away, threaten or manipulate to suit oneself. Indeed, everyone must safeguard this gift of life from its beginning up to its natural end. We therefore condemn all those practices that are a threat to life such as genocide, acts of terrorism, forced displacement, human organ trafficking, abortion and euthanasia. We likewise condemn the policies that promote these practices.

Moreover, we resolutely declare that religions must never incite war, hateful attitudes, hostility and extremism, nor must they incite violence or the shedding of blood. These tragic realities are the consequence of a deviation from religious teachings. They result from a political manipulation of religions and from interpretations made by religious groups who, in the course of history, have taken advantage of the power of religious sentiment in the hearts of men and women in order to make them act in a way that has nothing to do with the truth of religion. This is done for the purpose of achieving objectives that are political, economic, worldly and short-sighted. We thus call upon all concerned to stop using religions to incite hatred, violence, extremism and blind fanaticism, and to refrain from using the name of God to justify acts of murder, exile, terrorism and oppression. We ask this on the basis of our common belief in God who did not create men and women to be killed or to fight one another, nor to be tortured or humiliated in their lives and circumstances. God, the Almighty, has no need to be defended by anyone and does not want His name to be used to terrorize people.

This Document, in accordance with previous International Documents that have emphasized the importance of the role of religions in the construction of world peace, upholds the following:

- The firm conviction that authentic teachings of religions invite us to remain rooted in the values of peace; to defend the values of mutual understanding, human fraternity and harmonious coexistence; to re-establish wisdom, justice and love; and to reawaken religious awareness among young people so that future generations may be protected from the realm of materialistic thinking and from dangerous policies of unbridled greed and indifference that are based on the law of force and not on the force of law;

- Freedom is a right of every person: each individual enjoys the freedom of belief, thought, expression and action. The pluralism and the diversity of religions, colour, sex, race and language are willed by God in His wisdom, through which He created human beings. This divine wisdom is the source from which the right to freedom of belief and the freedom to be different derives. Therefore, the fact that people are forced to adhere to a certain religion or culture must be rejected, as too the imposition of a cultural way of life that others do not accept;

- Justice based on mercy is the path to follow in order to achieve a dignified life to which every human being has a right;
- Dialogue, understanding and the widespread promotion of a culture of tolerance, acceptance of others and of living together peacefully would contribute significantly to reducing many economic, social, political and environmental problems that weigh so heavily on a large part of humanity;
- Dialogue among believers means coming together in the vast space of spiritual, human and shared social values and, from here, transmitting the highest moral virtues that religions aim for. It also means avoiding unproductive discussions;
- The protection of places of worship – synagogues, churches and mosques – is a duty guaranteed by religions, human values, laws and international agreements. Every attempt to attack places of worship or threaten them by violent assaults, bombings or destruction, is a deviation from the teachings of religions as well as a clear violation of international law;
- Terrorism is deplorable and threatens the security of people, be they in the East or the West, the North or the South, and disseminates panic, terror and pessimism, but this is not due to religion, even when terrorists instrumentalize it. It is due, rather, to an accumulation of incorrect interpretations of religious texts and to policies linked to hunger, poverty, injustice, oppression and pride. This is why it is so necessary to stop supporting terrorist movements fuelled by financing, the provision of weapons and strategy, and by attempts to justify these movements even using the media. All these must be regarded as international crimes that threaten security and world peace. Such terrorism must be condemned in all its forms and expressions;
- The concept of citizenship is based on the equality of rights and duties, under which all enjoy justice. It is therefore crucial to establish in our societies the concept of full citizenship and reject the discriminatory use of the term minorities which engenders feelings of isolation and inferiority. Its misuse paves the way for hostility and discord; it undoes any successes and takes away the religious and civil rights of some citizens who are thus discriminated against;
- Good relations between East and West are indisputably necessary for both. They must not be neglected, so that each can be enriched by the other's culture through fruitful exchange and dialogue. The West can discover in the East remedies for those spiritual and religious maladies that are caused by a prevailing materialism. And the East can find in the West many elements that can help free it from weakness, division, conflict and scientific, technical and cultural decline. It is important to pay attention to religious, cultural and historical differences that are a vital component in shaping the character, culture and civilization of the East.

It is likewise important to reinforce the bond of fundamental human rights in order to help ensure a dignified life for all the men and women of East and West, avoiding the politics of double standards;

- It is an essential requirement to recognize the right of women to education and employment, and to recognize their freedom to exercise their own political rights. Moreover, efforts must be made to free women from historical and social conditioning that runs contrary to the principles of their faith and dignity. It is also necessary to protect women from sexual exploitation and from being treated as merchandise or objects of pleasure or financial gain. Accordingly, an end must be brought to all those inhuman and vulgar practices that denigrate the dignity of women. Efforts must be made to modify those laws that prevent women from fully enjoying their rights;

- The protection of the fundamental rights of children to grow up in a family environment, to receive nutrition, education and support, are duties of the family and society. Such duties must be guaranteed and protected so that they are not overlooked or denied to any child in any part of the world. All those practices that violate the dignity and rights of children must be denounced. It is equally important to be vigilant against the dangers that they are exposed to, particularly in the digital world, and to consider as a crime the trafficking of their innocence and all violations of their youth;

- The protection of the rights of the elderly, the weak, the disabled, and the oppressed is a religious and social obligation that must be guaranteed and defended through strict legislation and the implementation of the relevant international agreements.

To this end, by mutual cooperation, the Catholic Church and Al-Azhar announce and pledge to convey this Document to authorities, influential leaders, persons of religion all over the world, appropriate regional and international organizations, organizations within civil society, religious institutions and leading thinkers. They further pledge to make known the principles contained in this Declaration at all regional and international levels, while requesting that these principles be translated into policies, decisions, legislative texts, courses of study and materials to be circulated.

Al-Azhar and the Catholic Church ask that this Document become the object of research and reflection in all schools, universities and institutes of formation, thus helping to educate new generations to bring goodness and peace to others, and to be defenders everywhere of the rights of the oppressed and of the least of our brothers and sisters.

In conclusion, our aspiration is that:

- this Declaration may constitute an invitation to reconciliation and fraternity among all believers, indeed among believers and non-

believers, and among all people of good will;
- this Declaration may be an appeal to every upright conscience that rejects deplorable violence and blind extremism; an appeal to those who cherish the values of tolerance and fraternity that are promoted and encouraged by religions;
- this Declaration may be a witness to the greatness of faith in God that unites divided hearts and elevates the human soul;
- this Declaration may be a sign of the closeness between East and West, between North and South, and between all who believe that God has created us to understand one another, cooperate with one another and live as brothers and sisters who love one another.

This is what we hope and seek to achieve with the aim of finding a universal peace that all can enjoy in this life.

Abu Dhabi, 4 February 2019
His Holiness
Pope Francis

The Grand Imam of Al-Azhar
Ahmad Al-Tayyeb

APPENDIX IV

FRATELLI TUTTI

SHORT SUMMARY OF POPE FRANCIS'S SOCIAL ENCYCLICAL

Fraternity and social friendship are the ways the Pontiff indicates to build a better, more just and peaceful world, with the contribution of all: people and institutions. With an emphatic confirmation of a 'no' to war and to globalized indifference.

By Isabella Piro

What are the great ideals but also the tangible ways to advance for those who wish to build a more just and fraternal world in their ordinary relationships, in social life, politics and institutions?

This is mainly the question that *Fratelli tutti* is intended to answer: the Pope describes it as a "Social Encyclical" (6) which borrows the title of the "Admonitions" of Saint Francis of Assisi, who used these words to "address his brothers and sisters and proposed to them a way of life marked by the flavour of the Gospel" (Par 1). The Encyclical aims to promote a universal aspiration toward fraternity and social friendship. In the background of the Encyclical is the Covid-19 pandemic which, Francis reveals, "unexpectedly erupted" as he "was writing this letter". But the global health emergency has helped demonstrate that "no one can face life in isolation" and that the time has truly come to "dream, then, as a single human family" in which we are "brothers and sisters all" (Par 8).

CHAPTER ONE: DARK CLOUDS COVER THE WORLD

In the first of eight chapters, which is entitled "Dark Clouds over a Closed World", the document reflects on the many distortions of the contemporary era: the manipulation and deformation of concepts such as democracy, freedom, justice; the loss of the meaning of the social community and history; selfishness and indifference toward the common good; the prevalence of a market logic based on profit and the culture of waste; unemployment, racism, poverty; the disparity of rights and its aberrations such as slavery, trafficking, women subjugated and then forced to abort, organ trafficking (see Par 10-24). It deals with global problems that call for global actions, emphasizes the Pope, also sounding the alarm against a "culture of walls" that favours the proliferation of organized crime, fuelled by fear and loneliness (see Par 27-28).

CHAPTER TWO: STRANGERS ON THE ROAD

To many shadows, however, the Encyclical responds with a luminous example, a herald of hope: the Good Samaritan. The second chapter, "A stranger on the road", is dedicated to this figure. In it, the Pope emphasizes that, in an unhealthy society that turns its back on suffering and that is "illiterate" in caring for the frail and vulnerable (see Par 64-65), we are all called – just like the Good Samaritan – to become neighbours to others (see Par 81), overcoming prejudices, personal interests, historic and cultural barriers. We all, in fact, are co-responsible in creating a society that is able to include, integrate and lift up those who have fallen or are suffering (see Par 77). Love builds bridges and "we were made for love" (Par 88), the Pope adds, particularly exhorting Christians to recognize Christ in the face of every excluded person (see Par 85).

CHAPTER THREE: VISION OF AN OPEN WORLD

The principle of the capacity to love according to "a universal dimension" (see Par 83) is also resumed in the third chapter, "Envisaging and engendering an open world". In this chapter Francis exhorts us to go "'outside' the self" in order to find "a fuller existence in another" (Par 88), opening ourselves up to the other according to the dynamism of charity which makes us tend toward "universal fulfilment" (Par 95). In the background – the Encyclical recalls – the spiritual stature of a person's life is measured by love, which always "takes first place" and leads us to seek better for the life of the other, far from all selfishness (Par 92-93). The sense of solidarity and of fraternity begin within the family, which are to be safeguarded and respected in their "primary and vital mission of education" (Par 114).

The right to live with dignity cannot be denied to anyone, the Pope again affirms, and since rights have no borders, no one can remain excluded, regardless of where they are born (see Par 121) In this perspective the Pontiff also calls us to consider "an ethics of international relations" (see Par 126), because every country also belongs to foreigners and the goods of the territory cannot be denied to those who are in need and come from another place. Thus, the natural right to private property will be secondary to the principal of the universal destination of created goods (see Par 120). The Encyclical also places specific emphasis on the issue of foreign debt: subject to the principal that it must be paid, it is hoped nonetheless that this does not compromise the growth and subsistence of the poorest countries (see Par 126).

CHAPTER FOUR: HEART OPEN TO THE WORLD

To the theme of migration, the latter, entitled "A heart open to the whole world". With their lives "at stake" (Par 37), fleeing from war, persecution, natural catastrophes, unscrupulous trafficking, ripped from their communities of origin, migrants are to be welcomed, protected, supported and integrated. Unnecessary migration needs to be avoided, the Pontiff affirms, by creating concrete opportunities to live with dignity in the countries of origin. But at the same time, we need to respect the right to seek a better life elsewhere. In receiving countries, the right balance will be between the protection of citizens' rights and the guarantee of welcome and assistance for migrants (see Par 38-40). Specifically, the Pope points to several "indispensable steps, especially in response to those who are fleeing grave humanitarian crises": to increase and simplify the granting of visas; to open humanitarian corridors; to assure lodging, security and essential services; to offer opportunities for employment and training; to favour family reunification; to protect minors; to guarantee religious freedom. What is needed above all – the document reads – is global governance, an international collaboration for migration which implements long-term planning, going beyond single emergencies, on behalf of the supportive development of all peoples (see Par 129-132).

CHAPTER FIVE: BETTER POLITICS

The theme of the fifth chapter is "A better kind of politics", which represents one of the most valuable forms of charity because it is placed at the service of the common good (see Par 180) and recognizes the importance of people, understood as an open category, available for discussion and dialogue (see Par 160). This is the populism indicated by Francis, which counters that "populism" which ignores the legitimacy of the notion of "people", by attracting consensuses in order to exploit them for its own service and fomenting selfishness in order to increase its own popularity (see Par 159). But a better politics is also one that protects work, an "essential dimension of social life". The best strategy against poverty, the Pontiff explains, does not simply aim to contain or render indigents inoffensive, but to promote them in the perspective of solidarity and subsidiarity (see Par 187). The task of politics, moreover, is to find a solution to all that attacks fundamental human rights, such as social exclusion; the marketing of organs, tissues, weapons and drugs; sexual exploitation; slave labour; terrorism and organized crime. The Pope makes an emphatic appeal to definitively eliminate human trafficking, a "source of shame for humanity", and hunger, which is "criminal" because food is "an inalienable right" (Par 188-189).

The politics we need, Francis also underscores, is a politics centred on human dignity and not subjected to finance because "the marketplace, by itself, cannot resolve every problem": the "havoc" wreaked by financial speculation has demonstrated this (see Par 168). Hence, popular movements have taken on particular relevance: as true "torrents of moral energy", they must be engaged in society with greater coordination. In this way – the Pope states – it will be possible to go beyond a Policy "with" and "of" the poor (see Par 169).

Another hope present in the Encyclical regards the reform of the UN: in the face of the predominance of the economic dimension, a task of the United Nations will be to give substance to the concept of a "family of nations" working for the common good, the eradication of poverty and the protection of human rights. Tireless recourse "to negotiation, mediation and arbitration" – the Papal Document states – the UN must promote the force of law rather than the law of force (see Par 173-175).

CHAPTER SIX: DIALOGUE AND FRIENDSHIP

From the sixth chapter, "Dialogue and friendship in society", further emerges the concept of life as the "art of encounter" with everyone, even with the world's peripheries and with original peoples, because "each of us can learn something from others. No one is useless and no one is expendable" (see Par 215). Then, of particular note, is the Pope's reference to the miracle of "kindness", an attitude to be recovered because it is a star "shining in the midst of darkness" and "frees us from the cruelty ... the anxiety ... the frantic flurry of activity" that prevail in the contemporary era (see Par 222-224).

CHAPTER SEVEN: RENEWED ENCOUNTER

The value and promotion of peace is reflected on in the seventh chapter, "Paths of renewed encounter", in which the Pope underlines that peace is connected to truth, justice and mercy. Far from the desire for vengeance, it is "proactive" and aims at forming a society based on service to others and on the pursuit of reconciliation and mutual development (see Par 227-229). Thus, peace is an "art" that involves and regards everyone and in which each one must do his or her part in "a never-ending task" (see Par 227-232). Forgiveness is linked to peace: we must love everyone, without exception – the Encyclical reads – but loving an oppressor means helping him to change and not allowing him to continue oppressing his neighbour (see Par 241-242). Forgiveness does not mean impunity, but rather, justice and remembrance, because to forgive does not mean to forget, but to renounce the destructive power of evil and the desire for revenge. Never forget "horrors" like the Shoah, the atomic bombing of Hiroshima and Nagasaki, persecutions and ethnic massacres – exhorts the Pope. They must be remembered always, anew, so as not be become anaesthetized and to keep the flame of collective conscience alive. It is just as important to remember the good (see Par 246-252).

"Just War"

Part of the seventh chapter, then, focuses on war: "a constant threat", that represents "the negation of all rights", "a failure of politics and of humanity", and "a stinging defeat before the forces of evil". Moreover, due to nuclear chemical and biological weapons that strike many innocent civilians, today we can no longer think, as in the past, of the possibility of a "just war", but we must vehemently reaffirm: "Never again war!" The total elimination of nuclear arms is "a moral and humanitarian imperative". With the money invested in weapons, the Pope suggests instead the establishment of a global fund for the elimination of hunger (see Par 255-262).

Death penalty

Francis expresses just as clearly a position with regard to the death penalty: it is inadmissible and must be abolished worldwide. Not even a murderer loses

384

his personal dignity" – the Pope writes – "and God himself pledges to guarantee this" (Par 263-269). There is emphasis on the necessity to respect "the sacredness of life" (Par 283) where today "some parts of our human family, it appears, can be readily sacrificed", such as the unborn, the poor, the disabled and the elderly (Par 18).

CHAPTER EIGHT: RELIGION AND FRATERNITY

In the eighth and final chapter, the Pontiff focuses on "Religions at the service of fraternity in our world" and emphasizes that terrorism is not due to religion but to erroneous interpretations of religious texts, as well as "policies linked to hunger, poverty, injustice, oppression" (Par 282-283). a journey of peace among religions is possible and that it is therefore necessary to guarantee religious freedom, a fundamental human right for all believers (see Par 279).

The Encyclical reflects, in particular, on the role of the Church: she does not "restrict her mission to the private sphere", it states. While not engaging in politics she does not, however, renounce the political dimension of life itself, attention to the common good and concern for integral human development, according to evangelical principals (see Par 276-278).

Lastly, Francis quotes the "Document on Human Fraternity for World Peace and Living Together", which he signed on 4 February 2019 in Abu Dhabi, along with the Grand Imam of Al-Azhar, Ahmad Al-Tayyib: from that milestone of interreligious dialogue, the Pontiff returns to the appeal that, in the name of human fraternity, dialogue be adopted as the way, common cooperation as conduct, and mutual knowledge as method and standard (see Par 285).

https://www.vaticannews.va/en/pope/news/2020-10/fratelli-tutti-pope-fraternity-social-friendship-short-summary.html

http://www.imankatolik.or.id/ensiklik.html

ABOUT THE AUTHOR

It was the best of times, it was the worst of times, it was the age of wisdom, it was the age of foolishness, it was the epoch of belief, it was the epoch of incredulity, it was the season of light, it was the season of darkness, it was the spring of hope, it was the winter of despair.

Charles Dickens, 1842

Sudibyo Markus, *Dunia Barat dan Islam* (PT Gramedia Jkt 2019); *Islam and The West* (Fons Vitae, Louisville, KY USA 2022)

Sudibyo Markus was born in the small city of Pare, in Kediri, East Java, Indonesia. He is a co-founder of Muhammadiyah's youth wing, the Ikatan Mahasiswa Muhammadiyah (Muhammadiyah University Student Association or IMM). Upon completing his studies at the School of Medicine, Gadjah Mada University, Yogyakarta, Indonesia, he worked for the Ministry of Social Affairs of the Republic of Indonesia, rather than the Ministry of Health. However, in order to broaden his humanitarian vision and networks, he decided to leave his post as Director of Civil Society Affairs and join the United Nations Development Program (UNDP) in 1988. His personal and his family's good interaction with the Harvard students at the multicultural small town of "Modjokuto" gave him the first impetus for envisioning the relation between Islam and the West.

This tiny old steam train is the MASCOT of the younger generation of Pare from the 50s to the 70s, including when the Harvard group was around at Modokuto. Without it, we could not have attended junior and senior year of high school, since Madjokuto had only elementary school facilities. I took the train from 1955-1961. The train stopped every two kilometers o pick up the students in the darkness of 5:00 am, where there was no electricity. We attended the 24 km distance from Modjokuto to Kediri, the district capital, two hours away. The train passed right in front of Geertz's rental house every two hours when he was there in Modjokuto (1952-1953).

His career with the United Nations Development Program has helped him enhance his humanitarian insight at the international stage. Meanwhile, his volunteer status and position as the Chair of Muhammadiyah's Council for Public Health (2000 to 2005), then as a Chair of the Central Executive Board of Muhammadiyah (2005-2010), and lastly as the Vice Chairman of Muhammadiyah's International Relation Office since from 2010 to 2021, has further enhanced his connections with numerous civil society and interfaith communities at the regional and international levels.

INTERNATIONAL ENCOUNTERS

As a member of international civil society and humanitarian networks, the International Council of Voluntary Organization (ICVA) in Geneva, Johannesberg-based Civicus International of NGOs Alliance, and with the Kuala Lumpur-based International Federation of NGO (IFNGO), Markus has had sufficient opportunities to expand, update and involve himself in broader international humanitarian issues and practices. Moreover, his strong background in multicultural affairs and encounters with the Harvard University students

387

at his early age in 1952, especially with Prof. Clifford Geertz, the author of the international best seller *The Religion of Java* (Massachusetts Institute of Technology, 1960), have helped him very much in promoting his multicultural, interfaith and humanitarian vision.

His involvement in founding the Humanitarian Forum (London, 2006), an East and West humanitarian network to represent Muhammadiyah in 2006, along with his western humanitarian NGO partners like ICVA Geneva, Oxfam GB, the Norwegian Refugee Council, the British Red Cross along with the Islamic Relief Worldwide (Birmingham), IHH Turkey, Kuwaiti International Charitable Organization, Qatar Red Crescent, Islamic World Youth Assembly (Jeddah) was indeed a remarkable opportunity. His involvement as member of the *International Contact Group* (ICG, 2009-2020) in support of facilitating the peace negotiation between the Government of the Philippines and the Moro Islamic Liberation Front (MILF) has provided him with in-depth best practices in promoting dialogue and negotiations between conflicting parties.

Sudibyo Markus has been assigned by the Indonesian Ministry of Foreign Affairs to deliver two presentations on behalf of the Indonesian delegates at two different events, the first at the Second Asia-Pacific Interfaith Dialogue in Cebu in the Philippines (2006), and at the fifth Asia-Pacific Interfaith Dialogue in Perth, West Australia in 2010.